Heiko Schrader

Changing Financial Landscapes in India and Indonesia

Sociological Aspects of Monetization and Market Integration

St. Martin's Press
New York

Heiko Schrader

Changing Financial Landscapes
in India and Indonesia

Sociological Aspects of Monetization and Market Integration

St. Martin's Press
New York

CHANGING FINANCIAL LANDSCAPES IN INDIA AND INDONESIA

St. Martin's Press, Scholarly and Reference Division, 175 Fifth Avenue, New York, N. Y. 10010

First published in the United States of America in 1997

Printed in Germany

ISBN 0-312-21016-7

    Library of Congress Cataloging-in-Publication Data
Schrader, Heiko.
  Changing financial landscapes in India and Indonesia:
sociological aspects of monetization and market integration / Heiko
Schrader.
     p.   cm.
  Includes bibliographical references and index.
  ISBN 0-312-21016-7 (cloth)
    1. Finance – India – History. 2. Finance – Indonesia – History.
3. Financial institutions – India – History. 4. Financial
institutions – Indonesia – History. I. Title.
HG187.I4S37   1997
332'.0954–dc21   97-25824
                                                          CIP

For my father

Contents

List of Tables

List of Figures

Preface

The transformation of primitive or peasant societies into modern market societies is a secular process. The European political economy made technical innovations and their socio-economic consequences, manifested in the Agricultural, Commercial and Industrial Revolution, responsible for this development. In this process the market-system becomes the prevailing dominant force of society, subsuming not only products but also the production factors land, labour and capital under its mechanisms.

This transformation process was not confined to Europe. However, the development paths in the center and periphery were not the same, as assumed by modernization theory, since with the incorporation of highly developed, non-European regions in the process of colonization these developed in dependence from Europe.

Transformation processes are accelerated or slowed down by specific social formations. The particular role of traders and financiers (who to my mind form a sub-category of traders) in this process was always of particular interest in economic history. This study is concerned with the changing financial landscapes in India and Indonesia over the last five centuries.

This kind of study in the field of economic history and economic sociology is not only relevant for historians. To my mind, contemporary financial landscapes and regional differences among them are largely the result of historical processes both on the national as well as the international levels. I intend to analyze the function of financial actors with regard to monetization and market integration, the appearance and disappearance of particular agents in certain historical constellations, their changing tasks, their relation to different classes, rulers, and so on. The discussion of both India and Indonesia is of particular interest because of their respective histories, and I am not the first to attempt such a comparison. Both countries participated in the long-established Far Eastern long-distance trade, which was in place well before Western incursion, and they are both shaped by their colonial histories, albeit under different authorities. Moreover, both countries gained independence soon after the Second World War. The question of special concern to me is whether these histories brought about similar financial landscapes as the result of a globalization process.

Before examining the cases of the two countries, I shall focus on moneylenders, credit and interest generally in **Part I**. At the outset I would like to invite the reader to follow me into the contemporary financial landscapes of the Third World. Chapter 1 outlines their structure and the types of financial actors and agencies involved and considers the paradigms of development finance. In Chapter 2, my research hypotheses regarding the changing socio-economic functions of particular financial agents will be specified.

Chapters 3 and 4 deal with the theoretical perspective on the two couplets 'money and credit' and 'capital and interest', respectively. I start by considering money and

11

credit in the context of the theory of exchange, and shall outline the changing qualities of borrowing and lending in the differentiation process of society and economy.
I discuss the theoretical perspectives of two major scholars, Karl Marx and Max Weber, who have decisively influenced the thinking of social scientists. Both referred
to the different economic development potentials of Europe and Asia. According to
Max Weber, the 'Protestant Ethic and the Spirit of Capitalism' and a rational type of
bureaucracy are unique to European development, while he presumed that the ethics
of Asian religions and their bureaucracies acted as obstacles to the endogenous emergence of modern capitalism. Scholars on India adopt this argument in the discussion
of Indian entrepreneurship. Marx took a similar position to Weber with respect to the
different development potentials of East and West. He maintained that large parts of
Asia were trapped in the Asiatic mode of production and that a change towards the
establishment of a capitalist mode of production in such countries could only be affected from outside. Nowadays it is commonly agreed that endogenous factors alone
are insufficient to explain the different development potentials of East and West. It
is argued that politicoeconomic factors on a world scale were equally responsible for
such developments. The macro perspective is taken in Part IV.

Part II (Chapters 5 – 8) consists of the case study of India. In broad terms, it
is an analysis of the financial landscape in pre-colonial, colonial and contemporary
India, the broad spectrum and hierarchy of financial agents and their changing socio-
economic functions. These agents cannot be separated from trade, many of whom
were merchant bankers, traders-cum-lenders or at least had their origins in trade and
eventually specialized in finance. Trade and finance were already highly developed
in pre-colonial India and it can be safely argued that the Muslim period in Northern
India was the heyday of Indian merchant banking (Chapter 6). During the colonial
period, indigenous high finance which used to provide loans for and invest in long-
distance trade, and its function as state bankers, experienced a set-back. The British-
Indian government, the East India Company, English private merchants and finally the
British banks incorporated a number of their former functions (Chapter 7). Nonetheless, medium-scale, mostly urban informal finance has continued to exist until this day,
which supplies credit to the service and smaller-scale secondary sectors. As a matter
of fact, often borrowers combine both formal and informal finance to maximize their
credit volumes.

We face a different situation with low-scale finance, particularly in rural regions.
This type of finance experienced considerable growth under colonial rule. One decisive factor in its success was the introduction of British legislation which provided
safe foundations for lending activities; other factors were growing market dependence
and the British revenue system. Moneylenders supplied loans to peasants and landlords in order that they could pay the taxes to the British authorities on time, and this
well-functioning revenue system was the backbone of colonial rule. The growth of
the rural credit supply, however, led to increasing rural indebtedness and land alienation, which was accompanied by peasant unrest in the course of the second half of
the nineteenth and early twentieth centuries. The British abandoned their premises
of Liberalism only very hesitantly and intervened in the financial market through
moneylenders', usury and tenant legislation, as well as debt relief, whereas the more

market-compatible strategies of public and cooperative credit provision remained underdeveloped. During the post-colonial period (Chapter 8), this interventionism was extended. In addition to moneylenders' legislation, subsidized credit programs were set up, private banks were nationalized and the national development plans placed an emphasis on the expansion of formal rural finance. On the whole, informal finance in India declined in the course of the twentieth century from more than 90 to around 50 percent.

Part III concentrates on the case of Indonesia. In contrast to India, the top level of informal finance was not well developed. The analysis shows that until the late nineteenth century private investment, whether Dutch or non-Western, was crippled by state enterprise in both production and foreign trade which peaked during the period of forced cultivation (Chapters 9 and 10). The entire economy was kept on the level of agricultural production and its processing (sugar, rubber etc.), whereas industrial development was neglected. My argument is that such an economy was not in need of nor provided opportunities for large-scale informal finance. However, to allow this state capitalism to function, the Dutch required *comparadores*, intermediaries between themselves and indigenous producers. This position was taken by Chinese migrants who became dominant in domestic commerce and moneylending (Chapter 11). Arabs and Indians also engaged in such enterprise but on a minor scale. To put it another way, almost the whole commercial sector was monopolized by aliens.

A closer analysis of Chinese enterprise reveals the existence of Chinese commercial-cum-financial networks, without producing large-scale specialized financial agents. Those who held the key positions in these networks were at the same time bureaucratic functionaries in the Dutch system of indirect rule, which offered them the opportunity to exert economic and political control over the Chinese community. Indigenous racial discontent articulated itself periodically against the Chinese community because of their economically prominent position and their cooperation with the Dutch.

During the second half of the nineteenth century the living conditions of the rural population worsened as a result of population growth, increasing scarcity of land, high revenue payment, decreasing world-market prices, and so on. To cope with the problem, the Dutch, in contrast to the British in India, did not hesitate to interfere in the financial market (Chapters 12 and 13). Not only was moneylenders' legislation immediately introduced, but they institutionalized a popular credit system expanding into the countryside at the turn of the century. Other political and infrastructural measures of the 'Ethical Policy' at the turn of the century, assisted the fight against rural indebtedness.

Private investment became possible with the liberalization of the economy during the late colonial period: Chinese and Western. Again the emerging capitalists were predominantly non-indigenous. Contrary to the Indian case where indigenous capitalists were involved in the independence movement, the Chinese were aliens and therefore did not show this inclination. Moreover, in spite of the large number of wealthy Chinese, they did not invest in heavy industry until much later, mainly during the post-colonial period. This can be explained by the very hostile environment which encouraged periodical pogroms against the Chinese. Nonetheless, they form one of the dominant capitalist groups in contemporary Indonesia upholding close relations with the government (Chapter 14).

Until the 1980s financial policy in Indonesia was heavily regulated. The government tried to capitalize rural regions by introducing heavily subsidized credit programs. However, they largely ended in failure, due to high default rates and unadjusted distribution of credit, nor were they very successful in putting a squeeze on informal finance and lowering its interest rates. The liberalization of finance during the 1980s and 90s caused the established and new banks in the cities to boom, but market-oriented rural finance continues to be a matter of concern in government policy. One pilot project in Indonesia relates to the use of existing rural structures, such as self-help groups, to qualify rural people as credit-worthy bank customers.

In **Part IV** I finally take up the international perspective to provide further arguments for an explanation of the differences in the financial landscapes of both countries under consideration. The analysis of the pre-colonial economic order demonstrates that South and Southeast Asia played different roles within the Far Eastern world-economy, which serves as a possible explanation for the lack of large-scale private finance in Indonesia, whereas it was highly developed in India (Chapter 15). With growing Western incursions into Asia, and particularly during the period of colonialism, these roles changed. Asian merchants were eventually squeezed out of long-distance trade and its finance, while the different European nations captured this trade by force, increasingly obtained an economic and territorial stronghold in these countries and finally subdued whole sub-continents. Within this process the highly developed and partly industrialized Indian economy was forced to revert to producing raw materials, while Indonesia was kept on this level within the colonial division of labour.

However, the economic conditions in both Britain and India were different too (Chapter 16). The British used the imports from the colonies to assist their own industrialization process and re-exported part of the processed goods for sale in the Commonwealth and their colonies. While the British colonial policy was largely mercantile until the mid-nineteenth century, Britain invested in Indian industries in the final stage of colonialism to exploit the availability of cheap labour. The Dutch, however, generally confined themselves to the level of mercantile exploitation. The state imported colonial produce and semi-processed raw materials from Indonesia to the Netherlands and sold them on the world market, thereby neglecting the development of Dutch industries at home and in Indonesia. This policy was successful for some time and the Dutch managed to maintain their primary position in world trade which they had earlier captured from Portugal. However, the British eventually succeeded in gaining dominance, at least as far as trade with India and China is concerned. The incorporation of Asia in the course of colonization is discussed with world-system theory and its critique (Chapter 17).

The dominance of European trade was similar under both colonial regimes. Nevertheless, colonial practice in both Indian and Indonesia differed. In Indonesia, the Dutch East India Company held the monopoly in foreign trade for a long period, while in India the monopoly of the English East India Company was short-term and, on the whole, left more room for private European initiative in seeking Indian partners with a knowledge of the market. These different conditions may again explain the different financial landscapes in colonial India and Indonesia.

With regard to the post-colonial development both countries took up a financial policy of heavy regulation which was directed to expand formal and extinct informal finance. The latter, however, has continued to exist and I argue that it is not only a residue of the past but moreover important for the functioning of capitalism. I conclude with the assessment that I expect a homogenization of financial landscapes on a world scale because of the ongoing process of globalization (Chapter 18).

Finally I would like to use this occasion to thank all the people and institutions helping me in completing this study. First of all, my thanks go to my wife Cordula and my then new-born son Malte who accompanied me in the ten months of material collection to Indonesia, Singapore, Thailand, India, Nepal, the Netherlands and London, and thus shared with me this important period of life. Next I would like to thank Hans-Dieter Evers with whom I discussed the progress of my work from the beginning until the end and who gave me a number of valuable inputs. I am also grateful for the financial assistance of the *Deutsche Forschungsgemeinschaft* (German Council of Research) which provided my scholarship grant (*Habilitationsstipendium*) and print support.

In the course of material collection I have accumulated a considerable burden of debt. My thanks go to the Population Studies Center (Sofian Effendi and his staff) and Dibyo Prabowo from the Faculty of Economics at the Gadjah Mada University in Yogyakarta. Our stay in Indonesia would have been less intensive without the hospitality of my former Bielefeld colleagues Werner Tießbohnenkamp and Helmut Weber. In Singapore we received support from the Institute of Southeast Asian Studies and by Gerwin Gerke. In Bangkok the staff of the Center of Social Development Studies, Faculty of Political Science at the Chulalongkorn University, my research assistant Nillawan Chuvanapirom at NIDA and my former Bielefeld colleague Hans-Dieter Bechstedt in Bangkok have my gratitude for their assistance. Special thanks to Carmen Hussain and family, and the then Regional Representative of the Friedrich-Ebert-Foundation in New Delhi, Heinz Bongartz. This list of acknowledgments should further include the staff of the Delhi School of Economics and the Center of Development Administration at Tribhuvan University, Kirtipur (Nepal), Rahman Mahadevan then at the Center for Development Studies in Trivandrum, Frits Bouman and Otto Hospes in the Department of Agrarian Law at Wageningen University, Dietmar Rothermund at the *Südasieninstitut* of the University of Heidelberg, Hans-Dieter Seibel from the *Arbeitsstelle Entwicklungsländerforschung* of the University of Cologne and Jan Pieter Krahnen from the Faculty of Economics of the University of Gießen, who provided me with valuable material and intellectual criticism. Liz King from the Faculty of Sociology, University of Bielefeld took on the sometimes strenuous task to sub-edit the manuscript. Last but not least I would like to thank my colleagues at the Sociology of Development Research Center for their critical comments, particularly (in alphabetical order) Erhard Berner, Gudrun Lachenmann, Helmut Buchholt, Rüdiger Korff, Günther Schlee and Georg Stauth, our guest fellows in winter 1993/94, Jennifer and Paul Alexander, our secretary Christel Huelsewede who helped me in a number of organizational matters.

**Part I   ON MONEYLENDERS, CREDIT AND
INTEREST**

1. A Preliminary Step into Financial Landscapes

1.1. Introduction

Rural (and to a lesser degree urban) finance forms nowadays one of the key concepts of development planning.[1] Identifying undercapitalization on the grassroots level as one of the main development impediments, access to capital has been considered as a means for development. At least until the 1970s economic growth and income growth were assumed to depend on the growth of factor inputs, of which capital input was treated to be the most important variable. Underdevelopment was considered to result from the 'vicious cycle of poverty'.[2] The only possibility to induce growth was seen by providing capital from outside sources. This capital was spent on technological improvements bought in the donor or lender countries in exchange for capital goods such as machinery. The planning concepts of the period aimed at a top-down capitalization, with major investment in the technology of large- and medium scale industries and commercial agriculture (production techniques, land reforms, marketing facilities, etc.). Eventually, it was assumed, smaller and small-scale enterprises as well as off-farm activities should profit from 'trickle-down' effects and a gradual spill-over of techniques, and the population should benefit from employment in the growth sectors.

In retrospective it is commonly agreed that this one-sided development strategy was too narrow and wrong in its basic assumptions. During the 1970s it became obvious that unintended counter-effects emerged, too, such as an increased dualism of the economy and society, poverty, unemployment, and land flight. The following development decade therefore changed the emphasis. The new strategy which was introduced by the UN/ILO, was the fight against poverty with a basic-needs and target group-orientation. In other words, the access to cheap credit on the grassroots level was identified as a necessary condition for development. Although the target groups were different, finance was still considered capital provision from outside sources, now to farmers and small businesses instead of formerly big enterprise and public institutions. The economic rate of return as the measure for success, which included macro-economic and public benefits such as health, employment, education, external effects, and so on, replaced the formerly used financial rate of return. Specialized subsidized development banks and programs were introduced to distribute credit. However, the success of these banks with respect to reaching the target groups was poor. Reasons were identified as ranging from economic limitations on the lenders' side, such as high transaction costs and risk involved, to causal limitations on the borrowers' side, such as high opportunity costs, inadequate bank's opening hours, time-consuming credit application procedures, non-adaptation to borrowers' credit requirements, resentments

---

[1] For a good summary of development finance until the 1990s, see Krahnen and Schmidt (1994).

[2] It was argued that the poverty of individual and public households results from low incomes, so that savings cannot take place which are necessary for investment. This again results in low productivity and low income, i.e. in poverty.

of customers because of the depersonalization of credit relations, and so on. Although an efficient operation of these institutions was not required by development policy, the default rates were so high that they were beyond toleration, very often accounting for more than 90 percent (see, for example, Adams et al. 1984). This has caused the development planners to shift their focus again. The main problem identified now are institutional impediments. The current approaches aim at higher efficiency, stability and autonomy of the existing and the development of new financial institutions. The policy applied will lead to the creation of self-perpetuating local income flows (the mobilization of the savings of the target group) to form a basis for the lending of the institutions involved, to make them independent from government subsidies.

Many development planners hold the black-and-white view that Third-World economies and financial markets consist of a modern and a traditional sector. It is assumed that the latter impedes development mainly for two reasons: the charging of exorbitant interest and the provision of consumer credit which does not generate higher future income to the borrowers and leads to increasing indebtedness. That matters are not so simple has been shown by various studies. The high interest rates are in many cases a result of high transaction costs, risk involved, and lender's opportunity costs (see, for example, Singh 1983 and Chapter 8.2.4), and a clear-cut distinction of production and consumer loans is difficult from the perspective of the household. Indeed, banks have certain advantages compared to informal lenders, such as the readiness to finance long-term and large-scale loans, to offer additional services such as consultancy, to be refinanced by the state bank, and so forth. However, informal lenders have certain comparative advantages, too. As they belong in many cases to the *Lebenswelt* (life-world) of their customers, they have good information and therefore low transaction and monitoring costs and the borrowers have low transaction and opportunity costs. Borrowing procedures are simple. There is personal knowledge of lender and borrower and no fixed office hours, and the borrower can go to see the lender under cover of night to avoid gossip in the village. Even the smallest credit can be obtained, and the repayment is adapted to the requirements of the borrower.

To overcome the financial dualism, three strategies have been suggested. One is the 'upgrading' of semi-formal financial agents and institutions to use the advantages of particular informal lenders (know-how and closeness to borrowers), another is the 'downgrading' of banks. A third one is the linking of formal banks with self-help groups to use peer monitoring (i.e. group-internal pressure to borrowers) as a means of reducing the risk of lending (see, for example, BMZ et al. 1987; Seibel 1989a,b; Krahnen and Schmidt 1994). Some politicians engage in heavy state interventionism to eliminate certain informal suppliers; some experts again rely on market forces to bring down the informal interest rates. The result of these options is the same. The dualism will be overcome in such a way that informal finance disappears eventually.

1.2. Definitions

Finance[3] is the monetary and inter-temporal decision aspects of economic processes. It comprises everything which involves saving, lending (credit) and the insurance of financial risks. Credit is therefore one component of finance only. The financial infrastructure includes all savings and financing opportunities and institutions which provide saving and credit facilities, as well as the valid norms and modes of behavior related to the financial system, i.e. political, legal, moral, etc. Financial agents may or may not be institutionalized and/or specialized on financial services or even particular financial services. Financial landscapes[4] are the broad spectrum of financial markets, financial agents and their clients (borrowers) and the financial infrastructure.

A term which has been commonly used for the description of financial landscapes is a dual approach (Kessler et al. 1985) which is analogous to the formal and informal sectors of the real economy: formal and informal finance and formal and informal financial sectors, respectively.[5] Following Germidis (1990), the formal financial sector of developing countries is subordinated to policies ranging from total regulation with extensive government control and intervention in the activities of monetary institutions (with the effect of hindering the development of financial markets, [Polak 1989]) to a higher degree of liberalization, of decision-making at the institutional level, and of market forces. It is obvious that the structure of the formal sector to some degree determines the extent of the informal sector, yet the informal sector has a certain dynamic of its own. One line of argument considers the informal financial sector to be a response to the shortcomings of the formal financial sector and therefore supplementary, the other line considers financial dualism to be a mirror of the economic dualism of developing countries, both sectors having been interpreted as being hardly related to each other. Reality, however, shows that the informal financial sector provides credit not only to those who have no access to formal credit at all, but that many borrowers combine formal and informal credit sources, or even use their access to formal banks or credit programs to obtain credit and on-lend to informal borrowers. Policy-makers consider financial dualism dangerous for the development of the economy, as it conserves sectoral and regional disparities (for example, capital-intensive – labour-intensive or urban – rural) and an unequal division of income, due to the fact that informal credit is more costly for the borrower. Furthermore, informal structures undermine the government's economic, monetary and fiscal policies.

The common critique of the concept of formal and informal real sector can be applied here, too. These categories should be used descriptively rather than analytically, and the boundaries of both sectors are not at all clear-cut (see Elwert, Evers and Wilkens 1983). The older line of argumentation, the perception of non-overlap

---

[3] The definitions of finance, financial infrastructure and financial intermediary are in line with the definitions of the BMZ et al. (1987). The other definitions have been supplemented by the author.

[4] The term 'financial landscapes' was suggested on the Wageningen Conference on 'Financial Landscapes Reconstructed', 17-19 November 1992, to replace the dual terms 'formal' and 'informal financial sectors'. It indicates the broad spectrum of financial agents. The analysis of the structure of particular financial landscapes can be considered to form maps of these landscapes.

[5] Another dualistic terminology that has been used analogously is 'organized' versus 'unorganized finance' (see, for example, Tun Wai 1980).

of both sectors (but not the dichotomy formal-informal) has recently been overcome with the question of linkages between both sectors. This linkage has always existed, after the emergence of formal finance, through financial intermediaries. This term will be applied to financial agents who are linked in one way or the other to both financial sectors or, to put it another way, those who have access to formal finance with formal incomes and savings or formal credit which they on-lend informally.

1.3. The Structure of Financial Landscapes

A common definition applied to formal and informal financial markets is very techno-cratic:

> "Financial markets (not institutions) are defined here as formal when they fall under the con-trol of the state credit and of related financial laws (. . .).[6] For formal financial institutions the government, or state, usually establishes a central bank as an instrument of central control. Conse-quently, financial markets are defined as informal when they operate outside such control" (Kropp et al. 1989: 27).

Another, to my mind more useful, definition has been recently provided by Krahnen and Schmidt (1994). They start from the realistic assumption of imperfect markets in which information is distributed asymmetrically. To obtain and maintain good infor-mation on the borrower (monitoring) is costly for the lender. Particular enforcement mechanisms of repayment may compensate for imperfect information.

> "There may be different types of enforcement mechanisms: social sanctions between mem-bers of a community, or a family, for instance; or an illegal, possibly violent form of prosecution by a gang; or legal prosecution through official agents like policemen or sheriffs.
> To give an example, loan arrangement can be supported by formal collateral if in case of non-fulfillment of contract terms the lender has the right, and indeed the practical opportunity, to liquidate the pledged asset. Here, the right and its enforceability are crucial. The same collateral will be of little use if the creditor is unable to execute his claim.
> A lack of enforceability using legal means, however, is characteristic of informal transactions. Social sanctions and norms, or moral or family ties might then substitute for legal enforcement (. . .) Apart from social and ethical norms, the absence of legally enforceable contractual stipula-tions induces economic agents to develop an intelligent contractual form that diminishes the risk of breach of contract by anyone party to the arrangement (. . .)
> A more precise definition of formal and informal economic activities can now be developed: A transaction between economic agents is called formal if for enforcement purpose it relies on the legal system of society. Otherwise it is called informal" (Krahnen and Schmidt 1994: 33).

To introduce a legal infrastructure, Krahnen and Schmidt (1994) continue, is quite expensive. Such a legal infrastructure in most developing countries therefore exists for specific economic activities or agents only. The other way around, most people cannot rely on the legal infrastructure. Either they cannot enter legal contracts for reasons of access and cost or such contracts do not give them security. Informality is thus characterized by a lack of legal infrastructure. This lack is compensated by longer-term inter-temporal relationships between the transacting parties. The time between the performance of one party and counter-performance of the other requires an explicit or implicit form of bonding such as the pledging of fields, crops, labour and

---

[6] For other scholars, the fact that they fall under the control of the state is more decisive.

life or the potential loss of social standing and honor. In certain cases such informal bonds are even stronger than laws such as the still existing – although prohibited – bonded labour in India. Another form of informal control is 'peer-monitoring', i.e. social control within a group which is positively correlated with group homogeneity of kinship, sex, age, ethnic membership, profession etc. Certain informal financial institutions such as rotating savings and credit associations and 'strategies' such as the linkage-concept which will be discussed later, make use of peer monitoring.

Worth noting is the plural form 'markets', which scholars mostly apply. This form shall refer to the different, in many cases not integrated, segments of financial markets (the imperfection of the market system with only limited mobility of capital flows from one segment to the other, different interest rates and borrowing conditions in different markets, limited information on the conditions in other markets, limited access etc.), which is true for many developing countries.

Among the broad distinguishing features of formal and informal financial markets which Kropp et al. (1989) list, are the following (exceptions exist of course): (a) Formal financial markets are highly centralized. Decentralization depends on the branches of the centralized institutions. Informal financial markets are atomized, with many different agents/institutions. (b) Both markets operate rather independently from one another, with different agents/institutions, clients, modes of operation, interest rates etc. (c) The target group of the formal market is the upper stratum of the population, such as formal sector employees and enterprises, including state institutions. However, many formal sector workers are nevertheless excluded from access. Informal financial markets are accessible to both upper and lower strata but mainly used by the lower strata of the population: rural and urban informal sector participants. Semi-formal institutions serve, in general, the better off of the lower strata. (d) Access to credit in the formal financial sector is handled much more restrictively than access to deposit accounts and this again much more than to saving accounts. The informal credit, deposit and saving possibilities form the only opportunity of access for the informal target group. (e) Both markets have certain strengths and weaknesses:

> "(. . .) formal financial markets excel in modernity, in access to national and international refinancing institutions and in access to other supporting institutions, none of which applies to informal financial markets. Informal financial markets excel in accessibility, popular participation, basic needs orientation, organizational flexibility, local adaptability, situational appropriateness and sociocultural integration at the local or regional level, none of which applies to formal financial markets. (. . . On the other hand, H.S.) formal financial markets comprise a powerful modern sector with the potential of contributing to the dynamic growth of the economy, but are limited to a few – and therefore are unable to initiate self-sustained development. Informal financial markets are open to all; but they comprise a weak indigenous sector, contributing mainly to survival through self-help and to slow development on the local level" (Kropp et al. 1989: 30-1).

The share of formal and informal finance with respect to both number of people involved as well as volume varies form one country to another. Nevertheless, various case studies reveal that both volume of informal finance and number of people involved exceed at least 50 percent in most Third-World countries (Pischke, Adams and Donald 1983), although the relative and probably also absolute shares have decreased during the last three decades. Nevertheless, their share reflects the financial

viability and adaptability of informal finance to their clients' needs and the cultural
gap between most formal financial institutions and many customers.

Considering the average level of nominal interest charged by informal agents and
institutions it has declined from 40 percent in the 1950s to 30 percent in the 1970s
with large deviations, but is still higher than formal interest rates. However, the gap between average formal and informal interest rates has narrowed during the past decades
(Tun Wai 1980: 260).

Germidis (1990) provided the following cross-cultural estimates of the share of
formal finance, approximated by the ratio of market capitalization to domestic credit.[7]

Tab. 1: Market Capitalization as Percentage of Domestic Credit in Selected Countries

Year	1981	1982	1983	1984	1985	1986	1987*
India	15.10	13.30	7.60	12.30	15.60	15.60	14.10
Indonesia	1.10	3.10	2.50	0.90	0.80	0.60	0.60
Philippines	10.60	6.50	7.10	6.20	12.10	24.40	26.70
Thailand	6.10	6.90	6.30	6.20	7.40	10.30	14.80
Zimbabwe	29.00	16.00	14.30	12.10	28.00	27.10	41.30
Nigeria	11.70	4.70	7.90	8.00	7.60	4.10	
Mexico	11.70	2.20	5.40	6.20	6.30	10.70	31.50
Brazil	17.80	13.40	22.60	49.90	61.40		

Source: International Monetary Fund 1989: International Financial Statistics 1988.
Note: * Estimates

1.3.1. Formal Financial Markets

Unlike the informal financial markets, the formal ones have been well documented.[8]
The major formal institutions comprise the central banks, commercial or business
banks, development banks, savings banks, cooperative banks, merchant banks, building societies, and the insurance and social security sector. Licensed investment companies, hire-purchase companies, public pawnshops (and sometimes private licensed
ones) and so on may also be part of formal financial markets. Financial markets of
their own form the capital markets (financial, bond and stock markets) which, depending on the country, are more or less developed. Formal financial institutions operate
in a commercial way such as commercial banks, or in a non-commercial way, such as
subsidized government credit programs.

The traditional role of the central bank is that of a monetary control agency. In
some countries such as Indonesia, it acts furthermore as a development bank, which
plans, monitors and evaluates development programs that are implemented by execut-
ing banks or non-banking institutions.

---

[7] This ratio reflects the relative weight of market mechanisms versus intermediation mechanisms as well
as the private sector in the economy.

[8] In the description I follow Kropp et al. (1989). Recently a valuable comparative study on informal
finance in Asia was published by the Asian Development Bank (Ghate 1992).

Commercial banks provide the services of savings and non-risky credit, trade shares and obligations, and do certain own businesses. In many developing countries they have been obliged to reserve a certain percentage of their lending budget for small entrepreneurs and farmers. Nevertheless, they work with the bigger clients only among this target group. It is not so much the risk involved than the high transaction costs for small-scale lending, with credit ceilings below market rates, that discourage banks from supplying the small-scale credit needed by small-scale traders, peasants, craftsmen, and so on.

Many development banks limit their activity to credit transactions with particular target groups and economic sectors and have run into difficulty because of poor repayment rates, scarce national and international credit lines and sometimes internal problems. Some have therefore extended their activity to savings and deposit transactions for small enterprises.

Savings banks, like post office saving banks work with the target group of small savers. They provide the service of savings only. Critics hold against such institutions – and this was indeed the cause of their initial establishment during the colonial period – that they drain away capital from the poor periphery of countries into their centers and raise a disposable fund for the government. Due to high inflation rates in many Third-World countries, which in many cases exceed the savings interest rates (negative real savings), the tendency to hold savings accounts has decreased.[9] As a consequence of this some of these banks were transformed into savings and credit banks.

Cooperative savings and credit institutions are formal or semi-formal institutions such as credit unions, *banques populaires* or *caisses rurales*. In Germany they go back to Raiffeisen and Schulze-Delitz and developed toward the end of the nineteenth century as a reaction to decreasing rural welfare, while in Britain, for example, this movement was associated with the Rochdale Pioneers. However, in most developing countries these institutions have been introduced from above. Many cooperatives fall under the cooperative law rather than under financial laws, especially if they are multipurpose cooperatives. Among the financial cooperatives, two categories – the savings-based and the credit-oriented organizations – have to be distinguished.

What has been summarized as the main strengths and weaknesses of formal financial institutions (see for example, Kropp et al. 1989: 37-8) is characteristic for banks and does not apply to institutions such as licensed moneylenders or pawnshops which only by definition may be counted among formal financial institutions. These strengths are:

- they provide modern services;
- they can finance long-term and large-scale businesses;
- they collaborate with national and international partners and have access to refinancing and other supporting institutions;
- they are integrated into the formal and public sector.

The main weaknesses are the following:

---

[9] The author carried out a quantitative, comparative pilot study on the financial structure of banks in developing countries, particularly in Asia (see Schrader 1993).

- they only reach a small number of small-scale enterprises, they are spatially and psychologically distant from informal small enterprises in particular and exclude them from their services;
- they ignore socio-cultural, socio-political and socio-economic conditions.

1.3.2. Informal Financial Markets

Informal financial individual agents[10] and institutions are usually grouped as non-commercial and commercial ones. In many cases they offer the financial service of lending only. However, again it is difficult with some agents to place them in one or the other category. Friends and relatives, for example, are usually considered to belong to non-commercial agents because they are expected to provide credit without aiming at profit.[11] What, however (as I observed during research), if somebody provides credit to his brother bearing 20 percent interest per month? Is such a loan non-commercial because of the closeness of social relation, commercial because of the high interest or even usurious? I assume in line with Mauss (1925) that non-commercial loans are not necessarily altruistic as commonly assumed. I consider them in the tradition of structural functionalism as an investment into social security under the aspect of future reciprocity. Commercial financial agents are then all those who aim at profit. Because of the difficulty to identify clear-cut boundaries Germidis (1990) added another category: the semi-commercial agent, which to my mind does not solve the problem. I suggest to take into consideration, the primary motivation of loan provision through lenders. Nevertheless a categorization according to this scheme should be avoided. Those who take profit from lending in one or the other way have often been named 'moneylender', which will be discussed in the following paragraph and analyzed in greater detail. The literature on India exhibits a category distinct from the moneylender, which has been called the 'indigenous banker', who is similar to the medieval merchant banker in Europe and provides an important category in this study.

Moneylenders

The terms 'moneylending' or 'moneylender' used in the literature are catch-all terms. Unlike most scholars, some (for example, Kropp et al. 1989) use the terms in a very narrow sense (purely professional lender of cash only). As will be seen, however, such a definition does not make sense, since most informal individual lenders combine commerce in one or another way with lending, so that a very loose use of the terms seems appropriate to me. I do not confine moneylending to monetized transactions

---

[10] Kropp et al. (1989) distinguish a third category: semi-formal financial agents which comprise government organizations and private voluntary, or non-government, organizations backed by international organizations or by bilateral support. They act like formal financial institutions but they do not fall under the credit law or under direct or indirect central bank supervision. But they are more than tolerated by the state which happens to most informal financial agents and institutions. Data reveal that once such institutions exceed a certain size, they become formalized.

[11] The criterion taken is either very narrowly confined to non-interest arrangements or to the profit orientation of the lender because in many cases friends and relatives obtain compensation for their cost. The latter seems more appropriate to me.

only, but shall apply it to transactions in kind or a combination of cash and in kind transactions, too. What is – strictly speaking – a contradiction in terms, makes nevertheless sense with regard to the business of moneylenders. **Credit (or loan) is then the lending of cash or kind, to be paid back after a period of time in cash, kind, or in a combination of both, with or without interest.**

Such a broad definition allows us to include a variety of functions that cannot be explained by a single monolithic model of economic theory alone, but comprises additional sociological and psychological factors, too.

From the perspectives of anthropology and sociology it is useful to count the lending of non-monetary objects such as commodities, non-commodified goods of prestige or sacred circulating (like in the *kula* or the *potlatch*),[12] and even services such as labour, help, etc. among credit. Many informal financial transactions are somewhat embedded in personal social relations and therefore more complex as is assumed by most economists. In addition to economic conditions they can comprise invisible elements of open or hidden social benefits and obligations, such as patron-client relationships, bonded labour, and so on.

The same is, of course, true for the question of interest that will be discussed later. Here it is sufficient to emphasize that in complex credit relations the level of interest may be irrelevant or even unknown, and that the calculation of an interest rate may be misleading in many cases, since in many transactions no direct relation exists between the duration of the loan and the interest rate. In embedded financial transactions social functions of credit provision may cover and modify the economic ones or even replace them. In such transactions the social goal of credit relations may be either to create dependencies (see, for example, Sahlins 1972: 208) or to establish or maintain interdependencies. Another fact which has been overlooked by many economists is that, in applying a macro-view on all credit transactions within a village, the distinction between borrowers and lenders in a particular setting often makes no sense, since most villagers are borrowers in some relations and lenders in other ones, or the position may change in time (see, for example, Harriss 1983; Jones 1994).

From a theoretical point of view there is of course a qualitative difference between cash and in kind transactions. However, assuming that moneylenders aim for profit, they have to do both cash and in kind transactions (and a combination of both), and this not only in incompletely monetized rural regions, but in every rural context. In many transactions in kind interest rates remain hidden, and some extra profits can be achieved by exploiting periodical price differences before and after the harvest. In this sense I understand moneylenders in a very loose sense: as lenders who aim for profit.[13] However, this is an insufficient criterion in a number of cases at least. One

---

[12] Here I refer to Malinowski (1964) and Mauss (1925). For a structure-functional interpretation of the gift as a credit transaction, see Chapter 3.

[13] 'Profit' will be used here in a narrow economic sense as the difference between turnover and costs. 'Costs' will include transaction costs and opportunity costs, too. 'Transaction costs' are the sum of providing a loan and collection costs, administrative costs, cost attributed to payments of loans and default costs. The simple relation exists that the smaller the credit, the higher the transaction costs as a percentage of the loan sum because this cost component can be assumed to be fixed and becomes less important with the loan size. 'Opportunity costs' are the potential profit, which could have been realized

can argue with Rothermund (1982a: 17) that moneylenders aim at creating continuous dependencies. To put it another way, it is not the recovery of the principal sum but a continuous flow of interest *because* the principal sum was not repaid, that is the strategy of many moneylenders. The category of moneylenders will include the following sub-categories: professional moneylenders,[14] i.e. pure lenders, and semi-professional moneylenders, i.e. those lenders, who combine commerce with lending. Professional moneylenders are fewer in number than semi-professional ones. Among the latter the profit motive does not necessarily correspond to high interest. Here the motive of creating dependencies makes sense in a way that lending may also provide a means of acquiring produce cheaply (this is, for example, the case with advances on the harvest by crop dealers, or production inputs on credit by input-output merchants), it may provide a means to secure deliveries, or it may primarily aim at maintaining or acquiring new customers (as in the case of shops). In any case, moneylending is hidden behind the facade of a shop or a commercial office. I want to emphasize that the history of moneylending (and indigenously developed banking, too) is indispensable from trade. However, commerce-cum-moneylending does not provide the only category of semi-professional moneylending. This type of moneylender belongs per definition to the sphere of non-producers. Landlord-lenders are another typical category of individual informal lenders. Most of them are not only rentiers in the Marxian sense (i.e. non-producers), but may run some commercial agriculture based on hired labour, too. Another non-producing contemporary category of semi-professional moneylenders are professionals and government servants (or more precisely: their wives), who prefer to 'invest' in moneylending rather than taking their savings to a bank account, since the returns of the former choice are higher. It should be emphasized here that the savings have been derived from formal incomes, while they are on-lent informally. Or, due to their regular salaries they have access to formal credit which also can be onlent with higher interest. From such a perspective this type of lenders belongs to the financial intermediaries. It can even be said that petty moneylending can be done by everybody who has some savings,[15] be they cash or in kind.

Excluded from the category of moneylenders will be friends and relatives (of whom many do not aim for profit) and pawnshops. The reason why the pawnshop forms a

---

with another investment alternative.

[14] This definition in the sense of the occupational structure of statistics inhibits the problem that moneylenders' legislation and the licensing of professional moneylenders may cause professional moneylenders to conceal this activity behind other professions. Another choice might have been to take the time spent with moneylending. Here again the question is what is the unit of reference, the individual or the family? In some cases the husband is an employee in the formal sector, while his wife is a 'housewife' working as a moneylender. Is she then a professional lender? To take the share of contributing to the household income as the distinguishing feature is difficult, too, with respect to civil servants or professionals whose official salary may be rather low, but whose professional status is high.

[15] In the Chinese empire, for example, no particular moneylenders class probably existed. Everybody who had some capital functioned as a lender. At the turn of the century a missionary reported that "the whole Chinese empire may be said to be in a perpetual state of borrowing and lending, and a large majority of its people are daily concerned with that most practical question of how they shall pay the interest to the minority who have lent them money" (quoted by Skinner 1976: 23). To my mind, such a bottom sphere of moneylending has been and can still be found in most developing countries. It may be headed by certain classes, castes or occupational groups, which are not necessarily pure lenders but belong to the class of non-producers.

category apart is that it is – strictly speaking – an agency based not on the provision of credit but on a purchase of an under-priced good with the temporary right of the former owner to re-purchase it at a higher price, the price difference being interpreted as an interest rate. Again, however, a clear-cut boundary of this category is difficult to apply. In many cases at least the moneylender-cum-trader (and to some extent indigenously developed banker-cum-merchant) takes collateral from the borrower to obtain better credit security, which may range from physical objects to land and real estate titles.[16] The latter, which are not taken into physical possession by the lender, are not pawns but mortgages. I see the institution of the pawnshop, be it public or private, as distinct from that of the moneylender because it provides the particular service of purchase with a re-sale option. In many countries the running of private pawnshops requires a license, while in some countries even government monopolies exist. A small paragraph on pawnshops in Asia will follow later in this chapter. Whether pawnshops belong to formal, semi-formal or informal financial markets, and are run in a commercial or non-commercial way, depends on the financial and civil laws. The same may hold true for licensed professional moneylenders.

Town moneylenders are sometimes pure lenders, but more often traders-cum-lenders. Many of them operate individually, others through a number of branches and agents. These operate in part with their own, in part with foreign capital. The smaller urban lenders provide primarily consumption loans, while the bigger ones operate in the same way as merchant bankers financing trade and commerce. Most of these advances are short-term to finance the transport of goods, and this type of lender usually ascertains the reason for which the loan is required. Loans are predominantly in cash. Deposits are rarely accepted. The default rates among these bigger town moneylenders are said to be low. After the introduction of moneylenders' legislation the number of licensed moneylenders has gradually increased. There is no clear-cut boundary to indigenous-style bankers.

It is not uncommon for small-scale traders to make deposits with 'mobile bankers', as reported from Africa (Miracle, Miracle and Cohen 1980). To avoid confusion with indigenous-style bankers I name them 'savings collectors', visiting their customers regularly on market days to collect the savings. They keep one deposit per period as their fee and return the rest in a lump sum at the end of the period. In other words: Savers obtain no savings interest, but they pay the savings collector for the service of safekeeping. This form of saving provides the benefit to customers that these savings are secure from theft in their homes, from moral claims of family members to redistribute them and from the own incapability to save individually and make a monthly budget plan. In some cases such savings collectors may also extend credit to depositors. Many of these are probably agents of town moneylenders aiming merely at raising working capital for short-term loans.

Prejudices against moneylenders are founded on their charging exorbitant and exploitative interest rates (and in some cases this is certainly true), that they sometimes offend against religious morality (particularly of Islam), that they are not interested in the use of credit, so that the loan is often for consumption/luxury purposes and

---

[16] For rural India, Bouman (1989), for example, used the terms 'moneylender' and 'pawnbroker' interchangeably.

counter-productive for rural or national development, and that it induces dependency. Development policy further relates moneylending to rural backwardness. Additionally, personalized relations with clients make it difficult for development planners to incorporate moneylenders into modernization programs. This may explain the aim of most planners to eliminate moneylenders who are considered to prevent the acceptance of formal and semi-formal financial institutions among the population (Pischke, Adams and Donald 1983: 229).

The World Bank studying formal and informal institutions in 1983 concluded it is not uncommon that such political attitudes depreciate

> "the functional role that informal lenders play during the incipient development of rural financial markets and may result in policies which displace informal lenders without offering alternate sources of institutional credit (. . .) In these circumstances, rather than substitutes for these formal arrangements, formal arrangements can and should complement these arrangements, supplement and strengthen informal credit sources, and compete with informal lenders" (World Bank 1983: 48, quoted by Kropp et al. 1989: 40).

Trade Credit

In many cases the dualistic structure of real markets is associated with a modern urban, industrial and commercial sector which is related to formal finance, and a traditional rural sector related to informal finance. This is not the case in reality, as urban studies reveal, but these have so far been neglected because of their small number. It is not only that urban commerce is largely financed by informal agents, but the urban industrial sector is highly imperfect, too. Only large-scale firms have access to banks, while the majority of medium- and small-scale enterprises have to rely on informal finance. One category of credit in the industrial and commercial sectors is trade credit. With such credit arrangements the creditor (an input supplier or a manufacturer) transfers on credit non-financial physical resources to the debtor (processing enterprise, wholesaler, retailers, or middleman). The debtor is not a consumer. He uses the physical credit either as an input for production or as items for sale to other traders or consumers. Such trade credit is usually short-term, and the transferred resources are used as part of the working capital. Together with savings and credit associations, trade credit can be considered as a sort of self-financing of particular groups/branches with similar interests.

It is typical of Third-World industrial production that customers do not immediately pay cash, i.e. they obtain trade credits. Lamberte and Jose (1988) found for the footwear industries of the Philippines that 84 percent of sales to customers take place on credit with a maturity between 30 and 60 days. This is not merely a matter of a friendly advance, but rather small manufacturers in particular are forced by bigger wholesalers or retailer to extend them trade credits which use to be secured in most cases by post-dated checks. In some cases the interest is hidden because cash payments obtain a bonus. In other cases the prices set for trade credit arrangements are visibly slightly higher than for cash payments. Most producers have to borrow themselves or apply for trade credit because a great part of their working capital is bound up in trade credit extended to customers. The scholars identified long credit chains ranging from department stores and supermarkets to manufacturers and input suppliers. While these credit chains are all found within the informal financial market, there are probably some linkages to formal finance, too.

Pawnbrokers and Pawnshops

In the villages and towns pawning is a daily affair. Anyone in need of quick cash pledges some valuables either to a private or public pawnshop, or provides a pawn as collateral to the pawnbroker-moneylender. As found by the Asian Development Bank (Ghate 1992) for the Philippines, and this also holds true for several other countries, individuals of even modest means use pawn brokerage as an additional income source.

Pawnbrokers and pawnshops estimate the value of the pawn and provide a certain percentage of the value to the customer. As already mentioned, from the theoretical point of view a pawn agreement is not a loan from the pawner's side but a sale under value with the right to repurchase (this is also true for mortgage loans). Pawnbrokers and pawnshops provide important financial intermediaries. They supply ready cash without long procedures to primarily low-income groups and often have been called 'financial institutions for the poor'. They seem to successfully handle small-scale lending and the problems related to it. For example, the transaction costs as a percentage of the loan sum are expected to be very high in small-scale operations in general and for the storage of pawns in particular. However, this can be compensated to some extent. Not every article is accepted as a pawn. Preferential pawns are small with high value because the storage cost is lower for such pawns. Pawnbrokers or pawnshops have no information costs on the borrower nor monitoring costs on the loan because the payment for the pawn covers a percentage of its value only. Therefore the risk involved in pawn brokerage is not the default of the pawner, which is compensated by the value of the pawn, but the incorrect pricing of the pawn by the pawnee or the taking into pawn of stolen items which, depending on the national laws, have to be returned to the original owner. Whereas pawn brokerage is widespread among a variety of informal lenders who take movable collateral into pawn as a security for the loans, pawnshops are institutions which confine themselves to the financial service of pawn brokerage only.

Considering the history of pawn brokerage, it is probably as old as property.[17] According to Skully (1994), the establishment of pawnshops as specialized institutions is, however, another affair. In Asia the pawnshop is probably older than in Europe, where such institutions emerged in Italy around 1000 AD. Like the first Italian pawnshops, the Chinese ones, probably the oldest in Asia, had a religious connection, and they did initially not aim for profit but had a charitable character. Chinese scholars found no interest mentioned. The gradual shift towards interest seemed to present no moral problem as it did in Europe. Early Chinese pawnshops seemed to be the reverse to the current ones. They hired out goods and animals, such as ploughing utensils and oxen, which belonged to the Buddhist monastery. To reduce the risks, pledges and third-party guarantors soon were required. Then a third change took place to arrive at what constitutes the contemporary pawnshop: the acceptance of goods, although

---

[17] Even the Bible refers to pawns (Exodus, chapter 22, verse 25: 'his clothes as a pledge of his repayment').

this acceptance was related to safekeeping in the early phase. The Chinese pawnshops were privatized in 600-900 AD. From the fourteenth until the seventeenth century private pawnshops flourished in almost every town, city and many villages.[18] In other Southeast Asian countries (Malaysia, Thailand, Singapore) the history of pawnshops seems to be closely connected with Chinese merchants.

In Malaya, Indonesia, Thailand and the Philippines pawnshops seem to have been farmed out long before the Europeans arrived. Dutch and British colonial practice took over revenue farms. In Singapore the government revenues from pawn brokerage were not very profitable compared to other licenses and farms (1824: pawn brokerage: $ 480; gambling: $ 26,112; opium: $ 23,100; spirits: $ 10,980). In Thailand and Hong Kong pawnshops go back to the nineteenth century, while local pawnbrokers are much older.

In time private pawnshops began to be condemned as usurious by the European population in the colonies. In the Netherlands Indies first experiments with public pawnshops date back to 1746. The pawnshop development in Thailand is similar to Indonesia, with a shift from private to public pawnshops. In 1985 King Rama V introduced the first pawnshop act,[19] which gave legal status to these institutions.[20] In 1955, in competition with private pawnshops, government pawnshops were introduced, which charged lower interest rates and gave a higher valuation of the pawn. In 1962 the Pawnshop Act of BE 2505 was enforced.[21] Nowadays public and private pawnshops still coexist, whereas private pawnshops are not allowed outside Bangkok and new registrations have been forbidden since 1978. Public pawnshops are again divided into federal government institutions and municipal ones.[22] Public pawnshops cover their costs. Since both public and private pawnshops in Thailand are strongly regulated, Sujariyapinum (1988) counted them as formal finance.

In contemporary Malaysia, the Philippines, and Singapore the pawnshop industry is exclusively private, in China we can find private and cooperative pawnshops, and in Indonesia officially only government pawnshops. Interest rates are regulated. They range from only 1.5 percent per month in Singapore to 3-4 percent for public pawnshops in Indonesia,[23] and from 3.6 percent for public pawnshops to 9 percent for private pawnshops in Thailand.

---

[18] By the early 1800s, 25,000 pawnshops were reported for China.

[19] As early as the Ayudhya period, already, a first law to regulate pawn brokerage was introduced, but it served more the pawnbroker than the customer. Night pawning was outlawed, and the pawnbroker and customer had to know each other personally to single out thieves from normal customers (Thakranonthachai 1982).

[20] Pawnshops had to register, obtain a license which had to be renewed every month, and pay a fee of Baht 50. Maximum interest rates were also fixed; however, pawnbrokers circumvented this regulation by taking a 5 percent service charge. The person in charge of the licensing of pawnshops had the name of *Praya Indrathipbodeesiharajrongmuang*. Due to the monthly fee many pawnshops continued illegally. By 1936 there were 88 legally registered pawnshops (Thakranonthachai 1982).

[21] All pawnshops under the regulatory control of the Registration Division which specified working hours, operation procedures, maximum interest rates, and so on (Thakranonthachai 1982).

[22] A very detailed account on pawning behavior in Bangkok has been provided by Sujariyapinum (1988). In the mid-1980s, 219 of around 330 pawnshops operated in Bangkok.

[23] That is to say, three percent per month for loans smaller than Rp 20,000, 4 percent for loans larger than Rp 20,000.

The number of pawnshops per country varies considerably: in 1990 Indonesia counted 505 and Thailand 361; in 1991 Malaysia counted 194 and Singapore 60. Common pledges in more advanced countries, such as Malaysia, Singapore and the Philippines were almost exclusively gold and jewelry, in Thailand electronics in addition to gold and jewelry, while in Indonesia a variety of household articles are pledged, too. Pawnshop owners prefer gold and jewelry because gold prices tend to rise consistently. The cash offered as percentage of value amounts to at least 30 percent in the Philippines (fixed by the government) to normally around 75 to 85 percent for gold and jewelry in Thailand (75-85 percent) and in Singapore (80-85 percent), while in Indonesia the government provides 84 percent for loans less than Rp 20,000 and 89 percent for loans more than this amount.

In India, as contained in the report of the Study Group on Indigenous Bankers (1971: 21ff.), pawnbrokers offer 70 percent of the value of gold ornaments and 50 percent in the case of silver. As the value of the pawn exceeds the loan by far, bad debts are rare. The boundaries between moneylender and pawnbroker are vague. In Madras Marwari pawnshops largely finance the small-scale vegetable trade. The vegetable vendors tend to pledge their jewels and clothes in the morning to obtain a small-scale loan of Rs 5 to 20 as working capital to buy their stock. The interest rate ranges from 1 to 2 paise per day, and the borrower pays interest and principal in the evening. This procedure is repeated the next morning. In 1943, the State of Tamil Nadu introduced the Tamil Nadu Pawnbrokers Act, according to which a pawnbroker is required to maintain certain books and is not allowed to take more than the simple interest of 12 percent per year (which amounts to one paisa per rupee per month). In spite of this strict regulation, the number of licensed pawnbrokers shows that this business is profitable.[24] Loans on ornaments and valuables range from 7.5 to 18 percent (7.5 to 12 percent in the case of gold), on jewelry 10 to 15 percent, on silver 18 percent per annum.

To sum up, pawnshops are either run by the government, by the municipality, or privately. In most Southeast Asian countries pawn brokerage requires a license. Whether pawnshops fall into the formal, semi-formal or informal financial market, and whether they can be considered commercial or non-commercial, depends on the particular financial and civil laws.

Savings and Credit Associations

It is commonly agreed that originally savings and credit associations were self-help emergency funds.[25] Nowadays savings and credit associations are found all around the world and among all parts of the population. In recent times, the majority of these associations have become pure financial institutions with the secondary function of insurance business. Many of them have been commercialized, too, being started or run by merchants, managing firms and even banks for the sake of profit, while the aspect of self-help has been totally lost. The various forms of savings and credit associations

---

[24] In 1969 this state issued 7,364 renewal licenses and 1,425 new licenses (SGIB 1971: 21).

[25] Seibel and Marx (1987: 15) even assumed that work associations are a basic form of savings and credit associations, which are found in less monetized regions and are organized in a similar way. In various cases they are combined with a savings and credit fund.

to my mind do not allow us to categorize them as commercial or non-commercial institutions. Nevertheless, most of these institutions are autonomous and therefore counted as belonging to informal finance. Most scholars agree that the participation in a savings and credit association may, at least to some extent, keep away low-income households from moneylenders.

The main distinction of savings and credit associations is between RoSCAs and ASCrAs, the rotating and the non-rotating, accumulating savings and credit associations, respectively.[26] The emphasis of each association may be on the savings or credit side. The recent discussion of RoSCAs and ASCrAs shows that a shift has taken place from the less calculable RoSCAs to the more calculable ASCrAs.

1.4. Recent Approaches to Development Finance

Nowadays scholars agree that subsidized credit programs have not fulfilled the assumption that subsidized interest rates induce more investment and produce more socio-economic justice. The reasons for the failure are the following. First of all, investment and savings are closely interrelated. However, low fixed lending rates also result in low savings rates which not only do not provide an incentive to open a bank savings account but it may result in more attractive investment opportunities for potential savers, such as informal moneylending and pawn brokerage. Second, financial repression has a negative impact on the quality of investment. Market rate lending singles out high-risk projects and those with very low returns. Third, interest ceilings for credit and credit rationing resulting from high demand for cheap credit may have counter-effects such as bribery, nepotistic lending, and so on. In addition to the negative effects on savings, investment, growth and distribution, subsidized credit may prevent the banking system to fulfill one main function, namely to collect idle money and to make it available for deficit households and enterprises. Low or even negative profit margins prevent the realization of economies of scale, so that only the larger customers obtain bank credit (a large part of transaction costs are fixed costs), while the majority of people has neither access to bank loans nor, in many cases, to deposit accounts (see Krahnen and Schmidt 1994).

A micro-economic reason for the failure of subsidized credit programs has been overlooked by most development planners. It seems to me that this is only due to their limited investigation of the borrowers' side and the concentration on the lenders' side. The reason for this is simply that low-income households not only combine different income sources to make a living but different credit sources, too. Under such an assumption, the risk that a borrower defaults in the subsidized credit program is the highest for two reasons. (a) Assuming that a borrower acts rationally he will repay the costly loans (i.e. the moneylender) first and the cheap ones last. (b) Assuming the 'safety-first' principle (Scott 1976) a borrower is more likely to be reliable in his long-standing credit line with his moneylender than in an unproved impersonal though cheaper credit line. Also economists have realized that the credit demand among the

---

[26] For a recent discussion of RoSCAs, see Schrader (1991); Pischke (1992), Bouman (1994).

poor population is highly inelastic to interest rate changes. This may explain the high default rates in subsidized credit programs.

The failure of subsidized credit programs has supported the assumption that, instead of considering the lack of capital as the primary development impediment, the financial system has to be reorganized. This means taking the whole spectrum of financial services into consideration. As a reaction to interventionism and regulation of finance, and with the decline of Keynesanism, the neoclassical faction among development planners recaptured the strongest position. Among them, the approach developed by the Ohio State University-circle around D.W. Adams achieved prominence. This approach considers the unrestricted financial market to be an efficient allocator of financial services. It recommends the deregulation of financial systems and leaving the rest to market forces. Only such systems, it is argued, will be able to mobilize savings, transform them into investable funds and channel these funds into socially valuable investment projects. Indeed, in recent years deregulation has been achieved in various countries of East and Southeast Asia.

Krahnen and Schmidt (1994) rightly criticized the 'Ohio State University Approach' in that it has not been theoretically grounded. The argument is mainly based on a critique of prevailing development policy. The implicit model being used is that of monolithic, profit-maximizing financial institutions which function in the same way as commodity markets (Stieglitz 1989). Krahnen and Schmidt held against this approach that deregulation alone does not solve the problems. They adhere to 'New Development Economics' (Stieglitz 1986) that is based upon New Institutional Economics. This view assumes that economic development depends to a high degree upon the availability of 'good institutions', a prerequisite of which is a good financial sector. Institutions, it is argued, are good if they provide incentives for savings, capital accumulation and allocation in such a way that they induce growth. (The term 'institution' is used in a broad sense. It includes markets, firms and governments, the financial system and its main elements). Krahnen and Schmidt held against deregulated financial markets that they do not only function in a non-optimal way but that they do not function at all. The reason for this is that credit and capital rationing can be expected in deregulated markets. Financial agreements in everyday life include elements which express the dangers of particular credit relations. This view assumes that financial markets are important, but they are imperfect in nature. The main issue is to analyze which institutions function in what way on the basis of what information. The existing institutions are considered to be the result of a long-term competitive and selective process. However, because of the imperfection of the financial market, the existing institutions do not function in an optimal way. Nor is the market allocation which these institutions take over optimal. This view is open for interventions which improve the allocation of resources.

The supporters of institution-building of course assume that financial reform programs have to be placed within a broader context of structural adjustment programs. With variations from one country to another, structural adjustment typically covers four areas: (i) macro-economic reform of the monetary, fiscal and exchange rate regimes and trade liberalization; (ii) real sector reform; (iii) legal, institutional and political reform; and (iv) financial sector reform. The latter comprises the following

components: (a) the rehabilitation of banks through financial and organizational measures; (b) deregulation and liberalization; (c) the strengthening of bank supervisory
institutions; (d) the limitation of government powers with respect to regulation; (e) the
lowering in entry and exit barriers of the banking sector (Krahnen and Schmidt 1994).

The three strategies for institution-building pursued until now by development
planners are 'upgrading', 'downgrading' and 'linking'. Institutions concerned in
these approaches are institutions from the formal and informal financial sectors which
are not financial institutions in the legal sense. One side consists of NGOs (non-
government organizations), PVOs (i.e. private voluntary organizations), self-help
groups and other informal-sector groups, donor-initiated rotating funds and credit
programs, cooperative-type organizations, and so on. This side is assumed to be close
to the grassroots level but the institutions lack professionalism, have high operational
cost and tend to be short-lived. The other side consists of banks and similar institutions
of the formal financial sector which are considered to be distant from the grassroots
level, but operate efficiently and are relatively stable.

The strategy of 'downgrading' banks relies on these attributes and aims at moving
them closer to the grassroots level. 'Upgrading' relies upon the closeness of informal
and semi-formal financial institutions to the grassroots level and seeks to make them
more efficient, professional and stable. Some development experts try to 'link' the
advantages of both types of institutions. For example, a bank will provide funding to
an NGO which on-lends for its own projects, or a bank may cooperate with informal
groups which will distribute or collect funds and acts as a guarantor for credit security
through collective responsibility or peer monitoring (see, for example, Seibel 1989a,b;
1990).

Among other arguments Krahnen and Schmidt (1994) held against these strategies
that the planners consider the institutions to be already in existence. The introduction
of an institution or new type of institution, as well as the reconstruction of an existing institution are also important. The only objective was to improve the social and
economic situation of the target population (target-group orientation). This depends
upon two factors, namely the presence of a political, institutional and economic environment, and the policy and structure of the particular financial institution. On the
operational level sustainability is equally important: a target group-oriented institution has to be professional and financially and organizationally stable and efficient.
Development policy, it is claimed, has to shift the emphasis from financial support to
technical assistance. Target group-oriented institutions should provide the following
services: deposit or savings facilities, credit or borrowing facilities, payment transfer
services and risk management and insurance services.

Institutional analysis and institution-building are to my mind a useful tool of development finance because this approach takes a broader perspective compared to the
earlier ones, starts from the realistic assumption of imperfect financial markets and
considers the strengths and weaknesses of particular financial institutions of both financial sectors and their ways of coping with situations such as risk. However, the
weakness of this approach and of most approaches by development planners is that
they largely ignore the perspective of the borrowers and confine themselves to partic-

ular institutions only – a perspective which results from the professional profile and economic training of development experts. However, a misconception of the borrowers' side may lead to erroneous assumptions in institution-building. Furthermore, the approach implicitly assumes that existing institutions and agents – be they formal or informal – do not work efficiently enough and have to be re-organized in one or the other way to fit in with the market or even be replaced. In most cases, too, economists leave the historical perspective out of consideration. What they overlook is that certain 'indigenous' financial agents and institutions have emerged in particular historical periods in relation to particular requirements of the economy and its actors. Over time some of them disappeared and others developed; others again have adapted themselves to changing circumstances and the requirements of the borrowers, which points to at least some efficiency of those who have survived. Institution-building is thus a long-lasting process which has been at work for some time, and is not merely a recent phenomenon. This process has produced the contemporary financial landscapes. To my mind, the multiplicity of agents and institutions cannot be explained by a period of transition of the developing economies in which old, inefficient agents and institutions are eventually replaced by newer, more efficient ones.

This multiplicity is a reflection of the different conditions and requirements of the population with respect to financial services. This means that formal and informal finance are somehow interrelated, be this relation competitive in some cases, or complementary in others. Such differences therefore require a perspective which assumes a different suitability and efficiency of agents and institutions for different target groups and the different requirements of such target groups in the financial markets. Let us take, for example, rotating savings and credit associations. From the economic point of view of undercapitalization impeding economic growth, one disadvantage of RoSCAs is the limited amount of money the participants have in turn available. However, subjectively considered, i.e. from the perspective of the single member, this disadvantage may be unimportant, if the amount covers his needs. Also RoSCA members may themselves determine which type of RoSCA they consider most appropriate for themselves. Those who require larger and more liquid funds may take part in larger RoSCA of the auctioning type. Similar subjective considerations from the point of view of borrowers are necessary to explain why certain types of commercial lenders have survived. For many borrowers the immediate availability of money is more important than the level of interest. They may even prefer a long-established credit line with high interest to new lending programs which have been institutionalized from above. Moreover, many small-scale borrowers can only exist on the basis of day-to-day small-scale credit which they use as their working capital and which banks cannot provide at reasonable rates because of the high fixed cost component. In spite of the high interest rates of such informal loans (if one calculates them annually), the productive input of the loan provides the borrowers with a sufficient income to make a living.

This study is concerned with a long-term view upon the development of financial landscapes in Asia. This view belongs to economic history, political economy and economic sociology. I believe that contemporary financial landscapes and regional differences result to a high degree from processes in the past taking place both on the particular national level as well as on a higher, structural level, and that past experiences and future expectations influence the present political decision-making of nation-states.[27] By comparing the particular cases of India and Indonesia and their pre-colonial, colonial and post-colonial economic histories I will investigate which processes are structural and which result from particular national developments.

Before guiding the reader into the fascinating financial history of India and Indonesia, Chapter 2 outlines the research hypotheses, while Chapters 3 and 4 reflect on money, credit and interest, and explain what is theoretically meant by processes occurring on the structural level.

---

[27] Certain financial policies in the Third World, for example, may have originated as reactions to imperialism. Sukarno's strict regulation of financial markets in independent Indonesia was legitimized as an anti-Dutch/anti-imperialistic policy (McLeod 1992), although – as will be shown – the Dutch colonial governments applied similar regulations.

2. Research Hypotheses

Development planners are concerned with a variety of activities related to finance. Whether they are involved in planning agencies or in projects, they take (and have to take) a narrow perspective that is determined by their professional profile, economic training and cost-benefit considerations. Their outlook, whether macro or micro, is mainly confined to the present and future of their specific setting: their country, region, town, village, target group, occupational group, and so on. They are concerned with socio-economic change (whereas the social and sociological aspects have increasingly been lost again with the revival of neoclassical/neoliberal thinking, re-emerging with the 'final victory of capitalism over socialism'). However, the past is only implicitly taken into consideration and upholds the dualistic stereotype. It is associated with traditional or at least value-rational action in the Weberian sense, while development is associated with means-end rationalizing and modernity.

My perspective of the past is different in that I place myself in the tradition of *longue durée* analysis, taking into account economic history and economic sociology. My view is that contemporary financial landscapes and regional differences are largely results of historical processes taking place both on the particular national level as well as on a higher structural level, and that past experience and future expectations influence the contemporary political decision-making of nation-states. I work in the tradition of great scholars such as F. Braudel and I. Wallerstein on a world scale or K.N. Chaudhuri for Asia, who related their studies to the emergence of what has been called the modern world-system or capitalist world-economy, which is seen to emerge from the commercial interaction of regionally confined world-economies (to use Braudel's [1982, 1984] terminology), in our context the European and the Far Eastern world-economy, and the step-by-step incorporation of the latter by the former in the course of colonization.

Critics may argue that such an approach may have been up-to-date in the 1980s but is now out-modeled. They may assert that Wallerstein's world-system analysis was too much a meta-theory which in the last analysis explained underdevelopment mono-causally as resulting from external factors, namely Western incursion into foreign cultures. Likewise he has been criticized because of his ambiguous understanding of 'system' (e.g. Nederveen Pieterse 1988). Furthermore, Wallerstein's (for example, 1984: 24-5) utopian view of the collapse of capitalism[1] (because of its too many self-contradictions and its reaching its utmost boundaries) has not only never come about until this day; rather, the opposite happened in that real socialism collapsed. While the third point of course is no proof of the quality of capitalism, it is treated as such by conservative politicians and scientists. The political events in Eastern Europe as well as the development success of the NICs (newly industrialized countries) have been

---

[1] In his essay on *'Patterns and Prospective of the Capitalist World-Economy'* Wallerstein developed the scenarios of a nuclear war or the transition to socialism.

seen as evidence for the non-validity of the left-wing meta-theories, *dependencia* and world-system theory, irrespective of their plausibility on important points. In Part IV I shall take a closer look to world-system theory, its critique and modification.

But what is the mainstream trend in the economic and social sciences? To my mind, in late 1993 and early 1994 (when I wrote the manuscript), it is no more than a neoliberal revival combined with an ideology of modernization, the belief in the self-vitalization and self-regulation of the market. David Ricardo's excavated theory of comparative cost advantages no longer articulates the unequal international division of labour but simply promises growth for all countries participating in the world market.[2] The 'deregulation' of the economies is proclaimed as the key to development and growth by the Word Bank and similar institutions. The soft approaches in development finance which I outlined in Chapter 1 fit into this picture of deregulation. Beyond this politicians can use this re-vitalized belief in the market to positively legitimize their passiveness (if not helplessness) in dealing with the socio-economic problems (Bonder and Röttger 1993: 62) like unemployment arising from the current structural crises of capitalism.

Returning to the scope of this study, I now outline my research hypotheses. I propose that merchant bankers are a structural phenomenon of expanding merchant capitalism (Schrader 1992). In line with Braudel (1981, 1982, 1984), I consider the transformation of the economy and society from subsistence to market orientation as a secular process which is constantly accelerated or slowed down by specific social formations. I argue that merchant bankers and large-scale moneylenders acted as accelerators. Perhaps they cannot be called 'entrepreneurs' in Schumpeter's (1912, 1974) sense,[3] but they financed others' entrepreneurial activities.

Once this transformation had been achieved, these merchant bankers and large-scale moneylenders were deprived of many of their functions and were increasingly substituted by bureaucrats and banks. They took up other occupations or continued their financial existence on an intermediate level of finance. On the low level of finance, various small-scale, mostly part-time, moneylenders who are as old as man continued to exist. Contemporary moneylenders and other informal financial institutions can be found in great numbers in developing countries, but small numbers can be found in industrialized countries too, and they experience a growth during economic crises wherever unemployment grows. Contrary to the thinking of modernizers, and in line with the '*Bielefeld Ansatz*' (AG Bielefelder Entwicklungssoziologen 1979), I reject the view that explains such financial agents as a remainder of the past, who slow down development and eventually disappear with the onset of modernization. I believe that such contemporary moneylenders and other informal credit suppliers are structurally assigned to the capitalist mode of production because they provide credit to marginalized people beyond the scope of banks. By supplying unsecured credit

---

[2] That growth may occur without development has already been shown by various scholars who adhered to these meta-theories.

[3] Schumpeter stressed the innovative character of entrepreneurs who are considered the engine of economic development. They push forward development by doing new things or finding new ways of doing old things. For a more detailed discussion of the theories on entrepreneurship, see Chapter 7.4.2.

to such people, the latter obtain purchasing power and are linked to the commodity market as consumers.

On the basis of this argumentation, my study will analyze the socio-economic function of Asian moneylenders and other financial agents in the long term. I think that one can discover generalizations and peculiarities in particular countries by comparative research only. The emphasis should be placed on the transformation process of economy and society and the changing functions of the financial intermediaries during this process. The outcome of my research is a comparison of changing financial landscapes in India and Indonesia in the long run, based on secondary material analysis (monographs, journals, government reports). This comparison is of particular interest because the country studies in Parts II and III exhibit the following differences between both countries: (a) a different social, economic and political structure of India and Indonesia in the pre-colonial period and therefore different positions within the world-economy of the Far East; (b) a colonial history under two different colonial regimes, the British and the Dutch; and (c) politically and economically different post-colonial developments.

The emerging questions with regard to my research topic are obvious. Did these different histories produce similar financial landscapes in both countries or are there any peculiarities? If yes, can we relate them to these different histories? The answers which I offer are based on plausibility chains. Because of the richness of the material used and the long-term process analysis I am aware of the fact that specialists in Indian and Indonesian history may find counter-examples to the ones I used and locate particular periods of change some decades earlier or later than I did. However, I believe that this kind of criticism does not act as a challenge to my line of argumentation.

3. Money and Credit

> "'Accumulate, accumulate! This is the golden rule' of the capitalist economy, wrote Marx. Just as golden a rule would be 'Borrow, borrow!'" (Braudel 1982: 386, quoting Marx 1970, I: Ch. 24, iii).[1]

3.1. Introduction

The list of economic, historical, anthropological and sociological literature on the origin or evolution of money, the emergence of financial institutions or the Christian condemnation of usury, is extensive. Every scholar defines money in his/her own way depending on his/her own background and these definitions and perceptions reflect the epochs of European thought on economy, society and the relation of the two.

Theories on credit, except for technical ones in business administration and financial science, are, however, largely absent. This is because most sociological and economic approaches treat credit as a corollary to the theory of money which in turn has been derived from the theory of exchange. In general I agree with this proceeding. Contrary to most economic approaches, however, I consider credit as not necessarily being monetized, and therefore it makes sense to start from the theories of exchange, treating theories on monetary exchange and money already as a particular case.

An important issue of this book is the process of monetization. While money was usually considered neutral in value, the process of monetization was hardly discussed in a value-neutral way. According to O. Harris (1989), the emergence of general purpose money has been interpreted either as a 'sign of alienation, individualism and the breakdown of social and communal values' (Harris 1989: 134) which destroyed an intact old socio-economic order. Or, according to Liberal philosophy, modern money is a symbol of society having made the step towards rationality, civilization and having liberalized itself from the bonds of dependency, marking the beginning of the modern era. One can assert with Parry and Bloch that 'money (...) is in nearly as much danger of being fetishized by scholars as by stockbrokers' (Parry and Bloch 1989: 3).

What was concealed in the discussion of 'traditional' versus 'modern' society, and symbolized with the use of money, was in reality the perception of **profit** in sales-purchase transaction and **interest**, its twin in lender-borrower transactions. Harris (1989: 236ff.) rightly argued that, on the one hand, money is a historical phenomenon but, on the other, it operates as a general signifier on many levels, standing for the profit motive, the market, the evil ideology of capitalism or even for the profane, the opposite of the sacral which is incompatible with money (so long as venality and commodification have not been extended even into this sphere).

---

[1] With Marx (1970, I) and (1970, III) I refer to *Capital*, Volumes I and III, respectively.

'Homo Sociologicus' and Homo Oekonomicus

General-purpose money and markets are closely linked. Their presence or absence marks two opposed socio-economic states – the self-sufficient society, based upon use values and governed by collective aims and morals, and the market society which is based upon exchange values and governed by individualism, means-end rationality, market laws and money (profit/loss as indicators of success in the market game). Throughout the history of the social sciences this dichotomy appears again and again,[2] whereas the individual scholar perceived the transgression of the former to the latter as either a step backward or progress in the evolution of society.

In his *'Politics'* Aristotle (1962), for example, took up the former position. Parry and Bloch (1989) summarized his thoughts as follows:

> "Like other animals, man is naturally self-sufficient and his wants are finite. Trade can only be natural in so far as it is oriented towards the restoration of such self-sufficiency. Just as in nature there may be too much here and not enough there, so it is with households which will then be forced to exchange on the basis of mutual need. 'Interchange of this kind is not contrary to nature and is not a form of money-making; it keeps to its original purpose – to re-establish nature's own equilibrium of self-sufficiency' (. . .) Profit-oriented exchange is, however, unnatural; and is destructive of the bonds between households. Prices should therefore be fixed, and goods and services remunerated in accordance with the status of those who provided them. Money as a tool intended only to facilitate exchange is naturally barren, and, of all the ways of getting wealth, lending at interest – where money is made to yield a 'crop' or 'litter' – is 'the most contrary to nature'" (Aristotle 1962: 42, 46, quoted by Parry and Bloch 1989: 2).

To sum up, Aristotle distinguished between the natural, *oikonomike,* use of money for the satisfaction of needs and the unnatural, *chrematistike,* use in which the acquisition of wealth becomes an end in itself. The position was revived by the Christian Church in the course of the late Middle Ages when the expanding economy and changing values questioned its authority (Le Goff 1980). Perhaps the most prominent proponent of this position was Karl Marx who witnessed the social consequences of the Industrial Revolution. His position on money, profit and interest will be considered in more detail later on.

The latter mainstream ideas put forward the liberalization of the economy from moral obligations and restrictions, and were articulated in the Enlightenment, Liberalism and economic theory. Adam Smith argued that the wealth of the nation and the happiness of the individual is founded on the individual's 'propensity (. . .) to truck, barter and exchange one thing for another' (Smith [1776] 1976: 17) and pursue monetary self-gain. Classical and neoclassical economic theories are based upon the idea that scarcity governs social and economic action. From such a perspective the making of money is considered natural, harmless and desirable. In its strictest ideological manifestation, the free market, any moral consideration (even Adam Smith's 'moral sentiments', a kind of instinct which prohibits *ego* to finally exterminate *alter* in the market fight) loses force, since the market (demand, supply and utility in classical or price in neoclassical economic theory, respectively) is defined as self-regulating (Adam Smith's 'invisible hand') and any imbalance is explained as being the result of

---

[2] Toennies, for example, (1959) called these two stages *community* and *society*, while Durkheim (1964) circumscribed them with *mechanical* and *organic solidarity.*

interference with the market. The state is ascribed no function other than to constitute the market system and to guarantee the framework for its functioning (law and order, free mobility of the factors of production, and so on).

Characteristic of 'modern capitalistic' societies, as Max Weber called them, is that 'man is dominated by the making of money, by acquisition as the ultimate purpose of his life. Economic acquisition is no longer subordinated to man as the means for the satisfaction of his material needs' (Weber in Andreski 1984: 114). The legal earning of money is the expression of virtue and proficiency in a calling. The conscious acceptance of these ethical maxims is a condition for the future existence of capitalism as well as of individual survival in capitalism. To offend against its premises means to lose. According to Weber, modern capitalism educates and selects the economic subjects which it needs through a process of economic survival of the fittest.

In economic anthropology these two mainstreams of thought merged into the antagonistic positions of **substantivism** and **formalism**. Substantivism understands 'economic' as an instituted process[3] of interaction between man and his natural social environment. Market systems, which are governed by the principle of means-end economizing, developed only during the process of the **Great Transformation**,[4] in which the economy became disembedded from society. Historical markets were *loci* of exchange which were not determined by the economic principle of maximization and sometimes even lacked the use of money. Social components played a similarly important role in the exchange as economic ones (Polanyi 1957: 248-50; 1978). One of the best-known discussions on the impact of Western money on a previously non-monetized subsistence economy is Bohannan's (1959) case of the Tiv in Northern Nigeria. Bohannan concluded that money is one of the shatteringly simplifying ideas of all time and creates its own revolution.

Polanyi (1957: 245-6) argued that from the formalist perspective the meaning of 'economic' derives from the logical character of the means-end relationship. It refers to a definite situation of choice between the different uses of means induced by an insufficiency of those means. If the choice is logically rational, we may denote this logic as formal economics in which rational action is defined as the choice of means in relation to ends. Assuming that the choice is induced by an insufficiency of means, the concept of rational action turns into the theory of choice. However, Polanyi warned that choice and insufficiency are not necessarily interdependent.

The dispute between both positions during the 1950s and 60s was finally a dead letter ending in the dogmatic controversy whether man's nature is *homo oekonomicus* or a self-sufficient being which aims for social security. However, recently Polanyi's thoughts were revived by scholars working in the substantivist tradition (see, for example, Polanyi-Levitt 1990), and further elaborated by economic sociologists. Granovetter (1985, 1992) rightly argued in his famous article '*Economic Action and Social*

---

[3] Polanyi (1957) defined a process as a movement of changes in location, appropriation or both. The instituting of this economic process vests that process with unity and stability and produces a structure with a definite function in society.

[4] Polanyi considered the Great Transformation as a relatively short period from 1815 to 1914. I believe that this process took much longer. It started slowly with the Commercial Revolution and ended with the First World War.

Structure: The Problem of Embeddedness' that Polanyi overemphasized the degree of embeddedness of the economy in marketless societies and that of disembeddedness in market societies. I take up this critique by arguing that the concept of embeddedness is even relevant for western and non-Western contemporary societies, when we dissolve the high level of aggregation of 'embedded' or 'disembedded society'. Instead I suggest to consider the degree of embeddedness of particular action or interaction. I assume a wide range of more or less embedded types of action or interaction that are characteristic for different institutional contexts (e.g. anonymous market, neighborhood market, family, network, etc.). A type of action or interaction is then a function of certain variables that are to some extent individually determined (e.g. closeness and distance to *alter*),[5] to some extent conditioned by social structure (the relation of individual and meta-preferences, conventions characterizing socially legitimate action, etc.). This type of action is then taken as social measure for real economic action in a certain institutional context. This modified understanding of embeddedness is applied in this book.

Interestingly neoclassical thinkers adopted Polanyi's position too. They use his claim of re-embedding the economy as a tool to legitimize the cutting of social transfer payments and public goods by getting family, kin and neighborhood to take over once more part of their (pre-industrial) security functions which the state fulfilled so far.[6]

3.2.   Exchange, Money and Credit

Economists consider modern, general purpose money as simultaneously fulfilling the following five functions: (a) the medium-of- (commercial) exchange function; (b) the means-of- (commercial) payment function; (c) the unit-of-(commercial) account (or reckoning) function; (d) the standard-of-deferred-payment function and (e) store-of value function. Theories on the origin of money which largely developed in nineteenth- and early twentieth-century Germany, make any of the functions of general purpose money responsible for the emergence of modern money. However, I do not want to analyze these types of money theories in detail, since they are hardly relevant for my study. What is important so far is that most theories, both commercial and non-commercial ones, identify the origin of money in a commercial or ritual exchange act.[7]

My first point is that, contrary to barter, both money and credit facilitate an exchange which involves time.

3.2.1.   Direct and Indirect Exchange

From the sociological perspective, exchange is one of the basic acts of man as a social being, a *total social phenomenon* (Mauss 1925, 1990). According to Max Weber

---

[5] Granovetter (1985, 1992) argued that action is usually embedded in a network of social relations. In the last analysis the degree of embeddedness of economic action is related to the degree of social distance.

[6] Elsewhere I discussed formalism and substantivism and its implications on exchange, trade and markets in more detail (Schrader 1994a).

[7] For a more detailed discussion on the origin of money and money objects, see Schrader (1990).

(1978: 71-4), it is a compromise of interests between two parties in the course of which goods or other opportunities are exchanged as a reciprocal compensation according to tradition or convention. Every case of rationally oriented exchange is the resolution of a previously open or latent conflict of interests by compromise, the 'continuation of war with peaceful means' (Thurnwald 1932). The object of exchange is everything transferable from the control of one person to that of another and *vice versa*. It is not restricted to goods and services, but includes all potential economic opportunities.

Economic theory considers an exchange act as two movements, the process of giving and of receiving.[8] In **direct exchange** or **barter** these two processes take place simultaneously, so that no future claim by one party and no liability on the other's part comes about. The perspective of objective value theory assumes that in free markets the exchange act is balanced.

While in *Capital I*, Chapter 3, Marx (1970) started his discussion of exchange from the perspective of objective value theory too, Simmel (1989: 60ff.) adopted a counter perspective from the subjective point of view. He maintained that exchange is as productive and value generating as production if one leaves behind the level of objective value theory. From the subjective perspectives of *ego* and *alter* goods (not only commodities) are obtained for other sacrificed goods, and given the condition of free exchange the final condition is satisfying more wants than the former one.[9]

The exchange act becomes trans-individualized in two-sided exchange. While it is objectively just, it leads subjectively to an increase of the cumulative sum of felt values. One individual gives what it considers unnecessary and obtains what is more scarce for the person.

Indirect exchange is defined as an act in which money enters the transaction as an intermediate medium of exchange. From the perspective of objective value theory, with the introduction of money as the general form of value (characterizing the price of a commodity), the exchange of two commodities becomes an indirect process, the metamorphosis or the circulation of commodities

Commodity – Money – Commodity, in short $C - M - C$ (Marx 1970, I: 108).

From the point of view of the first commodity, the relation $C - M$ characterizes the first metamorphosis or the sale, the relation $M - C$ the second, final metamorphosis or the purchase.

The metamorphosis $C - M - C$ means that an equal value of a commodity C which is sold for money M returns in the form of another commodity to the former seller

---

[8] Simmel (1989: 73-4) claimed that such a view is too simple from the sociological perspective. It is not just the addition of the two movements, but a new, third thing, in which each of the two processes is at the same time cause and effect of the other.

[9] The economic value is never a value per se. Its nature is a certain quantity of value which can only be determined by the difference of two intensities of wants – receiving and sacrificing. The value of a certain thing means that this thing has some value for myself – that I am willing to sacrifice something for this thing – a subjective value. The price correlates with the objective economic value. From the individual point of view the equivalence of exchange does not exist. The exchange partners are only willing to exchange if each of them has a higher preference for the state after the exchange act than before (Simmel 1989: 77-9).

who is now in the position of a buyer. Marx maintained that the movement of commodities is a circular. Money, on the other hand, progresses from the starting point, the exchange between two individuals, to other exchanges. Currency is the circulation of money from one hand to the next (Marx 1970, I: 116-7).[10]

Arguing from the point of view of subjective value, Simmel (1989: 126) took a broader perspective: Money has a dual role, within and outside the exchange relation of objects. In the former case it functions as a means of exchange. However, by this role it develops as an independent value with its own demand and supply, its own market and an interest rate (expression of its value). In other words, the dual role means: (a) it measures the relation of value between exchangeable goods; and (b) it becomes commodified itself. Its value is determined by the exchange relation with goods and manifestations of money (loans, foreign exchange, and so on).

According to Simmel (1989: 210-11), the medium-of-exchange-function of money brings about the socio-economic position of trader and money itself. The trader is the differentiated role bearer of the exchange act which was initially carried out directly between producers. We might say with Simmel that the trader is just placed in between the two subjects of exchange, while money is placed just in between the two objects of exchange.

Since general-purpose money constitutes an intermediate means (or medium) of exchange, time may be involved between the first and second metamorphosis. However, these two processes are distinct and no future claims and liabilities continue to exist in each of them once the transaction is finished as compared to credit-involving transactions (whereas it is unimportant so far whether money enters the exchange act).

3.2.2. Credit

As outlined in Chapter 1, it does not make sense for pre-modern and even developing societies to define credit in a modern economic sense as 'the purchasing power without the possession of money against the promise of compensation in future' (Sombart 1927: 175). It is more useful to include non-monetary transactions too which similarly engender claims and liabilities between the exchange partners. An example of a broad understanding of credit is provided by Raymond Firth's definition. Credit is

> "the lending of goods and services without immediate return against the promise of a future repayment. It involves an obligation by the borrower to make a return and confidence by the lender in the borrower's good faith and ability to repay. The return may be the same article or service as lent, or a different one. It may be equivalent in value to the loan or augmented in value above the loan (i.e. with interest). The augmentation may be voluntary or prescribed, and it may be proportionate or not to the amount of time for which the object lent has been held. The repayment may be contractual and enforceable at law, or it may not have a legal backing but be socially binding. Such a list of alternative elements indicates not only the possible variations in the structure of credit transactions in an economy, but also various points at which such variations may be conditioned by social forces" (Firth 1964: 29).

However, it is useful to apply an even broader understanding of the term credit than Firth employed. In Chapter 1 I simply defined credit as the provision of goods and

---

[10] Note, he treats the circulation of capital as a separate theme; see the discussion in Chapter 4.

services against the promise of future compensation. Credit relations comprise a broad spectrum of variations. The compensation may be in the form of the same or another good (cash, kind or in a combination of the two) or service, interest may be involved or not, the debt may be documented or not, the loan can be provided on personal security or against collateral and the terms of repayment (one lump sum or installments, the date of repayment, and so on) may be fixed or left open. All this demonstrates that credit relations are very complex. It is in many cases not the level of interest which is most important for borrower and lender, but other liabilities linked with the credit relation; for example, to assure a future reciprocity in case of emergency credit or, in case of traders to bind their customers to their supply.

In primitive and peasant societies borrowing for consumption purposes (including social events) is as a rule distinguished from borrowing for investment and both are often morally valued and priced differently, although the distinction between these forms is in many cases not clear-cut. Dalton and Bohannan (1964), for example, worked out the separate spheres of exchange and possible conversions. In case of emergency credit within a community, claims and obligations used to be balanced over a life time. Sometimes, but not generally, consumption loans do not incur interest, while with a loan for productive purposes, the lender will be compensated from the productive benefit.

The Gift – A Reciprocal Credit Transaction

In the first part of this chapter I shall not consider the issue of interest. According to Einzig (1949), non-monetary and non-commercial credit existed from the earliest phases of economic activity. This is convincing if we think of ritual, inter-temporary exchange as, for example, in the case of the gift.

To distinguish a loan from a gift in the sense that a loan causes liabilities while the recipient of a gift is free of any obligations, is too superficial, if one draws attention to the structure-functionalists' relation of the gift and reciprocity. In his essay on '*The Gift*' Mauss (1925, 1990) analyzed the gift as what he called the most elementary form of exchange. What seems to be a voluntary act in the ritual exchange of primitive societies was in reality a claim on the recipient of the gift which he had to reciprocate in the future. Mauss derived his theoretical implications from ethnographic descriptions of ritual exchange, such as Malinowski's *kula* ring from Polynesia or Boas' *potlatch* among the Northwest American Indians.

With regard to Boas' description,[11] Mauss argued that one important element in the *potlatch* is to create (ritual and economic) dependencies (claims) and humiliations. The latter are expressed in an inflated counter gift always exceeding the gift in value. Since there is a time interval between gift and counter gift, one can interpret the relation as a credit transaction, the inflation of value as an 'interest rate' and the creation of claims as 'investments' or 'insurance'. The reciprocation in the *potlatch* was not at all a voluntary act. Non-reciprocation was sanctioned with loss of rank and even the status of a free man (Mauss 1990: 100). With regard to the ethnographic

---

[11] Boas, 5th report: 38; 12th report: 54f., see Mauss (1990: 82, FN 122).

material, Mauss (1990: 122) maintained that gift exchange was characteristic of societies which had left the state of 'total presentation' (an exchange from clan to clan, family to family) behind but had not reached the phase of individual contracts, money markets, buying and selling, fixed prices, and so on. Principally, however, he interpreted gift exchange and commerce as complementary. This was misunderstood by many social scientists and, according to Bloch (1989: 168ff.), it became the 'received wisdom' in anthropology that gift exchange preceded market exchange. Mauss' view was moreover bound up with the aspect of the presence or absence of general purpose money, and hence dualistic concepts emerged as outlined at the beginning of this chapter. In my opinion the dualism is in many cases the result of the reduction of complex argumentation to catch words in which this complexity gets lost.

3.2.3. Trust

Since in transactions involving no credit (barter and cash payment) no claims and obligations arise between the exchange partners, the questioned integrity of the exchange partner refers to aspects of the appropriateness of measures and the money used and quality promises. In credit-involving transactions, however, it is commonly assumed that the time gap between the two processes of exchange requires trust in the willingness of the exchange partner to fulfill his obligations.

According to Luhmann (1973a), trust principally plays an important role in the functioning of society. He called trust a 'mechanism' of cooperation which reduces societal complexity and increases the individual's toleration of uncertainty. He distinguished everyday trust (on the level of credit-involving transactions between exchange partners) and system-trust on the societal level.

In a later article, Luhmann (1988b: 94-107) came to distinguish familiarity, confidence and trust which are different modes of self-assurance. Familiarity is an unavoidable fact of life, confidence is the expectation of not being disappointed (i.e. in a contingency of events) and trust is the solution to specific problems of risk (i.e. to be responsible for the consequences of one's own action). Risk does not exist by itself but is only a component of decision and action, an internal calculation of external conditions. The importance of these three factors changed with the differentiation process of society. Luhmann claimed that trust was non-existent until the emergence of capitalism. It differentiates people into more risk-taking and risk-avoiding ones and marks the transition from adventurous enterprise to risk-taking capitalism.

The relation between trust and confidence changed when the predominant type of social differentiation shifted from stratification to functional differentiation, since the formerly defined socio-territorial setting was dissolved and people had to gain access to different functional systems. Trust has remained important in interpersonal relations, while functional systems require confidence. The important point of depersonalized trust and confidence in functional systems will be discussed later in this chapter, while I now consider the element of personal trust in the exchange act.

On the level of exchange in primitive and peasant societies,[12] in which a distinction between familiar and unfamiliar predominates, uncertainty in time-involving exchange was reduced by either personal knowledge of the exchange partner (which I count as familiarity) or, because of the absence or inefficiency of civil legislation, by sanction mechanisms which ranged from physical force to social sanctions, such as the threat of loss of social prestige. The 'embedded' (Polanyi 1957) or 'moral economy' (Scott 1976) of primitive and peasant societies is based, among other principles, on reciprocity,[13] and to offend this basic principle means to insult the social code of conduct. Examples of pre-modern sanction mechanisms in India are provided in Part II of this study.

I argue that the access to such social sanction mechanisms depends on whether or not the creditor belongs to the debtor's solidarity community.[14] On the other hand, the alien status of a creditor may make it easier to legitimize the use of physical force or permit an insistence on balanced or even positive reciprocity (Sahlins 1972)[15] in the exchange act, which may offend against another basic principle of moral economies: redistribution among kin or community. The latter point was focused on and elaborated in the theory of the *Traders' Dilemma* (Evers 1994) as a stepping-stone for traders to accumulate profit, which will be discussed in this book at a more appropriate place.

By analyzing the role of trust in contemporary Chinese foreign business, Menkhoff (1993: 40ff., 145ff.) rightly questioned the usually assumed importance of trust in credit-involving exchange acts. He argued that perceptions of trust are often not reliable reflections of reality, since they include false interpretations or expectations of others' behavior. Hence, the element of trust is substituted to some degree by other mechanisms, for example, by testing the credit-worthiness of the exchange partner, and finally by establishing long-term trading relations, which are based on experience rather than trust.

---

[12] The concept of peasant society is wider than that of primitive society in so far as it includes monetary economic systems and production for the market (Firth 1964: 16ff.).

[13] Polanyi (1957) identified three functional patterns of exchange, namely reciprocity, redistribution and (market) exchange. Reciprocity denotes movements between correlative points of symmetrical groupings. Redistribution is the pattern of appropriational movement towards a center, dependent on some measure of centricity in a group. (Market) exchange refers to vice-versa movements in a market-system (Polanyi 1957: 250-252). While scholars used to interpret an evolution from one form to the next, a careful study of Polanyi points out that he disapproved of such an approach. Indeed, reciprocity and redistribution exist in market societies too, although the dominant pattern is that of market exchange.

[14] Exceptions are of course trading entrepots, where the hegemonial power introduces a legal code of conduct which offers a certain measure of security to alien traders and sets aside the social code of conduct.

[15] Sahlins (1972) elaborated Polanyi's concept of reciprocity. He realized that reciprocity is not necessarily balanced. He argued that a material transaction is usually a momentary act in a continuous social relation. The social relation may dominate the flow of goods. Thus, he introduced a continuum of reciprocity exchanges ranging from negative reciprocity to positive reciprocity. Sahlins went as far as to argue that everywhere in the world the indigenous category for exploitation is 'reciprocity'. One particular form of interest is generalized reciprocity. It forms the solidarity extreme in that the individual's counter-claim remains undefined and confined to a particular situation. The clearing of claims and liabilities occurs on society's level only. In modern society, the social security and insurance systems are based on the principle of generalized reciprocity.

To summarize this point: With regard to credit transactions, I put forward that familiarity and traditional sanction mechanisms, as well as risk-avoiding strategies in modern credit transactions, be they on the personal level or based on confidence in the legal system, all aim at reducing uncertainty and increasing the element of calculability or probability of being compensated in future. One such effective mechanism is the taking of collateral for an unfulfilled claim which usually exceeds the value of the claim. Werner Sombart (1927) argued that trust is not necessarily tied to the personality of the debtor but may comprise 'objective' circumstances like property of the debtor, his business standing or – one could add – a regular salary. However, in primitive and peasant societies and among poor borrowers, this option very often does not exist. The provision of collateral depends on the existence of private property rights, scarcity of the collateralized good and, of course, the ability to provide collateral. Typical collateral in modern credit transactions are land or house mortgages. In pre-modern societies, however, land very often either belonged to the ruler, or there may have been an occupancy right which was, however, not alienable. Here again, land may have been abundant and therefore was not valuable at all. All these issues are discussed in Parts II and III of this study.

Another mechanism to minimize trust in exchange relation is the maxim of many Chinese shops with a signboard above the counter: 'Cash, no credit', i.e. the complete elimination of credit sales.

3.2.4.   Money and Credit in the Differentiation Process of Society

One topic in Simmel's *'Philosophy of Money'* which is relevant to this study with regard to the changing functions of financial agents, is the role of money in the differentiation process of society. Since I treat monetary credit as an extension of money, Simmel's hypotheses may be applied to credit too. To begin with Simmel (1989: 375ff.) interpreted the development of social relations as a process of constant change of obligations and freedom. What is often felt as a freedom is indeed no more than a change in obligations. More or less every obligation is at the same time somebody else's claim on the person with liabilities. Three different patterns of obligations exist: (a) a claim on the body of the obliged person; (b) a claim on a certain product of his work; and (c) a claim on the product independent of the input of work of the obliged person.

An extreme example of the first case is slavery, another one is bonded labour which was and is still common in India. Although formally it is a temporary obligation only, it lasts as long as the debtor does not repay a loan and the debt/bonded labour relation may even be hereditary. The step to the second stage is a temporary limitation of labour, such as corvée labour. Part III of this study refers to the Cultivation System in the Netherlands Indies, which was based on compulsory labour and production. At this stage, argued Simmel, there is a shift from the temporary obligation of the person to the obligation to offer a certain object; for example, a fixed amount or a share of the harvest. Although this kind of obligation is probably more difficult to fulfill, it gives him more individual freedom.

The differentiation process of society is linked to an increasing spatial distance between subject and property. A landlord who leases his land and is compensated with a share of the harvest is still closer to his property than the owner of company stocks (I broadly understand both a lease and stocks as credit). Only money and monetary credit permit the owner and his possession to widely vary, and only with the inheritance of property (and one may add, claims and liabilities) does it extend beyond the individual and begin an existence of its own.

According to Simmel (1989: 463), the success of the money economy is related to the fact that money is a substitute for the dependency on the traditional solidarity system which was based on reciprocity. In the market the individual may purchase social security or obtain such from the state,[16] furthermore, the individual may liberate himself from social obligations towards the solidarity community by using a paid recruit as a substitute.

The same is true for punishment. Criminal law came into being with the emergence of a hegemonial power which, contrary to civil law, is not directed towards compensating for individual damage, whereas the hegemonial power punishes an offense against public peace and order (Simmel 1989: 495). In this study this becomes relevant with the introduction of Western law in non-Western societies, which replaced traditional rules of compensating for damages.

3.2.5. Financial Intermediaries and Their Position in Exchange

Simmel (1989: 210-11) placed the trader between the two subjects of exchange and money between the two objects of exchange. How then can we understand financial intermediaries in the exchange act?

In defining a financial intermediary as somebody who trades in money (money is commodified), one might superficially assign him the same role as the trader. However, it is somewhat more complicated. Isolating the exchange act of money against a promise of repayment or collateral (at this stage it is unimportant whether or not interest is involved), the relation depends on the type of financial intermediary. A moneylender or indigenous-style banker who works with his own money is one of the exchange partners. However, the loan money engenders another exchange act for the person who is currently short of cash. If such a lender takes part in the latter exchange act, his role is confined to financial intermediation.

The trader-cum-moneylender, on the other hand, combines both the position of trader and moneylender. He sacrifices goods and postpones his claims on other goods or money resulting from the exchange act.

Commercial banks and other financial agents or institutions working with borrowed capital have a specific position in the economy because they manage their customers'

---

[16] The introduction of a social security system by the state and provision of public goods, on the one hand, and the collection of revenue, tax, etc., on the other, is nothing but the commodification of generalized reciprocity (Sahlins 1972).

money.[17] Their claims in credit transactions are in reality claims on their customers and liabilities to banks are in reality liabilities to other bank customers. In addition to the management functions, banks hold further functions. They influence the process of currency circulation via the interest rate, have access to refinancing possibilities with the state bank, trade in securities and engage in other lucrative financial operations. Almost all banking assets and liabilities become eventually 'fictitious', i.e. only a title to value which can no longer be re-converted into money.

Another exchange act which becomes important in this book is revenue payment to the hegemonial power. What is superficially seen as a one-sided movement of goods, services or money is, from the point of view of generalized reciprocity, a credit-involving exchange act, where the reciprocation of the exchange act by the authority is postponed and the claim remains undefined. Contrary to the voluntary exchange act in which, from the neoclassical perspective at least, the two parties involved have the same rights and power,[18] revenue payments are obligatory and one party fixes the conditions of the exchange.

3.2.6.   A Sociological Theory of Money and Credit

Klaus Heinemann (1969, 1987) developed a complex, elaborate sociological theory of money in the code of system theory. Although he referred to credit in an indirect way only, I summarize his contribution because he combined many of the aspects discussed so far. Heinemann started from the point that an exchange act controls the behavior of others. In direct exchange it is based upon the right of disposal of scarce goods, which requires a preference structure. However, the dependencies which result from the preference structure, and which provide the opportunity to control others' behavior, vary considerably and cannot be standardized. They depend upon the supplied and demanded goods, the preference structure and the possibility to substitute wants. Since claims have to be met at the same time in direct exchange, time differences in the satisfaction of wants can hardly be bridged.

Market exchange is characterized by functional-specific, affectual-neutral and mostly short-term social relations. The securing of claims on the exchange partner is no longer guaranteed by non-market social relations. This requires the clear documentation and (legal) security of claims. Such a document is a certificate which institutionalizes and formalizes modes and contents of communication (Heinemann 1987: 325-6).[19] Money itself is an example of such a certificate.

The acquisition of money is only the means to achieve ends and not an end in itself. Simmel rightly emphasized that its intrinsic value (means of status, symbol of prestige, and so on) stems from its character as a medium. Wants can only be satisfied

---

[17] Baecker (1991) emphasized that banks are highly dependent on the trust of others. He hinted at the paradox that banks persuade their customers time to borrow and to save at the same time.

[18] Interestingly neoclassical economists raise the question of power when they consider moneylenders and the provision of consumer credit. The perception of moneylenders in most cases is that they exploit their customers, see Part II.

[19] Certificates are reduced to generalized texts or symbols, such as numbers, which symbolize a claim and a liability and certain modes of communication.

indirectly through money. The motivation to accept money in an exchange act, or even to exchange, originates in the motivation to achieve the freedom of general choice.

To cut short Heinemann's analysis, in market exchange money becomes a generalized medium of control:[20] (i) It has been continuously secured as an expression of economic opportunities to control others, it is always and timelessly available, it is neutral to time differences; (ii) as a measure of quantities (value) money is neutral to specific qualities of goods and services; (iii) money is neutral towards persons with whom the exchange takes place. This allows to conclude that (iv) money is an objectively and personally generalized medium (Heinemann 1987: 329).

Money provides the freedom of choice. It is independent of close social relations and norms of reciprocity or redistribution. Due to the large number of preferences, products, means of production and manufacturing technologies available, money has the important function of solving these problems in the framework of prices, the discussion of which I leave out of consideration. The price system is a condensed form of various sets of information: market exchanges, market relations, the assessment of goods and services, aims of market participants, preferences, etc. as far as they are relevant for all participants. Economists circumscribe this framework of information (called purchasing power) as an index of scarcity.[21] To take this framework of information as a guideline for individual decision means finally that the individual orients itself by plans and decisions of others (Heinemann 1987: 332).

Money neutralizes personal relations (which are found in the norms of reciprocity) and enables the individual to adapt to the changing circumstances and wants – an individualization, which is simultaneously opposed by an increasing socialization of individuals in the sense that forever new, extended forms of social relations and bonds, new constraints of integration, coordination and assimilation emerge. Money substitutes social-normative relations with functional dependencies and institutionalizes a stronger economic integration with the closer interlocking of interests. Liabilities and dependencies are depersonalized, although, they do not disappear. With the use of money an individual is socially bound in a three-fold form: by social relations with the exchange partner, by the fact that the possible claims which result from the possession of money are not directed toward a certain individual but remain undefined, and by the fact that money creates a joint feeling for all those who use the same currency. The individual will only accept money as a means of payment if he can expect future exchangeability for the satisfaction of wants (Heinemann 1987: 333-4).

When I discussed money as an indirect medium of exchange, I argued from the perspective of two exchange partners that no future claims and obligations arise with either of the exchange partners. However, this is different from the level of society and economy – and here we come back to the point of system-trust or confidence into functional systems. Heinemann (1987: 334-5) argued that money –useless in itself – becomes the symbol for a claim which is only secured by system-trust which is not so much directed in the legalized future acceptance of money by other individuals, but

---

[20] Luhmann (1973b, 1988a) applied the term 'generalized medium of communication'.
[21] According to Luhmann (1988a: 253ff.), scarcity is a temporary/factual/social problem, developing when somebody prevents someone else from future access to resources. Luhmann understands money as a regulative instrument of scarcity.

rather to the functioning of the economic system itself. This is what Luhmann (1988b) called confidence.

The changing physiognomy of money makes an increasing system-confidence apparent. Early modern money consisted of full-bodied coins, whose face value was an expression of the substance value. Eventually token money, paper money and plastic money (where the nominal value is much higher than its substance value) came to replace full-bodied coins. The stamp of the hegemonial power came to symbolize the guarantee for the future value and acceptance of the currency. This already requires a high degree of system-confidence.[22] In the times when the West-European political and economic systems where less stable than the modern Western states, the high level of system-confidence was reduced in that bank notes were for a long time a legal claim to an equivalent in gold and the national banks were obliged to keep a gold store equal in value to the real money supply. Most Third-World state apparatuses and economies, however, are very unstable and the less than full convertibility of their currency, the strong regulation of the money market and the investment of citizens in a more stable currency and gold are an expression of this.

However, in case citizens lose their confidence in the stability of the national or even international economy, the state or law and order – if society and economy become disequilibrated as the economists call it – this causes a run on the savings and other claims and banks, and with them the whole monetary system, collapses. Like banks, the state cannot simultaneously fulfill its liabilities towards the holders of obligations and the banks.

What has been said here with regard to changing confidence in the process of evolution of modern money can be applied to changing confidence in credit-involving certificates, such as formalized promissory notes, letters of credit, debentures, and so on. A verbal promise of one exchange partner has limited value only if he cannot prove his claim. For example, in the case of usufructuary mortgages, the customary rule in Indonesia suggested that a mortgagor should mark fruit trees which he gave into pawn with his sign to demonstrate his future right to redeem the pawn (see Part III). Another example is, a reliable person witnessing the credit-involving transaction to convince public opinion if necessary. To simplify the regulation of claims and liabilities in civil justice, standardized written promissory notes were introduced very early on. Part II provides examples of mortgage and sales deeds in medieval India and Nepal. The formulas did not only call the gods to witness the transaction, but human witnesses were invited too. Such standardized notes presupposed the existence of legal institutions and confidence in justice. I do not want to go into too much detail; what I want to emphasize is that with the evolution of the legal sub-system during the differentiation process of society, familiarity with the reliability of the exchange partners became increasingly substituted by system-confidence: confidence in the general validity of the certificate, its recognition by the legal authorities, their incorruptibility and power to force debtors to fulfill their liabilities, and so on.

---

[22] An expression of this system-confidence is perhaps the imprint on Dollar notes 'In God we Trust'. I interpret it as a substitute of an ancient confidence-generating mechanism: the temple as a place of exchange, where the exchange act took place under the eyes of the God who functioned as a witness.

Heinemann (1987) expressed the increasing system-confidence (which he called trust) as follows. The more complicated and complex the economy, the more it is not a matter of knowledge or experience, since social life is rarely based on proofs. Social action always involved uncertainty. However, to some extent this uncertainty is compensated by 'social certainty' because it generates an expectation in the behavior of others. Perhaps it is this 'social certainty' that the promise of a certificate can be taken for granted, that individuals have confidence in money and the economic system which permits planned action.

4. Capital and Interest

4.1. Interest and Interests

'Interest' or 'interests' is a central and controversial concept in economics, social science and history. The term came into widespread use towards the end of the sixteenth century and is derived from the Latin word *interesse*. At that time it had not much in common with our contemporary understanding of interest. Following Hirschman (1986a: 35ff.) the term was applied to the forces, based on the drive for self-preservation and self-deification which motivated or should motivate actions of princes or the state, of individuals and later on groups of people with a similar social or economic position (classes, group interests). In modern terms this action can be called self-centered, rational or instrumental action. In this connotation I will use the plural form to avoid confusion.

On the individual level the term was applied as an euphemism to make moneymaking in general and the taking of interest on loans in particular, respectable which had so far been called 'usury'. Various descriptions imply that the perception of profit and credit in ancient and medieval societies is somehow related to two essential factors: a religious ethic, on the one hand, and the development of commerce, on the other – or, more precisely, the decline of a particular mode of production (called 'feudal' by Marx) and with it, traditional elites (the rentiers) and the growth of another mode of production (merchant capitalism) with a new, commercial and financial elite.[1] Usury was defined strictly as 'where more is taken than is given' (Le Goff 1980: 29). This definition is similar to the contemporary understanding of interest and has nothing in common with the present connotation of usury.

Eventually economic requirements engendered the legitimization of exceptions of usury in commerce, such as the buying of annuities, the taking of land in mortgage, the use of bills of exchange, partnership arrangements, risk premium and delayed repayment, and so on. Towards the end of the thirteenth century, and particularly during the fourteenth and fifteenth centuries, there was a gradual separation of economic from religious morality. In everyday-life it was more and more obvious that society and economy could not function without loans. Financial agents and institutions were a necessary precondition for an expansion of trade and commerce and *vice versa*.

Max Weber (1964: 251ff.) explained the final abolition of the prohibition of loan interest as the resolution of the antagonism between inner and outer morality in society. The formal equality of all individuals eventually led to the abolition of the prohibition to take interest from brothers (inner morality) but similarly helped to overcome the unrestrained personal appropriation and usury in external relations. However, this

---

[1] See Böhm-Bawerk (1970), Braudel (1982, 1984), Homer (1963), Le Goff (1979, 1980, 1988, 1989), Shatzmiller (1990), Sombart (1927), and Weber (1950, 1964).

was a long-term process which I described elsewhere (see Schrader 1994b). It was strictly opposed by the Church (see Böhm-Bawerk 1970; Hirschman 1986a, b; Weber 1950, 1985). Nevertheless, it finally engendered the Protestant Ethic. The spirit of capitalism might be interpreted as a result of adapting to the devotional calling of making money, which the capitalist system demands (Weber in Andreski 1984: 123). Closely related to Max Weber's theory of the 'Protestant Ethic and the Spirit of Capitalism' are various theories on industrial entrepreneurship which I shall discuss in Chapter 7.4.1.

Finally the initial connotation of the interests was blurred (see Hirschman 1977). In economics the term took the dual, value-neutral connotation of interest from capital investment (natural interest) and money interest. This distinction goes back to the discussion of interest as an income obtained without work. Profit, wages and surplus value, and a theoretical distinction between money interest and natural interest, were the main topics which finally led to the labour and exploitation theory in *Capital*.

As will be shown in Part II, the ancient and medieval Indian aversion to interest was not as strong as it was in medieval Europe. Malamoud (1981) and Shah (1981) argued that the distinction between *artha* and *dharma*[2] liberated commerce from moral, sacral sanctions. Parry (1989) suggested that the doctrine of *karma*, with its different concept of time/eternity and inequality, does not consider money as inherently dangerous and polluting and legitimizes interest too.

> "Far from being an outsider to society as was the Jew in medieval Christendom, the financier tends rather to be a paragon of religious orthodoxy (. . .) Unlike the medieval friar or the Buddhist monk, the Hindu ascetic has few qualms about handling money, and both temples and monasteries have often been engaged in large-scale trade and moneylending (. . .) [in which Buddhist monasteries were involved too, H.S..] (. . .) Nor, despite often extremely high rates of interest, has moneylending ever been condemned by Hindu thought with any of vehemence of Aristotle or St Bernard (. . .) On the contrary [the moneylender, H.S. . . .) is often seen as a public benefactor" (Parry 1989: 78, 79).

4.2. Marx on Capital, Credit and Interest

Let us now return to Marx and his discussion of capital, natural and money interest. He focused his analysis on surplus value appropriation which he considered the chief characteristic of capitalism. In *Capital I*, Chapter 4, Marx came to distinguish money and capital. Money as currency and money as capital have two different forms of circulation, the former C – M – C, the latter M – C –M', which he called the metamorphosis of money into commodities and transformation back into money, buying something to resell it (Marx 1970, I: 174). This process makes sense only if there is some surplus value (Marx 1970, I: 149).

---

[2] In contrast to medieval Europe, where only a gradual distinction between sacral and profane legislation occurred, there was a clear-cut distinction in ancient Hinduism. Material means of the realm of *artha* (i.e. the realm under the jurisdiction of the king) were separated from the realm of *dharma*, over which the Brahman resides. These two spheres were linked in so far that the means of *artha* should not become ends in themselves. They should always be in conformity with the superior*dharma*.

Marx concluded that money, whether in the form of currency or commodities, is transformable into capital, on the basis of capitalist production. It produces profit, i.e. the capitalist is able to extract and appropriate from the workers a certain proportion of unpaid labour, surplus product and surplus value (1970, III: 338). With this function of potential capital – a means of producing surplus – money becomes a commodity, but a commodity *sui generis*.

Marx's discussion of credit, however, is separated from his discussion of exchange, money and capital, and it appears in *Capital III*. Considering the place of credit in capitalist society, he identified a financial capitalist behind the industrial capitalist whose function is the financing of the latter. Therefore he receives a share of the profit called interest.[3] Marx polemically called the financial capitalist a parasite and an honorable bandit (Marx 1970, III: 350) in the medieval tradition, in that such a person neither (physically) works nor makes others (physically) work for him.

The key issues of large parts of *Capital III* demonstrate that the analysis is not generally valid but confined to the capitalist mode of production. Since large parts of this study on changing financial landscapes in India and Indonesia are concerned with the transformation process of economy and society, Marx's remarks on pre-capitalist conditions are perhaps more important here than his analysis of credit in capitalist society. In *Capital I*, for example, Marx saw the exploitation of East India by the British as belonging to the 'rosy dawn of the era of capitalist production' (1970, I: 703), the process of so-called primitive accumulation. This era followed the trade war between European nations, and the different instances of primitive accumulation are more or less linked in a sequence across the commercial empires of Spain, Portugal, Holland, France and England, which engendered the process of the transformation of a feudal into a capitalist society. This transformation process was based on violent action (Marx 1970, I: 703).

According to Marx, what was decisive for European colonial expansion was the introduction (or more precisely, the improvement) of the system of public credit, the '*credo* of capital' (1970, I: 706), which during the eighteenth century experienced an integration between the European commercial centers. The balancing of public debt was to be achieved with a more efficient fiscal system which, as a consequence of the continuously increasing public debt, tended to over-exploit the populations, particularly in the colonies. The third mechanism in the process of European colonial expansion was the policy of protecting the expanding European domestic manufactures which began to organize capitalist production (ibid.).

In various paragraphs Marx emphasized that 'merchant capital', which consists of commercial capital and interest-bearing capital, historically preceded and even created the conditions for the capitalist mode of production.

---

[3] The circulation of interest producing capital may be expressed as follows (Marx 1970, III: 340): M – M – C – M'- M', where person B borrows some money M from A and circulates M – C – M'. The owner of money lends his money to another person and commodities it as capital for himself and the other person, as a value which is able to produce surplus and profit, a value that continues to exist (Marx 1970, III: 343). Money lent to person B by person A as a sum A returns as A + 1/xA to person A (Marx 1970, III: 341).

> "'Interest-bearing capital, or usurer's capital, as we may call it in its antiquated form, belonging together with its twin brother, merchant capital, to the antediluvian form of capital, which long precede the capitalist mode of production and are to be found in the most diverse economic formations of society'. Thus the medieval usurer, who is to the merchant as the financial capitalist is to the industrial capitalist, 'converts his hoard of money into capital for himself' according to the formula applicable to all capital, M-M', with the surplus m being in this case interest" (Brunhoff 1973: 77, quoting Marx 1970, III: 593, 598).

Marx argued that under the pre-capitalist mode of production two kinds of usurious capital exist (which recur on the basis of capitalist production, although as subordinate forms only): Usurious capital by lending to spendthrifts of the upper classes and among these, in the first instance landlords; secondly, usurious capital by lending to small-scale producers who possess their own conditions of labour. These include the peasant and the artisan. Whether or not this usury transforms the old mode of production into the capitalist mode of production, as it did in modern Europe, depends on the historical stage of development and its conditions (Marx 1970, III: 594).

> "Usury thus exerts, on the one hand, an undermining and destructive influence on ancient and feudal property. On the other hand, it undermines and ruins small-peasant and small-burgher production, in short all forms in which the producer still appears as the owner of his means of production" (Marx 1970, III: 596).

Usury centralizes monetary wealth where means of production have been destroyed. It does not change the mode of production, but it lives off the debtors and forces them to reproduce in the most miserable conditions. This is the reason for the widespread hatred of usurers.

Usury in pre-capitalist modes of production has a revolutionary effect in so far as old forms of property are destroyed. Under Asiatic forms of production usury can continue to exist for a long time without producing anything but economic decay and political decline. Only once the other prerequisites of capitalist production are fulfilled, does usury come to assist the establishment of the capitalist mode of production (Marx 1970, III: 597).

Marx maintained that the main domain of usury is the function of money as a means of payment. Every payment (rent, tribute, tax, and so on) payable on a specific date had to be made in cash. As will be shown in this study, during the period of colonialism one decisive element in the monetization of rural regions was the reorganization of the revenue system in that the peasants had to provide cash payments to the colonial government. The requirement of monetary payment forced peasants into cash-crop production, and the temporary gap between expenditure and income urged them to take up loans from moneylenders.

Marx continued that the development of a (formal, H.S.) credit system may be understood as a reaction to usury. In this credit system the interest rate is accommodated to the conditions of the capitalist mode of production. However, argued Marx,

> "usury as such does not only continue to exist, but it is even freed, among nations with a developed capitalist production, from the fetters imposed upon it by all previous legislation. Interest-bearing capital retains the form of usurer's capital in relation to persons or classes, or in circumstances where borrowing does not, nor can, take place in the sense corresponding to the

capitalist mode of production; where borrowing takes place as a result of individual need, as at the pawnshop; where money is borrowed by wealthy spendthrifts for the purpose of squandering; or where the producer is a non-capitalist producer, such as a small farmer or craftsman, who is thus still, as the immediate producer, the owner of his own means of production; finally where the capitalist producer himself operates on such a small scale that he resembles those self-employed producers" (Marx 1970a, III: 600).

Marx emphasized that credit has an ancient and a modern aspect. The modern one, corresponding to the capitalist mode of production, has a certain specific structure such as paper money, book money, financial markets, and so on, while interest-bearing capital, however, is a general phenomenon as old as commercial production, as, according to Marx, the only condition for its existence is the simple circulation of money and commodities. The functioning of credit in the capitalist mode of production is not merely the modern form of merchant capital. A real break takes place when merchant capital is incorporated into capitalist production and begins to function merely as its agent. This break, which Marx referred to and which I consider as a process of change, is of particular importance in this study. It is related to my hypothesis that professional moneylenders and merchant bankers are pioneers in expanding capitalism who are replaced by banks in the long run.

Marx distinguished between commercial credit and banking credit. Commercial credit is rooted in simple circulation when money acquires the function of a means of payment. The seller becomes the creditor, the buyer the debtor. Credit-money emerges from the function of money as a means of payment. Debt certificates (for example, bills of exchange) begin to circulate on their own. Both money as a means of payment and credit-money begin to extend, the latter of which in our time has reached unimaginable proportions in the form of book money, while the actual money supply has been restricted as an instrument of monetary policy.

Following Brunhoff (1973: 81-4), Marx (1970, I: 137-8) saw commercial credit to be on the border between monetary system and credit system. The circuit of financial transactions in commercial credit, which from a theoretical point of view forms a zero-balance, is, however, in fact never complete for several reasons. One main reason is price fluctuation, another is the diversity of branches of production, and a third one delayed payment. Therefore, Marx, and even Brunhoff two decades ago, believed that credit cannot substitute money, since ready cash is needed for various expenses, such as wages, taxes, and so on. Gaps have to be bridged with money, and money reappears as the general equivalent settling the transactions. The means of payment function involves the availability of cash. However, the credit card and electronic cash have revolutionized the money market and have to some degree deprived the use of cash in payment interactions of its function.

4.3. The European Perspective on Asian Development

Many scholars working on Asia were influenced by Max Weber's thinking in that they saw Asian countries as static societies. The same view can also be found in the Marxist concept of the Asiatic mode of production which enjoyed prominence until the Second World War. To sum up, Weber (1947, 1964, 1968, 1972), Marx (1970) and Wittfogel (1931, 1957) assumed distinct development paths of the Occident and Orient. The former produced modern capitalism, the latter was trapped in stagnation. Modern capitalism was finally introduced from the outside.[4] I do not wish to go into the discussion of whether or not the stagnation-hypothesis can be maintained. What is important from my point of view is that most scholars were influenced by either of these perspectives. However, in Parts II-IV I am concerned with the question of why the Europeans were eventually successful in incorporating and peripheralizing large parts of Asia.

Here the Marxist and the Weberian positions differ. The latter makes endogenous factors responsible for this development. I recapitulate that, according to Weber, the Protestant ethic and European history engendered a rational bureaucracy, a particular type of capitalist spirit and a rational business organization. The two most important trading societies, the Dutch and the English East India Companies, were molded in the Puritan type of Protestantism. They prospered in the course of the seventeenth and eighteenth centuries and increasingly monopolized foreign trade in Asia, thereby eliminating non-Western businessmen from the market. Based on the Weberian perspective, as will be shown, scholars made the Western type of joint-stock companies and their capital basis responsible for the final dominance of European capital in India, while non-Western merchants and financiers continued their traditional organizational forms with a capital basis that sufficed for the financing of trade but not industries.[5]

In contrast to the Weberian endogenous explanations for the final superiority of Western dominance in Asia, Marxist scholars stressed exogenous factors for technical superiority of the West, namely physical force and coercion. These theories are related to Marxist theories of imperialism. They consider imperialism as an important feature of capitalism at a particular stage of development and some scholars, such as Hamza Alavi (1962), went as far as to maintain that the industrial revolution in Europe would not have taken place without colonial expansion and the exploitation of the colonies. From a general perspective Lenin detailed the following characteristics of imperialism: a concentration of production and capital as well as monopolization tendencies; the merging of banking and industrial capital and the emergence of a financial oligarchy based on finance capital; a strong increase in capital exports in response to the stagnation of domestic economies; and the formation of transnational enterprises and capitalist associations. Marxist theories consider imperialism as the final stage of perverted capitalism before the revolution. Imperialism is usually divided into colonialism and neo-colonialism, the latter being characterized as the continuation of imperialism without territorial control which is closely related to the critique of the new international division of labour.

World-system theory, which I shall consider in detail in Part IV, is derived from this background. On a whole, there is now a common agreement that stressing either

---

[4] See Masubuchi (1966), Otsuka (1966), Shiozawa (1966).

[5] In the European history of banks the common argument is that, as long as financial institutions largely served commerce, merchant banks were sufficient. Joint-stock banks emerged only with capitalist production because the need for large-scale and long-term investment increased considerably (see Schweppenhäuser 1982; Sombart 1919, 1927).

endogenous or exogenous factors alone is too short-sighted and that these perspectives are not necessarily mutually exclusive.

Part II   INDIA

5. Moneylenders and Indigenous-Style Bankers

Indian literature provides two broad categories of indigenous financial agents, which have had a long tradition and can still be found in contemporary India: moneylenders and indigenous bankers. As will be seen, strictly speaking the latter term is inappropriate because many of these merchant bankers operated in a 'foreign' context – be this in the context of another country than India such as Burma, Malaya, Singapore or Sumatra in the case of the Chettiar, or be it in another place than that of their origin on the Indian subcontinent, such as the Marwari in Calcutta or the Gujarati Shroffs[1] in Bombay. It does not make sense to take the Indian nation as the defining criterion of an alien, since this nation is a political construct. More important for cohesion and the definition of aliens are ethnic and caste criteria. In this sense the term 'indigenous banker' should be interpreted as an abbreviation of 'indigenous-style banker', as used by Timberg and Aiyar (1980) to distinguish their mode of operation from Western banks, or more precisely, an abridgment of 'indigenously developed' or 'non-Western banker'. To avoid confusion I bypass the commonly applied term 'indigenous banker' and instead apply the expressions indigenous-style banker, indigenously developed banker and non-Western banker interchangeably. Another term which seems appropriate to me for many of them at least until the late nineteenth century is the term *merchant banker*, since many of them were involved in merchandising and banking, in a way similar to medieval European merchant bankers.

However, a clear-cut legal definition of moneylenders, on the one hand, and non-Western bankers on the other, does not exist, and for some time scholars applied various opposing definitions. Some scholars made a distinction according to the amount of capital involved in business. Jain (1929), for example, defined indigenously developed bankers as individuals or private firms providing loans and the service of *hundi* business[2] and/or accepting deposits. A moneylender, on the other hand, neither receives deposits nor deals in *hundis*. The Indian Central Banking Inquiry Committee (1931) provided a definition similar to Jain, whereas different provincial banking inquiry committees used the following characteristic: the acceptance of deposits or *hundi* business or the provision of productive loans. Such definitions, however, are inadequate, since commercial and cooperative banks deal in *hundis*, too. Taking the criterion of deposit business alone, postal savings banks, finance corporations, commercial banks and non-Western bankers offer this service. Ghose (1943) took *hundi* business alone as the decisive criterion for indigenous-style bankers.

---

[1] *Shroff* is the English version of the Hindi term *sarraf* or money changer. The Oxford Dictionary defined a *Shroff* as a 'native expert employed to detect based coins'. The assaying of the coins in use was the skill of goldsmiths and *sarrafs* and some of the wealthy *Shroffs* originated from the goldsmith's caste. In the following I maintain that indigenous-style bankers and moneylenders originated from the traders' caste. Goldsmiths were on the one hand producers, on the other they traded in precious stones and metal and – in a broad sense – can be counted among traders.

[2] *Hundis* are indigenous negotiable instruments of short-term credit, a kind of bills of exchange, which shall be discussed later.

The Study Group on Indigenous Bankers (hereafter SGIB) combined many of the criteria just outlined in the following working definition, which is in line with the *'Cambridge Economic History of India'*, Vol II (Kumar 1982):

> "The primary distinction between the moneylender and the indigenous banker is that while the former lends his own funds, the latter acts as a financial intermediary by accepting deposits or availing of bank credit; in other words the indigenous banking system is truly a financial intermediary in the sense that its ability to purvey funds is largely dependent on the resources it is able to mobilize. Another distinguishing feature is that transactions of moneylenders are conducted in cash while those of the indigenous banker are based on dealings in short-term credit instruments for financing the production and distribution of goods and services. The definition of indigenous banker adopted for this study covers those individuals and firms who accept deposits or rely on bank credit for the conduct of their business and are close to or on the periphery of the organized money markets and are professional dealers in short-term credit instruments (*hundis*) for financing the production and distribution of goods and services. This includes the Multanis, Gujarati Shroffs, Nattukottai Chettiars, Kallidaykurichy Brahmins and the Marwari bankers of Assam known as '*kayas*'" (SGIB 1971: 9)

As a matter of fact it was not until the investigations of the Indian Central Banking Inquiry Committee in 1931, that indigenously developed bankers as a category distinct from moneylenders came into the focus of official policy. The list of literature on such bankers is long;[3] however, only few authors go beyond purely operational definitions. Apart from the technical definitions above, however, it seems to me that many scholars have implicitly applied the rough, simple distinction that indigenous-style bankers largely confine themselves to the financing of small and medium-scale trade and operate with a larger amount of capital than moneylenders,[4] while village moneylenders largely provide consumer credit and agricultural loans.

The Indian terms *baniya, mahajan, bohara, seth, sahukar, sarraf* and others are Hindu caste names or honorable titles. They were and are still applied to indigenously developed bankers, moneylenders, dealers in grain, *ghi* (butter), groceries and spices (which were very often traders-cum-moneylenders) and other merchants, which supports Krishnan's (1959) argument that the distinction between moneylenders and indigenously developed bankers is not an emic one. The term *baniya* originates from the Sanskrit term *vanij,* which means merchant. In West India the *baniya* is called *vania* or *vani*. *Mahajan* means 'great man' and is a honorific title applied to moneylenders and bankers, while *seth* is honorifically used for great merchants, moneylenders, indigenous-style bankers or industrialists. *Sahu, sao* and *sahukar* symbolizes honesty and uprightness and is applied to some moneylenders, too. In Bengal *baniya* is a functional catch-all term applied to all moneylenders and indigenously developed bankers. Elsewhere, however, it is strictly a caste name.[5] The *baniya* caste occupations are tra-

---

[3] To mention some authors: For the ancient and medieval period, see e.g. Bhargava (1934); Goldsmith (1987); Habib (1960, 1964, 1990); Leonard (1979, 1981a,b); Subramanian (1987); Torri (1991); for a general description or specific case studies, see Cirvante (1956); Cooper (1959); Evers (1987); Ghose (1943); Goswami (1985, 1989); Hwa (1967); Jain (1929); Karkal (1967); Krishnan (1959); Mahadevan (1976; 1978a,b); Menon (1985); Panjabi (1961); Pavadarayan (1986); Rau (1938); Rudner (1989); Sayers (1952); Schrader (1989, 1992); Timberg (1978); Timberg and Aiyar (1980); Weerasooria (1973).

[4] Therefore indigenously developed bankers usually do not finance petty traders. They obtain their loans from moneylenders.

[5] The caste consists of various sub-castes. Some of the most important sub-castes like the Agarwala, Oswal and Parwar are frequently known by their sub-caste names, although the caste term is still applied as an affix among them.

ditionally merchandizing, trade and moneylending, and more than other castes most *baniyas* are still engaged in one of these (Russel 1975: 111-3; Enthoven 1979, vol. 3: 412-22).

Summarizing the distinction between moneylenders and indigenous-style bankers, I suggest refraining from an analytical distinction. I apply these categories as descriptive ones only, with an understanding that a continuum exists ranging from the small-scale village moneylender to the large-scale urban moneylender and indigenously developed banker, and that it is sometimes difficult to categorize one credit agent as a banker, and another agent as a large-scale town moneylender.

Until the late 1960s, formal banking was to a high degree a matter of metropolitan and to some extent urban areas, while rural regions and urban informal-sector enterprises were supplied by indigenous informal finance. The systematic expansion of the banking infrastructure into rural regions and large subsidized credit programs have increased formal finance in India. The implications of this extension of informal finance will be discussed later.

Part II investigates the history of indigenously developed bankers and moneylenders in India. By drawing on a number of English colonial sources, we should be aware that many of these scholars had a particular perception of India which was a reflection of colonialism. This is apparent, for example, in the discussion of rural indebtedness, which rose in the late nineteenth century. The image of the peasant is that of an extravagant, uneducated person who is to some extent responsible for his own living-conditions and, on the other hand, is the innocent victim of scrupulous moneylenders. According to Rudner (1989: 418), the following stereotypes were applied to moneylenders, which complete the image of the uneducated peasant, and to some extent these are still prevalent. One portrays them as systematically pushing their clients further and further into debt, and finally sucking them dry of money, property and freedom. Another one identifies them as unreliable and irrational, but rational in respect to their usurious practices. It was a common view to place the exploitative practices of moneylenders on the border between moral economy and market economy.[6]

Such images reflect the attitude of English colonial policy aiming at educating India with the introduction of Western-style institutions and administration. Only then, it was assumed, could India be successfully guided to independence. The Eurocentric view of the efficiency of Western institutions had an impact on the English perception of indigenous-style bankers. Although they were admired by English scholars for their long tradition and efficiency, and their financial networks initially used by the East India Company until a Western banking structure was implemented, they were nevertheless considered traditional and therefore inferior to Western banks. Such perceptions predominated in reports written by colonial officers and committees on particular problems, such as the increasing rural indebtedness and land alienation, in the course of the late nineteenth century. On the other hand, we can find many valuable accounts of colonial officers who were scientists rather than administrators in

---

[6] For the moral economy, see Scott (1976); for its critique, see Popkin (1979); for a further development of the argument see Evers and Schrader (1994).

their educational background. They provided very detailed information on various aspects of India. Another source of information are the gazetteers, district reports to the central government. Since these reports reflect the administrative side, their treatment of particular problems and their settlement, such as riots against moneylenders and moneylenders' legislation, express the deterioration of the living conditions. The reports of the committees of the early twentieth century, which were set up to investigate particular problems, are different. An example is the Indian Central Banking Inquiry Committee Report (1931) which examined the financial landscape of India. These committees usually consisted of British colonial officers, honorable Indian persons and both English and Indian experts, and very often minority positions of Indian members were appended to the reports.

Contemporary Indian scholars are running the risk of falling into a pattern of catching up with the colonial past and, based on *dependencia*-theoretical thinking, making only the British responsible for the state of underdevelopment. Or on the other extreme, because of their modernistic education, they consider indigenous institutions and actors as traditional and impeding development.

I venture to make another general, non-ethnic remark on the perceptions of moneylenders and indigenous-style bankers, in which scholars are also partly trapped. For the European high middle ages and the 'long sixteenth century', Braudel (1982: 375-81) and Le Goff (1989) gave a detailed description of trading and financial hierarchies, ranging from top merchants and merchant bankers down to peddling traders, petty moneylenders and pawnbrokers. The public perception of financial agents developed in line with these hierarchies, part of them being prosecuted as usurers, part of them being accepted as respected persons. In the same way one can assume that indigenously developed bankers and large-scale moneylenders ranged in their self-perceptions and in the public opinion somewhere in the upper range of this hierarchy as respectable, honest and often charitable persons, while ordinary small-scale village or peddling moneylenders ranged somewhere at the bottom.

Last but not least, contrary to the negative perception of colonial scholars and most contemporary development planners who consider moneylenders to be exploitative and impeding development, one should be aware that local people on the street usually hold an opportunistic, ambivalent attitude depending on their current relation to the lender. Case studies reveal that borrowers who wish to take up credit or want an extension of their credit line praise the noble character of their lender and his business practices, while those who do not get an extension or even lost their property to the lender provide the reverse image of the same person.

From this a point of view I argue with Gregory (1988) that

"Moneylending in the abstract is neither good or bad. For some people it has been the source of great wealth and prosperity while for others it has been the source of great poverty and misery. What is crucial for understanding the social consequences of indebtedness is the power relationship between the borrower and lender. If the power relationship is unequal, then obviously the potential for the exploitative use of the debt relationship is much greater than if the transactors are from the same class. Other relevant factors to consider in a comparative analysis of moneylending are the social forces that motivate lender and borrower, the nature of the security offered and the sanctions available to the lender" (Gregory 1988: 52-3).

6. Finance in Ancient and Medieval India

6.1. Ancient India

Literature on finance in ancient India[1] is rare and largely confined to indigenously developed bankers. Bhargava (1934) made a detailed analysis of the ancient religious scripts which reveals a mosaic of information from two millennia. I do not want to go too much into detail but shall confine myself to some important aspects. It is obvious that merchant bankers established their networks all over India and beyond even before Christ.[2] The *Arthashastras* (third century BC) and *Dharmashastras* (between 1 – 2 century AD), for example, reported a number of specialized bank employees: accountants, loan deed writers, representatives, debt collectors, cashiers, clerks, and so on.[3] These descriptions point to lively economic activity in particular regions which were involved in long-distance trade, and with Braudel (1984) I assume that not the entire economy but only the highest plane was integrated with trading regions in other countries. These scripts probably referred to the top level of merchant banking only.

Merchant guilds already appeared in the *Vedic* literature. A differentiation between the moneylender guild and traders was made sometime between 200 B.C. and 300 A.D. with the development of cities. Initially the goldsmiths were the minters of regionally valid coins and acted as moneylenders to the princes. Later a guild of bankers emerged. These guilds possessed considerable powers. Bhargava (1934) referred to several documents in which it was maintained that a king was afraid to return to the capital after a defeat to face the guild of indigenous-style bankers. However, I assume that creditors to powerful, despotic sovereigns always ran the risk that they would cancel their debts by decree or even imprison or liquidate them. According to Max Weber (Andreski 1984: 91, 100), the guild organization neither brought about city autonomy nor social and economic organization as it did in the Occident. The power of the bankers' guild remained based on the control of money without being backed by a political organization. The caste system restricted them, and eventually the guilds were turned into castes. Banking became a hereditary sub-caste occupation of the *Vaisya* (traders') caste since, according to the Manu Code, moneylending was prohibited to the two highest castes, *Brahmans* (priests) and *Kshatriyas* (worriers) (Habib 1964: 411). Borrowers belonged to almost all castes and occupations.

---

[1] I consider ancient India along the lines of the *'Cambridge Economic History of India'*, Vol. I (Raychaudhuri and Habib 1982) as extending to the rise of the Delhi Sultanate in the thirteenth century.

[2] Buddhist scriptures mention rich bankers conducting banking in various trade centers like Rajagraha, Vaishali, Patliputra, Kampa, Kosambhi, and so on. Later, during the Muslim period, great banking houses called *kothewalas* existed in Murshidabad, Dacca, Agra, Delhi, Multan, Rewari, Lahore, Lucknow, Surat, Ahmedabad, Aurangabad, Sironj, Calicut, Jaipur, Jodhpur, Udaipur, Bikaner, Ramghar, Malapura, and Pali.

[3] Manu, viii, Shukra, ii and iii and Narad Vivadpad; Arthashastra, iii, quoted by Bhargava (1934: 72-3). The ancient texts in what follows have all been quoted by Bhargava (1934). I did not list them in the references.

Merchant bankers provided the following financial services:

- lending;
- accepting deposits;
- discounting bills and promissory notes;
- providing guarantees;
- issuing drafts, letters of credit and circular notes;
- accepting bills on behalf of their customers drawn on the authority of *hundis*;
- changing money; and
- safekeeping of valuables.

Some top bankers took additional functions for the state:

- the royal treasury;
- minting;
- state revenue-collection; and the state's finance of wars.

The *Vedic* scripts do not mention any security like mortgages or pledges for loans. The personal knowledge of the borrower and the threat of severe punishment in case of default – enslavement according to the *Vedas* –probably provided enough security for a lender. Eventually things changed.

The *Dharmashastras*, the law code, written during the first two centuries A.D., maintained that regular law courts were established in every headquarter of villages and town, which regulated debt cases among other things. Trials were decided on according to the employment of loan deeds,[4] witnesses, responsibilities of relatives to be liable or not for the debts of the accused, and fines for false statements. Whether or not such law suits were a common affair or the exception is difficult to assess. During this period there appeared loans secured by usufructuary mortgages, pledges, personal liability of a guarantor and on personal security to persons to whom the bankers had great confidence. The transfer or potential transfer of land is, of course, closely related to the existence of landed property rights. The ancient literature discussed extensively whether the ruler was the sole proprietor or only an administrator (who was permitted to take land revenues) and whether the user was a tenant or had an occupancy right to the land. These scripts mentioned that cultivators sold or mortgaged their land (any adult member of a Hindu family could provide land for mortgage), the existence of simple and usufructuary mortgages (limited in time or indefinitely),[5] and the existence of a land sale tax. These facts contradict the common argument that only the English mobilized and commodified the production factor of land.

Worth mentioning are the banker's possibilities to recover a loan in accordance with the Manu Code.

> "A banker was given very big powers to recover his debt outside the law courts, and Manu says: 'By *dharma* (the use of inoffensive persuasion or mediation of friends), by suit in a court, by

---

[4] No loan was to be given without the execution of a loan deed. It took the following form: "I . . . .. son of . . . .. by case . . . .. of . . . ...gotra . . . .. alias (upnam) . . . .. have to-day (miti or date) . . . .. month . . . .. paksha . . . .. borrowed from . . . . son of . . . .. by caste . . . .. of . . . .. gotra . . . .. alias (upnam) . . . .. the sum of . . . .. repayable as . . . .. with interest at . . . .." (Bhargava 1934: 57). Some loan deeds required a witness, others did not.

[5] Brihaspati, i, 1, 28

artful management (. . .) or distress, banker (creditor) may recover the loan and fifthly by force'.[6]
By the first method, the banker was to bring friendly pressure on the debtor to liquidate his debt;
by the second method he was to file a suit in a King's court; by the third method the banker was
permitted to use crafty methods i.e. of taking away a certain article by misrepresentation from
the debtor and then refuse its return till the loan was repaid; by using such methods as lying
down before the house of the debtor (. . .) without food or drink till the loan was repaid. This last
method to a certain extent is even now resorted to by a certain class of creditors like the Kabuli or
Peshawari Pathan itinerant moneylenders. By the fifth method the creditor had the power to beat
or use other kinds of force to recover his money or to force the debtor to take employment under
the banker for the liquidation of his debt. This law, however, did not apply to cases of *Brahmans*,
and debts due by *Brahmans* were to be paid gradually. These powers of the bankers remained
intact till the sixteenth century" (Bhargava 1934: 90-1).

From this description I assume that moneylenders and bankers in the everyday-life
of ancient India had to personally persuade or force their customers to repay loans,
although there was also to some extent the possibility of calling in the judicial court.

The repayment of debt is considered a sacred obligation by Hindu social theory
and it is morally abject to die with debts. During the first two centuries A.D. usury
and interest were discussed and condemned at great length on the basis of religious
considerations.[7] Perhaps one can relate this condemnation to the theory of moral
debt in Hinduism, the natural debt of man to the gods (see Malamoud 1983), which is
similar to the Christian fall of man. More important from my point of view is that these
religious disputes were accompanied by the setting of interest rates and the maximum
amount for an accumulation of debt.

To provide some examples of interest rates: In ancient India the legal rate for secured loans, whether by pledges, movable properties or mortgages, was 15 percent per
annum.[8] For unsecured loans the rate was much higher. According to Manu, the caste
of the borrower was taken into consideration, in theory at least. A *Brahman* had to pay
two percent per month, a *Kshatriya* three, a *Vaisya* four and a *Shudra* (cultivator) five
percent.[9] The practical idea behind this interest rate diversification was that, the higher
the caste, the less risky the loan. Several centuries before Kautalya's *Arthashastra* did
not mention any rate diversification according to caste and spoke of five percent interest per month on monetary loans, whereas it was usual to fix a maximum compound
interest equal to the principal loan. Manu and Kautalya agreed that their rates should
be applied for ordinary transactions only, while for risky borrowers[10] the interest rates
were allowed to be considerably higher. Interest rates in kind were fixed, too, but the
rates given in the scripts of different periods were highly divergent.[11] Interest rates

---

[6] Manu, viii, 49

[7] For example, according to Manu 'weighted in the scales, the crime of killing a learned Brahman against
(the crime of) usury, the slayer of the Brahman remained at the top, the usurer sank downward' (Manu,
iv, 224, quoted by Bhargava 1934: 99).

[8] e.g. Vashishtha, ii, 51; Gautama, xii, 29; Manu, viii, 140; Arthashastra, xi, 174, 221.

[9] Manu, viii, 142

[10] Kautalya mentioned shippers (sea-faring merchants) and forest explorers, for whom the interest rates
per month were fixed at 20 and 10 percent, respectively.

[11] Interest rates in kind were grain, flavoring substances, flowers, fruits and roots tripling the original
price, products of animals, wool, produce of fields and beasts of burden five-fold of the value of the
object lent (Gautama, chap. xii, 36, 44, 45, 46, 47). Manu set the following rates of interest in kind:
loans in grain, fruit, wool or hair, on beasts of burden etc. – to be repaid in the same kind – not more
than quintupling the debt.

beyond the limits were considered as invalid, and the lender was fined 'at most to five in hundred'.[12] In contrast to these commercial loans, there existed social interest-free loans.[13] Manu and Kautalya agreed that debts which were not recovered within ten years should be canceled. In how far, however, lenders accepted these rates in practice or were legally fined is difficult to assess from these sources.

Taxation and the licensing of moneylenders and bankers is an indicator for the legal acceptance of these occupations and the participation of the administration in their profits. There is no evidence for the regulation of moneylending and banking before the Manu Code. According to this code, bankers had to pay a moderate business tax[14] in addition to the regular taxes in exchange for the protection afforded by the king – for example, with his legal courts. Eventually banking became a privileged profession which required a royal warranty.

It is worth mentioning the involvement of Hindu temples and Buddhist monasteries in moneylending, too. These temples were multi-functional institutions, which performed many non-religious, economic tasks. In this way moneylending was not only a matter of charity, but a means of self-financing for these religious institutions. Spencer (1968) went as far as considering the Hindu temple as a major institution through which early Indian economic life was organized. Singh (1989) described the involvement of village deities and temple committees in contemporary moneylending.

6.2.   Medieval India and the Emergence of British Rule

Medieval India, as Habib (1964) defined it, spans the period of about the mid-thirteenth to the eighteenth century, i.e. the Muslim period from the rise of the Delhi sultanate to Mughal India until the introduction of British rule, and this period was the heyday of indigenous-style banking. Medieval India had a monetized economy and was heavily involved in long-distance trade, which accelerated particularly during the first half of the fourteenth century (Habib 1982: 82). The Delhi sultanate introduced a tax and revenue system which comprised land revenue, house tax and cattle tax. These revenues were collected in cash, so that the peasant was forced to sell part of his produce in the market. The situation of the peasant was such that while land was abundant, the payment of revenues caused him considerable hardship.

The extensive agricultural revenue and its appropriation made possible the existence of large unproductive classes, urban centers such as Delhi or Lahore and the expansion of urban manufacturing (see, for example, Khan 1976). The commercialization of agricultural and artisanal production intensified domestic and long-distance trade. The economic climate stimulated the existence of different types of rural moneylenders who, in addition to granting consumer credit, advanced the land revenue payment to the peasantry, and merchant bankers, who largely financed trade.

---

[12] Manu, viii, 151-2, Gautama, xii, 31; xii 36. Kautalya's limits were 'equal to twice the share or principal' (Arthashastra, xi, 174, 221).

[13] These loans were provided to 'persons who are engaged in sacrifice', people suffering from disease, people who 'are detained in the house of their teachers' (scholars), or minors and poor (Arthashastra, iii, Manu, x, 117).

[14] The Manu Code mentioned the thirty-second part of their profits.

Since from the perspective of a sociologist the economic conditions and the administrative system during the era of the Delhi sultanate are basically the same as in Mughal India, and since the latter period is documented in much more detail and makes particular reference to indigenous-style bankers, I shift my attention to the period from the sixteenth to the eighteenth century. I shall start with a general description of the economic climate which is necessary to understand the particular roles of indigenously developed bankers and moneylenders in late medieval India. In this chapter, however, I shall largely confine myself to the domestic perspective, while in Part IV I move on to the world-perspective to explain the important function held by indigenously developed bankers from India's role in the Asian 'world-economy' (Braudel 1984) of the fifteenth to the eighteenth century.

6.2.1. Primary Production in Mughal India

The Mughal Empire under Akbar the Great took over and further developed the land revenue and tax system and its administration from the Delhi sultanate. It introduced a common monetary system and a more or less similar system of land allocation and taxation throughout the empire. Goods and money continuously flowed from the periphery to the center through the efficient revenue system. Raychaudhuri described the Mughal state as

> "an insatiable Leviathan: its impact on the economy was defined above all by its unlimited appetite for resources. In a predominantly agrarian economy these resources were extracted primarily from the agricultural sector, in the form of land revenue assessed as a fixed share of the produce" (Raychaudhuri 1982: 173).

For the urban population taxes were considerably lower than for the peasantry and did not exceed five percent of their income.

The land assessment varied from one third to one half or even more of the output, depending on the quality of land and the crop raised. Originally thought to be a share of the factual outputs, *zamindars*[15] (state revenue collectors) soon introduced average pre-assessments which, during bad harvests, caused severe hardship to the peasantry. Additional costs of collection, which were also imposed on the cultivators, amounted to 25 percent of the land revenue. One quarter or one third of the revenue was transferred to the government while the rest remained in the pockets of *zamindars*, moneylenders, agricultural castes with superior land rights[16] and the ruling class (military, nobility, religious elite)[17] which was paid by the emperor with life-time or temporary territorial assignments (*jagirs*) and the right to collect revenue.[18]

---

[15] *'Zamindar'* was a term applied to all landlords who were authorized by the government to maintain control over a particular local area, officials of previous regimes who had established a hereditary right to estate, and so on, and to collect revenue for the state (Rothermund 1978: 12).

[16] Rural society in Mughal India was stratified. Habib (1964) identified four different agrarian classes: (a) *zamindars*, moneylenders and grain merchants; (b) well-to-do or rich peasants; (c) the majority of the peasants, poor cultivators or small landholders; and (d) landless labourers or agricultural workers.

[17] This ruling class was Muslim in a Hindu society and recruited from abroad.

[18] Such assignments date back to the Delhi sultanate. Both terms *zamindar* and *jagirdar* are Mughal terms. However, these terms have been commonly applied to other political systems too.

In the course of the Mughal period a large part of the area under land revenue came under the *jagir* system. Instead of a salary the grantee obtained the right to extract surplus from a defined area and in turn maintained troops which had to assist the central government in case of war. Because of its merely temporary nature (sometimes a lifetime) the *jagirdars* (grantees) pursued only the short-term objective of squeezing the maximum from the peasantry. Another land tenure pattern in the Mughal empire was the *jjara* system, the farming out of a particular region for revenue collection. A revenue farmer (*jjaradar*) stipulated the price of the auction to the government, while he obtained the actual revenue or at least a share of it. Bankers and speculators used to invest in this lucrative business.

Raychaudhuri (1982: 173-6) concluded that the revenue system extracted most from those who had almost nothing. Agriculturists with superior rights to land, *jagirdars*, *zamindars* and *jjaradars* were able to shift part of their own burden to the small peasantry. Another factor which increased the unequal division of income were the flat rates of land revenue. The monetization of revenue payments forced the peasantry to sell part of their produce to grain traders or to take up a loan, and rural indebtedness (understood as a permanent rather than only a temporary condition) rose in Mughal India.

However, to consider 'the Mughal state as a mere incubus sucking the lifeblood of the peasantry' (Raychaudhuri 1982: 175) is wrong, too, since its politics contained welfare elements. For example, it guaranteed the security of tenure, in that *jagirdars* were forbidden to transfer peasant proprietors' land into land which the same persons tilled as hired labourers or dependents only. Land belonged to the peasantry which had a hereditary occupancy right and could not be displaced as long as the revenue was paid. Non-payment, however, was treated as an act of rebellion against the government and punished by expropriation, enslavement or even death (Dhanagare 1991: 26-7; Goldsmith 1987: 94-112).

Eventually a development occurred which was opposed to the initial structure of the landed pattern and land revenue system: the growth of 'property' rights and a market in these, although these 'property' rights were confined to particular rights and were not yet an alienable and unrestricted claim over land. In this process *zamindari* rights became heritable, salable and mortgagable. Since Mughal finance depended heavily on such intermediaries, the state had to make concessions to these revenue collectors. Eventually a stratification in *zamindar* rights occurred. Some had to pay tributes, some obtained their land as *jagirs*, and others obtained life-time but non-hereditary rights from the government. With the introduction of tax farms the *ta'alluqudari* system emerged, which was the purchase of the right to engage on behalf of other *zamindars*. All these rights were alienable and created a market of 'properties'. Before the *jagir* system collapsed in the course of the eighteenth century, *jagirdar* titles also became hereditary to some extent because the central administration was weak and required the support of the nobility, but the titles were not alienable (Raychaudhuri 1982: 176-7).

6.2.2. Trade in the Mughal Empire

Although Mughal India was commonly described as being agriculturally based, it was heavily involved in Asian trade, Asia-European trade and domestic country-city trade. According to Habib (1990: 371-9), the monetization of land revenues and the residence of elites in urban centers generated an extensive domestic trade in agricultural produce, which was handled by Hindu and Jain village, town and port-based merchants from the *baniya* caste. These were differentiated in a number of sub-castes, named after places, villages and settlements. One side-line of the *baniyas* was that of the *sarrafs*.[19] To put it more precisely: according to Habib indigenous-style bankers were differentiated from the *baniya* caste whose concern was land trade. This caste formed a category separate from maritime long-distance traders. While this is largely true for North India, the case of the South Indian Chettiar (see Schrader 1995) speaks against a generalization for the whole of India, since they are said to originate from maritime traders.

Among a sub-caste it was normal to have a sense of solidarity, to help each other and maintain its prosperity. There was no obstacle to having close business relations with other sub-castes or even other faiths. This is true both for trade and financing. Thus in addition to sub-caste solidarity, there was solidarity among the commercial class.

Two factors which have been identified by many scholars as being characteristic of Hindu mercantile enterprise and non-Western banking are (a) the intensive on-the-job training of sons and the transfer of collected experience from father to son; and (b) the development of values which are found in the Protestant ethic, too.

> "The major reason for their success surely lay in the training they received from early childhood in arithmetic, accountancy, and methods of business, sharpened by constant, acute competition with their peers (. . .) (These merchants combined, H.S.) two Calvinistic virtues, namely, thrift and religious spirit. The *baniyas* would carefully refrain from display of wealth and not spend lavishly on anything, except jewelry for their womenfolk (which was a form of saving). They were equally careful in points of ritual and prescribed diet (. . .) Clearly, the *baniyas* were well placed to command a very large part of Indian commerce, although we have no evidence that they enjoyed any exclusive legal rights or officially sanctioned privileges, let alone monopolies" (Habib 1990: 383-5).[20]

While the *baniya* usually appeared as an individual merchant, broker, or banker, in many cases his family (Hindu joint family) owned the firm. Another form of business organization was the partnership firm. Scholars generally assume that, until the early twentieth century, the individual firms, the joint family firm and the partnership firm were the only organizational forms. In Europe, on the other hand, the development of banks and merchant companies with share capital and bonds in the course of the 'long sixteenth century' (Braudel 1981) increased the capital basis of these enterprises and differentiated the owners of capital and its managers. Max Weber (1964) made the

---

[19] The Indian case suggests that traders and financiers should be considered one single, although differentiated, commercial category (emerging from traders and being involved in trade and finance or specializing in the trade of money and capital), at least until the development of industrial capitalism.

[20] Such values have been ascribed to Marwari and Chettiar, too.

Protestant ethic and its 'spirit of capitalism' responsible for this process of development to modern capitalism. The limitation of the Indian firms' own capital compared
to the European joint-stock trading companies' shareholder's equity is usually considered as having forced the former out of competition in the Asian trade. Habib held
against this view that

> "the absence of joint-stock companies did not prevent the growth of large *baniya* firms,
> whether of the individual, family or partnership type. In such a firm the *sahu*, or principal, had a
> number of factors (*bapari* or *vapari*)" (Habib 1990: 390, referring to Arasaratnam 1979).

In addition, caste solidarity and caste or ethnic networking compensated for this
lack of capital so that, for example, indigenously developed bankers with a temporary
shortage of capital could easily borrow from other bankers of the same caste. If a
business opportunity exceeded the capacity of the own firm they handed it over to a
larger firm and received compensation.

Asian long-distance trade was conducted by another class of highly skilled professional Muslim and some Hindu traders. Descriptions reveal that they were the more
important carriers of long-distance trade than independent merchants. Most of them
were financed by or sometimes acted on behalf of large merchant-bankers (*sahus*)
from the *baniya* caste (who were involved in the trade to the ports) and speculative
aristocratic officials. Contrary to their thrifty Hindu counterparts, Muslim traders had
the image of spendthrifts. According to Chaudhuri (1985: 182), this long-distance
trade in the Indian Ocean was based upon the logic of flows of goods from certain
surplus-producing areas to chronic deficit areas. A deficit area of consumption goods
was the Middle East, and there was a continuous flow from India, the Indonesian
archipelago and China to the Middle East which was balanced by precious metal.
This resulted from continental trade revenues. The Middle East again seemed to have
had a positive balance of trade with the Christian East, Central Asia and the city-states
of West Africa.

The Indian subcontinent was the leading exporter. In Gujarat, Cambay was the
leading port until the end of the fifteenth century. Due to silting this port found its natural death and Surat emerged as the new main West Indian entrepot. Other important
ports on the west coast were Goa, Calicut and Cochin, on the East Coast Chittagong,
Hugli, Massulipatam, Pulicat and Madras. Confining myself to Surat and its key role
in Indian long-distance trade, its business world was multi-ethnic, comprising Parses,
Jews, Armenians, Muslims, Hindus, Jains and other merchants. The Mughal empire
offered a variety of export goods in high demand, such as cotton textiles, foodstuffs,
and industrial raw material, which exceeded imports by far. The positive balance of
trade resulted in a continuous flow of bullion to India and during the seventeenth and
eighteenth centuries some of it was spent on imports from Java, Sumatra, Malaya,
China and the Philippines.

The Mughal state appropriated immense trade revenues. Customs duties were
charged as well as inland tolls. In addition to a proportionate income tax, Hindu
traders were taxed higher than Muslims and Europeans. However, profits from long-
distance trade were high enough to absorb these costs. Since Indians and Europeans
catered for different markets and Indian traders had comparative cost advantages to

European traders, the lighter taxation of Europeans was no heavy burden for Hindu merchants (Raychaudhuri 1982: 188-91).

Following Chaudhuri (1985) like in the case of domestic trade, supply and ownership of capital for long-distance trade remained largely in the hands of individual merchants. These required certain facilities in the port cities to make business. First of all, this was a 'spot' or forward market with clear price indicators and a continuous supply. Second, they required banking facilities which provided credit against bills of exchange. The settling of accounts and the recovery of bad debts necessitated binding agreements and legal courts. They needed a market for freight business, too, since many merchants with high value freight used to spread the risk by transport on different ships.

Capital was accumulated by merchants and non-Western bankers in different ways: one way was within the family or trading community to which the family belonged. This led to the formation of family firms, caste, ethnic or language group trading networks. Another possibility was the acceptance of deposits or the investment by rich landed classes and the ruling elites in the firm. The third way was by taking a chance, risk investments, good information on the markets, and so on.

Important for wealthy merchants and bankers was the political patronage of government officials to be protected from unwelcome state interference and to obtain privileges in official monopolies, revenue farms or with particular government tasks. Merchants and their capital, however, were vulnerable to shifts in policy and the favor of politicians.

> "Social conventions and the financial needs of the state defined the relationship between Asian political rulers and merchants (. . .) Trade remained a specialized occupation below the possession of arms (and, H.S.) of administration (. . .) If the political or social attitude towards the trading community was generally hostile in Asia, its origin lay in the supposition that the accumulation of capital, and even of commercial profits, were made at the expense of the public (. . .) Perhaps the most immediate and powerful means of self-protection available to merchants was their command over money" (Chaudhuri 1985: 214)[21]

and their ability to withdraw it. I show in this chapter that this is what precisely happened during the late Mughal period.

Having so far described the economic climate of the Mughal empire, I now shift my attention to the particular spheres of finance.

6.2.3. Credit in the Mughal Empire

Credit to the Peasantry

In addition to short-term consumer credit requirements to bridge the income gap until the next harvest if the reserves (cash and kind) were insufficient, many peasants had to borrow to be able to pay the high taxes and revenues and to finance social events (marriages, funerals, rituals, and so on). Various semi-professional lenders, such as

---

[21] Dasgupta's (1982: 422) view that the Mughal state was largely indifferent to traders, at least until the years of the beginning dissolution of the empire, contradicts this.

village headmen, well-off agriculturalists, village and town *baniyas, zamindars* and some professional moneylenders, were the rural credit suppliers. The government provided agricultural loans for the clearing of untilled land (for example, seed or cattle), and an instrument which was common to mitigate the effects of natural disasters was the temporary exemption or reduction of taxes. The rates of interest of *mahajans* in Bengal villages, for example, were reported to be 150 percent simple interest per year, whereas the actual loan period was two or three months. In case of late repayment interest was added to the principal, and a fresh bond was taken from the borrower (compound interest). As usual for ancient and medieval India, principal plus interest were not allowed to exceed double the amount of the principal at the end of ten years (Habib 1964: 394-5). However, Hamilton, at the end of the eighteenth century, reported for Bengal moderate interest rates of 12 to 18 percent per annum for secured agricultural loans, and 12 percent for secured non-agricultural loans. The interest rates for unsecured loans, on the other hand, were higher than forty percent. Most loans to cultivators were unsecured, since land was not transferable to the lender. (Bhargava 1934: 103-4, 114). Compared with present bank rates, these rates are very high, but not necessarily from the subjective point of view of borrowers and lenders. Cultivators lacked alternative sources of credit and had no security to offer. Repayment took place in kind, by labour service or sometimes by the sale of the debtor's children (Goldsmith 1987: 113).[22] It seems that moneylending in medieval India was part of everyday life of the Indian village. Depending on the pattern of land tenure, moneylenders sometimes advanced land revenues to whole villages. In such cases not an individual, but the whole village was the debtor.

Commercial Credit

While the financing of cultivators was handled by moneylenders in various shapes, the domain of indigenous-style bankers was the financing of non-Western domestic and long-distance trade. Wealthy aristocratic officials, large-scale moneylenders and the state took part in the financing of trade, too.[23] Commercial credit of indigenously developed bankers, however, was largely found at the international and interregional levels only. Most bankers were merchant bankers comparable in their mode of operation to the European merchant bankers of the late medieval period. They traded themselves or financed other traders, particularly the maritime long-distance traders, by sharing the risk and obtaining a large share of the profits,[24] they discounted *hundis*, which were usually drawn to purchase goods, or sent remittances to bankers in other places, and some of them accepted deposits, too.[25] The provision of financial services crossed caste barriers. Most firms were family firms and the larger ones had branch networks or interrelations with non-Western banking firms in distant places. Secured commercial interest rates in land trade varied according to place, and between 1624

---

[22] This shows that there was not then any distinction between substantive and personal law.

[23] A document from the fourteenth century, for example, points out that the state occasionally ordered particular goods and provided the finance for the purchase. The trader had to deliver the goods at a fixed price.

[24] This is similar to the European late medieval trading society.

[25] While scholars assumed that no deposit interest was paid since safekeeping was itself a service, one source from the mid-seventeenth century reported deposit rates of 5 to 8 percent per annum.

and 1665 the reported rates ranged from 0.5 to 1.25 percent per month. The usual bazaar rate was probably one percent per month. Habib (1990: 393) called these rates fair, although the level of interest was higher than in England or the Netherlands. The different rates point to different money supply and demand relations and borrowers' lack of knowledge about money prices in other commercial centers. Risky commercial credit, such as sea loans in long-distance trade, involved interest rates of up to 40 to 60 percent per trade venture. Like most factors in overseas commerce, demand for such loans was seasonal since trade depended on the seasonal winds.

In addition to the financing of non-Western enterprise, indigenous-style bankers financed European private merchants and trading companies, too. The Portuguese, the Dutch, the English and the French arrived one after the other on the subcontinent in the sixteenth and seventeenth centuries and founded trading settlements. In Surat and Bengal, for example, each of them had a trading settlement, temporarily at least. They required finance for their trading enterprises and for armed confrontations among each other or with Indian rulers, and they used the networks of indigenous-style bankers in particular to transfer funds from one trading settlement to another. It was reported by the English and that is probably true for the other Europeans, too, that they had difficulties negotiating with the indigenous-style bankers because they did not understand their strange modes of operation. Initially they were regarded with skepticism by the bankers who had no knowledge of their creditworthiness.[26] Comparatively speaking, the interest charged to these aliens was slightly higher than the common market rates (Habib 1964: 402-3, tables; Rau 1938: 290).

The Finance of Artisans

Even before the appearance of the Europeans, there existed vertical links between merchandise and production. Great Indian merchants had agents or brokers on a commission basis in the port cities who advanced working capital to weavers and other artisans to produce goods on order and deliver them on the specified date. This system has been called the Indian version of the *Verlagssystem* (putting-out system) in Europe. Contrary to the latter, however, the producers were paid in cash rather than in production inputs.

The Europeans extended this system as follows. To enforce the standardization of cloth and textiles ordered, both the English and the Dutch gave contracts to Indian merchants eight to ten months before the arrival of the European ships. Prices, quality and quantity were fixed in advance. These merchants in turn gave orders and advances to the producers as described above. When the cloth was delivered to the European warehouses, the officials sorted the delivery according to the samples seen before, and any deviation was either rejected or the prices reduced. In the course of the eighteenth century, the English even locked up the rejected delivery until the order was completed. This practice became to be known as the 'muster system' (Chaudhuri 1982: 406).

---

[26] Habib (1964) reported loans amounting to no less than Rs 200,000 per firm.

Credit to the Elites

In addition to the finance of trade, indigenous-style bankers provided considerable non-agricultural consumer credit to the nobility. Lending to them was very risky, since they had the political power to default without any judicial consequences. Indeed, the mortgaging of titles theoretically provided legal credit security. However, the Mughal courts were very susceptible to bribery. Habib (1964: 413ff.) reported that a Mughal administrator who decided in favor of a lender, used to claim one-fourth of the amount of debt for himself. The other way around, wealthy borrowers bribed the judge and obtained their right in case this was cheaper than to repay the debt. Poor people, however, were always disadvantaged. Because of this lack of security of loans to the nobility, the interest rates charged were probably substantial. In situations of hardship or military excursions the nobility could obtain long-term credit from the treasury up to ten years at the modest rate of between 6 and 11 percent[27] (Habib 1964: 398-409; Goldsmith 1987: 114-5; Rau 1938: 290).

State Banking

Some top indigenous-style bankers were treasurers and minters of the Mughal emperors and the financiers of the government production units (*karkhanahs*), the extensive and expensive Mughal architecture (mosques, tombs, pleasure gardens) and the frequent wars. Before the days of Akbar some had also been assayers, money changers and tax collectors – functions which were already outdated because of a single currency and the introduction of *zamindars* and *jjaradars*. But the revenue farms provided an investment opportunity for the well-off bankers and the nobility.

Moneylending and Islam

According to Chaudhuri (1985: 210-1), Islam contains the paradox that the Qur'an encourages trade but prohibits *riba*, the taking of interest.[28] The Qur'an's explicit prohibition of *riba* is valid until this day. Its consequences on the economic life of orthodox Islamic countries are such that Islamic banking has been developed as an alternative form to Western banking. It is in line with the prohibition of *riba* since it is based on the risk-sharing principle (see Mallat 1988; Baldwin and Wilson 1988).

In Mughal India like in other countries heavily involved in trade, the paradox between trade and *riba* was resolved in different ways, such as operating through bankers of different faiths (Hindus or Jains), the risk sharing in commercial finance, or the introduction of secular in addition to Muslim judges for commercial law. Claims to recover debts were usually treated by the secular offices of the administration. A

---

[27] The Ain-i-Akbarik mention the following rates of interest for loans from the treasury to officials and royal households: 1st year 0 percent, 2nd year 6.25, 3rd year 12.5, 4th year 25, 5th to 7th year 50, 8th to 10th year 75, 10th year and after 100 (Bhargava 1934: 103).

[28] According to Baldwin and Wilson (1988) some Muslim scholars translate *riba* as excessive interest, while the more orthodox are of the opinion that the prohibition comprises all interest. The Qur'an assumes that God has provided humankind with abundant resources, so that the fulfillment of a certain need is not at the expense of others. Competition is therefore not an element of natural order. Instead, man is to a certain extent socially responsible which does not, however, imply the renunciation of private property.

document from this period shows how a Muslim theologian coped with the paradox. At the beginning of the document he strictly condemned usury but, after a longer discussion of the matter, decided that it was the matter of the law-enforcing secular authority to decide whether moneylending and gambling should be forbidden (Habib 1964: 413-8).

To sum up the financial landscape of medieval India so far: in spite of a Muslim elite, it consisted of a complex web of cash and kind credit ranging from the village level to the highest commercial plane. Broadly speaking, three types of financial agents predominated: (a) moneylenders for consumer credit to peasants and the advance of revenue payments; (b) indigenously developed bankers for the financing of trade and the nobility; and (c) certain top indigenous-style bankers for the financing of the state and European trading companies.

The West Bengal District Gazetteers of Hoogly (1972: 325-6) and Malsa (1969: 21ff.) demonstrate the multi-functionality and changing functions of top indigenous-style bankers. While around 1600 they were engaged in the exchange of cowries and silver coins and acted as bankers, transferred money for others from one town to another or traded in *hundis*, some particular functions ceased to exist until the eighteenth century, while other functions were added. Until 1778, for example, the payment of land revenues from the revenue collectors to the Company functioned via the *shroffs*. The banking house of the Jagat Seth, a Marwari, established a quasi-banking and money-changing monopoly over the whole province of Hoogly and over great parts of Bengal. His agencies ranged from Dakka to Delhi, and he employed other indigenous-style bankers as his factors. He was the treasurer and minter of the Nawab and his house provided a number of revenue farmers and *zamindars*. He was among the primary Indian creditors of the Dutch, the French and the English and involved in *hundi* business. When the latter established control over Bengal and transferred their treasury to Calcutta, the House of the Jagat Seth practically ceased to act as the bankers of the Company. Its wealth declined and various smaller indigenously developed bankers took over the money-change. With the emergence of the agency houses and joint-stock banking at the turn to the nineteenth century, the indigenous bankers suffered a serious set-back.

6.2.4.   The Great Firm Theory

With her 'great firm theory'[29] Leonard (1979, 1981a,b) went beyond a pure description of non-Western bankers during the Mughal period and made them at least partly responsible to the decline for the Mughal Empire in the course of the eighteenth century. She argued that bankers and merchants are usually considered to form unproductive, segmental rather than strategic elites, being autonomous, apolitical, passive and parasitic in character and profiteering from the imperial powers (Leonard 1979: 154), or they are even classified as being traditionally minded, non-entrepreneurial, and conspicuous, impeding capitalist development. Such perceptions on merchant capital

---

[29] Scholars, for example Timberg (1978) in his study of the Marwari, applied this term to multi-functional business firms being engaged in various enterprises such as trade, banking, revenue collection, and so on.

and common explanations for the decline of the Mughal empire (like the exploitative revenue system, which increased rural indebtedness, led to peasant rebellions, and an inflated superstructure) neglect the importance of mutual dependency of indigenous-style bankers and the state.

Leonard's argumentation runs as follows: The rise and maintenance of the Mughal empire had required the coalition with strategically important groups and institutions to keep down various oppositional elites. To maintain power a strong central administration was introduced. Traders and bankers were important for the provision of goods and cash to the unproductive class. A monetized market economy and a complex system of credit were already in existence. The 'great firms' supported the rise of the Mughals and their consolidation of power and in turn obtained personal and political patronage. However, from the late seventeenth century onward trade opportunities in Surat harbor began to decline. Leonard relates this to a minor state protection, which is too short-sighted to my mind. While in the course of the sixteenth and seventeenth century such declines were of a temporary nature only due to confrontations between the Mughals and the European companies,[30] this decline was structural because of a decreasing demand for Indian export items and therefore not caused by the Mughal emperors. Whatever the reason, this decline in the importance of Surat harbor was perhaps the first visible sign of the fall of the Mughal empire in the course of the eighteenth century. Whether or not the 'great firms' anticipated this fall, they began to look for better business opportunities. Many of them drained away their capital to other emerging powers and commercial centers in India, such as the Marathas from the Deccan (Central India) or the East India Company in Bombay.

This already shows the flexibility of indigenously developed bankers to always adapt to the changing circumstances. If in the past it was the profitability of non-Western banking which probably caused the differentiation of some sub-castes into pure bankers or merchant bankers, the expectation of greater prosperity in other regions and of other powers caused the 'great firms' to move their business to other places, in the same way as the declining market shares of indigenous-style banking towards the end of the nineteenth and early twentieth centuries caused them to withdraw from banking and invest in industry.

Leonard's argumentation was supplemented by Subramanian (1987). Both scholars agreed that the indigenous-style bankers' switch of support played an important role in Indian politics. Subramanian went so far as claiming that the rise of the English East India Company on the West Coast was due to the finance of the Surat and Benares bankers, and that they accelerated the fall of the former rulers by cutting their credit lines. She argued that the Company's shortage of money on the West Coast was, among other things, due to the fact that Bombay as a trading settlement had no hinterland which allowed for the collection of land revenues. This necessitated

---

[30] Confrontations between one of the companies and the Mughal rulers was frequent and affected the interest of the traders. If the Indian merchants were incapable to resolve such confrontations by mediation, the Mughals cut off the supplies of food and other daily necessities to the European factories. These called in their warships which either blocked the port or captured Indian merchant vessels. These confrontations normally ended in a compromise without an escalation of violence (Chaudhuri 1982: 394).

a continuous draining of money away from the Supreme Government in Bengal to Bombay. The bill-of-exchange business between Calcutta and Bombay via the non-Western bankers' networks functioned in a way that Calcutta diverted part of Bengali revenues, in the form of specie, to buy *hundis* from the local Indian businessmen. These bills of exchange were sent to Surat and sometimes to Bombay, and reconverted by the indigenous-style bankers into coined silver.

Torri (1991: 376-83) held against this view that, from the macro-economic perspective, such an exchange meant in the long run a permanent negative balance of trade for Bombay and a positive one for Calcutta if the movement of goods or bills of exchange from the West Coast to Calcutta did not counterbalance this flow. Therefore he argued that these transfers can be interpreted only within the context of the Middle East – Surat – Bengal commodity trade. He related the *hundi* business connecting Calcutta and the West Coast with the silk/cotton trade between Bengal and the West Coast and the Surat – Middle East trade, all of them together constituting an integrated business network. The *hundi* business was mainly in the hand of Hindus and Jains, the Middle East trade was dominated by Muslims and Parses, and the silk/cotton trade by Hindus and Armenians. In spite of this ethnic specialization, these groups all belonged to the same system.

The arrival of the British in India threatened this long-established network. From the 1770s to the early 1780s the Middle East trade declined, since trade to the Middle East had become more expensive and more risky. The silk trade from Bengal to the West Coast declined, too, because the British transferred revenue to England in the form of silk and piece goods. This and additional customs duties increased the prices which almost produced a collapse of the whole branch of trade and forced Calcutta to abolish the duty on trade coming from Bengal. The gap between the value of the Bengal – Surat trade in cotton and the counterflow eventually increased by such a large margin that in 1790 Calcutta merchants carried gold and *hundis* via Benares to Surat and Bombay to finance the trade on the West Coast. During the late eighteenth century the Surat bankers were trapped in this declining system, and a series of bankruptcies occurred.

Subramanian (1987) maintained that, by the end of the eighteenth century, the indigenously developed bankers who had moved to Bombay had consolidated their role in policy and were heavily involved in the financing of the newly established direct India-China trade. The *baniyas* were fully aware of their indispensable economic position and, if necessary, reminded the Company authorities of this fact.[31] Subramanian called this mutual support of both non-Western bankers and the Company the 'Anglo-*baniya* order.'

Towards the end of the eighteenth century, however, the British started to reflect on how they could free themselves from the dependency on indigenously developed bankers. To raise independent finance they began issuing government bonds and setting up their own banks. The decreasing dependency of the British coincided with a step-by-step reduction of the functions held by indigenous-style bankers in their terri-

---

[31] When in 1795 in Surat riots took place against indigenously developed bankers they petitioned for help by East India Company and reminded it of their close relation.

tory, which had already begun in the Mughal period. Revenue farms were abolished in 1778, export/import trade and minting rights were eventually monopolized by the Company, and a single currency was introduced for all-British India (1835). In addition the British renounced the takeover of debts of former rulers to indigenous-style bankers. One could argue that, once the power of the Company was consolidated and the export market and Indian market established – in other words: once the risk was reduced – British banks took over the financing of trade and of the colonial administration.[32]

While Leonard and Subramanian emphasized the dependence of the political powers on the economic powers, at least for some time, Torri (1991) considered the position of the indigenously developed bankers in late Mughal and emerging British-India weak. First of all, they turned to Bombay not of their own free will but as a consequence of declining Surat business. Second, in British-India they neither formed a class nor had they any lobby (e.g. a strong professional organization or representatives in the Bombay government). They pursued their individual interests which were opposed to the unified body of the East India Company. For some time the English had to rely on the *shroffs* and these in turn had to collaborate with the British given the decline in Surat trade, but this temporary symbiosis of both bankers and the Company was not voluntary as it is assumed by Subramanian. Therefore Torri rejected her assumption of the 'Anglo-*baniya* order'.

To my mind the question of whether the indigenous-style bankers' position towards the Mughals and the Company was strong or weak is not as important as their shifting the coalition from a politically and economically declining to an emerging power and region. This reorientation was possible because of the mobility of their property and business-mindedness. Nevertheless, the advantages of this new coalition were short-lived.

---

[32] It seems to me that such a development took place in the Indian colony Burma and in parts of Malaya one century later, according to the same pattern outlined here.

7. Formal and Informal Finance in Colonial India

Most historians find it easy to mark the beginning and end of a period by particular path-breaking events. From their perspective medieval India relates to the Muslim period in North India, which lasted from the rise of the Delhi sultanate until the consolidation of British power in Bengal with the victory at the Battle of Plassey in 1757.[1] The *'Cambridge Economic History of India'* has underlined the importance of this year symbolically by the ending its first volume and beginning of the second at this point. Even Wallerstein (1989) whose work is more process- than event-oriented, chose this year as the beginning of the incorporation of the Asian external arena into the modern world-system (see Part IV).

The preceding chapter described the role of moneylenders and indigenously developed bankers in ancient and medieval India. I argued that the top bankers of this period supported the rise and fall of rulers, particularly the Mughal dynasty. A powerful state could confer on them certain privileges, such as state banking or revenue collection, but could equally limit their functions and subordinate certain tasks to civil servants. The indigenously developed banker, however, could easily compensate for the 'nationalization' of particular tasks by large profits from investment in maritime and land trade. They were more affected by the decline in trade with Arabia and the loss of shares to Europeans in the inner-Asian trade, the effects of which were felt in the early eighteenth century. This represented the first sign of the fall of the Mughals and caused a shift in the business orientation of the 'great firms' towards other emergent powers, in particular the East India Company.

The important functions of these top bankers in economy and state, with their control of money and their active participation in writing Indian history, are criteria to identify them as a 'strategic group' (Evers and Schiel 1988), which always supported the party from which they expected the maximum personal/business advantages (whereas the personalities and firms were often difficult to distinguish). Even Torri's (1991) criticism that their political position was weak compared to the East India Company cannot contest this view point. Indeed, they faced the dilemma that their profession had had its heydays and that its opportunities were in decline. The dilemma resulting from this structural change, was that none of the three choices they had – to continue supporting the declining Mughal dynasty, to shift their capital to other Indian rulers or to come to an arrangement with the East India Company – were in the long run promising compared to their position in medieval India. The former two choices meant betting on the wrong horse, and in the short run the third choice was preferable. In the long run, however, the East India Company, once it had consolidated its power, freed itself from its dependency on non-Western finance by institutionalizing banks

---

[1] In the 1750s the Anglo-French confrontations led to the policy of each side supporting the succession claims of another dynasty, and it was finally the revolution of Plassey which established English territorial control in Bengal.

which incorporated further functions that had been formerly fulfilled by indigenous-style bankers, and largely restricted the latter's involvement in foreign trade.

Of course, only the contemporary scientist is aware of this dilemma, while the indigenous-style banker decided on ways of how to restructuring his business in line with short-and medium-term expectations. This dilemma was a long-term process which affected several generations. It first arose in the early eighteenth century, came to a head from the second half of the eighteenth century onward and finally caused the reorganization of indigenous-style banking. This process crossed the boundary from late medieval to early modern India.

While the shift of political support was primarily the concern of the 'great firms' who were state bankers and financiers of long-distance trade, the majority of their colleagues were largely engaged in financing inland and overseas trade, both on a smaller level. They too felt the effects of the declining maritime trading volume due to Arabian market saturation, the declining interregional trade on land caused by lack of foreign demand for export goods and the continuous disputes of succession in North and Central India.

However, this structural change does not imply that indigenous-style banking disappeared step-by-step. It found its place within a newly emerging division of labour among commercial and financial agents and institutions. The SGIB (1971: 13) argued that the ultimate reason for its survival was its maintenance of a separate existence without establishing any link with the early European banks. This is incorrect in so far that links between formal and informal finance existed and still exist; for example, the possibility of indigenously developed bankers of rediscounting *hundis* at commercial banks. But it is generally true that, until this day formal and informal finance, and particularly banks of any style and indigenous-style bankers, largely (but not exclusively) serve different clienteles.

I go a step further than the SGIB (1971). I argue that, although their heyday had gone, indigenous-style bankers continued in existence thanks to the emerging economic structure in British-India, the division of labour between the British and the Indians, which left sufficient room for profitable indigenous enterprise and facilitated the coexistence of both Western and indigenous-style banking. To reduce this division of labour to a colonial division, with import-export trade being totally controlled by the British and domestic traders being the brokers for the British exporters, is an oversimplification, which is true only for the period from the 1750s until the 1810s, during which the East India Company monopolized India-England trade.

What I have roughly outlined here will be looked at in greater detail in this chapter. In Chapter 7.1 I take a general view of Indians' trading opportunities in colonial India, since trade and its financing always provided the chief enterprise for indigenously developed bankers. Chapter 7.2 summarizes the emergence of Western-style banks in India. In Chapter 7.3 I consider rural finance and rural indebtedness with regard to the changing agricultural conditions in colonial India, the answer of the colonial government to this challenge and its impact on moneylending. In Chapter 7.4 I analyze the emergence of Indian-owned industries and the role of indigenous-style bankers in this process.

7.1. The Pattern of Trade in Colonial India

In this chapter I shall concentrate on the analysis of commerce and largely neglect the monetary aspect.[2] To describe the politicoeconomic conditions in early modern India is difficult because they varied considerably in different parts until the British had extended their control all over the subcontinent and applied more or less the same rule. The Penguin History of India therefore speaks of British-India only after 1818. On the whole, the period from the 1757 until the mid-nineteenth century was characterized by political instability. The British expanded their power at the expense of the Mughal empire and other Indian rulers whose collapse led to attempts by other Indian sovereigns to extend their sphere of influence. Various independent regions existed or were affiliated to the British while maintaining autonomous status. Generally speaking the regions which were under British control left less room for Indian involvement in both foreign and domestic trade, while those regions which were not controlled by the British experienced a growth in domestic trade compensating for the loss of foreign trade involvement to some extent. Indian merchants and bankers adopted the role of brokers for the British and the organizers and financiers of up-country trade. So far I have largely confined my description to North India (including West and East India) and I shall continue to do so for the moment.

According to Chaudhuri (1982: 804ff.), the period from the Plassey events (1757) until the Charter Act (1813) was characterized by the establishment of British superiority in the subcontinent and the attempt to enforce an exclusive trade monopoly between Britain and India.[3] Rothermund (1989: 16-8) argued that the Company acted like a parasite profiting from the decay of the preceding rulers and benefiting from the existing system without changing it very much. Instead of stimulating the economy it simply collected tributes like the military feudal predecessors. 'But whereas these predecessors had spent that tribute in India, the Company transferred it abroad' (Rothermund 1989: 18). For a long time the Company maintained the duties on internal and foreign trade[4] and taxes on artisans' products. The Mughals' land revenue collection was also adapted. 'They did exactly what these predecessors used to do, only they were more exacting in collecting whatever was assessed' (Rothermund 1989: 19). The revenue policy impeded the production and circulation of commodities. Many Indian Marxist scholars take the same perspective as Rothermund, while the more conservative scholars challenge this approach with the Ricardian theorem of comparative cost advantages in that both England and India profited from the colonial division of labour.

---

[2] For the monetary aspect see, for example, Rothermund (1992).

[3] This attempt, however, was challenged by the complicity of the Company's own servants in the illegal trading of private merchants.

[4] Until 1757 the Hindu paid higher customs duties than the Muslim traders, but the English abolished these differences. Before the reforms of 1846, however, each province had its own regulations on customs duties. In Bengal, for example, British imports obtained preferred import rates in the second decade of the nineteenth century and foreign vessels were obliged to return from the big Indian ports without additional coastal trade. The decline of trade in other European countries largely resulted from this tariff policy and these regulations. In Bombay and Madras the regulations were similar. At the same time goods manufactured in India were placed in a disadvantageous position in comparison with imported goods by imposing higher transit duties on them.

According to Chaudhuri (1982: 806ff.), the pattern of foreign trade generally followed the traditional channels, while the share of Europe-Asian trade increased continuously. It consisted of the export of textiles, foodstuffs and other raw materials as
well as the import of bullion and some manufactured goods.

> "However, the East India Company's effort to combine its political role with that of a commer-
> cial organization and the practice of financing a large volume of trade through the public revenues
> of its Indian possessions caused serious distortions both in the internal economy of these provinces
> and that part of their external trade which was carried on legitimately by private traders. It was
> largely as a result of the political pressure exercised by the latter and the decline of mercantile
> doctrines in England, that the Company's exclusive monopoly in Indian trade was abolished in
> 1813 and the Company debarred from trading altogether in 1833. Thus the period of really mod-
> ern development in the history of Indian foreign trade can be said to begin only with the passage
> of the Charter Act of 1813" (Chaudhuri 1982: 806-7).

In the mid-eighteenth century the situation in India was such that three groups
dominated trade. Trade with Europe was increasingly taken over by English, Dutch,
French and other trading companies, most of which enjoyed domestic monopolies to
protect their position from private competition in their countries. The second group
were Asian, non-Indian merchants, such as Armenians and Arabs trading with the
Middle East. The third group were Indian merchants who were engaged in domestic
and foreign trade, the latter with declining fortunes. The most important Indian trading castes and groups were according to Chaudhuri (1982), the Gujarati in the north,
followed by the Chettiar merchants in the south and the Hindu traders of Bengal. A
fourth group, less important than the other three, were European private traders operating under license of their companies in Asian inter-port trade. The latter supplied an
important volume of carrying trade to Indian merchants.

By the time the English incorporated Bengal, it had already supplanted Surat as
the primary trading province of the Mughals. The English victory in the war with the
Nawab of Bengal and successful negotiations with the Mughal emperor, strengthened
the economic, political and financial position of the East India Company. In 1780-90
trade to and from Europe was distributed as follows. Foreign companies, excluding
the East India Company (Dutch, French, Portuguese, Danish), had a share of 41.5 percent of all imports and 37.6 percent of all exports, while the Company alone had shares
of 14.4 and 26.8 percent, respectively. English trade under foreign flags (clandestine
trade) had import and export shares of 25.7 and 27.3 percent, licensed English private
traders of 18.4 and 5.5 percent. Both Company servants, whose involvement in private
English trade was eventually checked, and private British traders dominated the maritime trade of Bengal, Madras and Bombay and generally greatly reduced the share
of Indian merchants (Chaudhuri 1982: 815-6). The Indian foreign maritime trade
from Calcutta in the early nineteenth century amounted to no more than five percent
in 1805, four percent in 1817 and 8 percent in 1825 (Bhattacharya 1982: 271).

Not only foreign trade, but also the domestic pattern of trade, was radically reversed, wherever the English had established control. Indian traders and indigenous-
style bankers were increasingly pushed into the position of Company brokers. Until
then free competition had existed in the local markets. The Company bought either
from independent Indian merchants in Calcutta or Hoogly or employed its own servants for the up-country purchase. This free competition was then increasingly re-

stricted and primary producers of export goods became obliged to sell to the Company at fixed prices. One means of doing this was the Company's provision of advances to the producers.

Until the Charter Act of 1813, which dissolved the monopoly of the East India Company, the Company built a system of trade which established a pattern of domination (scholars called the pattern 'domination effect'). In the production field it began to dominate the market as the largest buyer. In the marketing field it began to control the supply of export goods which were smallholders' produce with the exception of tea,[5] and the terms where and how such goods were obtained. The producer became increasingly dependent on the Company by advances which determined production decisions and marketing. To establish and maintain this control, Indian trading capital was largely excluded from the spheres dominated by the Company.

"So far as Indian trading capital was concerned this system meant either extrusion from spheres claimed by the Company or subordination to the Company and European private capital (. . .) Indian capital was perforce confined mainly to internal trade and unorganized banking, servicing petty commodity production in agriculture and artisanal industry" (Bhattacharya 1982: 289–90).

The increasing integration of India into the modern world system, argued Chaudhuri (1982), more clearly defined the subordinate role of indigenous capital in the emerging international division of labour. The European demand for export crops (especially cotton, indigo, sugar and later opium), coupled with a government policy of raising cash revenue, required the monetization of rural regions, cash-crop production, processing and marketing. These activities provided opportunities for entrepreneurs. To strengthen their position, British and private merchants began to form agency houses. While these houses initially supplied imported goods to Company agents, they soon came to act as bankers[6] and contractors in the export trade. However, the Europeans and Indians borrowed from Calcutta agency houses and indigenous-style bankers for the working capital requirements of factory production and advances to the cultivators. Once this pattern of domination was established, the Company fixed the terms of exchange in the particular fields under their control. Wages in commercial production were pushed down to subsistence level.

The newly emerging pattern of trade was closely connected with a financial hierarchy, ranging from the petty village and itinerant moneylender via the town moneylender to the entrepot moneylender and indigenous-style banker. It is important to emphasize the vertical links between them. For example, village moneylenders were financed by or even agents of town moneylenders, and these again obtained their working capital from the higher level. In other words, while it is true that most indigenous-style bankers were not directly involved in financing agriculture, they participated in an indirect way. An example of such a financial hierarchy was that of Bengal in the second half of the eighteenth century. At the top level was the banking

---

[5] The growth of cash-crop production, particularly in Eastern India, had generally no stimulating effect on traditional agriculture. Capital inputs of Europeans were mainly confined to production processes of semi-manufacture.

[6] The first English bank, the Bank of Bombay, was already established in 1720, but it survived only for a short period.

house of the Jagat Seth. On the second level were other indigenous-style bankers and large-scale moneylenders involved in money-changing (which was still lucrative until the standardization of currency in 1834/35), trade finance and *hundi* business. The third level was composed of various small moneylenders in the towns and villages (Bhattacharya 1982: 273-5, 291-3). Like commercial agents, the financial agents increasingly formed a *compradore* position in the colonial economy – an intermediary position between the British colonial system and the indigenous population.[7] The importance of moneylenders for cash-crop production and land revenue collection is considered in the Chapter 7.3.

With regard to the financial position of the Company, until the establishment of control over Bengal it paid the bills with bullion imports in the same way as other companies. Subsequently, however, it obtained the right to extract revenues from the province, which were used to balance the trade accounts. This right made the government increasingly independent on the support of indigenous-style bankers in transfers from Calcutta to Bombay. In addition to the financing of Indian exports, these revenues were deemed to suffice for the payment of Chinese silk and tea, so that bullion flows could be stopped. The volume of imported goods increased, too.

In the course of the eighteenth and early nineteenth centuries, domestic trading in northern India was largely in the hands of Indians until this region was step-by-step incorporated by the British, too. Long-distance trade and interregional trade of bulky goods along potential trade routes, such as the Ganges river, were controlled and financed by merchants and indigenous-style bankers in court cities and other important towns along the major trade routes (see Kessinger 1982: 242ff.).[8] The merchants' and indigenous-style bankers' networks provided the channels for the passing of *hundis*, which were used as means of payment in distant places and for the remittances of tributes and revenues to local authorities. Trade in northern India was occasionally very insecure and halted completely due to political instability. The British establishment of control in Bengal caused an eventual orientation of trade towards Calcutta even in independent regions. The existing production and distribution networks in non-British-controlled India on the whole showed considerable commercial integration in itself, although they were only partly linked to each other. Regional differences in consumption patterns and poor infrastructure formed obstacles to the integration of larger regions.

In western India domestic trade was in the hands of particular trading castes and communities, such as the Marwari Vanis, Bohoras, Parses, Khojas and Memons of Gujarat. The emergence of Bombay as the main British-Indian commercial center on the west coast and simultaneously the declining trading opportunities in Gujarat, Sindh and other regions attracted different indigenous-style bankers from the northwest. While Shikapuri and Gujarati Shroffs settled in Bombay, Marwaris spread all over the Deccan as rural crop merchants and moneylenders and settled in Calcutta and

---

[7] The term *compradore* originates from the Portuguese language. It was initially applied to the Chinese who functioned as middlemen for European firms in the Chinese market.

[8] Statistics from the period 1827 to 1847 reveal that, of the 200,000 inhabitants of Benares, for example, 19.1 percent were engaged in trading and banking, of which 9.2 percent were indigenous-style bankers, moneylenders and merchants; in Lahore 21.1 and 19.82 percent, respectively (Kessinger 1982: 244).

Madras as merchant-bankers. The leading contemporary indigenous-style banking castes, all of which were already bankers during the colonial period, are reviewed in Chapter 8.1. It will suffice here to emphasize that until the turn of the century, if not until the inter-war period, indigenous-style banking concentrated on the financing of and participation in its traditional activity, trade. Until the emergence of western-style banks the agency houses were also involved in finance but confined themselves to British business.

In 1813 the Charter Act removed some of the chief institutional restrictions to private trade, both English and Indian, the former enjoying privileged conditions.[9] It was followed by a rapid expansion in imports, exports and agency houses in Calcutta. To some extent these were also linked with Indian capital. In every crisis indigenous-style bankers withdrew their capital, reclaimed their loans or increased the interest rates. Indian capital was provided mainly on a short-term basis, compared to European investments which were on a partnership basis. This interlinking functioned very well as long as there was no crisis. However, in crises the agency houses ran into difficulty. They therefore put pressure on the government to be given public grant loans to survive such crises. However, the indigo world crisis in the second half of the 1820s led to the collapse of most agency houses.

Seen on the whole, the entire period until independence was characterized by a series of uneven spurts, fluctuating in line with European trade cycles. In other words, this is an indicator to the emergence of a world market. For example, the European crisis of the late 1840s resulted in a crisis of western-style banks, which also spread over to indigenous-style banking. During the first half of the nineteenth century fundamental structural changes occurred in the composition of imports and exports. India was gradually transformed from an exporter of manufactured goods (largely textiles) into the supplier of primary commodities and importer of finished consumer goods as well as certain intermediate and industrial goods. The British forced India into the partaking in the international division of labour.

Indigo, raw silk, opium and cotton dominated the exports, amounting to around 60 percent of the total value. In contrast to raw silk and cotton, indigo and opium were almost totally dependent on foreign demand and susceptible to crises.[10] The indigo cultivators obtained credit from European processing firms. This working capital originated from the agency houses which managed the marketing and shipping. Opium was almost as important for export as indigo.[11] While the indigo and opium trade were largely in British hands, the cotton trade and production which were centered

---

[9] While the official monopoly was abolished in 1813, the Company continued to trade until 1833 for technical reasons.

[10] Cotton and opium provided the basis of the triangular trade between India, China and Britain. Since Indian cotton was unsuitable for British machinery, it was exported to China, while the imports for British production originated from the southern States of America. After 1850 the Indian demand for cotton increased heavily, so that its production and processing sector became less dependent on the world market.

[11] Traditionally the cultivation and trade in opium were government monopolies, but were before 1760 largely farmed out to Indian merchants who gave advances and generally organized its production. With the opening of the China trade after the two Opium Wars in 1839-40 and 1855 to force the acceptance of counterbalancing the trade bills with opium instead of bullion, it amounted to 20 to 30 percent of all exports.

in and around Bombay were dominated by Indian entrepreneurs. While raw silk was processed in foreign-owned factories, its trade was free from monopsonistic control. Exports of raw silk boomed in the first quarter of the nineteenth century, but its share declined dramatically be the 1850s. The position taken by indigenous-style bankers towards Indian industrial entrepreneurial activity will be discussed later.

With the customs reform in 1846 the duty on Indian exports (with the exception of indigo) and discrimination in favor of British shipping were abolished, so that Indian trade and its finance had the chance to recover again from previous oppression. The financial difficulties after the Mutiny reintroduced customs duties, however without discrimination against Indian merchants and domestic trade. Indian merchants, and to some degree producers, benefited from these reforms on the whole.

During the second half of the nineteenth century an infrastructural development in India (railway construction) and abroad, and technical innovations (industrialization, steam ships), had the effect of stimulating both domestic and foreign trade and its finance as well as the rise of industries. With the opening of the Suez Canal the share of exports to Britain decreased, since European countries took up direct trade rather than importing Indian goods from England. By the end of the nineteenth century the old triangular Britain-India-China connection declined.

Chaudhuri (1982: 848-9) called the late nineteenth and the early twentieth centuries 'the great age of multilateral trade and international payments'. Rapid industrialization in Western Europe, the United States and Japan created a great demand for raw and semi-processed materials and foodstuffs. From the late nineteenth century until World War I imports and exports increased considerably. Within the composition of exports a diversification occurred. Food grain, oilseed, tea, hides, skins and manufactured cotton goods appeared on the list, and many of these goods had passed through a stage of semi-manufacture in India.

The two world wars had the effects of stimulating particular production and trade (raw cotton, jute, food grain, steel, etc.). The inter-war period was characterized by worldwide reorganization, by growing bilateral trade relations, a policy of tariff protection and foreign exchange controls. The boom in trade continued until 1920, followed by a heavy decrease of real import values and a slight decrease of export values. After 1924 the import trade began to revive once more. The Great Depression of 1929-30 inflicted heavy losses on India and other food-exporters and had a severe impact on rural indebtedness and rural finance. On the whole, trade fluctuated heavily in this period. Until the Great Depression the managing agencies offered everything which was in short supply in India: industrial capital, technical know-how, management, and so on. They obtained ten percent of the managed firms' turnover. After some time these enterprises had accumulated knowledge and creditworthiness to raise new companies which existed on paper only but had a number of shareholders while the managing agency kept only some shares. Profits and losses could be shifted from one company under its control to another, thus manipulating the balance sheets (Rothermund 1989: 62-3).

7.2. The Emergence of Formal Banks

As outlined in the previous chapter, the agency houses were the prototypes of western-style banks until the first commercial banks emerged during the second half of the nineteenth century. Before the Indian Companies Act of 1913 and its amendment in 1936, these were largely unregulated with regard to their minimum capital and cash reserves etc., which resulted in the continuous failure of banks. The commercial banks I consider are the quasi-official Presidency Banks of Bengal from 1806, Bombay from 1840/1868 and Madras (1843), the Indian joint-stock banks and the foreign-owned exchange banks.

The Presidency Banks enjoyed certain privileges like the monopoly of government banking business or the issuance of bearer notes and, after the passage of the Paper Currency Act of 1861, the government monopoly of issuing money. On the other hand, their business was restricted. For example, they were prohibited to deal with foreign exchange,[12] to borrow abroad and lend for periods longer than three months (until 1907), and later six months. Interest charges were limited to a maximum of 12 percent, and loans could not be secured by immovable property, personal security or one-name paper of goods, unless the goods of and titles to the borrower were deposited with the bank. Another restriction was that discounted bills were to be paid in India only. These banks therefore played a minor role in private financing.

In 1921 the three Presidency Banks were amalgamated to become the Imperial Bank of India, whereby the Imperial Bank of India Act of 1920 was by and large based on the Presidency Banks Act of 1876. The two basic lending rates of the Imperial Bank were the bank rate for loans against government securities, and the *hundi* rate for the discounting of indigenous-style, first-class commercial bills extending up to 90 days. In general the *hundi* rate was the same as the bank rate, which during the busy season amounted to 7-8 percent. The Imperial Bank of India Act was amended in 1934 and replaced by the Reserve Bank of India Bill of 1933. The Reserve Bank of India was formally established in 1935 and the banking of the Imperial Bank lost the function of government banking (Chandravakar 1982: 776-9).

After the recognition of limited liability in 1860, the growth of Indian joint-stock banks continued at a slow pace until about 1900. After the bank boom in the period 1863-5, which followed speculation in cottage trade during the American Civil War, 23 of the 25 joint-stock banks collapsed again, and at the turn of the century no more than nine survived. The *swadeshi* movement[13] of 1906 promoted the development of Indian banks until World War I. But again various banks collapsed. During the war and the inter-war period Indian joint-stock banking flourished once more, but many of them failed again in the post-war depression. The Indian Central Banking Inquiry Committee summarized the failures of these banks as resulting mostly from individual imprudence and mismanagement. Despite all these setbacks, the share of deposits of joint-stock banks to total deposits increased from 31 percent in 1930 to 40 percent in 1936, whereas the share of the Imperial Bank fell from 32 to 29 percent. Tomlinson

---

[12] The Bank of Madras formed an exception in dealings with the Bank of Ceylon.

[13] *swadeshi* (Hindi): the indigenous production of all essential commodities (import substitution).

(1979) emphasized that several owners of these banks were former indigenous-style bankers who had reorganized their business under a new legal form.

The historically negligible role played by Indian joint-stock banks in India's foreign trade was due to the strong position held by foreign exchange banks, which are categorized in two groups. The first group was formed by British banks (Chartered Bank of India, Australia and China from 1853, the National Bank of India from 1863, the Honk Kong and Shanghai Banking Corporation from 1864, the Mercantile Bank of India from 1893, and the Eastern Bank from 1910), while the second group specialized in trade of their countries of origin with India (such as the Comptoir National d'Encompte de Paris, the Yokohama Specie Bank, the Deutsche-Asiatische Bank, the International Banking Corporation from America and the Russo-Asiatic Bank).

Witnesses before the Indian Central Banking Inquiry Committee proclaimed the discrimination against Indians by these banks.

> "Among the more typical complaints were: that Indians, unlike foreign customers, were required to deposit 10 to 15 percent of the value of merchandise with the exchange banks in order to get a confirmed letter of credit opened; that import bills were drawn in sterling at relatively high rates of interest (around 6 percent); that exchange banks furnished unsatisfactory references abroad regarding Indian business houses; that they discriminated against Indian steamship and insurance companies; that they did not offer responsible posts to Indians; that exchange banks were not subject to any legal restrictions in India and were exempt even from the rather limited statutory obligations imposed on Indian joint-stock banks; that no protection was afforded to their Indian depositors; that no separate information was available regarding their Indian business" (Chandravakar 1982: 783).

7.3. Moneylenders and Rural Indebtedness

7.3.1. Introduction

The question of moneylenders and increasing rural indebtedness 'was the bugbear of nineteenth-century administrators throughout India', argued Cheesman (1982: 445-6). To my mind, most scholars do not distinguish between the cause and symptoms of rural indebtedness. The assumption that moneylenders are responsible for rural indebtedness cannot be upheld if we consider the facts. I shall show in this chapter that moneylenders existed in large numbers even before the colonial period. I am arguing that the cause of rural indebtedness is related to the transformation process which both cultivation and moneylending underwent: from a more embedded condition in the village community to a more disembedded one in the more advanced economy, to modify Polanyi's (1957) concept. Traditionally moneylending, understood as the lending of cash or kind, formed an essential service within the village: to bridge households' income gaps from one good harvest to the next. It is commonly assumed that subsistence-oriented societies set up communal 'insurance mechanisms' to cope with natural disasters (e.g. grain stores) because individual households were unable to make long-term budget plans. It seems possible to me that moneylenders fulfilled a similar function of risk management within the village community. I argue that according to the social code of conduct of the village community, the 'moral economy' (Scott 1976), a wealthy peasant or moneylender was expected to lend to needy villagers in occasional situations.

The process of the disembedding of moneylending was related to socio-economic change following the principles that govern market production. They challenged the moral economy and the embeddedness of moneylending. This change depended on at least three variables: increasing monetization and market-integration, increasing hegemony of the state (see e.g. Weber 1947) (manifesting itself among other things in a legal framework) and the degree of freedom of the market (depending on state policy, differences becoming apparent in comparative research). A fourth factor, which was related both to advanced economic integration and population growth, was an increasing scarcity of land. To my mind it is oversimplistic to regard the transgression from the pre-colonial to the colonial period as the step from an embedded to a disembedded economy, since this process of transformation took longer and these terms should be applied to certain economic relations rather than to the economy as a whole. I showed that even in Mughal India certain rural regions had been partly monetized and were producing cash crops, while the emperors had developed an efficient administration and monetary revenue system. Nevertheless, the introduction of British rule led to major changes in the economic and legal field which will be discussed in the next paragraphs.

Before going into greater detail, I venture to make another preliminary comment which has an important bearing on this chapter. Most colonial scholars were not aware of the relation between debt, investment and indebtedness. Their lack of knowledge about the theory of finance led to the apparent paradox that – contrary to the assumption that cash-crop production led to progress – the degree of 'indebtedness' was higher especially in such market-producing regions than in subsistence-oriented ones. This seeming paradox is also disregarded by many contemporary surveys on rural indebtedness. I therefore suggest a short working definition of the relation between debt, investment and indebtedness. For most economic activities, including cultivation, there is a large gap in time between income and expenditure. If the reserves are too small to bridge the income gap, one has to procure a loan. In this sense I consider debt as a temporary budgetary deficit, which is bridged by a loan.

If a future income in the long run is not higher than future expenditure, the borrower will be unable to repay the loan. Indebtedness represents a permanent situation of debt. Relating this to the question of loan purpose, it is obvious that in the less developed regions the loan purpose is basically one of consumption. In most cases a consumer loan does not generate a higher future income, while a production loan is by definition an investment to achieve higher returns in future.[14] By applying this definition most rural credit surveys in fact only reflect rural debt at a specific time. It is only if particular indicators are taken into consideration, such as loan purposes, duration of debt, relation of household income and expenditure, farm size etc., that one can dis-

---

[14] Of course, the definition of consumer and production loans is very vague. Food, for example, reproduces manpower and therefore generates an income. Human or social capital formation may yield higher income returns in the far-off future, etc. Nevertheless, in more market-producing regions most loans are used for productive purposes, such as irrigation, tools, wage payments etc., and generate higher future outputs or incomes.

tinguish debt and indebtedness. Stokes (1978: 245) rightly argued that the volume of debt, which in early twentieth-century India was highest in market-producing regions, is not identical to the grade of dependency, which was highest where the moneylender held a monopoly position, and this was in more remote regions.

During the Great Depression, in particular, rural indebtedness became a serious problem and under these special circumstances, which were related to world market developments, export-crop producing areas were indeed most severely affected since agricultural prices were very depressed, while the dues (revenue payments and/or rents) were eased only eventually.

7.3.2. The Pre-Colonial Period

Various scholars relate the question of monetization and rural indebtedness to British rule. In 1910, for example, Dodell argued that,

> "until the establishment of British revenue methods, there was no special reason why money should be used at all. Taxes were largely paid in kind. The work people of the village, the black-smith, the potter, the leather worker, were (. . .) paid by a fixed quantity of grain at harvest-time (. . .). Money in those times was only a store of value, not a medium of exchange. When by some happy accident money did come into the villages, it was promptly converted into ornaments (. . .) or otherwise hoarded. Then came the regular system of collecting the revenue in cash (. . .that, H.S.) formed the most powerful cause of introducing a money economy into the rural districts" (Schrieke 1966: 98, citing Dodell 1910).

This view is oversimplistic because moneylending, a monetary revenue system and a hierarchical and stratified agricultural society existed already during the pre-colonial period. Suroyo (1987: 73-5) rightly argued that the British in India adapted the prac-tice of money revenue collection by the various preceding rulers in different regions, but they raised it to a more efficient level. The first step was the legal fixation of land rights which obliged land holders to pay land revenue and tenants to pay rent. This made land mobile, i.e. salable, mortgagable and transferable. In the case of non-payment of land revenue, the land could be sold by decree to be set off against the debt. What was thought to be helpful for revenue collection, equally benefited landlords and moneylenders.

If we take a short look at pre-colonial practices of revenue collection (Rothermund 1978: 34f.) it can be argued that usually Indian rulers applied a pattern that established different modes of collection in regions close to the center of power and more remote ones. The Mughal rulers initially adapted the collection pattern of their predeces-sors in that they appropriated one third of the produce and for annual cash provided commutation on the basis of current prices. Under Akbar this system experienced problems because of the vastness of his empire. He therefore decentralized the system and relied on the cooperation of the *zamindars*. However, they neglected to report the necessary information. Therefore Akbar changed the *zamindari* system by paying them a cash salary and by introducing revenue collectors. In addition he abolished the annual cash commutation and based the revenue assessment on the decennial aver-ages of agricultural production and prices. This system, which became the backbone of Mughal revenue collection, was effective in the central regions only, while in the remote regions the assessments were made on whatever data were available.

The Maratha revenue practice was different from that of the Mughals and aimed at a refinement of the crop-sharing method. Fields were assessed according to the quality of the soil and productivity, and the actual assessment was announced annually as soon as reliable estimates were possible.

> "The Mogul system, where it really worked well, permitted a forecast of revenue income whereas the Maratha system meant a fluctuating income. On the other hand the Mogul system implied an uncertainty about the actual collection of the assessed amount, while the Maratha system eliminated this to a great extent because whatever was assessed on the spot and in full knowledge of the seasonal conditions could also be collected by a decentralized administration. The actual fluctuation of revenue income was probably more or less similar under both systems" (Rothermund 1978: 35).

In South India a variation of the Mughal system was common, while in Sikh territory the rulers dealt directly with the peasantry.

As Stokes (1978: 245) pointed out for Central India, the Maratha revenue practice and the absence of a powerful landlord class made the peasants dependent on moneylenders, so that rural indebtedness occurred as a problem already in pre-colonial India that was carried over from the Maratha into the British period. The rates of interest charged by moneylenders before the colonial era had been high because of, among other things, lacking credit security for lenders. Nevertheless, there was a qualitative difference of being indebted in pre-colonial or colonial India. Under the former governments where civil legislation was only marginally developed, a creditor was not able to fall back upon legal institutions to reclaim the loan plus interest. Land usually could not be appropriated as a compensation for the loan and was not even a desirable commodity, although the sale of land was possible in principle. The reason was simply that land was neither scarce, nor valuable and therefore not traded as private property. There was therefore no incentive for moneylenders to appropriate land. Moreover, in many cases land was communally owned, or the person who cleared the jungle for cultivation was simply able to claim ownership.

The lack of mortgaging, argued Darling (1977), was to a high degree replaced by

> "security in the triple chain of caste, custom and character, which in India binds the cultivator to the soil: only the direct necessity will make the peasant part with his land, and a person who will not part with his land must sooner or later pays his debt" (Darling 1977: 7).

Darling's arguments seem to me valid only for regions in which the cultivator had a long-established property right or occupancy right, or land was already scarce like indeed in many parts of India. During the colonial period, however, settlement and migration policies promoted the commercialization of agriculture and colonial exploitation. In the case of pioneering cultivation as, for example, in the Burma Delta, a migrant peasant cultivator did not establish close ties with his soil. Once indebted, he simply left his field to the lender, moved away and cleared a new plot of land to claim as his own. He could borrow again under a new identity and the same process would be repeated. Land transfers were not much of a problem for the cultivators as long as land was not scarce.

Many scholars romanticized the pre-colonial relations between moneylenders and agriculturalists as friendships, despite the fact that interest rates were very high. Raju (1941), however, argued – and this seems plausible to me – that the nominal interest rates were not identical to the amounts which the lenders used to recover because there were no legal institutions to force repayment. Instead a lender had to rely on the moral obligations of the borrower and perhaps the collective pressure of the entire village on him. In many cases debts existed for generations and the lender was content to maintain the debt relationship and to collect the interest.

According to Raju (1941), a borrower used every possible excuse not to pay the interest, and the lender on his part even applied physical force to collect it. The descriptions of travelers in the pre-British period who observed confrontations between creditors and debtors are colorful.

> "When some perverse debtor obstinately refused to pay anything and heavy arrears had accumulated, the creditor had recourse to *sat darna* by sitting on his doorstep till his debt was paid, or appealed to some influential person who would see that justice was done; otherwise a *panchayat*[15] was held which decided the case to everybody's satisfaction and there was an end of the matter" (Raju 1941: 135).

The following description has a similar tenor:

> "When a debt had to be repaid the debtor would say that he had no money at the time and would ask for grace. Further time would be granted once and even twice, and when the money was still not forthcoming the lender would make an unauthorized arrest. The borrower could not eat or drink without the permission of the creditor, who also starved with him. Otherwise, debtor and creditor stood in the sun each with a stone on his head, or walked around till one of them was exhausted or fainted; or both performed penance on one foot. Finally, the debtor, unable to put up with it any longer, would settle at least a part of the claims against him and promise to pay the rest later" (Raju 1941: 140).

To call these borrower – lender relations friendship relations is certainly besides the point. In addition bonded labour was wide-spread, which is similar to a master-slave relation and mainly common with landlord-lenders. Such masters had an interest in this relation continuing, since the appropriation of unpaid labour formed their basis of life in the same way as moneylenders were interested in maintaining the debt relation, since they lived from a continuous flow of interest payments. From such a perspective, bonded labour and debt relations can be considered as patron-client relations (Wolf 1966). Since they lived within the village among their debtors, they were morally, and also from the point of view of self-interest, obliged to keep the debtor alive. Even if a borrower had a large debt, the lender would not deprive him of his means of survival and instead defer part of his claims. This was especially true in the case of natural disasters. I call this state of moneylending 'embedded'.

According to Raju (1941: 138), in pre-colonial Madras state the usual interest rates varied from 8 to 12 percent p.a., while a higher rate was usually charged for short-term loans of only a few months. The law of *damdupat*, which was applied in large parts of India, maintained that the compound interest should never exceed the principal sum. When the usual interest rates rose considerably because the rulers had imposed a

---

[15] This is to say, the village assembly.

heavy increase on taxation and revenue payments, they fixed the maximum rates at 8 percent for one month, 18 percent for six months and 30 percent a the year. However, legal rates do not reflect the real rates which, depending upon the extent of control, used to be higher.

In Tamil Nadu, as elsewhere in India, the temple, which was one of the most ancient credit institutions, was the safekeeper of savings and valuables, a kind of reserve fund for times of need.

> "Money was lent and the interest on the money lent was utilized for occasional repairs of the temple or the irrigation channels damaged by floods. Money was lent with or without security but in all cases the social standing and the credit of the borrower was counted. Not only individuals but also the village assemblies borrowed money from the temple" (Gazetteer of India 1972, Tamil Nadu, Madras: 379).

7.3.3. Moneylenders and Rural Debt in Colonial India before the Great Depression

Explanations for Rural Indebtedness

During the colonial period moneylenders were usually considered to have become increasingly parasitic and usurious, thereby impeding rural development, which finally led to a 'de-peasantization', reducing the status of peasants 'to cultivators working for the barest subsistence return under a form of debt peonage' (Stokes 1978: 243).

Explanations for rural indebtedness are manifold but in many cases unfortunately mono-causal. To my mind, at least three factors contributed to its increase: the definition of property rights, which mobilized land and clearly defined the revenue payers; the increasing commercialization of agriculture, which was accompanied by population growth, both factors giving rise to increasing land prices, so that land became eventually a desirable asset for non-cultivators, too; and the application of Western civil and criminal law which made debts and foreclosures enforceable. Let us review these and some explanations of other scholars.

The changed property rights (Transfer of Property Act, rent acts and tenancy legislation) after the establishment of British authority mobilized land and re-organized the revenue collection. These property rights were based upon Western civil law and resulted in a re-organization of the agricultural classes. With regard to the upper class, the politicoeconomic position of the 'lords of the land' was transformed into one of 'landlords' (Rothermund 1978: 12). While in pre-colonial India their power depended on their relations with the government (temporary and life-time grants or particular tasks) and the land usually belonged to the ruler, their politicoeconomic function was reduced by the British to landlords, mere rentiers of their 'real estate' who obtained 'rent' from their 'tenants'. While formerly the relations between the lord of the land and the peasant was a patron-client relationship, the landlord was now protected by law. Many of these landlords were absent from their real estate and settled in cities, accepting their destiny as rentiers and trying to consolidate their power over their land by exploiting unprotected tenants (ibid.: 113, 184).

Another affair was the definition of hereditary and transferable property rights among tenants. Following Rothermund (1978: 87ff.), with the beginning of British rule the position of the landlord was initially strengthened with regard to revenue payment. Almost all tenants were regarded as tenants-at-will.

> "The Indian peasantry had normally been undisturbed in its right of occupancy, but as far as the collection of the share of the lord was concerned a show of force was often resorted to and every lord had a band of armed retainers. *Pax Britannica* eliminated such means of coercion and the modern landlord sued his tenant in a court of law or issued a notice of eviction instead of pouncing upon him in his field or village. Usually he would win the case because he had more money and under the British system of jurisdiction investment in lawyers is most important in order to get the desired verdict, the more so when land law is concerned which can be stretched to fit the party which can pay for the better argument" (Rothermund 1978: 88).

On the whole, three land tenure systems were introduced one after another and these provided different rights to particular tenants: the *zamindari*, the *ryotwari* and the *mahalwari* or *malguzari* systems. The *zamindari* system was introduced in Bengal in 1793. *Ryots* were defined as tenants to the *zamindars* and subject to rent increase or eviction. Following Dhanagare (1991: 31-34), under the Permanent Settlement of Bengal *zamindars* were declared the full owners of the land with absolute property rights. Similar rights were given to *talukdars* in Oudh. Before bureaucrats were institutionalized for the collection of land revenue, they had to collect them for the government. The *ryots* saw this as an injustice because their occupancy rights were totally ignored and they were reduced to peasants-at-will on their own fields.

Some time later another revenue system was applied in Madras and Bombay including Gujarat and Berar: the *ryotwari* system, which eliminated the landlord and declared the *ryots* themselves the owners with hereditary and transferable rights (this meant that the landed property of small peasants became mobile) thus being directly responsible for land revenue payments. This system led to a tenancy stratification. Various categories of tenants were formed, such as 'protected', 'occupancy', 'ordinary' and 'sharecropper tenants'. While the higher stratum of the peasantry enjoyed hereditary and alienable rights, the lower stratum, tenants at will, sharecroppers, and so on, were not protected at all. The third type of land settlement was the *mahalwari* or *malguzari* system in the United Provinces (excluding Oudh), Punjab and the Central Provinces (now Madhya Pradesh), excluding Berar. In these regions villages were inhabited by members of the same caste, kinship group, lineage or tribe, land was cultivated on a cosharing basis and revenue payment was based on the village unit. Due to the increasing scarcity of land, protected tenants began to sub-let the land to unprotected ones, eventually adopting the position held by former landlords.

The provincial differences make it difficult to establish general trends. Nevertheless, Rothermund (1978: 96) provided a very rough classificatory scheme comprising five ranks. Rank I consisted of tenure holders, substantial *ryots* and ex-proprietary tenants with holdings of more than 30 acres. Rank II contained occupancy *ryots*, normal *ryots* and statutory tenants with holdings of between six and 30 acres. To rank III belonged ordinary tenants, non-occupancy tenants, and so on, enjoying some protection but no hereditary rights. They held land of the same size as those of rank II. Rank IV consisted of unprotected tenants-at-will, under-*ryots*, and so on, with holdings of three to six acres. To rank V finally belonged the subtenants and sharecroppers with only small plots of land who cultivated other people's land to make a living. Rothermund

(1978: 37) concluded that the innovation in the inherited pattern of revenue collection was its greater rigidity and diminished tolerance which was precisely the cause of increasing rural indebtedness in the last quarter of the nineteenth century.

The tenancy rights of a particular stratum of the peasantry enabled moneylenders to secure a loan with a land mortgage and, if necessary, to enforce the transfer of land. It is certainly true that land transfers occurred before the British period too. The difference, however, was that no land market existed. With such a land market, credit on mortgages began to extend beyond the customary limits. According to the principle of Liberalism, the courts valued the freedom of contract very highly and protected the moneylenders' claims.

The revenue-paying peasant on a whole was confronted by a typical dilemma-situation. If he did not borrow but could not pay his revenues, his land was sold by the revenue office. However, if he borrowed but was finally unable to pay his debts, he lost his land to the moneylender (ibid.: 39) – comparatively speaking perhaps some time later.

Cheesman (1982) rejected this viewpoint. He maintained that, in spite of the implemented legal framework which laid the judicial basis to force the repayment of a loan, it was disadvantageous for the lender to regain the principal with a civil law suit because it was costly and even uneconomical from his point of view.

> "It positively went against a *baniya*'s interests to have a debt discharged. It would be like killing the goose that laid the golden egg for the interest (...) The *baniya* is commonly referred to as a 'moneylender', but it is a sorry moneylender who cannot recover his initial loan after ten years. If one thinks of a *baniya* as a shareholder, then his system makes more sense. His loans to the client would represent his investment and the interest gave him an extremely good return" (Cheesman 1982: 459).

I think that the potential to institute legal proceedings was probably pressure enough on the borrower to pay regular interest. I argue with Raju (1941) that, while formerly nominal interest rates could be hardly realized, under British rule they began to constitute the real rates. The existing legal maximum, such as the fixation of 12 percent per annum or the adaptation of *damdupat* law, were circumvented too easily.

> "Whenever the interest equaled or exceeded the principal, the old bond was canceled and a fresh one was drawn up in which the whole amount would be put down as principal. Very often a premium of 1 to 6 percent was charged, and deducted before the payment of the loan. The actual rate of interest paid by the debtor was (usually, H.S.) between 18 and 24 percent. On the security of jewels it was 8 to 24 percent, and on mere personal credit as much as 35 to 60 percent and occasionally even a 100 percent (...) If a *ryot* borrowed 2 maunds of grain valued 2 or three rupees, it was converted into a money debt by 'tricky proceedings'. As the interest accumulated, fresh bonds were executed in which interest and principal were consolidated till the debt amounted to Rs 50 or more. The *ryot* was now completely in the creditor's power and was compelled to give up all the produce of his lands beyond what was necessary for mere subsistence" (Raju 1941: 138-9).

However, economic conditions did not remain the same during the entire colonial period. Eventually land became a valuable asset, the value of which continuously increased. Raju argued that moneylenders changed their business strategy from appropriating a continuous flow of interest to the acquisition of land from defaulting

borrowers by court decrees for speculative purpose in many cases. The former small-
holder was even able to rent the land, so that the new landowner was also recipient of
a continuous flow of tenancy payments, too.

This was indeed true during the Great Depression and some previous minor depressions. In general, however, one has to distinguish strategies according to particular
types of lenders. As has already become obvious and will be restated at the end of this
chapter, British colonial rule engendered particular types of lenders, while other types
of lenders declined in importance. In particular these new types were the agricultural
lender and the trader-cum-lender. I support Raju's view that agricultural lenders might
have had an interest in increasing their landed property. However, I do not agree with
him about traders-cum-lenders. Since these were long-established traders, they were
generally reluctant to invest in land and agriculture. They were not only inexperienced
in such economic activities, but more importantly they did not want to fix their capital, especially when nineteenth-century India was shaken by one economic crisis and
natural disaster after another, so that very often land could not easily be reconverted
in cash. The acquisition of land by court decree was therefore used as a last resort
measure only to safeguard their claims. For example, the great famine of 1868-9 in
Central India led to an increasing number of land transfers to Marwari moneylenders
(Stokes 1978: 249-50). The foreclosing of mortgages and taking of property titles was
the second-best choice only compared to incomes from interest rates. Four decades
later various Marwari firms in Jalaun district had fixed all their capital in unprofitable
land. The inability of their borrowers to repay due to the various crises required them
to take the land, which in turn meant that they were unable to finance their ordinary
moneylending business any longer.

The replacement of customary rule by British-Indian law and its eventual effects on
everyday life contributed to the disembedding of moneylending: the replacement of
personalized borrower-lender relations by impersonalized ones. As argued elsewhere
(Evers and Schrader 1994), the moral economy characterized a condition in which
traders and moneylenders faced problems in accumulating private capital within the
own community. The transgression from a moral economy to the market economy is
a long-term process. This process can be explained with Simmel (1989) as a continuous change of binding and solving, of obligations and freedom. Simmel maintained
that what we often perceive as a freedom is indeed no more than a change in obligations. The individual was freed from the sanctions of the moral economy, while legal
sanctions were introduced. The other way around, obligations towards the community
were replaced by obligations towards society and the state. While the moneylender
increasingly came under the supervision of the state, he could now fall back upon
British-Indian law if a borrower was unable or unwilling to repay. While formerly
he had to personally face the borrower and to find ways of pursuing or forcing him
to repay the debt, often with the support of public opinion, the enforcement of debt
became an impersonal affair by using the legal framework. In this process of change
moneylenders unfortunately lost their moral obligations towards the peasantry, such
as to adjust their claims to the agricultural calendar or to postpone them in times of
need. For example, it was reported from Muzaffapur in the second half of the nineteenth century that *zamindars* fought rent-suits against peasants just when their store

of grain had been exhausted (Chaudhuri 1969: 225), while formerly loan repayment would have been adapted to the agricultural calendar and, in the case of disasters, moneylenders would have even postponed their claims.

Moneylenders played an important role in the British-Indian revenue system through timely advances for the land revenue payments of cultivators, of landlords and sometimes of whole villages.

> "Pedder pointed out pertinently how, without moneylenders, 'the land revenue would never be realized fully or punctually'.[16] William Wedderburn, the district judge, was another nineteenth-century official to promote a strongly functionalist view: 'the existence of the moneylender in the village polity', he argued, 'is as essential as that of the ploughman'"[17] (quoted by Charlesworth 1985: 86).

Charlesworth (1985: 86-7, 94) rejected an explanation linking the increasing rural indebtedness to the colonial apparatus of revenue collection. He provided another reason for the rise of moneylending during the nineteenth century: a lack of investment opportunities for small sums of money. Moneylending formed one such opportunity. The lender in the villages was mostly a man with only limited means. Charlesworth explained this lack of investment opportunities macro-economically from a neoclassical point of view. Capital was scarce and the security which cultivators had to offer was poor. Both conditions produced the high level of interest. At the same time he rejected the often assumed monopoly power of village moneylenders, since in nineteenth-century India various kinds of moneylenders competed against each other for clients in the villages. To put it another way, Charlesworth argued implicitly that neither the British nor moneylenders were directly responsible for an increasing rural indebtedness, but that it was the product of economic development which the capital market expansion could not keep pace with. To my mind, Charlesworth's explanation of capital scarcity is too mono-causal.

Other scholars isolated the destruction of subsistence production and introduction of cash crop production as the decisive factor for growing indebtedness because the latter producers became increasingly dependent upon world market prices. Several depressions during the second half of the nineteenth and early twentieth centuries significantly lowered agricultural prices, and thereby the household income of cash-crop producers, while the expenditure including revenue payments either remained stable or even increased.

In this chapter I largely draw upon British colonial literature. In the introduction to the Indian country study I already referred to the British perception of moneylenders. Broadly speaking, one less prevalent stereotype considered them traditionally minded and harmless because the relations to their customers were embedded in the village community and bound by moral sanctions.[18] Another more prevalent stereotype portrayed them as rational with regard to their usurious practices, pushing their

---

[16] IOL, Political and Secret Department Library, Papers of Sir William Lee-Warner, Deccan Riot Series, No. 2. W.G. Pedder, Note on the Indebtedness of the Indian Agricultural Classes, its Causes and Remedies, 29 July 1875: 5.

[17] Wedderburn, W. 1880: A Permanent Settlement for the Deccan, Bombay: 7.

[18] Rudner (1989: 417ff.) illustrated this attitude with R.K. Narayan's novel 'The Financial Expert' (Narayan 1952). It described the moneylender Margayya, running his business as a broker in the twen-

customers further and further into debt, and finally sucking them dry of money, property and freedom (see Darling 1977). British scholars even transferred the image of the ancient grasping Jewish usurer to the Indian rural moneylender (Cheesman 1982: 450). A third, more contemporary stereotype prevalent in rural finance is the image of the moneylender as an independent, strictly small-scale entrepreneur whose business activities are confined to small-scale credit transactions with his client agriculturalists neglecting their organization to form a powerful economic network (see Michie 1978).

The perception of the peasantry by British colonial scholars also deserves a mention. While it was, on one hand, the innocent target group which had to be protected from unscrupulous moneylenders, peasants were simultaneously

> "myopic, extravagant persons who, if allowed easy access to credit from unscrupulous moneylenders, would eventually become impoverished by debt" (Ravaillon 1990: 179, referring to Darling 1977).

It was argued that this was rooted in the extravagance in disproportionate ceremonial expenses which were financed by loans. Due to their unproductive nature, debtors were unable to repay their loans. Various contemporary writers have shown that the extravagance-hypothesis cannot be upheld.

Primary Sources from the Second Half of the Nineteenth Century

To illustrate the British discussion during the colonial period, which related rural indebtedness to the operation of moneylenders, let us consider some primary sources from the second half of the nineteenth century – the Bombay, Bengal and Madras Gazetteers which are representative for great parts of India to provide a broad picture of the matter. Various Gazetteers of the Bombay Presidency[19] of the later nineteenth century distinguished a broad spectrum of financial agents who originated from various ethnic groups and castes. They served various borrowers, such as cultivators, government servants, hereditary holders of allowances, traders, artisans, domestic servants, and labourers. As mentioned earlier, 'moneylending' is a catch-all term for various activities linked in some way with finance. The leading lenders were Brahmans, Gujarati Vanis, Marwari, Jains, Lingayats, Musalmans, and Parses. Most of them combined moneylending with another economic activity: land holding, trade and land holding, village shopkeeping or liquor selling. Another classification was based on their financial activity: indigenous-style banker (*sahukar*), pawnbroker (*jansau sahukar*), 'usurer' (*kisatia*), denoting a town lender who provided credit on installment, and village moneylender (*marwari*, the ethnic term of the majority of these lenders being applied as an occupational term). Beginning with the indigenously developed bankers, whom I have largely excluded from this chapter on rural indebtedness, the interlinkage between town and village moneylenders to whom they supplied working capital was already emphasized in Chapter 6. In addition, some indigenously

---

tieth century more with an eye to the goddess Lakshmi than with 'economic rationality' and by this satisfying all participants. However, by the time he started capital accumulation, destiny turned against him. In the end he was forced into insolvency by his clients.

[19] In what follows I shall refer to Vol. II (1877), Gujarat: Surat and Broach: 185ff; Vol. VIII (1884), Gujarat: Khatiawar: 202; Vol. XVII (1884), Deccan: Ahmednagar, 293ff; and Vol. XIX (1885), Deccan: Sátára: 181ff.

developed bankers used to advance land revenue for particular districts to the government like they did in medieval India. In such cases they obtained a charge of five percent discount, twelve percent interest and the cost of collection.

Most lenders were Hindus or Jains, although some Muslims were also involved in moneylending. In the Ahmadnagar District of the Deccan about sixty percent of the moneylenders combined trade in one form or another with lending. Marwari and Gujarati Vanias were mostly traders-cum-lenders or crop dealers-cum-lenders. Pawnbrokers were primarily Gujarati Vanias and Kanbis, but some Brahmans and a few Shravaks and Parses, too. In practice they only accepted gold and silver ornaments as pawns. Loans usually amounted to no more than ten percent of the value of the ornament, and interest was rather low, at four to six percent per annum. Many of them were widows of well-to-do traders, prosperous cultivators and artisans. The town 'usurers' were Gujarati Vanias, Kanbis and Marwar Shravaks. Many of them employed clerks. The village moneylender was either Gujarati Vania or Marwar Shravak (trader, crop merchant and moneylender. Brahmans, Kanbis and Marathas were often landlord lenders or large cultivators and Parses liquor sellers. They tended to invest in land and eventually acquired such a high status in the villages that they were honorably called 'Seth'. The Marwar Shravaks were the most numerous. In Ahmadnagar District, Marwaris constituted fifty to seventy-five percent of all moneylenders.

The rates of interest reported in the Deccan for 1839-40 for Ahmadnagar District, were collected in cash, grain, or a combination of both. The rates for cash interest varied broadly from ten to 80 percent p.a. depending on various factors; for grain from seventy-five to 150 percent, whereas grain loans lasted for only a few months, after which they were either settled or transferred into cash transactions. Mixed interest ranged usually from 120 to 192 percent p.a. These loans rarely lasted beyond one year, but if they were would be transformed into cash transactions. If security was provided (mortgage or pawn), the interest rate was often no more than one percent per month. In 1862 Marwaris who themselves borrowed from indigenously developed bankers for the purpose of on-lending, had to pay a quarter to one percent per month, while Marwaris usually charged an interest of one and two percent per month to common borrowers. Some lenders took an additional fee which was subtracted from the loan amount. For 1884 the following rates of interest were reported: in small transactions with pawn 12 to 24 percent p.a.; for petty agricultural loans with personal security 15 to 24 percent; with a lien on crops 18 to 75 percent; for large transactions with the security of movable property 15 to 24 percent; for loans with mortgages on houses or land with property right ten percent; and on land without property right about 33 percent. A grain loan for seed and home use, to be returned after the harvest, exacted an increase of 50 percent. Rates of interest usually rose sharply if the peasant failed to repay at the date agreed to.[20] The mortgaging of labour was found among the lower classes of husbandry men and labourers.[21] In 1870 Surat and Broach (Gujarat), for example, all informal lenders, with the exception of the indigenously developed

---

[20] Chaudhuri (1969: 232-4) provided an example from Bengal where the postponement of repayment until the next harvest increased the repayment by 150 percent.

[21] The report mentioned one case in which four persons, two brothers and their wives, mortgaged their joint labour for a period of twenty-five years against an outstanding debt of 90 Pounds (GBP, Vol. XIX, 1885, the Deccan: Ahmadnagar: 293-302).

bankers and the pawnbrokers, were considered by the courts to make unfair contracts and to take compound interest.[22] Here the usual interest rates in 1876 were as follows: loans to artisans and well-off cultivators which were secured by pawns were reported to amount to nine to 18 percent p.a., to poor cultivators 24 percent. In the case of personal security only, well-off borrowers used to pay 24 percent, while poor people were charged 75 percent. For large transactions with movable property, the interest was nine to 18 percent, for cattle loans twelve to 24 percent.[23]

Increasing land transfers to non-producers in the second half of the nineteenth and twentieth centuries changed the land tenure pattern. It was not only peasant smallholders who were affected but landlords, too. The formerly powerful Rajput landholding class lost most of its control over tenants from other castes and was driven back to the boundaries of their land which they cultivated themselves. Even during the early 1870s in Hongshangabad, for example, non-agriculturalist Brahmins held 29 percent of the land, and the land ownership of Marwaris in Jabalpur led to an official inquiry, which reported that 211 villages were in the hands of these moneylenders. However, these transfers peaked in 1893-1903, a period which was characterized by natural disasters, such as floods, droughts and famines (see Stokes 1978: 269).

In Bengal and Bihar, the regions from which British rule expanded, moneylenders were locals, mostly peasant proprietors, but hardly *zamindars* (Chaudhuri 1969: 224-5), in contrast to the Bombay Presidency, this pattern being the reflection of the land tenure system. With regard to agricultural crises Chaudhuri (1969: 254) reported that lenders in Bengal (and of course elsewhere, too) adopted a cautious lending behavior. Credit supply was cyclical according to agricultural conditions, while credit demand was anti-cyclical. In other words, credit contracted in cases of natural disaster and expanded with a prospective good harvest.

Chaudhuri therefore called moneylenders during the second half of the nineteenth century non-entrepreneurs. They were pure creditors because their aim was not agricultural prosperity, but the security of a good return on their loans. Even provided that the moneylender obtained the land of his debtor, he scarcely tried to increase productivity. The indebted peasant continued with the cultivation on a share-cropping basis. For agricultural moneylenders the transfer of land and enrichment did not induce increased productivity either. Such moneylenders tended to dissociate themselves from agriculture, letting their land to tenants on a share-cropping basis. As already seen, indebted landless labourers were employed by their creditors to work off the debt (Chaudhuri 1969: 227-57).

A report from the Madras Presidency for 1895 listed the following lender-borrower relations: masters to servants, landlords to tenants, *ryots* to *ryots*, *sowcars* to clients,

---

[22] For example, a case from 1827 showed that a cultivator had to pay twelve-and-a-half percent interest for six months. If it was not repaid after this period, interest was added nominally at the rate of twelve, but really at the rate of 24 percent. At the end of the year, in case of non-repayment, principal sum and interest were added up and the interest charged was 25 percent p.a. In practice the rates for small-scale loans were much higher (GBP, Vol. II, 1877, Gujarat: Surat and Broach: 203).

[23] GBP (Vol. II, 1877, Gujarat: Surat and Broach: 203)

brokers to producers, cattle-dealers to *ryots*, cloth-sellers to buyers, shopkeepers to buyers, and domestic and petty lenders to customers.[24]

The rates of interest observed varied considerably, depending on the type of borrower, of loan, of security, and so on. For larger loans above Rs 100 with mortgage security, most interest rates ranged between nine and twelve percent per annum, up to Rs 100, as well as for loans with simple bonds from nine to 18 percent. To sum up, smaller loans during the late nineteenth century were more expensive than the larger ones, and loans on simple bonds with good knowledge of the customer were often cheaper than small mortgages. Nevertheless, it is not obvious from the sources whether the interest rates mentioned were indeed the real rates.

For the Madras Presidency the small case suit records mentioned the following lenders' and borrowers' castes. About 17 percent of the lenders were Brahmins, 27 percent Chettiar and *vaishyas*, almost 8 percent Muslims, and 48 percent various other castes. Of the borrowers, more than 64 percent belonged to the agricultural class, almost 15 percent were traders, and about 21 percent had other occupations. In Tinnevelly District most loans (56 percent) were short-term (for a period of between six and twelve months). The average term for mortgages without possession was about two years, with possession about five years. All ordinary village loans did not exceed one year, all grain loans were understood to last for six months or for the full length of the crop season (RLAC 1895: 234-6).

What becomes obvious from the primary sources of the Bombay, Madras and Bengal Presidencies is that most moneylenders were aliens, who combined moneylending with trade, such as Marwaris, Gujarati or Parses in the Deccan or Chettiar even in Burma. The phenomenon of the 'alien' was already discussed by Georg Simmel (e.g. 1989) and reinterpreted in the 'traders' dilemma' hypothesis (Evers 1994) as a strategy to escape the moral economy requirements. Many Indian moneylenders were already formerly heavily engaged in trade, in many cases in their places of origin. The decreasing trading opportunities for Indians from the mid-eighteenth century onward and increasing business opportunities in a transitional rural economy from subsistence to cash-crop production made many of them migrate to settle as crop dealers and merchant-lenders. According to Catanach (1970: 14ff.), the Deccan was a region which largely lacked local moneylenders. Gujarati migrated even before the incorporation of the region by the British, while Marwaris largely followed after its incorporation. As migrants they were 'aliens' who were not bound to the moral economy of the local population. To put it another way, they disembedded the lender – borrower relation.

Merchant Lenders and the Exertion of Commercial Control

Taking the view that many moneylenders were merchant lenders, one could perhaps agree with an argument in the contemporary discussion of rural finance that loans from shopkeepers and crop dealers to farmers are provided as a means of introducing or maintaining a business relation and to secure deliveries, rather than primarily for

---

[24] Report Regarding the Probability of Introducing Land and Agricultural Banks into the Madras Presidency 1895, Vol. I, Madras: 230), hereafter RLAC.

the sake of profit with interest. Cheesman (1982: 450) assumed that a similar strategy was pursued by nineteenth and early twentieth-century traders and moneylenders from Sindh. Indeed, their strategy was the acquisition of land not for speculative purposes but to guarantee their access to agricultural produce for trade with the export harbors. Many of these traders-cum-lenders started small estate production and even invested in semi-processing industries like cotton-gins and rice-husking factories.

> "A pervasive network of agents linked the large European, Bombay and Sindhi trading houses of Karachi with the village *baniyas* in the countryside. The agents, living in market towns, bought agricultural produce from the village *baniyas* and forwarded it to the main offices; they did not have direct contact with the agriculturalists. The village *baniya* was the linchpin of the system, occupying a pivotal position as merchant and moneylender. As merchant he was a middleman. He bought produce from the cultivators at the threshing floor; some he kept for retailing locally, the rest he re-sold to the dealers. His position as a trader made him a natural source of credit and so he was also a moneylender, providing, among other things, the investment which enabled agriculture to develop. The arrangement suited those involved in trade very well. It saved the great merchants from employing a large body of agents to go shopping around the farmlands and it provided the *baniyas* with secure trading contracts. But it was less advantageous for the producers" (Cheesman 1982: 450).

Farmers with debts to traders-cum-lenders could not freely sell their produce in the market. They were bound by their creditors to settle their accounts. The calculations were complicated since the prices fluctuated throughout the year.

Charlesworth (1985: 88-9) supported this argument. Moneylending in nineteenth-century India was directed at obtaining social power and commercial control. Marwaris in Poona, for example, fixed loan terms according to which a cash loan which was not repaid within a fixed period was changed into a grain loan. This offered certain advantages for the crop dealer. Not only did he secure his supply of grain, but the value of the debt was credited at harvest time when agricultural prices were low. Another advantage of a grain loan was the high inflation of the Indian currency, while agricultural prices tended to increase continuously, at least until the late nineteenth-century depressions. Mixed cash-kind relations were applied to revenue advances, too. For example, an arrangement between a lender and a borrower could involve the latter obtaining a loan of Rs 300 and the creditor paying three quarters of the revenue assessment for the 4.5 acres of land, whereas he obtained three-quarters of the produce as interest payment.

However, the implications of socio-commercial control went further. A moneylender could even force peasant debtors to raise crops in demand on the world market to fulfill his obligations (see Rothermund 1982b: 129; 1989: 45). The peasant's production decision therefore became independent of his subsistence requirements. Market demand was again in many cases dictated by the requirements of the colonial division of labour. Charlesworth concluded, similarly to Chaudhuri (1969), that the rationale of the moneylender even inhibited the development of an Indian domestic market.

Taking a more comprehensive view, I argue that moneylenders had an ambivalent relation to the economy. With the support of the colonial division of labour they indeed hampered the development of the Indian economy. Similarly, however, they helped to push subsistence-oriented producers into cash-crop production. I take my argument even further. Their 'non-entrepreneurial activity', to use Chaudhuri's (1969) terminology, supported the incorporation of India in the modern world system and its peripheralization.

7.3.4. Peasant Unrest in Late Nineteenth and Early Twentieth-Century India

In what follows I focus on peasant unrest, a phenomenon which occurred with increasing rural indebtedness and land alienation from the second half of the nineteenth century onward. High revenue demands from the government were a burden for almost all agrarian strata, although the lower strata of the peasantry were more severely hit than the upper one until the Great Depression. According to British-Indian law those who were unable to pay land revenues could be evicted from their land. The land could be sold by auction to the upper agrarian castes to recover the debt to the government. Peasant unrest was either directed against moneylenders or the rural population as a whole rioted against the state. However, the rioting was restricted to the local area or regional and never developed into an all-Indian revolt. The riots were usually severely oppressed by the government, and the conditions after the riots were often even worse than before. After the Santal uprising in 1855-6, for example, the British approved the wholesale appropriation of land by *zamindars* to recover revenue dues and by urban moneylenders as a compensation for their claims, which deeply wounded the peasantry's sense of justice. The great Oudh Mutiny of 1857 and its cruel suppression was another important example of the unyielding British stance in taking vigorous action (Dhanagare 1991: 34-43).

In the decades following the Mutiny, the power of the landowners and merchant class in rural areas continuously increased. Dhanagare (1991) identified the following reasons: first, the change from subsistence production to commercial agriculture, which increased the demand of credit and required the marketing of the produce; second, an alliance between landlords, moneylenders, and the British in the collection of land revenues; and third, the increasing scarcity of available land. The victims of these developments were the small landholders, tenants or subtenants and sharecroppers, whose land passed into the hands of moneylenders and large landowners.

In summary, rural riots in the second half of the nineteenth and early twentieth centuries resulted from increasing rural indebtedness and land transfers, whereas the explanation of the root-cause of this indebtedness was controversial. Contemporary scholars largely agree that it was to a large degree caused by the introduction of British rule and its social implications. Administrative and legal reforms such as the new system of cash revenue collection and the *laissez-faire* policy of the government, strengthened the position of the moneylender and weakened that of the borrowing peasant. Two case studies will illustrate peasant unrest and the discussion of it, the Deccan Riots and the Punjab situation.

The Deccan Riots

While sporadic individual attacks on landlords and moneylenders had already been common before the Deccan Riots, the new momentum in these riots was the more widespread and joint action of a number of villagers in the Poona and Ahmadnagar

Districts. Catanach (1970) analyzed the Deccan Riots in detail. In 1875 the first rioting against moneylenders occurred in a single village close to Poona. It was followed
by thirty riots in other villages in the Deccan which were primarily directed against
Gujarati and Marwari moneylenders. They had established a trading and credit network. As aliens they fell outside the local moral economy and had no scruple falling
back upon British law. From the Deccan, rioting spilled over to other provinces.

> "The pattern followed in most of the riots was that men began congregating in the afternoon,
> sometimes within a village, often just outside it. When dark came, there was a noisy rush on
> the moneylenders' houses. Often a hundred or more men took part (. . .) The moneylenders were
> generally warned of what was to come; many of them seem to have complied with the rioters'
> demands, which were normally limited to the surrender by the moneylenders of their 'bonds' and
> other documents – the written evidence of indebtedness – and the destruction of those documents.
> Little violence followed (. . .) If the moneylenders did not comply with the rioters' demands, or
> had left the village earlier, the rioters would use their lighted torches to set fire to the moneylen-
> ders' haystacks (. . .), ladders would be brought so that the rioters could enter the moneylenders'
> comparatively opulent two-storied houses, doors and shutters would be priced open with iron
> bars, and then the moneylenders' houses would be set on fire. Even in these cases, however, there
> was little real violence: according to government records, only one moneylender was seriously
> injured" (Catanach 1970: 10-11).

Scholars argued that the riots served as evidence of social breakdown following
credit extension and increasing indebtedness in the region and could be considered
a regional agrarian revolution. The Deccan agrarian society had been transformed
through the British government's legal and administrative reforms and these reforms,
accompanied by massive land transfers, caused the agrarian unrest (West 1892; Kumar
1965). Charlesworth (1985: 100ff.) rejected this view. He analyzed the land transfer
statistics. In contrast to the common assumption that peasants were rapidly losing
their land and continued to work as tenants or landless labourers, he held that an only
very limited free sale of land took place during the period under consideration and that
suits of lenders against debtors, which rose by 100 percent between 1860 and 1873,
were for sums not exceeding Rs 20, which did not involve land transfers. Even if
lenders obtained court decrees these were not necessarily set into force.

The data that Charlesworth presented indeed show that landed property held by
Marwari moneylenders in the Deccan did not rise significantly. Moreover, Catanach
(1970: 14ff.) maintained that the transfers which occurred were less to alien merchant-
lenders than to local agricultural lenders. This might support an ethnic explanation
that discontent of the agrarian population exploded against aliens. Of course, such a
reason cannot be denied. But one can also assume that the riots were aimed at seizing
the moneylenders' bonds, unfulfilled decrees, accounts, etc. Such legal documents
formed a new form of dependency, a continuous psychological threat by moneylenders
to call in the judge.

Actual rioting was confined to 33 villages only, and Charlesworth (1985) believed
that the social significance of the Deccan Riots was overestimated by both administrators and scholars. He explained the upheavals as follows. In part they were a
response to higher revenue revision settlements and population pressure. Agricultural
prices had fallen during the period 1860-75. Moneylenders were also adversely affected by these sinking prices because credit became much more insecure and credit

in kind was affected by low market prices. As a consequence of the economic crisis one can assume that moneylenders contracted their credit supply. And it was at this point perhaps that the fear of peasants to lose their land began since, according to the Land Revenue Code, non-payment of land revenues resulted in its confiscation and sale by the government. Seen in this light, he explained the rioting as a symbolic act by peasants against foreign moneylenders to force them to further advance the land revenues on their behalf instead of contracting the credit supply.

However, the social demography of the rioters (peasants, artisans, labourers, etc.) reveals that many participants would not have been encouraged to participate by the fear of losing their land because they did not hold any land titles. Therefore I assume that an explanation for the riots must include the different aspects outlined.

As usual in such cases the government reacted quickly by investigating the case. The Deccan Riots Commission remarked that the deterioration of relations between moneylenders and peasants was caused by the introduction of British notions of land law. The riots were structurally explained by debt accumulation and loss of land. Some scholars made forced sales by the government responsible for the riots, an argument which was rejected by Metcalf (1979).[25] The final report of the Deccan Riots Commission led to the introduction of the Deccan Agriculturalists' Relief Act of 1879. The courts were advised to thoroughly investigate the background of debt cases. Imprisonment as execution of a decree was abolished, debtors with debts exceeding Rs 50 could be declared insolvent, moneylenders were advised to run personal accounts for their clients, and land (unless specially pledged) was exempted from attachment for sale in case of debt. The commission recommended two possible ways of dealing with moneylending. One way was to regulate their activities and to introduce certain laws and regulations, the other was to compete with them for the provision of credit and set up a public or cooperative credit system. With regard to the former, the transfer of land to non-agriculturalists became prohibited in the Deccan, although the identity of agriculturalists was not clearly defined.

The Punjab Case

The Punjab, which was the mainstay of British authority in India, was a region experiencing agrarian unrest some decades later. Half of its land was cultivated by tenants-at-will. While in 1874 a million acres of land was mortgaged, in 1891 it was already four million acres. Warned by the Santal uprising (1855-7), the Mutiny and the Deccan Riots, the government quickly acted by introducing the Punjab Regulation of Accounts Bill of 1900, a prototype of the Deccan Agricultural Debtors' Relief Act. All moneylenders were obliged to hold regular account books. Every debtor was to receive his personal account, in which all transactions were listed, every six months. Untouched by this bill were sales on credit even if interest was charged.

---

[25] According to Metcalf (1979: 130-1), who investigated the riots in the North-Western provinces, forced land sales by auction were not such a common occurrence as it may seem. In many cases the government had to purchase the land because much land was over-assessed or depreciated, or the inhabitants were so rebellious that no buyer was found. In many cases such land purchased by the government finally passed back into the hands of the former owners.

Other acts followed in the inter-war period (see Report of the Punjab Banking Inquiry Committee, 1929-30, and Tab. 2).

The Punjab Regulation of Account Bill permitted the transfer of land to agriculturalists only, but it was clearly defined by caste names and communities – in contrast to the Deccan Relief Act – which belonged to the agricultural classes. However, the act brought only some relief to the peasantry and did not stop land transfers. The only effect was that merchant-lenders were replaced by agricultural ones.

In 1907 fierce rioting broke out. Dhanagare (1991: 43-3) maintained that the partition of Bengal had radicalized the national movement in the Punjab, and the riots can be interpreted as neither a purely agrarian nor a purely nationalist revolt, but as a weak combination of both.

The Punjab case was discussed in particular, because of Darling's (1977 repr.) *'The Punjab Peasant in Prosperity and Debt'*, which was based on a study carried out in 1918-19,[26] i.e. after the unrest. This study was preceded by several other ones, of which the most well-known was Thornburn's (1886) *'Musalmans and Moneylenders in the Punjab'*, which, however, was seen by the Punjab government as overstating the situation. Unfortunately, Darling's survey was based on members of cooperatives only, but this did not stop him from making generalizations for every peasant society (Darling 1977: xiv). His study of the Punjab had

> "application to the whole of Southeast-Asia and to wide areas in Africa – probably indeed to wherever peasants living in primitive or backward conditions are suddenly brought into contact with the modern world" (Darling 1977: xix).

Unfortunately many scholars also accepted Darling's generalization, although the general validity of the data is put in question for several reasons. One important deficiency was that the data were based on peasant proprietors only. A further weakness was that the burdens of debt were expressed as multiples of land revenue payments. The latter varied, however, from one province to another.

More important than the data is Darling's distinction between the debts of large and small cultivators. From the interpretation of his data he raised the seeming paradox that larger proprietors were indebted to a larger extent than smaller ones. On the other hand, taking the debt as a multiple of the land revenue payment, the smaller proprietor's debt was higher than the larger proprietor's. He concluded that it is much harder for the smaller proprietor to stay solvent than the larger one (ibid.: 12).

> "The volume and burden of debt were positively related with prosperity in the Punjab, and the explanation of this 'apparent paradox' is not difficult to seek. For, 'the fundamental fact of rural finance' was that though the *existence* of debt was due to *necessity* (arising out of the smallness of holdings and their fragmentation, recurring losses of cattle, insecurity of harvest, improvidence and extravagance, etc.) its volume depended upon credit. With the establishment of foreign rule the rural economy became monetized, and land which was of little value in the past now commanded a high price. In these conditions the moneylenders did their utmost to make the cultivators borrow, and the latter found it difficult to resist the temptation. In other words, an environment was created in which 'money was plentiful, security good, credit easy and borrowing

---

[26] The book was celebrated, among others, by Myrdal (1968, Vol. II: 1042) and Dewey (preface to Darling 1977), but recently it came under strong criticism.

uncontrolled. Now experience shows that when these conditions prevail rural debt invariably increases' (Islam 1985: 84, quoting Darling 1977: 210).

Islam (1985) rejected Darling's major hypothesis. He made a similar distinction between debt and indebtedness to mine. From this perspective one can expect that larger peasants had higher debts since they made productive investments. However, to conclude that they were more indebted is wrong. For example, proprietors obtained more favorable terms from moneylenders than tenants because they could mortgage their land and because their rates of repayment were higher. This resulted in a lower debt/asset ratio and not in an accumulation of debt. For small farmers just the opposite was true because they borrowed for consumption purposes, which did not lead to higher returns in the future. The fact that the productivity of credit and the rates of repayment increased with the size of land holdings was indirectly confirmed by the All-India Rural Credit Survey (1955: Vol. 1, Part 1: 264).

To sum up, Darling's hypothesis has to be reversed. Although larger farmers have larger debts, their burden of debt is comparatively smaller than that of small farmers. Assuming that larger farmers were drawn more into the market than smaller ones one can also argue that in the long run farmers who were more market-integrated had a lower burden of debt than those who were less-market integrated. The value of Darling's contribution is his distinction between the volume of debt and burden of debt and its link with the question of cash crop production.

7.3.5.   Rural Indebtedness and Unrest During the Great Depression

In the inter-war period and particularly during the Great Depression years, agrarian unrest continued. This was a reflection of the worsening living conditions of the rural population and the growing importance of the nationalist movement which mobilized the peasantry. A detailed account of this period was provided by Rothermund (1992: 79-134) whom I follow in this section.

During the Great Depression agricultural prices fell sharply. The income of the market-producing rural population was cut by 50 percent and then remained at the pre-war level, whereas tax and rent were kept at the pre-depression level for some time and loan liabilities were not eased until government action was taken to help the rural population (ibid., see also Rothermund 1982a: 19; 1982b: 129).[27] During the 1920s agricultural prices had been twice as high which had increased the peasants' credit volume, and many of them had accumulated debt. However, until the Great Depression this posed no severe problems. Moneylenders-cum-traders had not reclaimed the principal and were content with a mortgage, the dependency of their customers in delivering the harvest to them at a lower price and a continuous flow of interest. However, during the depression many of the creditors began to foreclose mortgages –

---

[27] The government argued that the rates were average rates which should not be adjusted according to short-term fluctuations. It should be kept in mind that the government budgetary situation was difficult during this period. Revenue-paying peasants were directly affected by this revenue policy, while landlords were able to shift their burden to their tenants through rent payments. However, rent adjustments were already restricted by tenancy legislation which stipulated that rent should not rise by more than one percent per year.

the last resort to redeem their claims, and the statistics show a significant increase in land sales.[28]

Mahatma Gandhi was involved in the development of peasant unrest which started in Barodi, Gujarat District, in the post-war period. It was caused by a new revenue assessment and an increase of revenues by 26 percent as the officer's estimate was based on the high post-war price level. Gandhi recommended that peasants stop paying any revenue, and the mass refusal to pay by the peasantry prevented the government from taking legal action against them with forced sale because the courts were simply overworked. Finally a compromise was achieved by setting up an independent inquiry commission. Until the final decision, the peasants had to pay the full amount, but the difference between the old and new amounts was treated like a deposit. In the end the commission suggested an increase of only six percent, but the report pointed at the arbitrary nature of settlement procedures. This was a victory for Gandhi and the nationalist movement. While from the administrative point of view the whole affair was a district government matter, the central government was involved in the plan too, because it was afraid that disobedience might also occur in other regions.

The salt march in spring 1930 which was brutally put down and their helplessness in coping with the economic crisis, came to question British authority in India. In the second half of the year agricultural prices declined sharply, which caused a rebellion in the wheat-growing areas of the Western U.P. The Gandhi-Irwing Pact calmed the tensions. This pact, which was criticized by many nationalists because it restricted the power of the Congress to mobilize the peasantry against the British, has to be seen in the light of consolidating the gains of the movement before it was crushed by military force and a decline in supporters' donations to the Congress during the depression to finance such campaigns.

In the first part of this chapter I already showed that the British, with their revenue system and definition of property rights, supported the stratification of the Indian rural population. Ironically the lower strata had some advantages during the depression. Sharecroppers were less indebted because they could not borrow large sums due to lack of security. Since they received a share of the crop rather than cash for their work they were less affected by falling agricultural prices. Most concerned were landlords and peasants under direct assessment, while tenants were to some degree protected by tenancy legislation, according to which they could not easily be deprived of their land.

An example of the degree of rural indebtedness for the year 1934 is given by the Preliminary Report of the Bengal Board on Economic Inquiry (1935, quoted by Rothermund 1992: 114). In the survey region 23 percent or 1.15 million families were not indebted (Category I); 43 percent or 2.15 million families were indebted to the extent of twice their annual income (Category II) with an average debt of 125 Rs; 16 percent or 0.8 millions were indebted to an amount up to four times their annual income (Category III) averaging 287 Rs; and 18 percent or 0.9 million families were indebted to more than four times their annual income (Category IV) with an average

---

[28] In cases of non-fulfillment of revenue obligations the government could force the sale of landed property, while tenants who did not pay their dues could be deprived of their occupancy rights. In the pre-depression period moneylenders had been the 'helpers in need' and, in such situations, had offered credit for the payment of obligations, but the contraction of credit now dramatized the situation.

debt of 411 Rs. Only Category II was considered to be protected by suitable legislation, while Categories III and IV had to sell at least part of their land.

On the whole the sum of the total of registered sales deeds for ten major districts doubled from 1930 to 1940, with 111,000 and 230,000, respectively. In the same period the number of mortgage deeds decreased by 79 percent (1930=148,000; 1940=31,000). The majority of occupancy *ryots* was involved in sales transactions. The dispossession of indebted peasants grew considerably.

The Report of the Agricultural Finance Sub-Committee (1945), hereafter called RAFSC, summarized the surveys conducted by the District Banking Inquiry Committees on rural indebtedness in the years of the Great Depression. In these reports the average rates of interest and types of credit varied considerably. In Maharashtra the interest rates in irrigated areas ranged from 12 to 24 percent, in famine areas from 18.75 to 36 percent per annum. Gujarat reported rates ranging from 9 to 18 percent. In the Central Provinces interest on secured loans was 15, on unsecured loans 18 percent. For Berar the same figures were ten and 15 percent respectively. In the United Provinces the interest rate on mortgage loans was six to 18.75 percent, while unsecured loans ranged from 18.75 to 37.5 percent (RAFSC 1945: 6).

The analysis of the reasons for borrowing provided the following picture: (1) the repayment of old debts played everywhere a significant role in borrowing; (2) a large proportion of credit was used for unproductive purposes, which led to an accumulating debt; and (3) the share of productive loans was much higher in cash-crop producing regions than in subsistence-oriented ones (RAFSC 1945: 14, 15).

7.3.6. The Government Response to Rural Indebtedness

The national and the provincial governments intervened very belatedly in rural indebtedness, and not consistently within the whole of British-India, since conditions varied from one region to another. Generally speaking two measures were open to the government. The restrictive one was the regulation of moneylending, tenure,[29] interest rates, land transfer, and so on, as well as the provision of relief to the indebted peasantry (i.e. setting the market principle out of force). The market-compatible measure was to institutionalize public credit to provide competition with informal lenders.

With regard to the former opportunity, scholars saw these attempts as very half-hearted, as they were only sporadically introduced from the 1870s onward. The pro-nationalist writer Raju (1941: 141-143) argued that unofficially various administrators looked on moneylenders with a friendly eye, as they were their allies by advancing the land revenue payment of the agriculturalists. This was also the main reason for continuing the policy of *laissez-faire* until the turn of the century, due to the government's dependence on this revenue.

The United Provinces Banking Inquiry Committee gave a precise description of the operation of moneylenders in the pre-depression period with its disadvantages and

---

[29] Some provincial governments passed pro-tenancy acts, which I exclude from my perspective. For a detailed discussion, see Rothermund (1978: 86ff; 1989: 45-7).

advantages compared to formal finance – a description, which to my mind is more complete and more adequate than many contemporary descriptions of moneylenders by scholars writing on rural finance.

> "He is certainly no philanthropist, his object is to make money, and he is not always particular regarding the means by which he does it. He will deduct future interest from the principal before he pays it; he will debit his client with all incidental expenses. He will cause an illiterate borrower to put his thumb-impression on a blank form, and subsequently fill it up with a sum in excess of the amount actually lent. He charges a rate of interest which is always high and often extortionate, and compounds it at frequent intervals. Nevertheless, when occasion arises he can and does show leniency. He will not, for instance, use his fraudulent bond unless the client by his contumacy forces him to go to law. Again, if his debtor is prompt and punctual in repayment he will often allow him rebate of interest when the account is finally closed. Meantime, it is to him that the needy peasant turns for help in every trouble. It is he who finances the marriage ceremony and law suits – one almost inevitable as the other. He does not keep the borrower waiting for his money till the time for its profitable spending has passed. He does not press for repayment at due date, if he knows that such repayment is inconvenient. He does not conduct embarrassing inquiries into his client's *haisiyat* (financial condition); for what it is worth, he knows it already, and the element in it to which he attaches most importance is the client's reputation for prompt and regular payment" (quoted by RAFSC 1965: 74).

The first British measures against rural indebtedness followed the usual pattern of setting up commissions which investigated the cases and produced voluminous reports.[30] The second step aimed at political negotiation or the prohibition of land alienation. The provincial differences in land tenure and damage done by the depression were reflected in a great variety of legislation concerning indebted landlords and tenants. There was a debate on central legislation which, however, brought no results, so that the provinces took their own legal action. An exception was formed by the Usurious Loans Act from 1918, although its effects were negligible since it did not define excessive interest (or legal maximums) and required proof for both the excessiveness of interest and the unfairness of the transaction.

Attempts at regulating moneylending – the Deccan Agriculturalists Relief Act of 1879, the Contract Amendment Act of 1899 and the Usurious Loans Act of 1918 – met with very limited success. The Congress Agricultural Inquiry Committee (1982: 74) argued that one important reason for the government abandoning its *laissez-faire* attitude was the fear of discontent among the rural masses, the spread of anti-British propaganda and rioting of the peasantry, which had to be suppressed with unpopular actions. It is not only that these acts were ineffective with regard to rural indebtedness, they even had counter-productive effects, which led to a further contraction of credit and rise in interest rates.

The Debt Conciliation Boards and Debt Relief Courts, which were introduced after the late nineteenth- and early twentieth-century riots, were based on the principle that borrowers had to take their case to these institutions, which hardly ever happened because of psychological barriers. They could only change the conditions of payment or scale down the debt amount, which were mere symptoms of the problem, but they

---

[30] During the 1930s they were already influenced by nationalist thought and partly made British rule and its implications responsible for rural indebtedness (e.g. Congress Agricultural Inquiry Committee 1982 [repr.]). Earlier reports, depending on the perspective of the writers, blamed the peasants themselves or moneylenders for increasing indebtedness.

were not able to alleviate the causes of indebtedness, such as non-adapted revenue payment, money and capital scarcity, and so on.

Only the period after World War I – or more precisely, the Great Depression – was marked by substantial intervention in moneylending and related matters. However, these measures were mostly limited as a provincial reaction to growing discontent, whereas a coordinated crisis management for all of rural India was lacking. Government legislation on behalf of the indebted peasantry was summarized by the RAFSC:

> "These sporadic and sometimes localized efforts (. . .) were mostly temporary palliatives which did not act on the whole problem and did not achieve anything permanent and substantial even within their limited fields. The setting in of the depression in 1930 produced country-wide distress and brought into bold relief the acuteness of the problem of agricultural indebtedness and the need to deal with it in a manner more comprehensive than had been attempted hitherto. The period, therefore, witnessed a great legislative activity in many parts of India, to afford relief to agricultural debtors (. . .) For instance, to make the Usurious Loans Act more effective, it was amended by various provincial governments making it obligatory for the court to use its powers under the Act if the interest charged was excessive or the transaction was unfair. Amendments made in some provinces also specified the rates beyond which interest was to be regarded as excessive. Further, the law of *damdupat* was made applicable in several provinces. In certain provinces provisions were made for abolishing the arrest and imprisonment of judgment debtors and extending the scope of the exemptions of properties from attachment or sale in execution of decrees. In some provinces the minimum amount of debt which entitled a man to apply for insolvency was lowered from Rs 500 to Rs 250. In one of them the upper limit of debt which entitled a debtor to be dealt with under the Section 74 of the Insolvency Act was raised from Rs 500 to Rs 2,000" (RAFSC 1965: 26).

On the whole one can distinguish between (1) acts defining interest rates, (2) acts controlling moneylenders, (3) acts providing debt management and (4) acts staying execution of decrees. Taking a particular look at the control of moneylenders, one can state that, although the moneylenders' acts varied from one state to another, the basic ideas were the following:

- Moneylenders had to register and, in some provinces, take out a license which was valid for a particular period only. Any offense against the registration was fined. In some provinces, non-registered moneylenders were prohibited from seeking justice at the courts. A registration certificate or license was canceled in the case of fraud or if in contravening to the regulation acts.

- Moneylenders were obliged to present regular personal accounts to their customers. An offense caused the legal penalty of loss of claims for any period without such accounts. In some provinces this offense could even involve a fine or imprisonment.

- Legal interest maxima were fixed for both secured and unsecured loans by amending the Usurious Loans Act or other acts. These rates varied considerably from one province to another.

These regulations seemed far-reaching but, compared to British legislation at home they constituted minor progress.[31] First of all, they were directed at 'professional moneylenders' only, who were defined as people whose primary occupation was moneylending. Therefore, the obligation to register only applied to a small proportion of moneylenders. Second, moneylenders found various ways to evade the regulations. They took

> "a fresh document for the total amount of principal and interest due showing the sum specified therein to have been lent in cash, securing bonds or sums much in excess of those actually advanced, obtaining documents showing outright sale of land with an oral undertaking to return the same on the payment of the loan at a rate of interest orally agreed between the parties, lending money on the pledge of gold without any record, making advances on mortgages with possession and collecting interest by way of rent, etc." (RAFSC 1965: 77).

The same report recommended that, since moneylending is often combined with the marketing of agricultural produce, regulations should include merchant-lenders.

With regard to debt management the unsuccessful operation of the debt relief institutions led the Central Provinces to abolish the voluntary clause in the late 1930s and with the Relief of Indebtedness Act empower the courts to reduce debts with respect to both principal and interest according to certain scales based on the date of borrowing, the *damdupat* law and the Usurious Loans Act. Other provinces followed with similar practices. On the whole, these government measures of the late 1930s and early 1940s seem to have provided some relief to the debtors. In the Central Provinces and Berar, for example, the total debt was reduced from about Rs 1,561 *lakh*[32] to Rs 775 *lakh*, in the Punjab from Rs 91.5 *lakh* to Rs 55.5 *lakh*, in Madras and the Central Provinces from Rs 931 *lakh* to Rs 444 *lakh* and Rs 428 *lakh* to Rs 230 *lakh*, respectively (RAFSC 1945: 28).

One recommendation of the RAFSC, which applies both to debt management and the staying of execution of decrees, was the regulation of mortgages. The practice was that these were either usufructuary or simple ones. In the former case the mortgagee took the 'fruits' of the land as interest, while the mortgagor remained the legal owner. If he or his heirs did not redeem the land within a period of 60 years, the mortgagee or his heirs would become the owner. Several provincial acts had already intervened in this practice. They claimed that the usufructuary mortgage should be limited to a particular period after which automatic redemption would take place unless the property was transferred to a member of the same agricultural tribe or a tribe of the same group as the mortgagor. The idea of these acts was that profits from the land should not exceed the principal plus a certain 'just' interest and that, as time passed, the debt would be continuously reduced.

In the case of simple mortgages, the property and 'fruits' of the land remained with the mortgagor who paid the interest at a stipulated rate. The creditor had to reclaim the debt within twelve years from the date of the last repayment; otherwise he would lose his claims. In practice, however, the creditor compounded the interest

---

[31] In Great Britain the previous *laissez-faire* attitude had been overcome with the British Moneylenders Act from 1927, which required the licensing of moneylenders and provision of records to the borrower and prohibited compound interest.

[32] *lakh*, British-Indian: Rs 100,000.

at regular intervals or forced the debtor to make a small repayment, so that the debt accumulated until it exceeded the market value of the land which was then transferred to the mortgagee. The Report of the Agricultural Finance Sub-Committee (1945) recommended the introduction of a time limit not exceeding 20 years to satisfy the creditor's claims.

A new round of legislation and reforms of the land revenue system was established with the reformed constitution, which provided provincial autonomy and offered a chance of elections. The diversity of land revenue collection and land tenure patterns called for different political measures, ranging from a revision of land revenue collection as the primary concern to relief of indebtedness by debt conciliation.

The drawback for Congress ministers was that they wanted to maintain a broad class alliance against the British with the support of all rural classes, including landlords, tenants and moneylenders, all of whom suffered during this period. They were therefore reluctant to severely restrict or even prohibit the business of moneylending.

Table 2 provides a list of Acts regulating moneylending in India between 1773 and 1953, which is naturally not comprehensive. From 1933 onward legislation was particularly concerned with debt management.

Bose's (1986) analysis of rural social and economic change in Bengal is relevant for my general perspective of changing financial landscapes. To sum up the main points:

- In ancient and medieval India there was a broad spectrum of different non-specialized lender types, such as lords of the land, trader- and merchant lenders. In the course of caste differentiation specialized financial agents emerged. On the lower financial level these were professional moneylenders who were the primary lender type in rural finance until the second half of the nineteenth century.

- Because of moneylenders' legislation, their importance decreased. From then until the 1930s, landlord lenders and trader-lenders were predominant. Bose called this period the 'heydays of the creditor'. Simultaneously tenancy legislation set limits to land rent increase, so that lending money became more attractive than the investment in land. As Bose expressed it, the old appropriation of tenant production by landlords was continued by new means. On the other hand, the expansion of cash-crop production enlarged the credit needs of cultivators who obtained credit in the form of advances on the security of the crop, inputs etc. from external merchants via small trader-brokers. Many country traders in fact turned into commission agents of the purchasing companies in an elaborate marketing chain.

- During the period 1930-45 the rural credit system collapsed. Due to the Great Depression trader-lenders largely disappeared, and lending was no longer profitable for landlord lenders because of the high risk involved. Nevertheless, in some regions where landlords had greater influence upon production (West Bengal), powerful lenders were able to maintain their control. Rich cultivators emerged as a new type of lender who provided loans in kind to the peasants. These were often said to aim at the acquisition of land.

To take a final note on the market-compatible strategy, the provision of public credit as an alternative to private informal finance: Since the government budget did not permit the institutionalization of large-scale government credit programs during the Great Depression, the strategy of cooperative credit was adopted. The question of agricultural banks and cooperatives had already been discussed around 1880. Various reports suggested that an All-India Cooperative Bank be set up or that cooperatives be attached to a Rural Credit Department of the Reserve Bank. The Government of India asked Sir Malcom Darling in 1934 to prepare a report on the organization of such a department. Darling analyzed various cooperative banks and concluded that only a small minority operated on a sound financial basis. He therefore suggested that the Reserve Bank should instead promote the development of the land mortgage banks that various provincial governments had set up. However, the Reserve Bank rejected this recommendation and classified the report as secret. Instead the Reserve Bank provided some support to the cooperative banks but suggested that they should raise deposits from the public rather than rely on financial support. In 1938, however, the Reserve Bank opened credit lines to cooperative banks and land mortgage banks, but this measure was restricted to the most financially profitable. What sounds reasonable in terms of the contemporary discussion on rural credit was a threat during the inter-war period, since only those were offered support who did not need it (Rothermund 1992: 56-58). On the whole, public credit was rather unimportant in colonial India.

Tab. 2: Regulation of Moneylending in India, 1773-1953

Province	Act	Year
	Various regulations for *taccavi* loans (government loans from land revenue)	1773
	Usury Law	1827
Bombay	Agricultural Debtors' Relief Act (Deccan)	1879
Punjab, U.P., C.P., Berar	Various Land Alienation Acts similar to Deccan Act	
	Land Improvement Loans Act	1883
	Agriculturalists Loan Act	1884
Bundelkhand	Alienation Act	1903
	Cooperative Societies Act	1904
Central	Usurious Loans Act	1918
Assam	Assam Moneylenders Act	1934
Bihar	Bihar Moneylenders Act	1938
	Bihar Moneylenders (Regul. of Transactions) Act	1939
Bombay	Bombay Moneylenders Act	1946
Madhya Pradesh	Usurious Loans Act	1918
	amended by C.P. Act XI	1934
	Madhya Pradesh Moneylenders Act	1934
	C.P. and Berar Protection of Debtors Act	1937
Madras	Usurious Loans (Madras Amendment) Act	1936
	Madras Debtors' Protection Act	1943
	Madras Pawnbrokers Act	1943
Orissa	Orissa Moneylenders Act	1939
Punjab	Punjab Regulation of Accounts Act	1930
	Punjab Debtors' Protection Act	1936
	Punjab Registration of Moneylenders Act	1938
Uttar Pradesh	Usurious Loans Act	1918
	U.P. Debt and Redemption Act	1940
	U.P. Regulation of Agricultural Credit Act	1940
	Jaunsuar-Beawar Pargana Debt Control Regul.	1948
	Dudhi-Robertsganj Agric. Debt Relief Act	1951
West Bengal	Bengal Moneylenders Act	1940
Madhy Barat	U.S. of Gwalior, Indore and Malwa Moneyl. Act	1950
Mysore	Mysore Usurious Loans Regulation	1923
	Mysore Moneylenders Act	1939
Travancore Cochin	Travancore Regulations	
	Cochin Usurious Loans Act	1936
Ajmer	Bombay Moneylenders Act	1946
Coorg	Coorg Moneylenders Act	1939
Delhi	Punjab Acts	
Himachal Pradesh	Him. Pradesh Debt Reduction Act	1953
Kutch	Bombay Moneylenders Act	1946

Sources: (1) Kumar (1982); (2) Government of India (1956)

7.4. Industrialization in India

The emergence of Indian-owned large-scale industries required higher-level finance
than that obtainable from long-established non-Western financiers of commerce. How
the financial landscape in India developed during the late colonial period, will be
considered in this chapter. However, I shall first take a general look at the discussion
of entrepreneurship.

7.4.1. Entrepreneurship

In his Ph.D. thesis on the Marwaris, Timberg (1978: 14-8) discussed the topic of entrepreneurship, which I shall summarize here and supplement with some points made
by Schumpeter (1912, 1990) who was probably the most famous contributor to the
discussion of entrepreneurship. In his 'Comments on a Plan for the Study of Entrepreneurship' Schumpeter (1990: 412-4) broadly defined entrepreneurs simply as
people doing new things or doing existing things in a new way. He distinguished entrepreneurs and innovators by saying that the latter produce ideas while the former
'get things done'. Schumpeter suggested several approaches of how to investigate
entrepreneurship. One approach is according to the fields of economic activity: commerce, industry and finance. Within these fields one can distinguish entrepreneurs who
introduce new commodities, those who introduce new technologies for the production
of existing things, those who introduce commercial combinations such as opening
new markets for products or new supply sources of materials, those who reorganize
industries, and so on. This shows that the term 'entrepreneurship' is not confined to
industrial entrepreneurship.

In his famous book 'The Theory of Economic Development' Schumpeter (1912:
213-4; 226-229) considered industrial entrepreneurs. He called them non-producers
who devise new combinations of production factors and finance these on the basis
of capital and credit. They do not contribute directly to the final product, but permit
the other elements to combine; they are so to say the catalyst element in production.
Entrepreneurship requires the purchase of the means of production and production
factors. In a pre-capitalist economy, an entrepreneur can neither purchase the means
of production nor borrow them because they are used by the producers. Entrepreneurs
are therefore characteristic of capitalism.

Schumpeter maintained that capital is the purchasing power for entrepreneurial activity which originates either from former profits or from loans. Capital is nothing
but the lever that will place the entrepreneur in the position of subordinating products
and production factors to his decisions. While in theory there are differences between
products and production factors, the entrepreneur's action towards both is the same:
he purchases them.

Most entrepreneurial activities are financed by means of credit. To put it another
way, potential entrepreneurs initially become debtors. With credit the entrepreneur
obtains access to the circular flow of goods before he has attained a regular claim
through his own purchasing power. Generally speaking, credit is not a symptom of

static (pre-industrial) societies because one production process follows another and profits of an earlier production process are consumed and used for the purchasing of production inputs. In practice there are of course overlaps because not every production process immediately follows another. In static economies, money is tied to the producer and idle during the period in which it is not required.

According to Timberg (1978) the discussion of entrepreneurs places the entrepreneur at the opposite end of the traditional businessman.[33] Gerschenkron (1966) maintained that one distinguishing feature is the planning horizon of the two categories. The former has a long-term planning horizon, while the latter is directed towards a quick speculative profit. Some time earlier Dobb (1974) had taken a similar position. Another distinguishing feature is that entrepreneurship is a specialized career with continuous specialized training for one's lifetime, while the traditional businessman confines his education, if any, to book-keeping. Hoselitz (1963) argued that bureaucrats find it easier than merchants to become industrial entrepreneurs because of their capacity for planning. Applying the same argument for Indonesia, Geertz (1963b) maintained that the administrative aristocrat under colonial rule (*priyaji*) had a better chance of becoming an industrial entrepreneur than the prosperous Islamic *santri* trader.

Max Weber (1950, 1964) and his school consider specific ideological and psychological climates that facilitate entrepreneurship, and which in turn promotes development per se (in contrast to Marxists who assume that entrepreneurs are by-products of the process of development). Weber implied a particular rationality of entrepreneurs, too. This rationality, found in the Protestant Ethic includes the positive value of hard work, thrift, saving and re-investment. Other authors maintained that this climate among the entrepreneurs is insufficient on its own, but that it had to be found in the whole society. Timberg lent support to this view.

> "In particular it would seem that the possession of a matrix of commercial interaction, a network[34] of contacts adapted to commerce, is a major qualification for business success. From his network a businessman can get the capital, intelligence, collaboration, and personal accommodation which he needs to be successful" (Timberg 1978: 28)

Another point of discussion is Weber's view that Asian religions are so otherworldly and irrational, from a psychological point of view, that they oppose the inner-worldly, secular ethic which industrial capitalism requires. The Weberian cliché of stagnant, irrational Hinduism is found implicitly or explicitly in the arguments of many social scientists.

Related to this point is the question of correlation between marginalized groups and entrepreneurs. Weber (1950) emphasized the pariah aspect of Indian entrepreneurs (certain castes and religious groups other than the mainstream), as well as their particular rationality (a specification of the argument of the Protestant ethic to India). Many Indian entrepreneurs are Jains or Parses, the former also constituting a large number of indigenous-style bankers. Weber argued that, in contrast to Hindus, Jains practice

---

[33] The following theoretical positions of different scholars were all described by Timberg (1978).
[34] 'Network', corrects Timberg himself later, is inappropriate, because it is defined as an unbounded structure in sociological terms. It is more appropriate to replace this term with 'resource group'.

an inner-worldly asceticism which is characterized by compulsory saving, thrift, investment capital rather than consumption capital, and so on. Prohibitions of excessive travel shifted their occupation from trade to sedentary merchandising, banking and moneylending. They developed a quasi-Puritan ethic which favored capital accumulation.

To my mind the ethical argumentation is of course important for cultures and periods in which religion and its ethic shape everyday life and thinking. However, at the same time Weber rightly pointed out that religion undergoes a continuous process of change, so that this argument should not be overemphasized either. As a matter of fact, new religions break away from old ones either as a reaction to the decay of values (the fundamentalist variant) or as a reaction to the rigidity of the older one. In this way Buddhism, Jainism and the Sikhs are an offspring from Hinduism. On the other hand, religions differentiate themselves into particular sects which are more adapted to the requirements of their members than the mainstream. The Chettiar, for example, managed to combine the other-worldly outlook and Hindu ecstasy with inner-worldly asceticism and business success (see Evers, Pavadarayan and Schrader 1994), and they belong to the Indian industrial entrepreneur communities in the same way as the Marwaris, many of whom are Jains. Moreover, Weber himself (in Andreski 1984: 117) emphasized that in all periods and cultures there existed capitalist acquisition and capitalists who defy all ethical limitations.

Sombart (1919) dealt with another criterion of entrepreneurship. A good merchant, he argued, must be able to organize, to calculate, and to speculate. The on-the-job-training in particular merchant communities has been well-described by various travel reports and scholars. Another, particularly Indian, factor supporting entrepreneurship is, according to Timberg (1978), the inheritance pattern which favored the preservation of joint-family property instead of dividing it among the male heirs. The Chettiar, for example, legally obtained the joint-family status which had particular consequences and advantages from the point of view of taxation.

7.4.2.   The Emergence of Indian Industries

This is not the right place to provide a review of Indian industrialization, and I refer instead to the excellent existing analyses (see e.g. Nafziger 1978; Morris 1982; Rothermund 1985, 1992; Goswami 1989). To sum up, the development of Indian and expatriate industries during the twentieth century, particularly from World War I until independence, is characterized by a declining share of British and an increasing share of Indian capital, while the share of mixed capital remained rather constant (Ray 1979: 52). India's fiscal autonomy in 1921 promoted this development. Some of the emerging Indian industries, such as iron and steel, obtained a certain protection and, for some time at least, a preferential rate of duties on exports to Great Britain. Nevertheless, until 1929 British firms continued to dominate industries.

Most of the industries in East India were British-owned and export-oriented, while most industries in the other parts of the country were Indian-owned and directed towards production for the domestic market. The British had comparative advantages in the former and the Indians in the latter sphere.

Fig. 1: Shares of Capital, India 1914-47

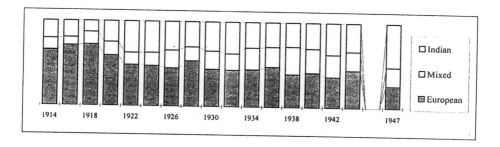

Source: Ray (1979: 52).

Before the First World War small firms had played a pioneering role in Indian-owned industries, many of which failed due to a lack of capital and business experience. Such low-capital industries continued to play an important part in post-war industrial development. In the field of big business which, according to Ray, played the pioneering role in new industrialization, Indian family businesses had very high growth rates, while European firms had high growth rates until 1922 and slow growth rates thereafter. At this time multinational groups, like Imperial Tobacco, Lever Brothers, Imperial Chemicals, Dunlop etc., entered the Indian market. Most of them were based in Britain and had already strong trading connections dating back to the years before the war. However, many of them switched to industrial production in India because wage labour was cheap and the country infrastructures were developed (Ray 1979: 259-99).

The leading indigenous industries until World War II were steel, textile, cement, refined sugar, matches and paper, and chemical industries, whereas the relative share of the dominant industries – textile, jute and steel – declined compared with the former. Indian industrial production was not as much affected by the inter-war depressions as other countries because it was more oriented towards Indian demand. At the end of this period the Indian textile industry around Bombay became almost self-sufficient in cotton textiles and began to export on a large scale during the Second World War. The Marwaris, Parses, and Gujaratis, who were among the early Indian industrial entrepreneurs, are still among the leading groups in modern industry, particularly in commercial centers like Bombay and Calcutta.

Although the Indian share of industries increased eventually, this process was rather slow. As shown by Morris (1982: 555, 598-9), various impediments of industrial development were on the supply side. Factors of production were expensive, skilled labour was scarce (which favored the managing agency system), and fuel and therefore domestic transport were costly. Only unskilled labour was cheap, and the cost relation of production factors impeded technical progress. But to explain the delayed Indian industrialization endogenously only does not reflect reality. One has to take into consideration the international dimension too. With regard to terms of trade, the Ottawa Conference, which gave way to a change in the British paradigm of free trade to protectionism, resulted in an unfavorable position for India. At the same time the exchange ratio of Pound and Rupee was overvalued, which benefited the sale of foreign goods in India and made the transfer of the Home Charges easier, while import substitution was impeded and the value of the foreign debt increased (for details see Rothermund 1992: 34ff.).

In what follows I take a look at the twentieth-century Indian financial landscape. It is generally conceded that the First World War, or the inter-war period, formed a structural break in the Indian economy. Tomlinson (1979: 8) characterized finance before the First World War as consisting of three different levels which were only weakly linked: (a) British exchange banks with their branches in India; (b) Indian import-export firms (managing agencies) and Indian and expatriate joint-stock banks; and finally (c) indigenous banks. He argued that, until the First World War, the upper level financed large-scale industries. In this sphere bank credit was rather easy to obtain. Neither British-owned industries, European managing agencies and bigger Indian industries nor the biggest Indian enterprises suffered from financial bottlenecks. On the second level, British exchange banks financed the import-export shipping. The Indian branches were supplied with capital from London to facilitate a higher flow of export goods. In normal years at the end of the trading season, their surplus balances were transferred to England. In addition to the British exchange banks, there were the major import/export firms and the Indian and expatriate joint-stock banks including the Presidency Banks of Bengal, Bombay and Madras. The largest international trading firms financed some overseas trade with advances to Indian intermediaries. If they had offices outside India they were able to provide foreign currency if required. Most import-export firms, however, were dependent on internal sources of finance. The Presidency Banks, which were prevented by statutes from dealing with overseas countries, discounted domestic trade bills, and most joint-stock banks were too small to do such a business. With the exception of Madras, Indians seldom borrowed from Western banks because most up-country traders and merchants did not fulfill the requirements of loan security. The indigenously developed bankers and Indian joint-stock banks financed, together with the trading firms, the purchase and transport of some goods from up-country centers to the ports and in the opposite direction. In addition, indigenously developed bankers dominated the trade in gold bullion, which was then and is still now the preferred form of saving for the rural population. Many of these bankers had overdraft facilities with commercial and presidency banks and discounted trade bills. However, they neither provided loans to the Westernized sector nor did they discount or purchase European commercial papers. Tomlinson (1979: 10) argued that the Indian segmented money market before the First World War was a reflection of how the growing international market for Indian products had helped to maintain and even strengthen traditional agencies. The stability and self-sufficiency of the informal money market kept the Indian money market as a whole and the domestic economy on traditional lines.

In contrast to Tomlinson's outline of the early twentieth-century Indian financial markets, I would like to propose another three-tier distinction: (1) an upper sphere being financed through banks and British import-export houses which consisted of import-export trade, expatriate and flourishing big Indian-owned industries and the colonial state; (2) an intermediate sphere for the financing of commerce and lower-level financial agents through indigenous-style bankers with certain refinancing possibilities at banks; and (3) a lower sphere for the financing of agriculture through moneylenders of different shapes.

From the point of view of the composition of indigenous capital, before the inter-war period Indian industrial capital was small compared to agricultural and merchant capital. Industrialization was not only impeded by the British, but the low investment in industries resulted from rising land prices, too, which fixed capital in land investment instead of channeling it into the commercial and industrial centers. According to the 1921 census, the number of non-Western bankers (which included managers, moneylenders, exchange and insurance agents and money changers) totaled almost 1.5 million. The Indian Central Banking Inquiry Committee (1931) estimated that informal finance in India financed as much as 90 percent of total domestic trade.

I shall now consider the different explanations for the emergence of Indian industries, particularly after the First World War. One standard explanation made the gradual collapse of the colonial administration and its replacement by a national government in India responsible for this development. Tomlinson (1981: 456) assumed that the expatriate firms foresaw this collapse and planned their smooth retreat for the last thirty years of British rule, repatriating profits and curbing their enterprise. Ray's (1979) 'Industrialization in India' made political unrest and uncertainty in India, and simultaneously more promising opportunities in other countries of the Commonwealth, particularly in Canada, Australia and South Africa, responsible for this retreat. Most foreign investment in India was by then no more than a reinvestment of part of the profits made or the salaries of Europeans.

Another explanation for the slow growth of Indian industries until the First World War is that the Government of India promoted infrastructural development to encourage the agricultural export sector rather than the development of an Indian industrial sector. During the war domestic industrialization policy changed because of the request that India contribute to the Allied war effort.

The position about the structural break in the inter-war period maintains that the old mercantile economy of the nineteenth century and its firms collapsed, and a new type of industrial-capitalist economy emerged. I concur with this structural explanation. However, a look at the old and the new structure alone does not explain the process of change, and to confine oneself to types of firms – besides European trading companies the Indian family firm as characteristic of the mercantile economy and 'modern' partnership firms (without kinship links) and particularly joint-stock enterprises as characteristic of the industrial-capitalist period – involves neglect of the importance of finance in the process of change.

I agree with Bagchi (1972: 440) who emphasized that, for the 1930s, the emergence of industrial entrepreneurs in India is far better understood if we connect their origin with trade in general (and one can use this term broadly and include the financing of trade) and the opening up of new opportunities in particular fields and regions rather than with specific castes. This is supported by Goswami (1985, 1989). He stressed that during 1935-40 indigenous-style bankers in particular diversified their businesses.[35] Most of these firms had accumulated their capital from trade, contracting, speculation and finance (Nafziger 1978: 42-7; Ray 1979: 276), and some had already gained a foothold in industries.

> "Especially prominent in this process of transformation of traditional merchant communities into modern entrepreneurial groups were the Gujarati Baniyas, whether Jain or Hindu, from whose ranks came Walchand Hirachand, Ambalal Sarabhai and Kasturbhai Lalbhai; the Punjabi Hindu Khatris, Aroras and Baniyas, among whom figured Lala Shri Ram, Karamchand Thapar and Gokulchand Narang; and most dramatically of all, the Rajasthani (including parts of Punjab) Maheshwaris, Agarwals and Oswals, both Hindu and Jain, grouped together under the generic name Marwaris, whose migrations throughout India threw up such large groups as Birla, Dalmia, Juggilal Kamlapat, Sarupchand Hukumchand, Surajmull Nagarmull, Jaipuria, Bangur, Goenka, etc. The Parsi houses, those early industrializers, fell behind in the race, except the giant house of Tata[36] (...) Bengali, Marathi and Tamil entrepreneurs, who built up some medium-size concerns (...), never succeeded in operating on a really large scale" (Ray 1979: 276-7).

The Marwaris are probably the most spectacular example of such Indian industrial entrepreneurs. During the 1930s and 40s they converted substantial speculative and trading profits into industries, by establishing their own enterprises and by acquiring shares in expatriate firms, joining the board of directors, increasing their equity shares and finally taking over these firms (Goswami 1985; 1989). Timberg's (1972) argumentation leads into the same direction (see Schrader 1994b: Appendix II). This period coincides with the phase in which the Chettiar in South India became involved in joint-stock banking. However, their major appearance in industries occurred as late as during the 1950s and 60s, when Chettiar nuclear families began to pool their capital in 'business combines' of related families (Ito 1966; Pavadarayan 1986).[37] The growth of Indian industries correlates with the growing importance of Indians in administration (Bagchi 1972: 440) and with the political independence movement (Ray 1979: 307).[38]

---

[35] A summary of the most important contemporary indigenous-style bankers who were all involved in finance in colonial India, too, will be given in Chapter 8.1.

[36] One of the most famous Indian industrial entrepreneurs was J.N. Tata, the founder of the well-known Indian steel enterprise in Bombay. His success was due –to some extent at least – to the increasing war demands.

[37] I explain this delayed entry into industries with the profitability of financing agriculture in Burma, Malaya or Ceylon until the Great Depression. Unfortunately, the defaulting of their borrowers during the depression turned Chettiar capital from liquid into fixed assets (land and some other immovable property).

[38] Indian industrialists formed the Federation of Indian Chambers of Commerce and Industry (FICCI) in 1925 as a counter-institution to the European Associated Chambers of Commerce (Assocham) in India, Ceylon and Burma. The executive committee of FICCI consisted of leading Indian capitalists, among others the Marwari G.D. Birla (Indian Chamber of Commerce, Calcutta) and Sir M.C.T. Chettiar (Southern India Chamber of Commerce, Madras), (see Ray 1979: 307-9). However, Rothermund (1992: 297) emphasized that the Indian capitalists had very divergent interests. Contrary to the Marwaris, represented by Birla, who supported the disobedience campaign, the Bombay mil owners and the Tatas depended very much on Indian protectionism. They favored the Gandhi-Irwing Pact.

Tomlinson (1981) argued that the official statistics, which usually form the basis of the argument of the structural break, are distorted because they only reflect the formal sector, and this sector was perhaps

"in reality no more than fleas on the buttock of Mother India; they have been replaced by parasites that have been more persistent and elusive, but that have not yet become a great deal more firmly established' (Tomlinson 1981: 486).

He suggested instead to have a closer look at both the expatriate and Indian firms' capital bases. I agree with Tomlinson that it is just as important for an understanding of the rise of Indian industries to take a closer look at their relation to informal finance and their possibility of self-finance. Timberg (1978), for example, argued that the Marwaris' access to capital, which they had accumulated through trade and speculation, was the decisive factor in their success over rival Indian entrepreneurs.

Until the inter-war period capital was scarce for Indian industrial entrepreneurs. According to Tomlinson (1979: 12-4), they neither obtained bank credit nor credit from indigenously developed bankers. The latter were reluctant to finance industries because they were traditionally involved in financing trade.[39] According to Tomlinson, this did not reflect their sheer conservatism, but their adherence to the old-established pattern was justified by India's growing importance in world trade during this period. To put it another way, until the Second World War the young Indian industries had difficulty in acquiring capital, while expatriate firms had access to formal credit from Western banks and British trading companies. During the war, however, the pattern of capital provision was reversed. Bank credit was now scarce, while indigenous-style finance, with its bad experience of the Great Depression with regard to trade, agricultural finance and investment in land, was prepared to finance Indian industries as a consequence.

Less than one decade later, however, Indian joint-stock banks became increasingly important as the financiers of domestic industry, for the Treasury Bill market and for the marketing of agrarian produce, while the importance of indigenous-style bankers went into decline at the same time.

"The development of financial institutions that occurred in the inter-war period, notably the 'modernization' of banking networks to integrate agricultural marketing into the rest of the economy and the growth of large institutions with interests in both trade and industry, had been part of the Government of India's long-term development plan for the economy since before 1914. It had been thought that once these goals had been achieved, hostile criticism of *laissez-faire* economic policy would collapse; ironically, because this growth was accelerated in the 1930s and 1940s thanks to a crisis in India's external and internal economies and in the relationship between them, its result was that *laissez-faire* had to be abandoned for ever" (Tomlinson 1979: 102).

To sum up, statistically considered it is true that the importance of indigenous-style banking experienced a severe decline in the inter-war period. Scholars adopted the Weberian argument that the financing of industries was beyond the capacity of traditionally organized, family-firm type indigenous-style bankers' capital and required the

---

[39] This attitude has been observed in Thailand, too, where Thai industries had to finance their operations through foreign banks until the 1970s, while Thai-Chinese banks largely confined themselves to financing trade (see Hewison 1988).

joint-stock financing of modern, Western-style banks which had a pool of investors' capital at their disposal. While this may be true for many smaller indigenous-style banking firms, it is not the case for the big ones with their extensive branches and networks.

In my opinion, another explanation might be more applicable. Generally speaking, I agree that the development of Indian industries required finance on a level to which indigenous-style bankers were not accustomed. In the case of the big banking houses, this was not so much due to lack of capital (the scarcity of individual capital was very often overcome by pooling the capital of different family firms and sharing the risk), but rather due to the fact that the financing of trade and industries was essentially different. The former is short-term in most cases. In the past it was limited to a particular trading venture, while in the present it bridges the gap between purchase and resale of goods. In addition to short- and medium-term finance (production inputs, wages, and so on), industrial activity also requires major long-term investment of fixed capital in the means of production, such as machinery, factory buildings, and so on. One can link this argument with the double nature of interest too (see Chapter 4). Until the early twentieth century indigenous-style bankers largely restricted their business dealings to loan capital and accumulated loan interest. However, they soon came to realize that profits can also be derived from natural interest by investing in industry.

To limit the argument to Weber's hypothesis that tradition inhibits the development of rational economic action is to my mind much too short-sighted. However, it is certainly true that various indigenous-style bankers reorganized their firms from the 1930s onward. They either opted for methods of operation, began to look for new niches in the field of finance or started up as industrial entrepreneurs. The top financiers among them diversified their enterprise into a number of different activities. This serves as a contrast to the theories of entrepreneurship put forward by Gerschenkron (1966), Geertz (1963b) and others, which I outlined at the beginning of this chapter. They not only considered traders to be conservative but even as impeding entrepreneurial activity.

Family firms were transformed into partnership firms or joint-stock companies. Part of the newly emerging Indian joint-stock banks were former indigenous-style banking firms which took new legal and organizational forms.[40] Marwari, Chettiar and other indigenous-style bankers turned into industrial entrepreneurs in textile or jute production, milling and other activities. A specific organizational form were the business

---

[40] In Statement II of the SGIB (1971: 114) report, the Commission listed the following indigenous banks in South India which reorganized themselves into joint-stock banks: (1) Karur Vysya Bank Ltd (1916); (2) Kumbakonam Bank Ltd. (1904); (3) South Indian Bank Ltd. (1903); (4) Chettinad Mercantile Bank (1933); (5) Illanji Bank Ltd., Tenkasi (1904); (6) Indo Commercial Bank Ltd. (1933); (7) Kulitali Bank Ltd. (1933); (8) Mannargudi Bank Ltd. (1932); (9) Rajapalayam Commercial Bank (1936); (10) Salem Bank Ltd., Salem (1925); and (11) Tenkasi Bank Ltd., Tenkasi (1933). The years of registration showed that most of these indigenous banks were transformed during the 1920s and 30s. Most of these banks, however, later on merged with larger banks. During the writing of the report, (1)-(3) were still functioning as scheduled commercial banks, while during the 1960s (4) and (5) amalgamated with the Bank of Madurai, (6) with the Punjab National Bank, (7) with the Indian Overseas Bank, (8) and (10) with the Indian Bank, Madras, (9) with the Tanjore Permanent Bank, and (11) went into voluntary liquidation in 1954.

combines,[41] an Indian version of family trusts. What they have in common is that they had in the past been traders and financiers, that the boundary between trade and finance had never been clear-cut, that they had never before engaged in productive activities, and that they were highly urbanized (Gadgil 1955, quoted by Ito 1966: 375). Very few of these business combines, however, entered heavy industries.

> "The reason why enterprises under the control of these business combines grow more rapidly than medium and small independent enterprises of the same size is that when a number of enterprises is concentrated under the control of a single decision-making 'authority', they cease to be a mere congeries of independent enterprises and are freed to a certain degree from capitalist free competition, gain stability and credit-worthiness, have easier access to foreign capital and technical collaboration (...) and, as a result of all these things, are able to accomplish a rapid elevation of their economic, social, and political position. In concrete terms, if a number of enterprises which have vertical and horizontal relations in matters of technology are under the control of a single decision-maker, it will be possible to make book-keeping and adjustments to a considerable degree when passing goods from one company to another within the group, and it will also be possible, to some extent at least, to make book-keeping and adjustments in regard to actual production and sales in the enterprises belonging to a single industry within the group, and in this way to disperse profits among the enterprises (...) The mobilization of funds for the enterprises in the group from sources both inside and outside the group by means of the group's own banks, investment companies, managing agents, etc., is an extremely profitable mechanism under the conditions of an economy in which investment requires immense funds in the light of present levels of technology and in which capital accumulation is lagging behind. What is more, all these things can be done quite legally" (Ito 1966: 378).

Because of the dual, partly overlapping structure of Indian finance, indigenous-style bankers played an important role in the Indian economy. However, for the government and the state bank, they were always a critical factor in economic policy, since they were largely beyond the control of government institutions and financial laws. Their integration in formal finance was therefore a topic of discussion as emerged in the report of the Indian Central Banking Inquiry Committee in 1931. This report recommended that their role be improved and that they be integrated in the Indian banking system. Moreover, it suggested that the indigenously developed bankers, commercial banks and cooperatives be brought in a direct relationship with the Reserve Bank and provided with rediscounting facilities.

The Reserve Bank of India took a confrontation course against these recommendations. It announced that indigenous-style bankers should confine themselves to particular bona-fide trade transactions. Commercial banks discounting *hundis* should present a list of *shroffs* with whom they maintained business relations and also a record showing the credit limits accorded to them and the type of business engaged in by the *shroffs* (SGIB 1971: 93).

This stance opposed the recommendations of the Banking Inquiry Committee and the wish of the government to integrate indigenously developed bankers. The Bombay Shroffs Association rejected the proposal that *shroffs* be placed below their competitors, the scheduled banks, in the relation to the Reserve Bank. This criticism resulted in an attempt to prepare a scheme for the direct linkage of indigenously developed bankers with the bank, but this attempt failed. The indigenously developed bankers

---

[41] According to Ito (1966), family business combines are formed by several blood-related nuclear families which pool their capital for economic investment.

did not want to be controlled by any institution. Similar attempts in 1941 and 1946 were equally unsuccessful.

7.5.   Conclusions to Indigenous-Style Finance

7.5.1.   Indigenous-Style Finance in Colonial India

The preceding chapters analyzed the development of the financial landscape in colonial India. From a macro-perspective I showed that, after the establishment of British authority in Bengal (1757), Indian business opportunities in trade continued to decline, at least until 1813, when the Charter Act dissolved the trading monopoly of the East India Company, if not until the mid-nineteenth century, when the Company finally wound up its activities. Within the sphere of organizing and financing trade, Indians were largely excluded from their traditional domain, the maritime long-distance trade. They were increasingly pushed in a *compradore* position between the Indian producer and the British (or other European) exporter. With regard to domestic production and trade, the British for a long time imposed trade restrictions, ensuring that British imports enjoyed an advantageous market position compared to domestic products.

The declining business opportunities of indigenous-style bankers and traders were to some extent compensated by an increasing volume of domestic trade to the three export ports of Calcutta, Bombay and Madras. In terms of geography, Bombay became the main center of indigenous-style banking, which led to the migration of various financial agents from the north-west to the west coast. It is probably not an accident that Bombay also developed into the center of Indian industries during the late colonial period. Calcutta provided less business opportunities for indigenous-style bankers, because trade and industries were largely monopolized by British firms.

In addition to the loss of foreign trade and its finance, indigenous-style bankers lost further former functions. While in the early period of British rule the top bankers held important functions as state bankers of both the independent and colonial states, the incorporation of the former and the liberation of the latter from this dependency on indigenous-style bankers deprived them of tasks like minting, state treasury, money-changing and, in particular, the continuous transfer of funds from Calcutta to Bombay.

With the exception of the loss of state banking, the emergence of Western-style banks to my mind constituted a minor threat to indigenous-style finance. The developing colonial financial landscape was largely dualistic. Western-style finance limited itself to Western enterprise, which was formerly financed by indigenous-style bankers to a minor degree. During the twentieth century the state and Western-style finance also supported well-established Indian industries, whereas non-Western finance serviced Indian commerce and agriculture. At least until the Great Depression Indian-owned industries largely lacked the finance from both financial spheres. However, there were various links between both indigenous-style finance and western-style finance, such as *hundi* discounting at banks or advances of indigenous-style bankers to managing agencies. Furthermore, Western banks employed indigenous-style bankers as guarantee brokers. The report of the Indian Central Banking Inquiry Committee (1931) even went as far as suggesting their employment in banks.

While the former functions of indigenous-style bankers in trade and government finance decreased on the whole, new business opportunities emerged in the field of agricultural finance. These opportunities were closely related to the transformation of subsistence-producing into cash-crop producing regions and marketing, as well as to the introduction of Western legislation with regard to land revenue collection, private property, land transfer, land mortgaging, and so forth. Such legislation incorporated the peasants in the market and prepared the ground for collateral lending and legal enforcement of claims. I argued that, while in pre-colonial India the lender-borrower relation was largely embedded in society imposing moral sanctions on lenders, it became increasingly disembedded in colonial India because lenders could avoid the personal confrontation with borrowers by simply applying to the courts. I considered moneylenders important supporters of colonial rule from the structural point of view, because they advanced the payments of the land revenue of landlords and cultivators to the government which, together with the opium and salt monopolies, formed the major financial basis of the colonial state.

The economic and legal conditions in colonial India led to an increase in rural indebtedness, which escalated during the depression and finally forced the colonial government to abandon its liberal *laissez-faire* economic policy which even supported moneylending for the above reasons. The government interfered in the financial landscape by introducing moneylenders' and tenancy legislation, usury laws, debt relief and a minor attempt at supporting financial cooperatives, which is, however, not at all comparable with public credit in the Netherlands Indies (see Part III). On the whole, the results of such intervention were meager. While professional moneylenders were restricted in their operation to some degree, as far as they did not find ways to circumvent the regulations, legislation supported the rise of a new type of lenders, agricultural and merchant lenders, the former particularly having an interest in acquiring the land of their customers.

A review of indigenous-style bankers' castes, such as the Gujarati and Shikapuri Shroffs, Marwari and Chettiar, reveals that particularly from the inter-war period onward a number of indigenous-style bankers once again re-organized their economic activity. I call this the second great turning-point in indigenous-style banking. An adaptation not far removed from their former activity was their involvement in Western-style banking. They either pooled their capital to establish their own banks, such as the Chettiar-owned Bank of Chettinad, a private company, or the Bank of Madurai, a joint-stock company, or they bought shares of other banks. An example of this are again the Chettiar, some of whom hold a number of shares in the Indian Bank and the Indian Overseas Bank. Another re-organization led them to the production sphere. The theory of entrepreneurial activity considers the reorientation from merchandising to industrial production as a distant step. However, the history of indigenous-style bankers and the formation of business combines shows that they were always quite flexible in adapting to changing circumstances.

However, I have to emphasize again that indigenous-style banking did not disappear during the inter-war period and continued to play a decisive role in the finance of trade and small-scale manufacturing. This will be shown in Chapter 8.

7.5.2. Indian Indigenous-Style Finance and the British Colonial System outside India

The analysis of indigenous-style finance in colonial India neglects the business opportunities the British colonial system offered to indigenous-style bankers and moneylenders outside India. To really understand the structural dimension of such financial agents within the colonial system, one should also include this perspective. I did this elsewhere by considering the case of the Nattukottai Chettiar (Schrader 1994b: Appendix I; 1995) who at the turn of the nineteenth century followed the British to Ceylon, the Malayan peninsula, some decades later to Burma (which was annexed between 1824 and 1886 and became an Indian colony) and to other places, where they established a well-functioning international financial network. Sandhu (1969: 77) argued that the change of political power in Southeast Asia from indigenous to colonial rule afforded better political and legal protection of business, which in turn prepared the ground for an expansion of the indigenous-style financial networks outside India.

The discussion of the Chettiar always placed the main emphasis on their role in financing agriculture, which categorized them as moneylenders. I reject this approach because of their additional involvement in commercial finance, their important exchange function in Ceylon and their elaborate financial branch networks, which is why I count them among indigenous-style bankers. I argued (Schrader 1992) that the Chettiar were pioneers in expanding capitalism. To put it more precisely, they provided the finance for the opening-up of lower Burma and other regions for cash-crop production. The contextualization of their indigenous-style finance within the British colonial economy pinpoints their *compradore* position. They had refinancing possibilities with British banks and channeled funds into the agrarian economy where the former did not operate.

But the Chettiar who dominated the non-Western financial scene in Burma, Ceylon, Malaya and so on, were not the only Indian financiers in British colonies outside India. For example, Marwaris, Shikapuris and Gujaratis were involved in the financing of Burma and Malaya trade, too, but largely confined themselves to the cities. Menon (1985) related the Chettiar foreign activities to the reduction of business opportunities in the Madras Presidency, but from the structural perspective this argument can be also extended to the other financial agents.

The decline in Chettiar indigenous-style banking and moneylending was largely attributed to political changes in the colonies and the effects of the Great Depression. I do not deny that these developments eventually put an end to their foreign activities. However, in the same way that I relate the rise and decline of indigenous-style banking to particular structural change in the period of capitalism (merchant and industrial capitalism), I interpret their decline within the wider process of particular regions being incorporated in the world-economy and their replacement by Western-style banks.

8. Contemporary Formal and Informal Finance

Estimates of the share of contemporary informal finance in India are very rough and inconsistent. According to Chandravakar (1982: 798), a sample survey of the Reserve Bank of India from 1951-2 on rural indebtedness assumed a share of informal rural credit of 90 percent. Two decades later, the Rural Credit Survey of 1971 estimated that 70 percent of all rural debts were loans from informal sources. Its share has decreased further because the Indian government pushed forward the banking infrastructure in rural regions. Bell (1990) even maintained that its share in the early 1980s was not higher than 24 percent, which to my mind is a considerable underestimate. It is safer to assume a share of around 50 percent.

It is difficult to assess whether this decline is only a relative one because of a major increase in available formal finance, or an absolute one since the tendency among different informal financial agents is not uniform (see Mamoria 1982). Case studies reveal that the number of rural merchant lenders, crop dealers, commission agents, hire purchase financiers, pawnbrokers, and so on has increased, while that of traditional indigenous-style bankers, professional moneylenders and landlord-lenders has decreased. Such structural change resulted from both changing requirements of society and economy, as well as state interference with the financial landscape.

In the first part of this chapter I shall reconsider the contemporary urban informal financial agents and institutions, which consist of indigenously developed bankers and finance brokers, finance corporations, *nidhis* (mutual benefit funds)[1] and *chit* funds (rotating savings and credit associations, which are often commercialized, see e.g. Nayar 1973). The latter two financial institutions have been excluded from this study. In the second part I take a look at the rural financial landscape. I include a few notes on formal finance, since its extension has affected informal finance.

---

[1] For a detailed description, see Report of the Study Group on Non-Banking Financial Intermediaries (1971).

Tab. 3: Estimate of the Number of Moneylenders (Incl. Indigenously Developed Bankers) in India, 1968

State	Total	Urban	Rural
Andhra Pradesh	4744	2241	2503
Assam	573	65	508
Bihar	1324	774	550
Gujarat	1559	1033	526
Jammu/Kashmir	118	72	46
Kerala	154	31	123
Madhya Pradesh	1704	1086	618
Madras	3967	2962	1005
Maharashtra	2593	2021	572
Mysore	1320	1090	230
Orissa	1610	544	1066
Punjab	438	161	277
Rajasthan	6191	1390	4801
Uttar Pradesh	4327	2839	1488
West Bengal	3119	2749	370
Total	33,741	19,058	14,683
Union Territories:			
Andaman and Nicobar	1		1
Delhi	100	99	1
Himachal Pradesh	9	2	7
Manipur	1		1
Tripura	55	16	39
Goa, Daman and Diu	1	1	
Pondicherry	31	4	27
Total	198	122	76
Grand Total	33,938	19,18	14,759

Source: SGIB (1971): 113

8.1. Urban Informal Finance

8.1.1. Introduction

A detailed analysis of indigenous-style banking in contemporary India was provided by the SGIB (1971). Considering the density of banks and indigenous-style bankers, their appearance is not mutually exclusive. Particularly in commercial and metropolitan centers, such as Bombay, Calcutta, Madras, and so on, the 1961 Census outlined the clustering of indigenously developed bankers.[2] The high level of economic ac-

---

[2] In 1960-West Bengal and Mysore, for example, about 80 percent of indigenously developed bankers were found in urban areas.

tivity in these regions facilitates the simultaneous existence of both indigenous and formal financial institutions.

Urban informal credit has been estimated at 42 percent (excluding black money) or 57 percent (including black money) of total urban credit, whereas the trade sector uses two-thirds of it. Urban household credit amounts only 1.5 percent of total urban informal credit. The proportion of consumer credit to total informal credit is therefore much lower in the urban than in the rural context. The urban informal financial sector seems to be rapidly growing (Ghate 1992: 66).

A break-down of indigenously developed bankers in India was provided by Timberg and Aiyar (1980) for the late 1970s. It shows only a small number in North India and a higher concentration in other parts. They counted 1,200 Multani bankers and more than 500 associated brokers, 5,000 Gujarati bankers and commission agents (the last-mentioned were not counted as indigenous-style bankers by these scholars), 2,500 Chettiar bankers and 25,000 pawnbrokers, 100 Marwaris in Madras plus various Marwari firms in Calcutta and other places and 500 Rastogi bankers (see Tab. 3). The few Kallidaikurichy Brahmins from South India went unmentioned.

These castes are all Hindus or Jains, but the assumption that there are no Muslim informal financiers because of the prohibition of taking interest by the Qur'an is refuted by evidence of Muslim moneylenders in India, such as the Pathans, Hadramouth traders and itinerant Muslim moneylenders in the Trichinopoly District of Madras (Chandravakar 1982: 776-7).

Only one decade earlier, the SGIB (1971), drawing upon the numbers mentioned by the associations of indigenous-style bankers, reported quite different numbers: 400 Multani Shroffs, 350 Gujarati Shroffs, 50 Chettiar firms, 400 Assam *kayas*, and 1,300 others, data which were adopted by Goyal (1979). The very different data are due to the application of different categories.

Multani Shroffs, Gujarati Shroffs, Nattukottai Chettiar and other indigenous-style bankers have organized themselves in associations, many of which go back to the 1920s and 30s. They take various functions which are carried out more or less strictly. They serve the exchange of information on customers, penalize the dishonesty of members (since it leaves a stain on the whole caste), sometimes fix maximum rates of interest, hold social functions, such as the organization of festivals, and form a political lobby to defend the interest of the caste occupation against government interference with their business. According to Timberg and Aiyar (1980), urban informal finance is highly organized (which contradicts the misnomer of indigenously developed bankers being 'unorganized bankers' as did, for example, Karkal [1967]). Associations are formed according to caste/ethnic background and special business lines in which particular banking castes have specialized. Examples of such associations are the Shikapuri Shroffs Association in Bombay, the Bombay Shroffs Association, the Gujarati Shroffs Association in Bombay, the Hindustan Chamber of Commerce in Bombay, the Merchants Chamber of Commerce in Calcutta, the Delhi Mercantile Chamber or the Kanpur Cloth Committee, which all have regulatory functions. The Bombay Shroffs Association has quite successfully tried to found a national organization of the local bankers' associations.

"In essence, these bankers perform functions analogous to a modern bank (if not on the same scale), *viz.*, receiving of deposits on current and fixed accounts, buying and selling of *hundis* – demand and usance –remittance of funds and in some cases accepting valuables for safe custody. Chequable deposits and term finance provided by commercial banks, however, are features not discernible in indigenous banking" (SGIB 1971: 22).

The primary business of indigenously developed bankers was and still is the finance of trade (retail and wholesale), including the movement of agricultural produce (for the history of indigenous-style finance, see Schrader 1994a, b). In addition they also finance small and medium-scale industries, but refrain from agricultural finance which is left to cooperatives and moneylenders. On the one hand, most indigenous-style bankers were even traditionally not involved in this field of activity, on the other hand, moneylenders' acts set certain limits to the financing of agriculture, requiring registration and licensing, and fixed interest rates. Definitions of categories affected by the moneylenders' acts differ from state to state. In Bombay, for example, a restriction of one's business to the finance of trade did not require a license (Bombay Moneylenders Act, 1946) but legal ceilings were nevertheless set. Other states fixed amounts up to which every commercial transaction is considered moneylending. Therefore many financial intermediaries, including indigenous-style bankers have limited their loans to minimum amounts of Rs 3,000.

The main activity of indigenous-style bankers is dealing in short-term financial instruments which have to be met on demand or by a certain date. Until 1970 the *hundi* was the usual credit instrument which was discounted to customers and with banks and it was used as an instrument to raise funds.

8.1.2. Hundis

Although inconsistent with the Negotiable Instruments Act of 1881, various forms of *hundis* exist. The SGIB (1971) maintained that a clear definition of a *hundi* has never been provided by any authority on banking.

Hundis perform three functions: (1) the raising of money; (2) the remittance of funds, and (3) the financing of inland trade. A principal distinction, which will suffice here,[3] is made between *darshani* (sight or demand) *hundis* paid by presentation and *mudatti* (usance) *hundis* to be paid after a stipulated period.

The duration of a *mudatti hundi* is normally 30, 60, 90 or 120 days, whereby 90 days are most common. Generally two persons are involved: the lender and the borrower. Its validity is confined to the local area. In the case of *darshani hundis*, three parties are usually involved: a drawing *shroff*, a paying *shroff* and a payee. This instrument performs the function to finance inland trade or to remit funds through indigenous-style banks from one place to another, for example for paying trade bills. *Darshani hundis* can be cashed at any time, day and night. In contrast to checks, they pass through many hands before being endorsed, are less costly in fees and cheaper to negotiate a settlement if they are not honored.

---

[3] For various sub-categories, see the SGIB (1971: 48ff.).

The whole *hundi* business is based on the assumption that the borrowers honor the letters of credit on due dates. Every endorser is liable for its payment to the holder. In case any drawer faces financial difficulties, an indigenous-style banker who endorsed the *hundi* with a bank, takes it back by paying the amount even before the due date. This is necessary to maintain his creditworthiness. The SGIB (1971) maintained that

> "The dishonoring of *hundis* is 'an event of rare occurrence'. If *hundis* are not honored on due dates the drawers are considered bankrupt. The drawee of the *hundi* may, however, refuse to accept it, if he does not hold funds in the form of any deposit for the drawer or no prior arrangement has been made for its acceptance. When a *hundi* is so invalidated, it is sent to the Sharafi (i.e. *shroff*, H.S.) Association of which the party is a member, for getting it protested. The presenter is required to fill in the Association's form and the Association inquires of the drawee the reason for non-payment and notes it down on the reverse of the form. The Association informs the party of the reply of the drawee and for this service the Association charges 15 paise. Thereafter at the request of the party the association grants a '*majarnama*' (certificate in proof of dishonor *vide* Exhibit 15) for which it charges 50 paise (. . .) The *majarnama* of the Sharafi Association is stated to have the weight of a court award, because invariably on the production of this *majarnama*, the maker of the *hundi* returns to the *rakya*[4] not only the original amount with interest, but pays '*nakarnamana shikaraman*' (damages of dishonor) according to the custom of the place" (SGIB 1971: 53).

However, government interference with the negotiation of *hundis* had severe effects on this traditional business of indigenous-style bankers. Until November 1970 the *hundi* discounting rate of the State Bank of India was 9.5 percent and left a margin of 5.5 percent until the legal ceiling for the indigenous-style bankers. In 1971, however, the bank discounting rate increased by 3.5 percent, whereas the legal ceiling was not increased, so that the remaining margin was now insufficient to run a profitable *hundi* business. In various cases this caused an offense against the legal ceiling, while on the whole a re-orientation of the business of indigenous-style banking occurred, away from the long-established dealing in hundis to the installment credit and commercial paper business, although the volume of *hundi* business is still considerable.

Additional financial services of contemporary indigenous-style bankers are the transmission of money from place to place without the use of *hundis*, the receipt of deposits, the issuing of letters of credit to merchants requiring finance at several trade centers, and so on. Most indigenously developed bankers combine banking with trade, commission agency business or hire-purchase financing. Only a minority are pure bankers like the Gujarati Shroffs of Ahmedabad.

Timberg and Aiyar (1980) explained the shift of orientation in many indigenous-style banking businesses by a shift of business orientation of their customers who nevertheless maintained their old-established financial links. In other words, in contrast to my opinion that many indigenous-style bankers should be considered entrepreneurs, they argued that the indigenous-style banker only reacted to the changing environment. Their long-established financial networks have permitted certain castes and groups to remain dominant in the finance of trade and industries and even to enter some branches of production. They have maintained a quasi-oligopolistic position in urban informal finance. The Chettiar, Rastogi and Kallidaikurichi Brahmins who were leading agricultural financiers, however, largely withdrew from these markets.

---

[4] A *rakya* is a person named in the *hundi* to whom or on whose behalf the amount of the *hundi* is to be paid.

8.1.3. Organization and Functions of Different Indigenously Developed Bankers

Like in medieval and colonial India, most contemporary indigenously developed bankers combine banking with trade or related forms, such as a commission agency business or hire-purchase financing. Only very few are pure bankers. They are still using their traditional mode of accounting, which was viewed with skepticism by many foreigners, since they could not understand it and was used as a kind of secret language. On the whole, there are three books, a cash book, a journal and a ledger.

In what follows I shall consider the leading banking castes one after another, whereby I largely draw on the report of the SGIB (1971) and Timberg and Aiyar (1980).

The Shikapuri Shroffs or Multanis

For generations the Shikapuri have been involved in commerce and finance. From Shikapur in Sindh they carried out business with, or had offices in, places in the north-west, such as Bokhara, Khurasan, Kandahar, Kabul, Tehran and Kashgar. Tradition-ally one of their activities was the provision of finance to local traders, shopkeepers, and so on. Their financial operations started with mere moneylending. By the time the Multanis shifted their activities from Shikapur via Multan to Bombay and as far as South India, they combined the finance of the movement of goods with trade. With the opening of banks, the transfer of funds lost importance. Instead they developed the *khata* business, the opening of current accounts in the name of business and trading concerns and the provision of advances to them according to their credit and capacity. At the second stage they took up the *hundi* business. Their success in the past was due to the discounting facilities of *hundis* with the Imperial Bank (now State Bank) of India.

Bombay business started around 1870, but remained only one of several centers of activity. Until the Second World War less than 50 firms were counted in Bombay. After partition, however, the city became the center of Multani commercial activity. Other Multani bankers own firms in Madras, Bangalore, Coimbatore, Secunderabad, Tiruchirapalli, Calicut, and various other places. A number of firms have branches in one or more of the major cities. According to Timberg and Aiyar (1980), a little less than half of the about 1,000 Multani firms (excluding the brokers) are organized in the Shikapuri Shroffs Association, which is quite informal.

The SGIB (1971: 21ff.) considered the contemporary activities of the Multanis as an important financial intermediary service to small-scale industries and retail trade by securing access to working capital, with a very mobile mode of operation. Credit can be obtained on *hundis* or other commercial papers in about half an hour. Multanis work with their own capital, through bank loans[5] and with investments by friends and relatives who in the early 1970s obtained interest of six to ten percent on their share capital. Deposit acceptance from the public does not as a rule form part of the Multani

---

[5] On average, total limits sanctioned by the banks amount to roughly twice the amount of the owned capital per firm, whereby most firms do not use more than 40 percent of these limits, since they are very anxious to keep their creditworthiness.

business. Until 1964 another means of raising capital was the *purja*, the selling of obligations to the public. The investor endorsed such a *hundi* with the Multani banker after the stipulated period and obtained interest. The Multani Bankers Association maintained that the *purja* business took an important function of savings mobilization with the small man who was unwilling or unable to deal with a bank (SGIB 1971: 26). This business was discontinued because the income-tax authorities no longer accepted the genuineness of this kind of sale. Since the dealing in *darshani hundis* was restricted by the financial authorities, too,[6] many indigenous-style bankers moved from ninety-day *hundis* to installment credit operations.

In contrast to many indigenously developed bankers, Multani bankers are pure bankers. As long as it was lucrative, they preferred the usance *hundis* to demand *hundis*, in spite of the stamp duties involved for the former. They had realized that it was exactly this stamp which gave their notes a higher degree of authority and allowed them to discount them at banks.

Every borrower obtains a maximum limit which is checked and revised every quarter of the year. Since most customers are traders and small- and medium-scale producers, most loans are used for investment purpose, although Multani bankers do not explicitly ask for the loan purpose. Many families run two or three firms. In the case of large-scale loans Multani bankers share the financial risk. This caution in their dealings has generally prevented financial difficulties if a borrower defaults.

For the Multani business, close contact and knowledge of the customers' business standing is very important. In Bombay and some other places, this closeness cannot be maintained, so that the Multani bankers operate through brokers. Most of them originate from Shikapur, too. These brokers who often specialize in a specific branch propose a potential borrower as a client and inform the Multani banker of his financial standing. Some of them are guarantee brokers,[7] others information brokers only.

In recent years some brokers developed their own independent business. They collect and accumulate idle funds from various sources and lend them to a smaller number of other sources. One can distinguish full-time and part-time financial brokers, ranging from those who work with large amounts on the intercorporate call money market and combine stock brokerage with brokerage of other financial commodities, others who work with fairly small sums in the cloth market or grain and jute market.[8]

---

[6] Panjabi (1961) reported for the early 1960s that the number of banks which were interested in dealing with *hundis* was small, due to highly regulated formal finance in post-colonial India which largely required the banks to borrow from the Reserve Bank against government securities during the busy season and to prefer loan applications from big industrial firms. By then Multanis paid themselves seven percent interest at the banks and took twelve percent interest from their clients. Taking into consideration stamp costs, brokerage, etc. customers had to pay well over 13 percent. Compared with other informal credit sources, which take 18 to 24 percent, the interest is rather low. Compared with bank rates to which some of their clients also have access, the rate is high.

[7] Interestingly, this broker position is similar to the *compradore* position of particular indigenous-style bankers themselves during the colonial period.

[8] Timberg and Aiyar (1980) reported that an average part-time broker works with no more than Rs 5,000 to Rs 25,000 working capital. Full-time brokers work with a minimum of Rs 5 *lakh*, at 8.5 to 10 percent interest with a-half percent brokerage.

Gujarati Shroffs

The Gujarati Shroffs, too, have a long-established banking tradition, and their mode of operation is very popular. Some of these firms called *pedhis* are 150 to 200 years old. While most of the 1,500 Ahmedabad firms are pure indigenous-style banks, the 3,500 Bombay firms combine banking with commission agency business for the marketing of agricultural produce and crops. Associations are the Gujarati Shroffs Association in Ahmedabad and the Bombay Shroffs Association. These perform key disciplinary functions of the members, such as penalizing their members and setting maximum rates of interest. On the whole, they are less organized than the Multani bankers.

The Gujarati Shroffs provide business which in many respects is analogous to modern banking: receiving deposits on current and fixed accounts, advancing money on call or for fixed periods on security or on personal credit, arranging for remittance of funds by issuing and collecting *darshani hundis*, acting as commission agents and financiers for certain products, and so on.

The pure bankers among them accept deposits and provide clean and secured advances. They issue *hundis* to customers against payment in cash or on credit for transferring money from one center to another, and for the purchase of goods they offer their customers sight *hundis* drawn on their or other Gujarati Shroffs' firms. They also honor *hundis* drawn on their customers for the delivery of goods.

The merchant-bankers combine commission agency business with banking. The former business was taken up because commercial banks grew significantly and the Indian financial laws increasingly restricted the *hundi* business. This supports my argument that, in the long run, indigenous-style bankers came to specialize in finance if this activity generated sufficiently high profits but differentiated their business again with the decline of indigenous-style banking. Commission agents are either purchasing or sales commission agents. The former purchase and deliver goods on credit to up-country customers according to order, and these repay the credit when they sell the delivered goods. The *shroffs* charge a certain commission plus extra charges and an interest rate.[9] The selling commission agents advance money for up to 80 percent value of goods on railway receipts of their up-country clients, sell the goods once delivered, and remit the balance between selling price and advances minus the commission charge and other charges to their customers. Commission agents-cum-bankers facilitate the flow of goods from centers of production to remote centers of consumption and from centers of primary production to urban centers. Different firms have specialized in different product lines. Most firms are partnership concerns. Large enterprises have more than 30 branches. In addition *shroffs* have arrangements of reciprocal accommodation for the acceptance and payment of *hundis*. This organizational form (branches and reciprocal accommodation) permits commission agency, exchange and arbitrage operations, and the raising and lending of funds in those places where they are idle and needed respectively.

---

[9] These rates amounted to 12 percent p.a. plus 0.5 to 0.75 percent of the value of the goods plus freight and handling charges in the early 1970s.

The SGIB (1971) reported a number of accounts per firm ranging from 50 to 3,000, while one big firm had around 15,000 clients all over India. The firm's capital consists of its own capital plus deposits from the public and interborrowing, whereas bank borrowing is hardly used. Deposit rates ranged from four to six percent for current deposits, six to eight percent for savings accounts, and ten to eleven percent for fixed term deposits. These interest rates were more attractive than those of commercial banks which did not pay interest at all for current deposits and an average rate of five percent for other deposits.

Characteristic of the Gujarati Shroffs is their own call money market, comparable to the inter-bank call-money market. This market efficiently allocates idle resources of one Gujarati Shroff on the demand of another and enables the necessary liquidity of firms for short-term demands of their customers. The rates in this call money market are determined and reconsidered every month by the Gujarati Shroffs Association and react strongly to seasonal changes of demand. During the investigations of the SGIB (1971), the rate for call deposits was 10.5 percent. In addition, the Gujarati Shroffs have reduced their overhead cost to a minimum and run a branch with four or five persons, and no more than 20 in the case of large firms. Bad debts are said to amount to no more than ten percent of the net profits.

Due to the decline in *darshani hundi* business resulting from government legislation, some Gujarati firms run a business which is similar to the Multani bankers. Each firm has 300 to 400 customers, and business also takes place through brokers. In the early 1970s, credit limits ranged from Rs 2,500 for small traders to Rs 5,000 for larger customers. Since both Multani and Gujarati Shroffs operate in Bombay and various other places in the same business lines, this might result in competition which reduces the interest rates.

Nattukottai Chettiar and Kallidaikurichy Brahmins

These two banking communities which are involved in similar operations both have their days of indigenous-style banking behind them, due to structural change, a regulated financial system in India and competition from the Multani Shroffs as well as commercial and cooperative banks in their territory.

The Nattukottai Chettiar had the most elaborate branch networks, but interestingly outside India. It was largely set within the British colonial context. Since they were heavily involved in the finance of agriculture, they were called 'moneylenders' which, to my mind, under-estimates their importance as financial intermediaries and ignores the international aspect of their activities in Ceylon, Burma, Malaya, Singapore and, to a lesser extent, Mauritius, Indo-China and Sumatra. In India, the Nattukottai Chettiar operated in the Tamil Nadu Districts of Madurai, Ramnad, Trichinopoly and Tanjore. The Kallidaikurichy Brahmin bankers, on the other hand, operated mostly in the Tinnevelly District. In addition to agricultural finance, both castes were involved in *hundi* business, the acceptance of current and fixed deposits, the honoring of checks, the provision of safekeeping facilities and acting as pawnbrokers of gold and ornaments.

Both groups organized business on the basis of joint families, and each firm was an entity in itself. However, strong community solidarity and mutual help accounted for their economic success at the same time. While the wealthier among the Nattukottai Chettiar operated their family or partnership firms, the less wealthy were employed as agents, with a salary and share in the profit. The extensive agency system of the Nattukottai Chettiar is characteristic of their business. The old Chettiar firms based on *hundi* business are said to be practically non-existent. The remaining Nattukottai Chettiar banking firms provide finance to small traders and artisans, and the business of most firms has changed from proprietary concerns to partnership concerns.

A category apart from the Nattukottai indigenous-style bankers are the numerous Chettiar pawnbrokers (see Table 4), most of whom belong to sub-castes other than the Nattukottai Chettiar. A detailed account of the latter was provided elsewhere (Schrader 1992, 1995).

Marwaris

Marwaris have been seen as the most important commercial caste of Western and Northern India. Being largely engaged in moneylending and crop dealing during the colonial period, the most successful became industrial entrepreneurs in eastern India who, by way of financing British firms, eventually took over British shares and even whole enterprises. One section of them, which has been often overlooked, were the Marwari *kayas*, who were and still are the private bankers of Assamese tea plantations. Another financial branch in Calcutta and Madras specialized in the discounting of commercial papers, checks, post-dated checks, truck receipts, and so on (see Timberg 1978; Schrader 1994b: Appendix II).

Another less important group of indigenous-style bankers, mentioned by Timberg and Aiyar (1980), are the Rastogis from U.P. who, like the remaining Chettiar bankers, finance small traders and artisans.

Having described the most important castes of indigenous-style bankers in contemporary India thus far, Timberg and Aiyar (1980) provided estimates for the late 1970s (see Table 4). To provide some additional data from the late 1970s, Multanis received Rs 3 to 6 *crore*[10] in bank refinance and had Rs 7,5 *crore* in deposits. Gujarati bankers had as many as Rs 800 crore deposits. They paid 7.5 percent on current accounts and up to 12 percent on longer term deposits. Gujarati pure bankers' annual *hundi* turnover in Bombay was Rs 1,000 *crore*, of bankers and commission agents Rs 600 *crore*. Of the Chettiar who are pawnbrokers, 25 percent of their lending was for commercial purposes; and the bankers among the Chettiar held Rs 250 *crore* deposits. Among other things the bankers refinance pawnbroker lending. Rastogi bankers had roughly Rs 55 *crore* in deposits on which they paid 12-20 percent deposit rates. They lending rates of 18-24 percent mentioned were for secured loans only, while rates for unsecured ones were much higher (Timberg and Aiyar 1980).

---

[10] British-Indian, 10 million.

Tab. 4: Volume and Rates of Credit in Indian Informal Urban Credit Markets

Caste	No. of firms	Credit extended (Rs crore)	Lending rates (Percent p.a.)
Shikapuri, or Multani Bankers			
- Local association members	550	60.0	21-37
- Non-members	650	65.0	21-120
- Brokers	550	125.0	21-120
Marwaris (Madras only)	100	10.4	28-44
Gujarati Bankers			
- Pure bankers	1,500	860.0	average 18
- Bankers/commission agents	3,500		average 18
Chettiar			
- Pure bankers	2,500	380.0	18-30
- Pawnbrokers	40,000	1,250.0	18-30
Rastogi Bankers	500	100.0	18-24

Source: Timberg and Aiyar (1980: 280); estimated figures. Selected data.

Finance Corporations

To clarify the term 'finance corporations' (which are often called 'finance companies'), such institutions collect savings from the public by providing high interest[11] and lend them to commercial customers or even speculate in risky ventures. Many of the owners of such companies have their origins in indigenous-style banking, and the difference to such bankers or financial brokers is often only a legal distinction of registration. Timberg and Aiyar (1980) assumed that in the late 1970s such companies numbered more than 2,000 in India. They are involved in financing retail and wholesale trade, agriculture and hire-purchase agreements for used cars. Furthermore, such companies discount and collect remittances and commercial papers, maintain deposit accounts, provide checks and run *chit* funds (commercialized rotating savings and credit associations). The financial development towards finance and investment companies has been observed all over the world as an urban phenomenon.

8.1.4. The Relation of Urban Formal and Informal Finance

Contrary to the commonly assumed hypothesis that informal credit is accessible quite easily and quickly, Timberg and Aiyar (1980: 259) maintained that, with the exception of metropolitan financial markets, informal loans are more difficult to obtain. An advantage is that urban informal lending takes place in many cases without any collateral. Some of the negative aspects of urban informal finance are the usually higher interest rates, the brief lending period and the essentially fixed terms of repayment.

---

[11] Nayar (1982) reported that the differences of effective deposit rates of finance corporations and commercial banks amounted to 6.7 percent for one-year deposits to more than around 20.5 percent for five-year deposits.

Most larger enterprises, which also have access to bank credit, too, make use of mixed formal and informal finance.

Most of the informal loans in urban areas are aimed at trade and industries (see Tables 4 and 5). Gujarati Shroffs predominantly finance wholesale trade in agricultural goods and craft work commodities, while Shikapuris Shroffs provide loans to a wide range of trades and industries. The Rastogis and Chettiar finance smaller traders and artisans. Shikapuri brokers and others finance a wide range of activities depending on the market in which they engage. Special demands on the informal markets come from exporters, builders and restaurants who have no physical security to offer. None of the groups provides agricultural credit to avoid conflict with moneylenders' acts.

Tab. 5: Destination of Informal Financial Market Funds (percent)

Financial Agents	Trade	Exports	Small-scale Industries	Large Industries	Other
Multani	32	20	16	7	25
Gujarati	60	10	5	10	15
Chettiar	45	10	5	20	20
Rastogi	55	12			33
Pawnbrokers	22		5		73
Finance Companies	40		8		52

Source: Timberg and Aiyar (1980: 295

Film finance is a very risky business and relies mainly on black money (estimates are around Rs 750 *crore*, of which two third is said to be black money).[12] More than 500 brokers, among them Chettiar, participate in this type of finance and take interest of 36 to 60 percent and sometimes even up to 120 percent. Most informal lenders are not involved in such risky business.

A break-down of the financing of particular branches showed that 50 percent of finance for the wholesale cloth trade and 20 percent of the grain trade in Calcutta came from informal sources. In other branches the share was 15 to 30 percent. A typical borrower had Rs 100,000 in assets. Loans per person ranged from the occasional Rs 100 (small shopkeepers) to Rs 1,000,000. The minimum loans of industrial firms were around Rs 100,000.

The Report of the Asian Development Bank (Ghate 1992) provided the following picture of finance for India in 1987.

---

[12] According to Sundaram and Pandit (1984: 676), the informal credit market consists of 'legal' (or, to be more precise, legitimate) informal institutions and illegal, black market institutions, the latter of which take lower interest rates since they operate with money which has been illegally obtained. This informal black money market is largely a response to government regulations, such as income and value-added taxation, restrictions on foreign exchange and import-export business, and so on. The suppliers and demanders are mainly businessmen who also have access to formal finance.

Tab. 6: Sources of Funds of Selected Branches in India (1987)

Sector	Own Funds	Formal Credit	Informal Credit
Road construction	62	6	32
Garment exports	31	26	43
Film finance	5	–	95
Powerloom units	43	10	47
Textile trade units	42	10	48
Housing finance of households	66	20	14

Source: Ghate (1992: 110)

Considering the costs of funds, the interest rate in the informal financial market is generally higher than in the formal one. The interest rate consists of the cost of funds, the risk allowance and monopoly profit. These components vary from one lender to another if not regulated by the particular association (see Ghatak 1976) or the environment. The SGIB (1971) mentioned the following factors which generally determine the cost of credit and the availability of funds:

"(1) elements of risk involved in lending, (2) credit-worthiness of the borrower, (3) nature of the security and also the liquidity of the security, (4) ratio of owned to borrowed funds with the lender, (5) site and period of the loan, (6) monopolistic and monopsonistic situations of the traders-cum-bankers, and (7) elasticity of demand for funds coupled with inelastic and limited supply of funds. The price of capital in the unorganized market is also conditioned by the ability of indigenous banking agencies to (a) utilize and invest available funds, and (b) recover capital losses incurred through bad debts" (SGIB 1971: 61).

Timberg and Aiyar (1980: 291) calculated the transaction costs of different formal and informal financial agents and institutions, which averaged between 3.5 and 5.5 percent. For small loans they are considerably higher. Comparatively speaking, the borrowing transaction costs of informal credit are lower because banks in India demand high extra charges, and a loan provision often involves a bribe.

Urban informal financial markets in India are strongly segmented in that they are localized and even sub-localized. Urban informal financial agents and institutions lend to and borrow from a limited number of parties, usually sharing the same occupational background, whereas particular banking castes have specialized in the finance of particular branches. Due to market intransparency and occupational segmentation, there is only a limited inter-market flow, so that the allocation of funds by indigenous-style bankers is not necessarily the most efficient one if seen from the national perspective. Exceptions are the contemporary Gujarati and Marwari networks who finance long-range trade.

Summarizing Timberg and Aiyar (1980), in the late 1970s the lending rates of indigenously developed bankers and brokers in India ranged from 18-24 percent p.a. for larger established traders and 24-36 percent for smaller artisans and traders. Checks and bills were discounted at 18-24 percent. Call money loans were sometimes provided for not more than 12 percent, while black money was available from 12 to 24 percent depending on the area. Commercial banks' lending rates were normally between 13 and 16 percent.

While banks take interest once the account is back in balance, Shikapuri bankers and some other lenders take interest in advance, which is disadvantageous for the borrower. Penal interest is uncommon except in hire-purchase financing. In some cases interest in paid on the basis of the initial loan amount and is not reduced as installments are repaid. In other cases they accord with the bank standard on the basis of actual liabilities. Additional fees that are common are brokerage (one half to two percent, whereby brokers do not guarantee the loan), charity charges and stamp duties. They may raise the cost of a loan up to six percent and are common with loans from commercial banks too.

Table 7 presents bank rates and bazaar bill rates in Bombay and Calcutta from 1929-1974, and in Madras from 1960-1974.

Tab. 7: Money Rates in India, 1929-1974 (percent)

| | Bank Rate | | Informal bill | | | | | |
| | | | Calcutta | | Bombay | | Madras | |
Year	High	Low	High	Low	High	Low	High	Low
1929	6.5	0.25	12.00	10.0	11.00	5.25		
1934	3.5	0.75	8.00	6.00	6.75	3.00		
1939	2.25	0.25	7.00	6.00	6.75	5.25		
1945	1.00	0.25	7.00	6.00	5.25	5.25		
1950	1.25	0.50	12.00	10.00	9.00	8.25		
1960	4.00	4.00	13.00	9.50	12.00	9.00	13.92	12.00
1965	6.00	6.00	15.00	15.00	15.00	12.00	19.80	17.40
1970	6.00	5.00	13.50	13.50	15.00	15.00	21.00	21.00
1974	9.00	7.00	19.50	18.00	21.00	17.00	28.80	21.00

Sources: Data for 1929-53: Cirvante (1956:35);
Data for 1960-74: Goyal (1979: 446 f.)

The money structure in these different informal financial markets and the formal one, however, is linked in various ways. Credit supply in the informal financial markets, for example, is very inelastic, and seasonally increasing demand can be satisfied only by diverting funds from the formal into the informal financial market. If credit contraction occurs in the formal financial market, the additional demand cannot be satisfied by the informal. A consequence is an analogous fluctuation in both formal and informal interest rates.

Politicians either aimed at regulating and suppressing the informal financial market (through moneylenders acts and other financial laws) or tried to subject indigenous-style bankers to the control of the Reserve Bank of India and link them with commercial banks. Both the 1929-30 Banking Commission and the SGIB (1971) promoted the linkage concept.

The linkage discussion, which started in the 1930s and was quite unsuccessful because indigenous-style bankers and their associations resented having to subject themselves to the control of the central bank (while the latter resented having to cooperate with the former), receded into the background with the nationalization of the major commercial banks and their expansion into particular priority sectors like small-scale industry and agriculture, the former being one target group of indigenous-style bankers. The recent report of the Asian Development Bank (Ghate 1992: 198ff.), however, suggested that the sound practices of indigenous-style bankers should exempt them from regulations and allow them to take deposits. It claimed that sufficient control of their business is exercised by their own organizations.

The small-scale and medium-scale trade sectors are still not adequately provided with formal finance. Hence, urban informal financial intermediation of indigenous-style bankers is still required for some time to come.

8.2. Contemporary Rural Finance

8.2.1. Finance Policy

In independent India, the financial system was until recently heavily regulated by the government and the Reserve Bank of India. This policy was accompanied by mounting efforts to eliminate informal finance by way of regional and national legislation. According to Balamohandas et al. (1991), the early development plans largely neglected the agrarian sector. They were designed to develop infrastructure and industries. Secondary-sector development was considered to provide the impetus for self-sustained growth. As a consequence, the finance of agriculture was largely left to informal finance.[13] Only with the onset of the Green Revolution did an awareness of the primary sector and backward areas increase.

The government applied a multi-agency approach to rural finance. In addition to the promotion of cooperatives, it encouraged commercial banks to offer more credit to priority sectors. In 1969 the government nationalized fourteen commercial banks, and six at a second stage in 1980. Thus the government systematically built up these banks' infrastructure in more remote regions. The number of offices rose from around 8,350 in 1969 to more than 42,000 in 1983, of which more than half were in rural regions and 9,000 in semi-urban ones. To put it another way, the share of rural branch offices increased by 32 percent from 22 percent in 1969 to almost 54 percent in 1983. The total outstanding advances increased eight-fold from 1968 to 1981, the share of agricultural loans amounting to 2.2 percent and 16.7 percent, respectively.

Savings mobilization was also encouraged. Between 1969 and 1982 the credit-deposit ratio in rural regions increased from 37.2 to 58.7 percent. However, as Bouman (1989) pointed out, due to the policy of interest rating, savings returns to borrowers are very low. This lack of incentive to maintain a savings account at a bank has led them turn to alternative private financial institutions which provide higher returns or

---

[13] In 1951 the All India Rural Credit Survey maintained that 93 percent of rural finance was provided by informal financial agents.

investments in gold and other valuables. On the whole, it should be clear that the lower agrarian strata do not yet have sufficient access to commercial banks. One main criticism is that rural bank branches are advised to transfer savings to urban regions, instead of increasing credit supply where the savings have been raised.

The Banking Commission thus raised doubts whether commercial banks could efficiently provide rural credit and suggested the introduction of a new category of rural banks in remote regions. In 1975 the Regional Rural Banks (RRBs) were instituted to provide credit for the weaker and neglected sectors of the rural economy in a rural environment.

In 1983 the number of RRBs was 142 (sponsored by 22 commercial banks and one State Cooperative Bank). From 1976 to 1983 their deposits and outstanding advances increased considerably (a 39-fold increase in accounts and 87-fold increase in amounts outstanding).[14] In 1983 the share of agricultural credit amounted to 44 percent, followed by retail trade, small business and self-employment (23 percent) and crop loans (17 percent). However, the loans to rural artisans and village and cottage industries are underrepresented amounting to less than six percent (Balamohandas et al. 1991: 1-55).

The quantitative extension of formal finance, however, caused qualitative concerning financial security and rentability. In 1993 the government banks' balance of payment was deficitary. While for 1991/92 they had published profits amounting to Rp. 800 *crore*, the following year exhibited deficits of Rp. 3,370 *crore*, because a large part of the banks' assets was 'lost', 'dubious' or simply 'non-performing'. The reorganization of the banking system has been estimated to cost Rp.12,000 *crore*. The main issues are pursued: the adoption of international guidelines of banking and the deregulation of formal finance (DSE 1994).

From the point of view of total debts, rural India is no longer the crucial problem area. From the early 1970s until 1982 the share of rural informal finance in India declined from three quarters of total debts outstanding to less than two fifths (Ghate 1992: 63). However, this does not mean that indebtedness has ceased to be an issue.

8.2.2. Rural Informal Credit Suppliers

For an understanding of rural finance, scholars (for example, Harriss 1981, 1983; Jones 1994) have emphasized that it is impossible to separate the financial from the commodity markets, since both are directly linked in various ways. In analyzing rural financial markets, one method of field research that takes these links into consideration is the identification of all those agents and agencies in a particular setting (village, region) which are in one way or another involved in finance. The majority of these are commercial-cum-financial ones.

The literature on rural finance in India is extensive and its analysis deserves a study of its own. In the context of changing financial landscapes, I shall largely confine

---

[14] Advances increased from Rs 711 *lakh* for 98,400 accounts to Rs 62,400 *lakh* and 3,845,000 accounts.

myself to some recent studies and surveys. In addition to formal rural financial institutions, such as banks or, depending on the legal definition, cooperatives, surveys and case studies from India report the existence of a variety of rural informal agents and institutions, such as landlords, agricultural moneylenders, professional moneylenders, traders and crop dealers, pawnbrokers, friends and relatives, and voluntary savings and credit associations, with a widely fluctuating range of importance depending on the area.

According to the Report of the Asian Development Bank (Ghate 1992) in 1982, landlord-lenders had on average a market share of ten percent in informal finance, agricultural moneylenders of 22 percent, professional moneylenders of 21 percent, traders-cum-lender of nine percent, friends and relatives of 23 percent and others of 15 percent.

Fig. 2: Types of Moneylenders in Rural India, 1982

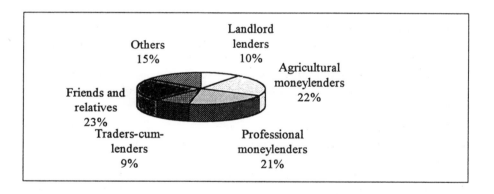

Data from Ghate (1992: 45, FN 2)

The most widespread credit instrument of village moneylenders is the promissory note, which is defined by the Negotiable Instruments Act, Section 4, as

> "an instrument in writing containing an unconditional undertaking signed by the maker to pay a certain sum of money to or to the order of a certain person or to the bearer of the instrument" (quoted by the SGIB 1971: 44).

Promissory notes are either payable on demand or after a certain period. Another common instrument is the bond or *dastavez*.

> "Bonds are written on stamped legal forms and are duly executed. All the terms and conditions of the advance agreed upon, such as the rate of interest, penalty for default, etc., are explicitly written in the bond. Bonds are used where it is considered safer to have all the terms of the advance clearly spelt out in writing. Where the borrowers are illiterate, the lender maintains 'bahis' or stamp books in which he obtains either the thumb impression or the signature of the borrower as evidence of the debt. However, it is not customary to mention the terms and conditions of the advance which are settled orally" (SGIB 1971: 44).

A third common instrument in rural lending is the mortgage or *rahan* of landed property, which is either simple or usufructuary. The loan commonly amounts to half of the market value of the land, and the interest is lower than in the case of promissory notes. A simple mortgage is allowed to run a maximum of 12 years.

Common among borrowing traders is the installment credit (*kist*) on daily or monthly repayment. The first installment is often reduced from the principal.

A relatively large part of informal credit is usually classified as consumptional. Consumption purposes are categorized as

- subsistence, emergencies (incl. medical expenditure) and other essential purposes;

- housing, education and purposes such as emigration;

- the purchase of consumer durable goods; and

- lavish, ostentatious or conspicuous consumption.

The latter is often associated with high expenses for social occasions. In India in particular life-cycle rituals such as marriages and funerals are a very costly affair and may indeed cause the indebtedness of a household, since the expenses are multiples of annual incomes. A study from Bihar on reasons for borrowing, for example, showed that marriage and funeral expenses accounted for 51 percent of all loans (Mundle 1979: 108).

The above categorization is not very meaningful because the hidden purpose of borrowing is in many cases an investment. For example, emigration is a tool for income generation, a bicycle at least saves public transport fares or may even constitute a means of production (for hire), expenses for education are human capital formation and even food can be considered as reproducing manpower. Furthermore, expenditures on subsistence of the family may reproduce the labour force. Ghate (1988) introduced a useful distinction between productive loans, consumer loans and productive consumer loans.

The recent study of the Asian Development Bank (Ghate 1992: 106) fell back on the 'standard' classification. It counted an average of 24 percent production loans, 65 percent consumer loans (including expenditures on housing construction and repairs, which together formed about 37 percent of total informal credit, and 57 percent of consumption credit), and 11 percent payment of past debts.

From the perspective of a borrower, such classifications make even less sense because he or she does not distinguish between such purposes. Another often neglected fact is that borrowers tend to combine different types of formal and informal loans in order to maximize their credit volume or maintain different credit lines. Borrowers

"tend to build around themselves protective networks of security, stretching from relatives and friends to patron and landlord, trader, shopkeeper, priest, fellow artisan. Such networks are necessary for sheer survival. In the context of these networks much community-based credit has social undertones and is generated on a basis of reciprocity" (Bouman 1989: 92-3).

Traders and crop merchants lend in cash or kind. They usually do not take collateral and may discriminate against some customers because of high demand. Barbara Harriss (1983) reported that the loan amounts are medium scale, interest rates remarkably consistent and not much above the legal ceiling (which was 12 percent at that time in Tamil Nadu). Repayment is normally in kind and takes place after the harvest. A delay in repayment for more than one month after the harvest (20 percent of the sample) gives rise to an increase in the interest rate.

A large number of traders and crop merchants can survive in the market only by providing credit to small farmers at low interest, and this is generally explained by the securement of agricultural produce.

Pawn brokerage is very common in India and practiced by every lender who takes physical or legal possession of movable property. Whether a financial agent is a moneylender, a trader-cum-lender or a pawnbroker is very often a matter of definition, and the declaration of a business as a pawnshop only a legal distinction.

Pawn brokerage has continued to flourish in India, probably as a result of the steep rise in gold prices, and is very often combined with goldsmithery, gold refining and jewelry. Lending on pledged valuables was part and parcel of the ancient profession of moneylenders. Pawnbrokers provide smaller loans than moneylenders and the latter do not even tend to lend such small sums. According to Harriss (1981: 166, quoted by Bouman 1989: 76ff.), until 1965 pawn brokerage/moneylending in North Arcot (Tamil Nadu) was primarily in the hands of Marwaris. Thereupon many newcomers from Tamil Nadu entered the business. These are mostly part-time lenders with a regular salary from their primary professions, such as officials, teachers, and clerks. Better-off farmers also tend to operate pawnshops. The increase in non-professional moneylending and pawn brokerage is, according to Harriss, a reaction to an increasing need for small agricultural loans. In Harriss' (1983) sample from Tamil Nadu, pawnbrokers charged an interest rate of up to 25 percent which was higher than bank interest charges. Sivakumar (1978: 847f.) reported of Marwari pawnshops that interest rates vary according to the pawn.[15]

Overall the number of licensed and unlicensed pawnbrokers in India increased during the past decades. Bouman (1989) took a particular look at informal pawn brokerage in Sangli District of Maharashtra, where this increase was stopped by the Debt Relief Act in Maharashtra State from 1976. Various moneylenders and pawnbrokers closed their shops or concealed lending activities behind a commercial front. This dried up a credit supply for poorer people.

The Reserve Bank of India fixed interest rates for licensed pawnbrokers. These rates, however, are unrealistic. Privileged borrowers, like farmers, will obtain preferential rates of nine percent only, while the pawnbroker has to pay 17 percent at the bank. To evade this act, the pawnbroker simply changed the profession of the borrower in his book and charged the maximum of 18 percent. In addition, many pawnbrokers make covert extra charges of two to three percent per month or even more for short-term loans (Bouman 1989: 91).

---

[15] For gold, the rate was 2.5 to 3 percent per month; for silver, 4 percent; for brass and copper, 6 percent; for durable goods, such as watches or radios, up to 10 percent (quoted by Bouman 1989: 79).

8.2.3.   The Relation between Rural Formal and Informal Finance

Considering the relation between formal and informal rural finance, it is obvious that formal finance has not substituted the informal one to date. Scholars take controversial points of view of the relation of rural formal and informal finance. A number of studies consider both formal and informal finance competitive. In her case study from Tamil Nadu, Harriss (1983), for example, found active competition among all the informal institutions and lenders as well as formal ones, and Iqbal (1988) added that the existence of banks in villages reduces moneylenders' interest rates.

Singh (1989: 293ff.) came to a similar conclusion by analyzing the data of an unpublished indebtedness survey from Kinnaur District/Himachal Pradesh in 1983.[16] No nominal interest of formal and informal sources was higher than 18.75 percent per annum. Formal credit (government, cooperatives, banks) ranged among the lower (3.13 to 12.49 percent), informal credit (landlords, agricultural moneylenders, traders, temple lending) among the higher interest rates (9.37-18.74 percent) (Singh 1989: 298, 202), whereas the standard deviation was rather low.

In Kinnaur the importance of village moneylenders has decreased in the course of time. However, Singh emphasizes that this type of moneylending carries no social stigma because village deities are also involved in moneylending. The existing moneylenders do not overexploit their customers. Interest rates reported are moderate (up to 25 percent until 1948, then usually 12.5 percent), which is partly due to legislation.

Worth mentioning is the informal lending of village deities (*devtas*) and their managing committees, because it has some characteristic features of traditional rotating credit associations. Singh (1989: 312ff.) argued that this type of lending did and still does not aim to acquire tribal property and to reduce borrowers to landless servitude, which I consider the aim of a number of landlord lenders and large agriculturalists. Rather it is to increase their portfolio for further lending. The lending procedure starts with the fixation of a date for loan distribution by the managing committee, which consists of influential villagers. Those demanding a loan apply at the secretary of the temple committee who writes a list. These applications are discussed and decided in an open meeting by the villagers. The rate of interest is announced before loan distribution.[17] Decisions are confirmed by the deity via a medium. At least ten to twenty

---

[16] The most popular credit agencies in the sample of 100 households were the government (23.53 percent of the loans) and the commercial banks (23.53 percent of all loans). Interesting is the complete absence of any non-local professional moneylender – a factor which Singh explains by competition of other formal and informal lenders and institutions. Most local moneylenders were landowners (23.43 percent). Other important informal credit suppliers were the *devtas*, village deities (17.65 percent), followed by traders (2.94 percent). On a whole informal credit sources accounted for almost half of the number of loan cases. Close to 50 percent of all loans were obtained on personal security, 27 percent on surety, security of guarantee by a third party, 21 percent on mortgage of immovable property and 6 percent without security. Relating these data to loan size, the added-up maximum loan amount (42 percent) was provided against third-party guarantee, 33 percent against personal security, 24 percent on mortgages of immovable property and the rest without security (Singh 1989: 297).

[17] The rates of interest of the *devtas* seem to have been rather stable. Cash loans had to be repaid cash, grain loans in grain or in term of their cash equivalent. The traditional rate of interest was 25 percent per annum. In 1948 it was reduced to 12.5 percent and once again in the 1980s to 10 percent.

percent of the fund are kept away for running expenditures and emergency cases. Loan transactions are recorded without mention of the interest rate.

Another viewpoint considers both informal and formal finance as complementary since they finance different segments of society (see, for example, Jones 1994). Studies taking this position found that informal credit supply by friends and relatives, pawnbrokers and traders-cum-lenders becomes less important the bigger the size of farm. Pawnbrokers lend to the poorer section of society, while small farmers borrow from traders-cum-lenders. Full-time moneylenders, on the other hand, are increasingly concentrating in the towns, and lend to larger cultivators, traders and small producers.

Roth (1983) analyzed rural credit markets in North India, and his sample survey produced quite different results from Harriss' (1983) rural financial market, that featured lively competition between formal and informal finance. In Roth's case the market was very inelastic. Most sample credit suppliers were large-scale farmers-cum-lenders. Moneylending is a very attractive form of investment for this category of lenders. They lend cash and in kind, and in many cases occupy key positions in the village administration. Typical interest rates charged for in kind loans were 50 percent of the amount for paddy consumption and 100 percent for seed paddy, to be repaid after the harvest (irrespective of the time of borrowing). 75 percent was taken for a mixed in kind loan for consumption paddy and seed paddy. The interest rates of the different moneylenders were generally the same. Factors, such as the bargaining power or land ownership of the debtor, had hardly any influence on the interest rate. Fluctuations in market prices for paddy did not affect the interest rates. Only cash loans were calculated on the basis of duration of credit and normally calculated per month. Cash loans as well as interest were principally repaid in cash. Cash loans in Roth's survey varied considerably from zero to 300 percent per year, depending on the supplier. General interest rates, here calculated on an annual basis, were 36, 60, 72, 75, 120, 150, 180 and 300 percent (ibid: 39ff.).

Roth (1983: 50ff.) compared the contemporary interest rates of Bihar and West Bengal with those collected by British civil servants and missionaries in 1827. He concluded that there was no significant change in the conditions of traditional village credit. Neither market integration and formal credit competition, nor specific acts against usury (for example, the Bihar Moneylender's Act of 1938 with a legal maximum of 12 percent) had an impact upon the actual interest rates of moneylenders.[18]

A challenging hypothesis was offered by Gregory (1988). With field work in Bastar District, Central India, this neo-Marxist scholar took the view that formal finance may even support the rise of moneylending and rural indebtedness. It is commonly assumed that World Bank medium-term and long-term productive loans will increase the efficiency of production and enable the agriculturalists to escape the clutches of traditional moneylenders. However, the operation of the World Bank-initiated Land Mortgage Bank produced just the opposite results. Instead of abolishing poverty through

---

[18] Rothermund criticized Roth's observations. He argued, Roth did not realize that the interest rates mentioned were only conventional ones and not the effective ones. Due to the fact that a moneylender wants to keep his debtor alive and to continue the flow of interest he is willing to reduce the interest after a bad harvest and to increase it once again after a good one (personal communication).

increased efficiency in production (from which the loans should be repaid), the bank caused an upsurge in village-based moneylending. Due to external effects and an unadjusted World Bank policy,[19] the borrowers are often unable to increase their productivity. For a timely repayment of the bank loan, they have to borrow from the moneylender.

Development agencies provide loans for productive purposes only. However, there is little demand in the village for such loans. Consequently, Gregory argued that such institutions have to create a demand. They sell their 'product' by raising unrealistic expectations among the villagers.[20] The inability to repay such unadjusted loans is one important reason for landlessness and poverty for Gregory, and this is not generally the outcome of moneylending business, in spite of land mortgages. The reason for this is that, as long as the moneylender belongs to the village, the lender-borrower relations are not so much subject to the laws of the market, but to some extent still embedded in social obligations. I once again refer to my modified concept of embeddedness in which the degree of embeddedness of an interaction is determined by social structure and social distance.

Taking a look at the interest rates, Ghatak (1983) conducted a comparative analysis of rural interest rates of India in 1962-63, based on the data of the All India Debt and Investment Survey. He found much lower results than expected. The average interest rates in fourteen Indian states ranged from 8.65 to 29.19 percent only, a figure which was distorted by the high share of interest-free loans from friends and relatives (20-25 percent). Nevertheless, the proportion of loans above 40 percent was low.

Harriss (1992) summarized the findings of various scholars in various Indian regions which link certain production and exchange types to particular types of credit. Differences occur in the form of financial contract, in the market power of lender and borrower, in the segmentation of markets by locality group, crop and collateral, in class discrimination in the market, in unanticipated repercussions of policies, in production forms and in the commodities loaned and repaid.

8.2.4. Cost Components

Considering the composition of interest, four cost components have been discussed in the literature: (1) transaction costs; (2) opportunity costs; (3) risk costs; and (4) the degree of market imperfection or monopoly profit.

(1) Transaction costs

Both lenders and borrowers have to take transaction costs into consideration, whereby I shall restrict my discussion to the former, because I believe that most

---

[19] The World Bank, Gregory (1988) argued, applies unadjusted theories which regard capital in technical relation to production only and misinterpret socio-economic conditions and processes. Recent neo-Marxist anthropology (e.g. Seddon 1978), however, interprets capital in the context of social relationships.

[20] Indeed, I see a parallel to the assumption of British colonial policy that the peasant has to be educated to escape the 'vicious cycle of poverty'.

informal borrowers are probably not aware of the transaction costs. Lender transaction costs consist of: cost of information (which are often zero because the lender generally has a fixed clientele and hence experience of former transactions or obtains information by living in the neighborhood, while he is also informed of interest rates in other markets), administration, monitoring and the enforcement of loans. Administration costs are increased by the taking of collateral (safekeeping, documentation, etc.), which in turn reduces the costs of enforcement and the risk premium. Repayment takes place either automatically by a crop sale to the lender, by labour provision, installments, and so on, or collateral or social pressure make repayment probable. To sum up, the transaction costs of informal lenders are relatively small (Roth 1983; Ghate 1992). Mathematically considered transaction costs as a per centage of loan size decrease with the size of loans. The same relation probably exists between interest rate and loan duration because of the fixed cost nature of transaction costs.

(2) Opportunity costs

Generally considered, opportunity costs are the loss of returns from an alternative action compared with the chosen action. For moneylending, this concept means that in a rural setting the interest of moneylending has to be compared with other investment opportunities, such as in land, the maintenance of a savings account, and so on. Since lenders have different opportunities, their opportunity costs vary considerably. Singh (1968), for example, estimated these differences in a village to account for 70 percent.

(3) Risk premium

The theory of finance maintains that, in the same way as insurance companies, a lender charges a risk premium for every borrower to be compensated for any defaults. According to Ghate (1992: 146), in India the risk premium is generally low, which does not apply in other countries. It depends on the default rate, which in turn is related to risk-reducing mechanisms like information, credit rationing (excluding risky borrowers), the taking of collateral, and social or physical pressure. A mechanism which significantly reduces the risk is social pressure applied by informal lenders, such as the threat to villagers that they lose social prestige or caste disapproval, pressure by the village panchayats, fear of borrowers to lose their credit source, and so on. (Balamohandas et al. 1991: 3). Even physical pressure is reported in different case studies of India.

Other lending strategies to reduce the risk premium are to make smaller and shorter-term loans and lend for purposes which increase the ability to repay, such as income-generating activities. For example, Iqbal (1988) found that farmers residing in areas using the Green Revolution technology are charged lower interest rates by moneylenders, because agricultural development seems to lower the margin of risk in general.

Contrary to high default and low recovery rates among formal institutions, the defaulting of informal borrowers is comparatively low,[21] while the recovery rates of

---

[21] The reason is that borrowers use to combine formal and informal credit. As the interest rates of the latter use to be higher, the rationale of the borrowers is to first repay the informal loans.

informal lenders are less high because they often prefer a long period of interest payment to the quick recovery of the principal sum. The default rates of low-income borrowers are not necessarily higher (Iqbal 1988).

(4) Monopoly profits

While the concept of opportunity costs includes a certain 'reasonable' profit margin between chosen and second-best alternative, any profit exceeding the sum of transaction costs, opportunity costs and risk premium is an extra profit called 'monopoly profit'. Generally speaking, monopoly profit depends on the market situation. In highly competitive markets it tends to be low, while under monopolistic or oligopolistic conditions it may be higher.

Scholars' assessments of monopoly profit vary considerably. Results are mainly based on their assumptions. Bottomley (1983), Harriss (1983) and Singh (1983), for example, maintained that monopoly profit is quite low. Singh provided a microeconomic analysis with a case study from North India, showing that the high interest rates of moneylenders are largely a function of opportunity costs and risk costs. On his sample he calculated annual interest rates as ranging from 134 to 159 percent (average 143 percent), irrespective of any moneylenders' acts. The marginal value productivity of capital on the sampled Indian farms was very high, which engendered a high share of opportunity costs averaging 77 percent. The average costs of distribution constituted 21 percent of the principal. The risk costs amounted to an average of 36 percent. The average monopoly profit was thus 9 percent only. I ask myself how far such calculations make sense from the point of view of borrowers and lenders. From another point of view, the interest rates in less productive regions are nearly as high, but the opportunity costs in particular are considerably smaller. Here the main share is probably the monopoly profit.

On the other hand, Tun Wai (1953), Nisbet (1967) and Lipton (1976), by making somewhat different assumptions about default rates and reasonable rates of return, concluded that monopoly profit plays a substantial role in rural lending. Roth (1983) took up the same view. He considered the rural informal credit market as segmented into smaller, regionally limited markets in which each village moneylender has, socio-economically speaking, a monopoly-like position. Cooperatives, which are usually assumed to be an instrument to combat moneylending,[22] provide no real competition since the richer farmers-cum-moneylenders hold key positions in these institutions.

> "Thus, the grotesque situation arises that one and the same group of people guard over interests which pursue opposite objectives, since the cooperatives were primarily organized in order to curb the power of the moneylender. It is a paradoxical situation in which those people administer the institution which was created to eliminate them" (Roth 1983: 26).

---

[22] The All India Rural Credit Survey (1955) recommended the establishment of multi-purpose cooperatives. The government followed this recommendation and started promoting cooperatives in the later planning periods. In 1979-80 there were 27 State Cooperative Banks, 337 Central Cooperative Banks, and 95,000 Primary Agricultural Credit Societies (PACS), with 55 million members. However, the results of the cooperative movement are rather meager. The cooperatives are financially weak with high overdue rates and defaults, the administration is far from being efficient, and the coordination within the cooperative framework is poor (Balamohandas et al. 1991: 4-6).

The fragmentation into small credit markets of limited extent is useful for the lender to minimize risk by personal knowledge of and the possibility to exert pressure on the customer. From the borrower's point of view the credit market is also fragmented. He can only obtain personal credit from moneylenders who know him. If he provides a mortgage title, only moneylenders in the neighborhood who can make use of the right to cultivate the borrower's land would offer credit.

Roth (1983) came to conclude that the high interest rates in his study can only be explained with a high monopoly profit. However, the motive of lending of most farmers-cum-moneylenders is not only a high return per invested capital, but also to create social obligations in the form of mortgages and underpaid or unpaid labour of the debtors. Voluntary credit relations are based on mutual familiarity and the possibility of the borrower to obtain credit whenever needed. Involuntary commitments are debt liabilities which reduce the freedom and income opportunities of the debtor. Often 'an initially voluntary agreement can turn into a personal liability, which obliges the debtor to pay off his old debts and arrears of interest by manual labour on the farm of the creditor' (Roth 1983: 36). Sometimes the third generation after the initial borrower has to work on the fields of the creditor and has no chance of freeing himself from debt bondage.

The Asian Development Bank (Ghate 1992: 149ff.) distinguished between a competitive and a transparent part of informal-sector finance and the non-competitive, non-transparent part. The former functions relatively impersonally and is not interested in the personal attributes of borrowers since it relies on collateral as a substitute for information. It consists of moneylenders lending on a collateralized basis, pawnshops, finance companies, etc. The latter part of informal finance is based more upon personal information than on collateral. Under such conditions every lender has a non-overlapping, quasi-monopolistic position in which demand reacts very inelastically to interest rate changes because the customers rely on their moneylender for future loans. The market for non-collateral based borrowing seems to have a cellular structure with the cells centered around each lender, and each cell contains the number of potential borrowers on which the lender possesses information. Among the borrowers of each lender is a core group for whom switching to another lender is too costly (e.g. long-standing tenants or employees), surrounded by a fringe of borrowers who have potential access to another lender.

8.2.5. Conclusion

Continuing Bose's (1986) analysis of change in rural finance for India in the post-independence period, one can safely argue that:

- Between 1945 and 1960, specialized lenders regained some importance, due to legislative measures after independence preventing landlords and traders to lend.

- From the 1970s onward, a diversification of lenders has been observed: moneylenders and pawnbrokers, rich cultivators, input entrepreneurs, cash crop brokers and traders. The relative importance of specialized lenders, which have been increasingly controlled by the government, has decreased, while that of linked credit-transactions (such as between cash-crop merchants and cultivators) increased.

This analysis of change in rural finance shows that, although the number of specialized informal financial agents decreased with the enforcement of usury legislation, it works counter to the intended aim, in that it raises the risk premium and interest rates and restricts wider access to credit. Furthermore usury laws force lenders and borrowers to work secretly, which further fragmented sub-markets. The report of the Asian Development Bank (Ghate 1992: 161ff.) therefore recommended the abolition of usury laws, while it was proposed that the registration and licensing for purposes other than deposit taking be voluntary. It argued that instead of the categories legal/authorized and illegal/unauthorized, a distinction should be made between registered/licensed and unregistered/unlicensed intermediaries, and the public should be aware of the costs and benefits involved in dealing with each category.

Part III   INDONESIA

9. The Pre-Colonial and Colonial Economy

A review of the literature on the Dutch colonial period in Indonesia reveals that formal and informal finance were less prominent a topic than in colonial India. Nevertheless, two main issues can be identified: (a) the general question of monetization and credit in a dual economy; and (b) the matter of rural credit provided by moneylenders and, after 1900, additionally by public institutions. Before I consider these two particular issues, I shall provide an overview of the pre-colonial and colonial economies of Indonesia until the introduction of public finance to demonstrate how the situation differs from India.

9.1. The Pre-Colonial Period and the Heydays of the Dutch United East India Company

In contrast to the highly developed economy of medieval India, scholars described pre-colonial Indonesia as a largely agrarian society which consisted of more or less isolated communities of subsistence producers, living closely and harmoniously together under the supervision of the village headman. They were said to have enjoyed a high degree of institutional and economic self-sufficiency, living on communally owned land, while agricultural labour was organized along the principles of mutual assistance and reciprocity. Scholars maintained that such villages existed until at least 1800. Some scholars argued that such societies were trapped in the Asiatic mode of production, which prohibited socio-economic change, while others pointed to a very gradual, non-cumulative process of change. Both agreed that a transformation *sui generis* was impossible (Breman 1980: 10) and that an external stimulus was required.

Such a static subsistence society, romanticized by Schrieke (1966: 95), had 'little need of a medium of exchange'. Fruin (1938: 107) expressed it the other way around, in that he saw such a society hampered in its development by religious and traditional values, by its pattern of redistribution of wealth and by its expectation of generosity. Since the community provided security, no savings or credit were necessary at the individual level. Where individual accumulation existed, it acted as a sign of prestige in the form of a large herd of cattle, foodstuffs, fine clothes, jewelry or gold coins. This perspective is close to what Scott (1976) later called 'moral economy'.

Recent village studies, however, show that the stereotype of egalitarian Javanese villagers under s strong headman is a myth. Breman (1980) went as far as to consider this stereotype as a European creation and construct of colonial policy that was promoted to permit more efficient colonial exploitation. The colonial government could negotiate with entire villages through the headman, both in tax affairs and matters of compulsory labour and forced production. Communal land could be more easily appropriated by the colonial government (see Suroyo 1987: 62ff.). The emergence of the

165

Javanese village stereotype in which the headmen held the key function can be dated to the time of the British interlude (1811-16), a period in which the country was transformed into the colonial state which necessitated an efficient top-down administration. Breman maintained that it is probably no accident that the British had shortly before discovered the *ryotwari* system in India. A closer look at the early colonial literature of the Dutch United East India Company (*Vereenigte Oostindische Compagnie*, hereafter VOC) period reveals that negotiations took place with central, later regional overlords. Village headmen as important institutions were not mentioned or seen only as relevant for the task of collecting revenue (Breman 1980: 10-11).

In the description of the Javanese village, Breman followed Onghokam's (1975) research from East Java. The village before the colonial period was stratified. Early writings also refer to intermediaries between state elite and village spheres. It is probable that there was a complex hierarchy of officials from the state level down to the village level. In this hierarchy, however, village heads were only *primi inter pares*. The peasantry seems to have been divided into vertical groups of territorially scattered and stratified *cacahs*.[1] In the most elementary cases they consisted of land owning and landless villagers, with complex patron-client relations between them, with the landless soon outnumbering the landowners. On Java there emerged a picture of 'loosely-structured, dynamic networks – with a fixed core but vague and overlapping peripheries'. Eventually the necessity to mobilize labour on a large scale to raise the export crops for the VOC and to carry out infrastructural works led to the introduction of direct taxation under the *cacah* system (Breman 1980: 18-23).

> "Only under the colonial regime did the village become a spatial and administrative standard entity (...) Local isolation increased during the last century through external pressure. Thus the process of localization and horizontalization – decrease of scale and social compression – produced 'the peasant community' as an archetype, in which a central role was apportioned to the village authorities. The reasons why the idea of a village-framework found acceptance at the beginning of the nineteenth century are, however, not the same ones that kept this notion alive later on. With regard to British-India Dewey [1972, H.S.] remarks that the idea of a local community has in the course of time become the subject of strongly fluctuating political standpoints" (Breman 1980: 42).

This stereotype of the static, self-sufficient, and egalitarian village was maintained by the 'Ethical School', by Indonesian nationalists and by post-colonial scholars, although far from being historically proved (Breman 1980: 10).

Wertheim's (1964: 91) description of the ancient agrarian economy already began to question this stereotype of a closed subsistence economy. Both *sawah* (wet rice) and *ladang* (shifting) cultivation were prevalent on Java. In the *sawah* cultivated areas external trade was less promoted by the chiefs who extracted their revenue from agriculture and corvée labour. Some of these areas developed into the typical despotic hydraulic societies which pushed ahead with the construction and maintenance of irrigation works, roads, temple building, and so on, without, however, bringing about socio-economic change. The *ladang* areas, on the other hand, produced only a limited

---

[1] *Cacah* originally meant 'amount of rice fields under cultivation' and later became the 'taxation unit', revenue being calculated on the number of peasant households working on it and being predominantly paid in kind (Suroyo 1987: 62-5).

quantity of food, and population growth was therefore slow. However, marketable production took place there. The profits from the exchange were appropriated by the chiefs of the productive inland states as well as foreign merchants and indigenous elites in the harbor principalities, the latter raising their revenues through tolls and harbor fees, cultivating the surrounding land with serf and slave labour, piracy (see Van Leur 1955: 75ff.) and the sale of local tax-farms. The turn of the eighteenth to the nineteenth century, which is usually seen as the important period of change, coincided with the winding up of the VOC and the take over of possessions and debts by the Dutch colonial state.

Recent research on ancient trade in the Indian Ocean confirmed that particular coastal regions of Java and certain Outer Islands participated more in long-distance trade and were more monetized than is generally assumed. Descriptions of pre-colonial Southeast Asian trade (Evers 1988; Meilink-Roelofsz 1969; Reid 1980; Van Leur 1955) provided a lively counter-picture of at least some regions that were involved in long-distance trade and some inland-trade. Traders from China, India, Arabia and mainland Southeast Asia were attracted by forest production, seafood, gold and spices. The fifteenth century cash-crop production, such as pepper in Sumatra, cloves in Banda and the Moluccas brought further incentives for trade. Sugar as a trade good was also established before the arrival of the Dutch. The ancient Javanese trading centers were located along the northern coast and in the districts of Mataram.[2]

During the sixteenth century Dutch colonization started from the North Coast of Java and in some sparsely populated regions, such as the Moluccas. They were preceded by the Portuguese whom they eventually expelled. In the early phase of Dutch colonialism, however, the Dutch were merely one trading group besides the Chinese, Gujaratis, Portuguese, Arabs, English and so on, and many Dutch trading companies competed with one another (see Part IV).

In spite of the commercial involvement of particular regions until 1870, the time of the introduction of the Agrarian Laws, money transactions were exceptional across large parts of Java and most of the Outer Islands (Van Laanen 1980: 14-5). However, coins were already in use. Earliest coins have been dated back to the Hindu arrival in 400 AD. During the Muslim era (after 1200 AD) coins were used in the coastal regions on trade routes and secondary trade channels. During this period the right of minting was often ceded to the Chinese. The Hindu-Javanese principalities levied taxes in kind, while the later Moslem rulers – like in pre-colonial India – introduced taxes in cash. On the whole, coins were only used at the top level of society and did not trickle down to the subsistence-oriented *desa* (village) community. Coastal trading in the harbor principalities and the use of money for exchange hardly affected the hinterland and was, if at all,

> "confined to the upper strata of village life. Apart from the *kraton* (courts) and the centers where the bureaucratic seats of government were located, coins were not in general use as a medium of exchange in inland areas. The fact that some of the taxes levied by the rulers and headmen had to be paid in cash forms no exception: the required funds were generally borrowed from moneylenders in exchange for agricultural products" (Van Laanen 1980: 14).

---

[2] Proofs for the linkages between pre-colonial inland and maritime trade on the Outer Islands were provided for the Sumatran Batak by Sherman (1990), for the Minahasa by Buchholt (1990).

This state described here remained more or less unchanged until the arrival of the VOC. Even during the days of the Portuguese in the seventeenth century money was predominantly in use in the port cities in exchange for goods to export. In the early days of the VOC this situation continued, and there was a constant flow of silver to Southeast Asia, since at that stage there was little demand for European products. However, in time these money flows extended to the main trading and production centers in the hinterland, and eventually cash-crop production developed.

The first period of Dutch hegemony got under way with the VOC, which was founded in 1602 as a large joint-stock company, two years later than the English East India Company. Initially it was granted the trade monopoly between the Cape of Good Hope and the Magellan Straits for twenty-five years, together with the power to build forts, maintain armed forces, to negotiate treaties, take possession of land and introduce officers of justice (see Hall 1985: 310-19). The Company's aim was to maximize profits with monopolies in purchasing produce and exporting to the Netherlands, as well as in inner-Asian trade. While the VOC everywhere based its monopoly trading on fortified 'factories' on the coast, Java was the only region where a territorial policy was adopted (Van Gelderen 1929: 91).

Trade privileges and monopolies were gained from the local rulers by negotiation and force. The maintenance of the privileges required an administration and armed forces.

> "Slowly (... the VOC, H.S.) developed from a trader into a sovereign. Its income assumed more and more the character of revenues in form of so-called contingents and forced supplies – even though payment was made – instead of trading profits resulting from exchange goods. Although the Company had little interference with the actual inhabitants and dealt mainly with the rulers and headmen, yet there was a far reaching influence exercised by its policy on the agriculture of the Indies. This policy robbed farming of its legitimate profit, rendered precarious the market for its products and thwarted individual initiative." (Van der Kolff 1929: 105).

The VOC negotiated or pushed the purchasing prices at very low levels, while the produce was not paid for in cash but exchanged against overvalued goods originating mainly from other Asian regions. In spite of the high trade profits, the VOC sustained heavy losses due to the high expenses for administration and armed forces to defend their monopoly trading position, corruption among the underpaid administrators, and the share of profits taken by various middlemen (Van der Kolff 1929: 102-5).

The VOC gave up part of monopoly trading as late as the 1740s to revive trade in the Netherlands Indies by competition between private free *burghers* (Dutch freemen) and Indonesians. However, this liberalization came too late and was only partially successful. While the trade of the VOC in the East Indies during the second half of the eighteenth century was characterized by stagnation and decline, the decline was more obvious when compared to the simultaneous growth of the English East India Company. The 'Fourth English War', as it is called by Dutch historians, finally gave the VOC the deathblow. Various Indian trading stations and those on the west coast of Sumatra were lost to the British. Ships on the voyage were sunk, and no Dutch ship in harbor dared to sail. Dutch Asian trade was at a standstill. The Treaty of Paris, which was signed in 1784, broke the Dutch monopoly system and British ships were granted free trade throughout the Indian Ocean (Hall 1985: 357-64).

> "For two centuries the wealth of the Netherlands had depended almost entirely upon the sale in Europe of the valuable produce shipped by the Dutch East India Company from the East. Nevertheless, the Company itself was insolvent, and when the French, after occupying the Netherlands in 1795, set up the Batavian Republic the Dutch East India Company disappeared, leaving its debts to be taken over by the Netherlands Government" (Mackenzie 1954: 117).[3]

During the VOC period revenue was appropriated in the following way. Regional rulers (*bupati*) had to provide rice, coffee, cotton, etc. and labour against small compensation (*contingenten*) or for free (*verplichte leverantien*), as well as plantation work (*cultuurdiensten*), from the early eighteenth century onward, and they in turn forced the peasantry to deliver these in addition to the revenue for the rulers.[4] Villagers were very often forced to raise produce that they would never have raised for subsistence needs, and such forced labour on the land deprived them of time to attend to their subsistence production. Compulsory labour, however, was not abolished with the winding-up of the VOC. It rose to its height under Van den Bosch's Cultivation System after 1830.

I hold that in spite of the ancient spice trade, Indonesia particularly before 1800 was on the whole less monetized, less industrialized and less well integrated into world trade than India.

9.2. The Cultivation and Consignment Systems

Similar to the later VOC period, the Dutch colonial government, after restoring Java to the Dutch by the British, was unsuccessful in extracting profit from the Netherlands Indies because of the high administrative costs and war undertakings compared to the trade benefits achieved until 1830. This initiated a controversy in The Hague of how to consolidate the finance of the colony. The liberal section, which demanded the abolition of state monopolies, was superseded by the conservative wing. In 1828, Van den Bosch, who had gained experience in such matters from his service in the West Indies, was appointed Governor General. Rejecting the liberal demands, he designed the Cultivation System (*cultuurstelsel*) as a strategy to revitalize the state treasury of the Netherlands Indies. In many respects this system was a step back to the colonial policy of the VOC in that it repelled and stifled any attempts to develop private economic initiative. The Cultivation System was introduced on Java in 1830 and lasted until around 1870. Under this system the agricultural production of certain crops became a large-scale monopolistic government enterprise.

The Cultivation System was characterized by traditional patterns of authority, obligations, tribute and labour services being incorporated in the system – administered by a handful of European civil servants who themselves employed and supervised the traditional Javanese elite –which came to be known as 'indirect rule'. The administrative system was based upon the *Controleur* and the *Vergaderingen* (conference of local officers). To introduce and control the forced cultivation on the village level, the

---

[3] According to Hall (1985: 365), the liabilities of the VOC had by then accumulated to 134 million guilders.

[4] For different accounts on VOC operations in eighteenth-century Indonesia, see Van Goor (1986).

Javanese and European administration both received percent payments of the delivered goods. But, 'although Van den Bosch dressed up native society in native clothes, it was a fancy dress, a masquerade of native institutions' (Furnivall 1939: 140).

Originally designed for export crops, the Cultivation System soon became one of forced cultivation and compulsory labour. According to Van Niel (1972: 90) the idea was that the Javanese village provided a portion of its land (normally one-fifth) for the planting of crops determined by the government. The produce was to be delivered to the government at a fixed price sufficient for the payment of land-rent owed by the entire village. The basic principles laid down by Van den Bosch, however, were in practice very quickly transgressed. The limits to per centage of land and labour per village for export crops were exceeded by far.

Indigo and sugar cane were introduced as the first export crops under the Cultivation System, followed by coffee. Further attempts to include tea, silk, tobacco, cotton, cinnamon, cochineal and pepper followed but these, as well as the attempt to introduce forced cultivation in the Outer Provinces, were quite unsuccessful and not lucrative. In these Outer Provinces the pattern was mainly one of voluntary production by indigenous people and plantation production. During this period West Sumatra, Borneo and North Sulawesi were increasingly drawn into the world market and their populations worked as labourers on large estates or were smallholders cash-crop producers (Van der Kolff 1929: 197ff.; Van Gelderen 1929: 91-3).

Van den Bosch rejected the British colonial monetary taxation which had been introduced on Java during the British interlude with only limited success. He maintained that the indigenous people were more content if they were allowed to pay tax in kind instead of cash. The produce had to undergo some processing before export which was placed under the Europeans and Chinese management with whom contracts were made to deliver the products at a certain price to the Dutch store houses. These industries were financed by government loans, which were paid off with the products delivered. The processed goods were exported by state monopoly to the Netherlands by the *Nederlandsche Handel-Maatschappij* (NHM)[5] to the Netherlands and sold on the international market.

During the first phase of the Cultivation System, from 1830 to 1840, there was a strong increase of exports both in volume and value, exceeding ten percent per year. However, after 1840, the system ran into problems, due to overextension, and adjustments of land rent assessment, which led to a reduction of land for government cultivation. The growth rate again decreased to almost zero, and the average for the period 1840-70 was only two percent. Coffee and sugar were the major staples. With the introduction of the Cultivation System market laws were set out of force. The entrepreneurial risk was taken over by the government. Price fixations replaced market prices, labour costs were minimized by compulsory labour, and demand was guaranteed by the government. Indicators of successful production did not exist (Van Niel 1972; Fasseur 1978; Boomgaard 1989; Booth 1989).

---

[5] This company had been established to compete with the British East India Company, but it operated unsuccessfully until the introduction of monopoly shipping, which came to be known as the 'Consignment System'.

Suroyo (1987: 61, 68-9) summarized Dutch colonialism, at least until the introduction of the Agrarian Laws in 1870, by saying that the exploitation consisted mainly of labour rather than land, while the British in India relied more on land exploitation based upon their land revenue system rather than upon the exploitation of labour. Four-and-a half million people were drawn in one way or another into the Cultivation System. In 1840, 57 percent of the Javanese population and six percent of the land area were involved. One decade later these numbers still amounted to 46 and four percent, respectively (Fasseur 1978: 16). Compulsion was reduced towards the end of the Cultivation System. Some of the compulsory labour was paid, although it was underpaid.

During the period of the Cultivation System, however, land revenue payments were not abolished. The Dutch reformed the land revenue system in such a way that the assessment was made by headmen and government officers, who could in certain situations like crop failure etc. adjust the revenue amount to the circumstances or permit an equivalent payment in kind to the cash revenue. The Cultivation System, however, offered many farmers some money from land lease or wage labour, to pay their *land-rente* (land revenue). On Java the remaining compulsory labour requirements were abolished as late as 1916 (Suroyo 1987: 69-75).

During the early period of the Cultivation System, reports and essays on the living conditions of the indigenous population appeared only sporadically, but the criticism of the system increased during the late 1840s and 50s as more information became available in the Netherlands. Although Dutch liberals, backed by a liberal Constitution which came into force in 1848 in the Netherlands, as well as a group of bankers, industrialists and merchants, who had profited from the Cultivation System but lacked opportunities to invest their capital in the Netherlands Indies, pushed for the system to be replaced by wage labour and free enterprise, it took a very long time for the Cultivation System to be finally abolished. Historians agree that many Dutch Liberals adopted Liberal positions not so much for ethical reasons but with the aim of liberating the economy from government monopolies and opening up the Netherlands Indies for private capital.[6] Characteristic for the thinking of the opposition to the Cultivation System during this period is Douwes Dekker's (pseudonym: Multatuli's) novel 'Max Havelaar',[7] which described the negative impact of the Cultivation System for Java. With the appointment of Van den Putte in 1863, the Cultivation System was legally brought to an end, although various government monopoly cultures continued for some time (Penders 1977: 8, 31ff.).

---

[6] Fasseur (1978) rejected this thesis. In the last analysis it was public pressure which abolished the system. Those entrepreneurs who held contracts in the Cultivation System profited from their position and cannot be considered to have been competitive, at least until 1850 when no more contracts were issued. The more liberal public opinion therefore clashed with the increasingly conservative attitude within the government.

[7] Multatuli (1958): *Max Havelaar of de koffieveilingen der Nederlandsche Handel-Maatschappij.* Rotterdam.

9.3. Monetization and Liberalization

The incursion of money into village life is generally considered to have taken place in the course of the nineteenth century. The penetration of money into Javanese culture first of all occurred in the *kraton* sphere and the bureaucratic centers during the nineteenth century, and later in the village sphere, too. As in the case of India, the process of monetization of rural regions went alongside with the collection of cash revenue payment. On Java and in some of the Outer Provinces, the change from revenue payment in kind to cash occurred during the mid-nineteenth century, and this requirement surely forced various cultivators to switch from subsistence to cash-crop production in order to generate a monetary income or, after the liberalization of the economy, to lease or let part of their land to Dutch estates. In contrast to India, the pre-colonial revenue collection of the indigenous rulers, however, had largely been in kind. This system was adopted by the Dutch, which replaced the British by cash payment (with limited success only), but revenue in kind was reintroduced during the period of the Cultivation System. Dutch policy was only after 1870 eventually directed towards de-feudalization and replacement of the command economy by a market economy, but this was subject to conservative setbacks throughout the twentieth century.

Wertheim (1964: 93) argued that with the Cultivation System the interior of Java became increasingly involved in the money economy, since the cultivators obtained partial compensation for their labour service or their provision of land for export cultivation. However, the wages and rents or leases were undervalued. The monetization process accelerated during the liberal period with a change from forced cultivation to private enterprise. On the one hand, the Agrarian Laws of 1870 protected the farmer from land alienation in that land transfers to foreigners continued to be prohibited.[8] On the other hand, however, the way was cleared for Western capital incursion into Java to rent or lease agricultural land for estate production. To state Robison (1986: 6), mercantile colonialism was eventually transformed into a capitalist enterprise. It was during this period that the large sugar, coffee, tea and cinchona plantations were established on Java as well as the tobacco plantations on Sumatra.

> "Nowhere in the Archipelago has the Westerner penetrated to the extent he has done in Java and this is especially the case during the last quarter of a century. Here this development has pressed back the elements of the higher developed home industries. The native export trade was destroyed and local industry disappeared before the wave of cheap mass-produced imports. The remnants of the native higher classes became civil servants in the state organization ruled by the Westerner. It is true that the unit of the life of the people, the *desa*, was interfered with only to the extent necessary for the delivery of produce" (Van Gelderen 1929: 99).

The Agrarian Laws replaced forced labour by wage labour, forced commitments of land by land rent and land lease and introduced the right of sale to indigenous people. Land occupancy was recognized as private property (*eigendom*) and all land where property rights could not be claimed was confiscated by the government. This land (*domeinverklaring*) was leased on a long-term basis (*erfpacht*) (Burger 1939, 1975; Van der Kolff 1929: 113-4).

---

[8] According to Kartodirdjo (1973: 14), the law was, however, not very effective because the population was highly indebted to Chinese and Arab moneylenders. This indebtedness promoted the rise of radical political anti-colonial and orthodox Islamic movements and leaders.

Population growth fostered land fragmentation. Many landholders could not survive with their small plots and let their land to somebody else or became indebted. During the second half of the nineteenth century land concentration was observed among well-to-do farmers and the rural elite, although on a smaller scale than in India. Rural indebtedness increased and public welfare declined. Instead of explaining this change in the context of the macro-economic situation of colonial exploitation and world market developments, the Dutch reacted with the Ethical Policy to increase welfare at the turn of the century. This again was to promote the growth of industries in the Netherlands (Suryo 1987: 273-4).

Many scholars have written about the impact of monetization on Indonesia. To begin with, the penetration of the money economy into village life cannot be generalized for the whole of Indonesia. Generally speaking, the Outer Islands were always more integrated into the world economy than Java, and particular regions and even villages were generally drawn more into the market than others. According to Fruin (1938: 107-8) the incursion of money into the village economy, which particularly resulted from the Agrarian Laws, had a severe impact on social and economic relations of villagers. While most scholars assumed that traditional social relations had been based on reciprocity, the effect of the transformation on rural society was, what Polanyi (1957) called the 'disembedding' of the economy from society. Labour was paid in cash or kind, tenants had to pay land rent in advance instead of a certain share of harvest. Production decisions were no longer determined by subsistence needs, but the market determined what should be planted, and so on. Schrieke emphasized the neglect of rice production for subsistence in favor of cash crops.

"We have to do with a revolution in spirit, similar to that of the early capitalist period in Europe, as indicated by Max Weber and Sombart. The 'economic mentality' has made its entry upon the scene" (Schrieke 1966: 99).

In short: the villagers became largely dependent upon money, wages, and the market. Nevertheless, the money economy only affected village life to a certain extent, since the villager did not necessarily work in a profit-oriented way, nor did he save or accumulate capital, and in certain domains he even continued to barter. The time-lag between expenditure (land revenue payment, land rent, production inputs, religious ceremonies, etc.) and income (marketing of the harvest), however, had to be bridged by savings or credit. Wertheim (1964) agreed that the Javanese peasant continued to maintain a passive attitude towards the incursions of the money economy and continued his self-sufficient life. He left profit-seeking to Europeans, Chinese and Arabs.

Bakker (1936: 21ff.) took a theoretical view on what was just described by applying Marx's circulation formulas. To restate it, the relation C-M-C[9] was valid for pre-capitalist society and the village sphere in the Netherlands Indies. People sold their produce to buy produce or products which they could not obtain within their community. As this stage was beyond direct exchange, both exchange acts fell apart. In such societies money had the quality of a commodity. While the villager at first tried to acquire this commodity within the village, eventually he began to work as

---

[9] i.e. commodity – money – commodity

part-time day labourer, small-scale part-time trader, and so on. Once he had obtained the money required he returned to the village to continue with subsistence production.

> "But by adopting this passive attitude he made himself to the defenseless victim of the middleman and the moneylender, both of whom were more calculating and more at home in the price system, and who also possessed some capital" (Wertheim 1959: 95).

The colonial government, and prior to that the VOC, always employed middlemen (Westerners, Chinese and *priyayi* [indigenous nobles]) in communications with the population.

The liberalization of the economy after 1870, in which the share of government production and trade decreased in favor of private involvement, coincided with a period of growing world trade, and Indonesia participated in the growth, whereby some changes occurred. While the traditional staples of tea, coffee and sugar declined in relative importance, trade in rubber, palm oil and petroleum products grew rapidly. Another development was that Java's dominant position compared to the Outer Islands decreased. Third, smallholders production grew more rapidly than estate production. Fourth, export trade with Asia increased while export trade to Europe decreased. Compared to other countries the growth of Indonesia's exports after the First World War was rapid. However, the commodity terms of trade declined sharply after 1913. The growth of cash-crop smallholders production was mainly due to the Outer Islands, while on Java land extension of *sawah* (wet rice) land was limited (Booth 1989: 68-78).

On the national level a significant decrease of indigenous welfare occurred towards the end of the nineteenth century. The sugar crisis in 1884, which sharply reduced wage labour, and a simultaneous population increase and ever-growing scarcity of land impoverished the rural population. Tax burdens during this period were particularly high, which was in part due to the high infrastructural expenditure of the state which in turn was a necessary prerequisite for private investment but paid for by the indigenous people. The situation was reflected in Boeke's (1926a) *Inlandse Budgetten* (budget studies) of the 1880s. By the end of the nineteenth century the colonial economy severely stagnated again and the colonial government was almost bankrupt. The considerable loss in government revenue caused by the abolition of the Cultivation System and several revenue farms were not compensated by another efficient system of taxation (Penders 1977: 31-4).

There was a call for state intervention on behalf of Javanese welfare in the Netherlands which seems to be a reflection of the *Zeitgeist*.[10] This call was made manifest in the 'Ethical Policy', the equivalent to the 'White Man's Burden' in the British colonial system. Here, too, Wertheim (1964: 96) related the Ethical Policy to Dutch capitalist interests. It was expected that increasing welfare in the Netherlands Indies might strengthen the demand for Dutch products. Four strategies formed the package of the Ethical Policy: improved irrigation, educational improvement, agricultural advice, and popular finance. The last strategy, which is of particular interest for this study and will be discussed in detail, manifested itself in the popular credit system, later

---

[10] The second half of the nineteenth century saw the birth of the European co-operative movement (Rochdale Pioneers, Raiffeisen, and so on). The core idea behind this movement was the protection of common people from the harsh effects of industrialization and market integration.

called *Volkscredietwezen* (People's credit System) and *pandhuisdienst* (government pawnshops).

During this period of growing Imperialism, the attention of foreign investors was drawn to the mineral wealth of the Outer Islands. At the same time Indonesian and Chinese estates and factories were established on the Outer Islands for the cultivation and manufacturing of rubber and coconut, for example, while Western plantations followed. The indigenous enterprises became eventually more or less dependent on foreign middlemen or large Western businesses, particularly during the 1920s when the plantations were brought under a coordinating superstructure of large syndicates and cartels from the Netherlands and other Western countries. However, according to Wertheim (1964: 100-3) these economic developments did not raise Indonesian welfare. Capital was constantly invested in estate agriculture and mining, and the government considered this to be the right strategy to increase welfare, while indigenous small-scale agricultural production, wet rice cultivation on Java and shifting cultivation on the Outer Islands, remained characterized by very low productivity. Technical innovations did not take place. In contrast to the British colonial system in India, industrial development was by and large neglected, although projected by the designers of the Ethical Policy. Impediments to industrial development were the established large estate capitalists who were afraid that the industrialization of Indonesia might increase their labour costs and thus reduce their export opportunities, as well as Dutch industrialists who were afraid of growing industrial competition from the Netherlands Indies which might substitute for the Dutch imports.

The Great Depression had severe effects upon the Indonesian economy. Scholars maintained that the Javanese peasant dissociated himself from the market and retreated into subsistence production, which was true at least for some regions (Van der Kolff 1937). In addition to the world crisis, the main problem of the agrarian economy was that the increase of arable land and agricultural output did not keep pace with the population increase, so that the population was not able to feed itself once labourers were set free from the plantations as a result of the crisis. For the indigenous population there was a large gap between money incomes and expenditures during the Great Depression. While prices for agricultural produce and wages dropped sharply, prices for consumer goods dropped only moderately, land taxes were adapted as late as 1932-33 to the hardship situation, and popular credit was contracted instead of being extended in accordance with the requirements of the people (see Gonggrijp 1957). During this period the peasant became increasingly indebted, as shown by the investigations of the Peoples' Credit Bank in 1935 (see Soenario 1939; Djojohadikusomo 1943). On Java, the scarcity of land and diminishing agricultural incomes forced many Javanese to take up retail trading, while others migrated to the cities and towns in search of wage labour. After the Depression, the small emerging Indonesian middle-class began to invest in small enterprises and provided new labour opportunities. However, it was difficult to gain a foothold in business because the Chinese had occupied such businesses some time ago and had accumulated capital to invest in new enterprises. Wertheim concluded that, seen as a whole, the ethical policy was a failure. Plantation work increased, while individual small-scale agricultural production decreased (Wertheim 1964: 97-9, 110-1).

The Second World War resulted in heavy capital losses of Western and Chinese investors. Plantation production was restricted by the Japanese occupiers to domestic consumption, while other production was reorganized for war requirements. Free trade within the archipelago was severely restricted, irrigation works and the fight against rats and weeds was neglected, and so forth. The period of occupation coincided with a series of droughts. The entire Japanese policy was directed towards a weak post-war Indonesia, that would be dependent on a strong Japan. This aim was to be achieved by weakening the Chinese economic and financial standing in Indonesia.

The post-war period until independence was characterized by continuous conflict between the Republican Government and the Dutch, and this situation again worked against private capital investment. The capital composition in later colonial and independent Indonesia is worth a chapter of its own (see Chapter 14.2).

10. Credit

Similar to India, various colonial scholars considered the need for credit as being due to particular psychological features of the peasantry, which was made responsible for the state of underdevelopment. A metaphor commonly used was the *geld and crediet honger* (hunger for money and credit) of the indigenous population.[1] The colonial writers of the Ethical Period regarded indebtedness as an outcome of the sudden incursion of money into traditional village life, an economic development which the socio-psychological development of the population could not keep pace. This gap was made responsible for the misuse of credit on the borrowers' side and considered as an opportunity for exploitation on the moneylenders' side. The result was increasing rural indebtedness and decreasing welfare. I would like to remind the reader of the British-Indian discussion of the 'extravagant', wasteful peasant that took place during the same period. While the language used was similar, the explanation of the peasantry's pattern of behavior underwent a slight change, to my mind. Darling (1977) and his contemporaries saw the behavior as rooted in the peasants' mentality and tradition, leaving any external influences, including the colonial system or the social consequences of monetization, out of consideration. Boeke and his contemporaries, on the other hand, considered the peasant as a victim of rapid economic change. In the same sense Ringrose (1940: 72) argued that the 'hunger for money' results from the collision of two social structures, which were linked to two different cultures. This is the typical dual view of society shaped by Boeke.[2]

In *Indonesian Economics* Boeke (1980) developed the theory of 'dual societies', which had considerable influence on early development theory and is regarded as a prototype of modernization theory. Although this theory was challenged as soon as it was published, the concept of dual economies is alive until this day in the modified version of two sectors, the formal and the informal one. Since most Dutch scholars during the period under consideration upheld the view of the dual economy (a view that was shaped as a 'theory' as late as 1940), it is useful to reconsider the assumed structure of the Netherlands-Indian economy. Boeke rejected both the position of particularizing social scientists, such as Clark (1907) who assumed a territorial or historical limitation of Western economic theories, as well as the stand of universalizing social scientists who presupposed the general validity of their position, for example, classical and neoclassical economic theory.[3] Both groups of social scientists supposed

---

[1] Other scholars, for example, Boeke, referred to the 'thirst for credit'.

[2] J.H. Boeke was a colonial officer in the Netherlands Indies. In 1920 he became the advisor for co-operative matters to the *Volkscredietwezen* (Peoples' Credit System) and was joined by Fruin, then adjunct-adviser of the *Volkscredietwezen* and later adjunct-director of the *Centrale Cas* (Central Cash Office). After retirement Boeke accepted a chair of colonial studies at Leiden University where, based upon his colonial experiences, he developed the theory of dual societies.

[3] For a good discussion of the particularizing and universalizing positions in the social sciences, see Wallerstein (1991: Part I).

the unity of society, in which economic phenomena occur. This contradicted Boeke's empirical findings in the Netherlands Indies.

> "Where is no such a unity, where (...) there is a sharp, deep, broad cleavage dividing the society into two segments, many social and economic issues take on a quite different appearance and Western economic theories lose their relation to reality – and hence their value. It is not the level of development of the members in such a society, but the isolation of their development, that creates the peculiar problems facing those branches of social science which choose that society as their object of study" (Boeke 1980: 27).

In dual societies, Boeke argued, the following antagonisms occur. The traditional sector is *organic,* a rural, agrarian 'goods economy' which is based upon *status,* the modern sector is *mechanical,* an urban trading and industrial money economy, based upon *contractus*[4] and both sectors hardly overlap each other.

> "In a homogeneous society the development of transportation, credit, marketing and irrigation system constantly takes place in connection and interaction with the development of agriculture, industry and trade. In a dualistic society, on the other hand, they are the result of governmental measures intended to bring such development about" (Boeke 1980: 33).

Boeke believed that the dualism could be overcome by modernization. In Chapter 1 I showed that many contemporary development planners believe the same with regard to the informal (financial) sector.

In another book Boeke (1942: 35-39) maintained that interest is a capitalistic phenomenon, whereby he used the term 'capitalistic' in a broad sense like Braudel (1981, 1982, 1984), for example. Boeke claimed that before Western incursion various transactions in time occurred on the Indonesian Archipelago without involving interest, such as mutual assistance, advances for seed, temporary loans of cattle, and so on, and some spontaneous transactions which involved interest in kind. Professional trading was completely absent, although some limited bargaining took place between producers and customers. This required a periodic market (*pasar*), a meeting place for producers and customers. The traditional village economy was vulnerable to natural disasters, but largely independent of Western trade cycles. The argument that such a description is based on a myth, has already been addressed in the previous chapter and will be amplified later in this chapter. Boeke (1942) considered 'Oriental communities', such as the Netherlands Indies, as 'dual societies'. In such societies

> "we find the forestaller or moneylender on the one hand and the native producer-seller-borrower on the other both feeling personally bound. The former will feel himself responsible up to a certain point for the latter, who on his part regards the forestaller or moneylender as a friend in need (...) The personal character of the relation makes any interference from outside difficult" (Boeke 1942: 38-9).

Here I argue as in the case of India that this description is too romantic. As long as the borrower-lender relation was embedded in village society, it was close to a patron – client relation, the two sides being mutually dependent, whereas power was of course unevenly distributed.

In his lecture on credit provision in the Netherlands Indies during the Ethical Period, Gonggrijp (1922) distinguished a three-tier structure of credit: (a) the bottom

---

[4] Here Boeke used the terminology of Durkheim's and Maine's dualistic concepts.

sphere, consisting of credit relations within the only partly monetized village; (b) a top sphere consisting of financing of colonial exports, infrastructural development and plantations; and (c) an intermediate sphere with links between western and village spheres. According to Gonggrijp, during the early twentieth century this intermediate sphere comprised more than nine tenths of the population of the Netherlands Indies, resulting form the process of modernization. Similar descriptions were provided by Burger (1939) and Ringrose (1940). To my mind, this distinction made by Gonggrijp is not meaningful. My main point of criticism is that he based the distinction on locational factors: village-internal, village-external and intra-village credit relations. Among credit in the village sphere, for example, he counted the mortgaging of land, houses and so on to wealthy villagers, regardless of whether or not interest was charged or the creditors were primarily interested in the debtors' land.

Contrary to Gonggrijp, I make an initial distinction between two levels of credit according to structural aspects, because to my mind it does not make sense to maintain a separate sphere of transactions for the village. The first level was an upper sphere of credit. It consisted largely of financing the exports, estates and the factories for the processing of export crops. It included Dutch loans to the colonial government for investment in irrigation work or transport (road and railway construction), for example. This sphere was connected with the majority of the population only through intermediaries, who handled the flow of goods to and from the ports and through whom money flowed into the villages (at least after the abolition of the Cultivation System and the introduction of the Agrarian Laws). The lower sphere of credit comprised (a) traditional credit relations in kind within the village, which were subject to moral obligations and customary law with respect to loan conditions and interest rates, and (b) commercial credit relations of merchants-cum-lenders and pure moneylenders. On this level of credit there were various small-scale credit relations similar to India.

10.1. The Upper Credit Sphere

The upper sphere of credit is comparable to the upper sphere of finance in colonial India: state credit, later credit of commercial banks (*cultuurbanken*), and advances by exporting firms to Chinese intermediaries,[5] estates and processing firms. Even during the period of the Cultivation System, some agricultural production and its processing were excluded from the government monopoly and sub-contracted to private entrepreneurs, initially mainly to the Chinese and later mainly to the Dutch. They obtained government credit and had to deliver the crops to government store houses. Exempted from government monopolies were sugar plantations and sugar factories, for example, which Fasseur (1978: 282ff.) investigated. The contracting factories processed the sugar cane which was produced through compulsory cultivation, and then supplied the refined sugar – all or only part of it – to the government. Sugar contracts were in great demand, because they promised large profits. Even *Residenten* (Commissioners) and other high-ranking government officials were contractors.

---

[5] Advances to Chinese merchants very often took the form of trade credit: goods for retail on ninety-day interest-free payment terms. These firms also provided cash loans to Chinese crop merchants who used to on-lend to the villagers. Loans were balanced with the harvest.

Sugar contractors obtained long-term government investment credit, which in 1844 amounted to seven million guilders and was interest-free. In 1847 the government abolished the provision of credit to new sugar industries. After 1850 no further contracts were issued at all. Until 1860 public credit was provided only for the working capital requirements of the existing sugar factories and for plant wages. This credit was set off against the sugar deliveries to the state.

With the abolition of the Cultivation System (accompanied by a cut of government credit to contractors) and the introduction of the Agrarian Laws, mercantile colonialism was eventually transformed into a capitalist enterprise (Robison 1986: 6) by opening Java to private Western large-scale cultivation and processing. The shortening of government credit and 'freed production' by way of the Agrarian Laws increased the cost of production and processing for the Dutch enterprises. From now on land had to be leased or rented for the planting of sugar cane, and the wage factor for hired labour during the harvest played a decisive role in the industry calculation. Capital, however, was easily obtained from Dutch import-export companies and Dutch investors because 'free sugar' provided a valuable collateral (Fasseur 1978: 68-70).

Although celebrated as a period of liberalization, Knight (1992) argued that the provision of land against rent was partly against the free will of the indigenous cultivators. It was induced by the state through fiscal pressure or direct force, assisted by village headmen. Land revenue was immediately collected in cash and it was only through the decreasing welfare of the indigenous population that, during the Depression, alternate payment in paddy was reintroduced. According to Van der Kolff (1929: 122-4), the sugar industry had a severe impact on the entire pattern of cultivation.

Considering the economic climate as a whole, the liberalization after 1870 increased the demand for investment capital. In 1882 Dutch merchants and estate owners applied to the government for the establishment of commercial banks. Private indigenous large-scale credit, as frequently obtained in British-India through indigenous bankers, probably played an insignificant role in financing the raising and processing of these export crops and for export.

Scholars emphasized that the credit requirements of many estates on the Outer Island were not very high, because the production was neither labour nor capital-intensive. According to Van der Kolff (1929: 116-7), the rubber plantations, for example, benefited from the practice of *ladang* (slash and burn) cultivation of the indigenous people who had cleared and cultivated plots of land over a period of two or three years and then migrated to form new settlements. The plantations put young rubber plants on these plots and left them alone until the trees were ready for tapping. This was done either by the plantation owner himself or by labourers who were paid in kind with half of their tapping. The production costs of such rubber plantations were thus minimized. Cocoa-nut and coffee were also low-cost estates. The sugar estates and sugar industry on Java, however, were labour-intensive and involved much higher production cost.

In 1892 the government introduced interest-free government loans to indigenous coffee producers worth up to a quarter of the expected harvest.[6] They were obliged to deliver their produce to the government store houses for a fixed price. Like with the contractors during the period of the cultivation system, credit was set off against delivery. This governmental action can be understood against the background of liberal thought which sought to strengthen indigenous enterprise and to prevent such entrepreneurs from taking up credit from moneylenders. However, it should not be overlooked that the government continued to harvest considerable profit from state trading.

10.2. The Lower Credit Sphere

10.2.1. Traditional Credit Relations

At least until the mid-nineteenth century most inter-village economic transactions and credit relations were in kind, such as borrowing rice from another villager for consumption or borrowing a buffalo for ploughing or breeding. With increasing monetization within the village and opening up for cash-crop production, these transactions became partly monetized and many of the credit transactions became mixed cash-kind relations.[7] In the traditional village, paddy became the substitute for cash. According to Van Deventer (1904: 228), paddy was borrowed for people's subsistence during the slack agricultural season, but it could also be used as seeds paddy. The loan period was normally six months, and it was agreed that double the amount of paddy would be paid after the harvest. Daily labourers were often paid in paddy, too. In his research on a village in late nineteenth-century Batakland (Sumatra), Sherman (1990) even showed that rice formed the general purpose medium of exchange, while gold and guilders were special purpose moneys within the prestige sphere of circulation only. In spite of the fact that in contemporary Batakland the Rupiah has become general purpose money, rice is still used as a mediator. Interest rates on land leases are expressed in terms of rice, although paid for in cash. What seems 'traditional' is even economic. The high inflation rate of the Indonesian currency, compared with the price of rice which has been consistently increasing over recent years, determines people's action.

Traditional, and to some degree mixed transactions were subject to the order of society and its protection, that is to say, they were embedded. This order was the *adatrecht* or customary rule. In former times the provision of credit in times of need was the moral obligation of the better-off, Burger argued (1975: 72). However, this moral obligation should not be confused with interest-free loans.

Gonggrijp (1922) described the mechanisms of how, in the absence of written law, a lender could force debtors to fulfill their credit obligations according to *adatrecht*.

---

[6] Van Deventer (1904: 232) reported that interest-free government credit to indigenous coffee producers amounted to f 192.000 in 1902.

[7] According to Van Deventer (1904: 28) a common mixed transaction was an agreement to repay every guilder borrowed before the harvest with one *pikol* of paddy after the harvest, or to repay a loan of f 10 with half *bahoe* worth about f 25. In the first case the interest is at least 50 percent.

These mechanisms were based on public opinion: the reputation of the borrower in the village community. For example, a creditor could be compensated for his claims by taking some of his debtor's property or its equivalent from the reserve fund of the community. If the lender was not from the same village he could take a member of the debtor's community hostage who would then be redeemed by the community in exchange for the debtor. There was no mention of what happened next to the debtor, but I presume that debt servitude was common. Gonggrijp reported from the Papuas that a creditor used to steal something from the debtor's house. Since the latter would then call on the community members to report the theft, the creditor would use the occasion to accuse the debtor of unreliability in front of the community. Public pressure would then force him to repay. All these examples which are similar to the Indian case, demonstrate that credit was common and that according to public opinion debtors were obliged to repay. What is less obvious is how far the taking of credit was neutral in value or whether credit was taken secretly and that the threat to publicize the debt was often pressure enough to secure repayment.

Gonggrijp also reported that claims on debtors were hereditary. Among the Karo Batak, a household head passing away would call his relatives to inform them of all demands and liabilities. If a claim on a debtor was not mentioned, his debt would be considered canceled. After his death, the heirs would be expected to visit their debtors to announce the transfer of claims.

Such episodes are a vivid illustration, how credit was secured without the chance of falling back upon written law. Nevertheless, I doubt that public opinion generally supported the creditor's claims. It is more probable that other factors than 'Justitia's incorruptible perception of moral justice' determined whom the community supported; for example, the closeness of lender and borrower to the village community and their status, the dependency of other villagers upon the same lender, or simply the highest bribe to the village leader.

10.2.2. Mortgages: Commercial Credit Relations?

Whether mortgages belonged to the sphere of traditional or to commercial credit relations depends, to my mind, upon the particular case, because a mortgage is an agreement of potential transfer of property right in the case of non-fulfillment of an obligation by a stipulated date or a transfer of use right (usufructuary mortgage) for a definite period or until the obligation has been fulfilled. Such an agreement is possible only if legal or occupancy property rights exist and are generally accepted. Since a mortgage is either a written or verbal contract, it says nothing about the intention of the mortgagee, whether he aims to secure a loan only, whether he aims to make profit or whether he even aims to acquire the land. To my mind, Gonggrijp's (1922) distinction of whether or not the transaction was at least partly monetized does not necessarily clarify whether a mortgage belonged to his category of 'village sphere of credit' or 'intermediate sphere of credit'. More important is the element of *contractus*[8] as the organizing principle, which substituted the element of familiarity with the

---

[8] To my mind, Maine's useful distinction, which was taken up and further developed by Toennies (1959), of *status* as the organising principle of the community and *contractus* of society, can be applied here.

debtor's willingness or ability to repay or for the sanction mechanisms of tribal rule by a mortgage contract.

In mortgage agreements it is no longer the status of the mortgagor which determines his creditworthiness, but the quality of the collateral offered. *Adatrecht* claimed that land mortgages to 'aliens', people who did not belong to the village community, were discredited, but mortgages to wealthy villagers occurred frequently. The incursion of money into village life and the liberalization of the economy eventually replaced this rule, as well as the Agrarian Laws which prohibited the transfer of land to national aliens (Ind.St. 1875 No. 179).

Considering the ranking of collateral according to *adatrecht* in the transitional Indonesian society of the nineteenth century, according to Gonggrijp (1922) highest-ranking was the mortgaging of high-quality land such as *sawah*, fruit trees such as coconut palm trees, a garden or an expected inheritance of high-quality land. In second place was the pawning of one's labour or that of a family member (which, in contrast to Gonggrijp, I do not call a mortgage) to serve the creditor until the debt was repaid. The danger of such temporary relations was that they easily turned into debt bondage, because debtors could not make sufficient surplus above their subsistence requirements to repay the loan as long as they had to provide labour to the creditors. In third place stood the mortgaging of a house, cattle, a boat, fishing nets, and so on.

Since written mortgages were the exception for a long time, there were frequent disputes between creditors and debtors about the fulfillment of obligations and the ownership of land. *Adatrecht* suggested some substitutes to demonstrate use rights. A creditor who had obtained a usufructuary mortgage on fruit trees was required to mark them with his sign to demonstrate his claim. A debtor who had mortgaged his land for an indefinite period (see the following types of mortgages) was to receive an annual small gift from the creditor to symbolize the prior right of ownership of the debtor.

Towards the end of the nineteenth and in the early twentieth centuries, the question of rural indebtedness was addressed by various scholars and reports. Discussed were declining social welfare and the question of mortgages. By the 1920s, Wertheim (1964) showed, landless peasants, coolies, the poor and peasants/semi-proletarians constituted 65 percent of the village population in a sample from Java and 51 percent in a West Sumatran sample, while a small number of people controlled the land holdings. Nevertheless, compared to India, indebtedness was discussed less directly.

In 1901 De Wolff Van Westerrode produced a comprehensive report on rural credit in the Preanger,[9] one of the regions with a high share of private landed property and therefore a priority area for the mortgaging of land. Most mortgages were hidden in sales-repurchase agreements to evade the Muslim prohibition to take interest (*riba*), and therefore any sale and purchase of land had to be registered after 1863. De Wolff distinguished three kinds of mortgages. The first one was called *djoeal-akad*, a mortgage which was concealed behind a sale with the indefinite right to repurchase the

---

[9] This report was titled *Gegevens uit het 'Rapport betreffende het Landbouwcredietonderzoek in de Preanger-Regentenschappen'*, reprinted in Adat Rechtsbundels II, Java en Madoera (1911), Serie B, West Java No. 2: 57-82, hereafter Adat Rechtsbundels (1911b). The Adat Rechtsbundels are collections of notes on certain legal topics as treated by *adatrecht*.

collateral at the same price. The mortgagee was not allowed to mortgage the land to a third party. The second form was called *djoeal-gade* or *djoeal-beuli*, a mortgage which was concealed behind a sale with a definite right to repurchase. After a specified period the mortgage was transferred to the mortgagee if the mortgagor did not fulfill his obligations. The third form of mortgage was *djoeal-toetoeng*, an agreement in which a productive immovable good, especially agricultural land, was mortgaged for a long-term period, whereby the debt was gradually written off (Adat Rechtsbundels 1911b: 58-63). This is nothing but a rent, with an advanced payment.

If the pawn was 'productive' (such as agricultural land, fruit trees etc.) and the produce was appropriated by the lender (usufructuary mortgage), no extra interest was charged. If the pawn was unproductive (such as a house), it remained in many cases in the hands of the borrower/seller, but he had to pay rent in cash or kind. The same option was open to the mortgagee of productive mortgages. In such cases the debtor's status changed from that of a proprietor to a tenant. He continued cultivating the land, and the creditor received a share of the harvest until the debt was repaid. Expressed in relation to the principal sum or amount borrowed, the rent or interest rate amounted to between 50 to 100 percent. As in the case of labour offered as collateral, mortgages with the exception of *djoelal-toetoeng*, could easily lead to a state of indebtedness and even result in the permanent loss of the land. Almost 80 percent of land mortgaged (9,079 cases) used to belong to the first form specified.[10] Although, according to *adatrecht*, this did not incur the permanent loss of property, the cultivator in fact remained a tenant. It is therefore not surprising that, over a period of 28 years of registration, only 15 percent of land mortgaged had been freed from debts and transferred back to the owners.

Van Deventer (1904: 228ff.) emphasized that in those regions with a high share of private landed property (West and East Java) land transfers and loss of land of small farmers to moneylenders increased after the introduction of private landed property, in spite of the fact that land transfer to aliens was prohibited by law. Foreign moneylenders, however, used to employ indigenous touts and registered the transfers in their names. Indigenous lenders who profited from mortgages were the *hajjis*, pilgrims who have done the expensive and strenuous pilgrimage to Mecca and therefore enjoy high status.

Another report on *Pandrecht in West Java* of 1911, according to *adatrecht* (Adat Rechtsbundels 1931) printed a standardized form of mortgage bonds declared as a sale with the right to re-purchase, which had eventually developed in Bandung and the Preanger. It is a declaration of the borrower, usually witnessed by a village administrator and the heirs. This mortgage bond was handed to the mortgagee.

A rough translation is as follows:

> "(a) I, (... name and address ...) who signs this document, recognize to have sold (... detailed description of the particular plot of land ...).
> (b) Sold to (... name and address of the creditor ...) for f ...
> (c) The agreement is: the land can be re-purchased (... conditions, period if agreed, additional labour services, interest rate if taken up, etc. ...).

---

[10] It is not obvious whether these 9,076 cases were all the registered ones in 28 years.

The purchaser will not be at any disadvantage" (translated from Adat Rechtsbundels 1931: 95).

The concluding formula or a similar one was added to guarantee, in the case of usufructuary mortgages, that the 're-purchase', the repayment of the principal sum borrowed, should not take place before the mortgagee had obtained compensation from at least one harvest. In most cases such contracts circumvented the explicit mention of interest rates. In some mortgage bonds the formula was even included not to call for the court. In the early twentieth century, there was a shift from interest and rent in kind to cash (Adat Rechtsbundels 1931: 98-9).

10.2.3. Commercial Credit Relations: Crop Dealers and Traders

What Gonggrijp (1922) called the intermediate sphere of credit, and I consider as belonging to the lower sphere in addition to traditional credit relations and mortgages, was a dense web of monetized credit relations. While economists usually consider the integration of subsistence economies into the market as advantageous for an economy, Gonggrijp warned that at least in the short run these advantages could involve various disadvantages resulting from a too fast monetization for social change to keep pace with.

One type of credit provision resulting from cash crop production and money in-comes in the village, was that of crop dealers and shop owners. De Wolff reported in 1901 that Chinese crop buyers had their agents in the villages. They organized the transport of the harvest, frequently provided advances on the standing crops, offered to provide production inputs on credit, and so on. (Adat Rechtsbundels 1911b: 79). Similar credit arrangements were reported from other regencies of Java and Madura, too.[11] A report on agricultural credit in Central Java of 1906 maintained that credit relations between Javanese villagers were also common and that the content of such agreements was similar to those with Chinese crop dealers, as expressed by the fol-lowing quotation.

"*De voorwaarden zijn meestal zoo bezwarend, dat zij gerust op één lijn kan worden gesteld met den woeker van Chineezen en andere particuliere credietgevers*" (Adat Rechtsbundels 1919: 71ff.).[12]

For seed paddy loans, an interest of 100 percent after the harvest was common. Even higher was the interest rate for planting seeds such as cabbage, potatoes, tobacco, onions and leek. The lender not only claimed half of the harvest, but in addition the planter had to deliver the other half of the harvest to him at a price well below the market value. Money loans were made against mortgages of land or shares of the harvest (Adat Rechtsbundels 1911b: 69).

---

[11] For reports from Banten, Batavia, Tjirebon and Preanger during the early twentieth century, see Adat Rechtsbundels (1911a: 26-55).

[12] A rough translation is as follows: 'The conditions are usually of a kind that these loans are on the same level as the usury of Chinese and other moneylenders'.

Typical were advances by Chinese crop dealers to cultivators on standing rice and other crops, which were called *ijon, idjon* or *ngidion*.[13] Strictly speaking such transactions are not credit relations but advances on a sale. *Ijon* is still customary in various regions of Indonesia. During the 1970s the Indonesian government decided to eradicate this system, but only with limited success.[14] The Chinese merchant usually combined merchandising and shopkeeping with trade, which kept his moneylending activities fairly concealed. In many cases the person who bought the harvest was at the same time the *toko* (shop) and *warung* (stall) trader. A common practice was that a cultivator obtained goods on credit and was thereby bound to deliver the harvest to the creditor. That means that the delivery of consumer credit and supplier credit was in the same hands. The setting-off took place after the harvest. This practice is still found across all developing countries. However, it is an oversimplification to call such credit relations exploitative in a two-fold manner, by taking hidden interest in the form of higher prices for the goods than in case of cash payment, and by way of undervaluing the produce after the harvest. As has already been mentioned in Chapter 1, shop owners and crop merchants of course aim to bind their customers. However, the reason may simply be that competition from other traders is too great, so that they have to provide either lower prices (their profit margins usually being too small for price reductions) or particular services to their customers, such as sales on credit, to keep their shop customers or to guarantee their supply of produce after the harvest. Burger (1975: 72) saw this as probable. He also added that such mechanisms to maintain relations also worked the other way around. Customers used to take up credit, even though they were not in financial need, because they wanted to tie the traders to buying up the whole crop rather than merely certain quantities of better quality. Another possible strategy of the borrower perhaps is to take up a small loan which is soon repaid as a proof for his credit-worthiness. Such repeated dummy loan transactions may qualify the borrower for a larger loan if required.

Burger (1975: 72) argued that, during the colonial period, many cultivators perceived mixed credit relations as containing an element of help. The peasant considered the moneylender

> *"als een uitkomst, als een houvast in de maalstrom, als een onmisbare gids in het labyrinth van het geldverkeer"* (Burger 1975: 71, quoting Boeke n.d.: 323).[15]

The traders-cum-lenders were aware of the peoples' perception of help and exploited the situation (ibid.). The same opinion was held by Heru-Nugroho (1993) for contemporary Java. To my mind, this view is an overemphasizing of only one side of the coin. The other side is the perception of the moneylender as a blood sucker. Which perception predominates always depends upon the particular position of the moneylender's counterpart. Someone who requires a new loan will praise the moneylender as his helper-in-need, while someone in debt who is unable to repay and will

---

[13] The term *ijon* derives from the Javanese word *ijo*, green. In the Preanger only few cases of *ijon* were reported, while they were common in Central and East Java.

[14] Partadireja (1974) has a broader understanding of *ijon*. To the form just mentioned, he added the advances on labour, handicrafts or the processing of foodstuffs.

[15] To put it in English, J.H. Boeke called the lender the indispensable guide of the Indonesian peasant through the labyrinth of the money economy.

not get any credit extension or somebody who lost his land to a moneylender, will call him blood sucker. Both perceptions are immanent in the mind of every borrower.

Scholars agree that traditionally mutual help was one organizing principle of communities. The understanding was that received help had to be reciprocated in the future. The intrusion of money into the village and the transition from subsistence to cash-crop production dissolved traditional forms of mutual help, such as joint labour gangs of cultivators during the harvest, and introduced the hiring of labourers. Labourers employed for the planting and the harvest season and for other types of works were frequently paid partly in cash, partly in kind. In the case of payment in kind, the labourer provided 'credit' to the proprietor, because he was paid after the harvest, while in the case of a cash payment the cultivator in many cases required loans from professional moneylenders to pay the labourers for their work.

11. The Ethnic Component of Moneylenders

As already shown in the preceding chapter and earlier in the Indian case, moneylending is closely related to trade. In everyday life it is often very difficult to categorize someone as a moneylender, since trading and lending are combined in many cases, for example, by crop merchants or shopkeepers, or moneylending may even be concealed behind another profession due to legal constraints. This chapter takes up the ethnic component of professional moneylending and trading-cum-lending.

11.1. Indigenous Moneylenders

The growth of credit relations and rural indebtedness went hand in hand with progressive monetization.[1] Trade and moneylending in the history of Indonesia was largely a matter of aliens, and the literature on Indonesia gives only marginal hints of indigenous moneylenders who provided credit on a level higher than in the neighborhood (Fokkens 1896; Knebel 1901; Seltmann 1987). Other indigenous moneylenders are a functional but not an ethnic category. Occasionally *hajjis* and village administrators were reported to be moneylenders.

Since European moneylenders worked secretly, so that hardly any data are available on them, I turn to the category of 'foreign Oriental' moneylenders,[2] which consisted of Arabs, Chinese and Indians, predominantly Chettiar.[3]

11.2. Arabs

The Arabs formed the second-largest 'Oriental' minority after the Chinese in the Netherlands Indies. Their number on Java (incl. Madura) and Indonesia rose from 6,000 and 9,000 respectively in 1860 to 18,000 and 27,000 in 1900, 42,000 and 71,000 in 1930 and 65,000 and 85,000 in the early 1950s, whereby the majority of the latter was born or grew up in Indonesia. Intermarriage between Arab men and Indonesian women was common. Most of them originated from Hadhramaut (Van der Kroef 1953: 300, 305). Their history on the Archipelago was already closely related to trade

---

[1] Indebtedness was discussed more indirectly than in India. Examples are De Wolff Van Westerrode's report from the Preanger (Adat Rechtsbundels II, 1911b), Vleming's (n.d.) investigations or Boeke's (1926a) budget studies. Other evidence after 1900 is the introduction of the popular credit system and anti-usury associations (see journal *De Woeker* and various reports of *Anti-Woeker-Vereenigingen*).

[2] Dutch colonial law distinguished between Europeans, natives and 'foreign Orientals'. The latter category included Chinese, Arabs, Indians and Malays.

[3] A few Sikhs were reported to operate as moneylenders, too. According to Coolhaas: (n.d. 114), Sikh moneylenders enjoyed a bad reputation. They concealed their moneylending business behind cattle holding but provided credit to most of the population, including the local rulers.

in the pre-colonial period, and many of them acquired considerable wealth. The arrival of the Dutch did not initially affect their position very much, but eventually the Chinese were favored to take up an intermediary position between the Dutch and the indigenous people. By the nineteenth century, the Arab merchant colony grew into a distinct minority. From the nineteenth century onward they became particularly involved in overseas commerce of certain export goods such as sugar, tea and rubber and in moneylending both in the cities and in the countryside.

In 1823 Chinese and Arabs were restricted by law (pass law) in their free settlement, travel and trade in Java. In 1835 a decree followed which forced the *freemde Oosterlingen* ('foreign Oriental' people) to live in their own quarters under officers of their own nationality. These officers were supposed to keep the peace among their ethnic group. A captain obtained powers to settle civil cases on the basis of ethnic rules or laws and was asked for advice by Dutch judges in criminal matters which were tried according to Dutch-Indian law. He was also empowered to order temporary custody (until Dutch trial), and ask the Dutch police to act against troublemakers. At a later stage he obtained his own police force. In addition, such officials were advised to collect information on troublemakers among their ethnic group whom the Dutch would then expel from the country. Such officials did not only enjoy high prestige but had a strong hold over their ethnic group in their particular region (Rush 1990: 86).

In 1863 the pass law was revised and extended; however, exceptions were made for involvement in agriculture and industry, revenue farms and public work. Although the pass law was abolished as late as 1915 (Ind. Stb. No. 212), this relaxation and the Agrarian Laws, which gave them the opportunity to lease and rent land, enabled Arab and Chinese traders and moneylenders to settle in rural regions. They began to form the links between the village world and the market economy as crop-buyers, merchant-cum-moneylenders or professional moneylenders.

The literature on Arab moneylenders is sparse. On Java they operated between Cheribon and Semarang and used to provide credit to factory workers and civil servants. Van der Kroef (1953) reported that on pay days the Arab moneylenders lurked for their customers in front of shops, plants and government and other offices to collect the installments. Whether prejudiced or not, colonial writers described Arabs as the most usurious and most violent lenders in Indonesia (e.g. Coolhaas n.d.: 113). It was often reported that they illegally searched the houses of those unwilling or unable to pay and forced customers by threat of violence to pay the installment. Van der Kroef (1953: 314ff.) provided some examples from the 1920s to underpin such opinions. In Jember, East Java, a borrower agreed to pay to an Arab moneylender a flat rate of 15 percent interest per month on a ten-month loan of 200 guilders (which is 180 percent per annum), another to pay 37.5 percent per month on a four-month loan of 35 guilders (which amounts to 450 percent per annum). A third one paid more than 11 percent per month on a six-month loan of 1,000 guilders (which amounts to 132 percent per annum). In Tengal rates of 200 percent interest per year were seen as 'reasonable' among Arab lenders. Another example from Cheribon, West Java:

"was that of a European who had borrowed 200 guilders, but had agreed to repay 320 guilders in eight monthly installments of 40 guilders. When after four months he had to ask for a temporary

extension on the fifth payment, his Arab creditor agreed only on the condition that henceforth his
monthly payments would be 48 guilders" (Van der Kroef 1953: 314).

Collateral offered, which might explain the large variation of interest rates, was
not mentioned by Van der Kroef, but he considered 100 percent for 10 months to be
paid in monthly installments as an interest rate common among Arabs. Some Arab
lenders had high amounts of lending capital outstanding; for example, a lender in the
Bangil region of East Java 300,000 guilders. It is not obvious from the description
of Van der Kroef whether these examples were representative or only the pinnacle
of usurious practices. The customers of Arab lenders were often gamblers, but also
factory workers and government officials.

The main obstacle to Arabs in moneylending and banking is the prohibition of *riba*
(interest) in the Qur'an. Van der Kroef (1953) reported that Arab moneylenders over-
came this obstacle by 'letting' money to somebody else, *sewa uwang*. To circumvent
legal proceedings against them, they made contracts which listed only the full amount
to be repaid without mention of the sum lent and interest rates. Borrowers rarely went
to courts because they did not want to lose their source of credit. Another common
practice among Arab lenders was the fictitious sale of goods with subsequent fictitious
re-purchasing, the price difference representing the interest rate.

> "The Arab may sell (. . .) *sarongs* with a value of 55 guilders for 90 guilders. The 'purchaser'
> (really borrower) signs a note for 90 guilders, and verbally agrees to make monthly payment of
> from 10 to 18 guilders. The Arab thereupon immediately buys back the sarongs for 50 guilders
> cash. The pseudo-sale thus is in fact a loan of 50 guilders, but 90 guilders must be paid by the
> borrower in the agreed monthly installment" (Van der Kroef 1953: 315-6).

To sum up, although my description of Arab moneylenders is based on one single source only due to scarcity of reports, it appears to me that they used to operate
individually without forming financial networks.

11.3. Indian Chettiar

What has been overlooked by researchers of the Chettiar is that some Indian-based
Chettiar agency systems were not only wide-spread in the British and Indian colonies
but that they also extended their outposts into the Dutch colonial system. Their business on the East coast of Sumatra, which started in 1879, was similar to that in other
countries. Elsewhere I discussed their Asian network and their Netherlands Indian
activities in more detail (Schrader 1994b: Appendix II; 1995). Here it will be sufficient to refer to the volume of their Sumatran business. The Chettiar had overdrafts
at banks and accepted deposits. Moneylending was normally on a scale ranging from
f 100 to occasionally as much as f 50,000, usually against promissory notes. Repayment was in installments or in a lump sum. Collateral was required for large sums.
Common interest rates of Chettiar loans were 12 to 24 percent p.a. for large loans
and higher for small amounts (Schoorl 1926). The total capital of the seventy Chettiar
who formed the Medan Chettiar community was estimated to be f 10 to 12 million.
Profits of a Sumatran agent after a three-year period usually amounted to between

f 20,000 and f 50,000, but sums of f 90,000 and even f 200,000 were also reported. From the macro-perspective, Westenenk (1922) argued that Chettiar activity on Sumatra drained millions of guilders from Sumatra to India. What he did not take account of was that Chettiar loans were mainly productive loans which were used to generate an income for the borrowers and therefore increased the gross national product of the Netherlands Indies.

11.4. Chinese

A similar pattern over almost all of Southeast Asia is the involvement of Chinese migrants in trade and related professions, and there has been much speculation about the particular business-mindedness of Chinese.[4] As in the case of cultural explanations of Indian commercial involvement, I reject such approaches of business success in the case of the Chinese. I argue with Chaudhuri (1985: 208) that Chinese migration and involvement in Southeast Asian trade can be simply explained by the attitude of the Chinese and the host states to traders and trade. Merchants in China were subjected to a high degree of government control, while such control was absent in India. This explains why Chinese migrated for trade which fits into the view of hypothesizing the 'trading foreigner'. In Chaudhuri's words,

> "one of the most advanced entrepreneurial groups in Asia was forced to operate outside the reach of the state system and to create its own system of self-protection. Indian merchants were not altogether free from state control; but in general they could trade wherever they pleased" (Chaudhuri 1985: 208).

This opens a new dimension of the theory of the *Traders' Dilemma* (Evers and Schrader 1994), which has not been considered so far, because these scholars applied a middle-range view: the escape of traders from their own moral economy of trade. Here the view is top-down. It is the dilemma of traders in relation to the state which sets the framework in which a trader can operate. Historically states tended either to promote free trade in order to share in the profits of this trade by revenue appropriation or, they did the exact opposite and simply monopolized trade like the Netherlands Indian government did during the period of the Cultivation System. I shall return to these political strategies in Part IV.

In terms of migration to the Indonesian Archipelago, two groups can be distinguished, the *peranakan*, off-springs of early Chinese settlers and the later settling *totok* Chinese. According to Suryadinata (1978: 82ff.) and Rush (1990: 83ff.), before the end of the nineteenth century the number of Chinese in Southeast Asia was quite small due to the poor infrastructure and the Imperial Decree of China, which formally prohibited the Chinese to leave their country. The Chinese migrant population in Indonesia during this period consisted of Hokkien, whose occupation was the Asian junk trade and commerce between the islands, the milling of sugar and rice, the manufacture of candles, and various other crafts. Before the arrival of the VOC some of the successful among them had already obtained revenue farms and concessions

---

[4] For a description of the occupational history of Chinese in Indonesia, see e.g. Cator (1936), Suryadinata (1978), Coppel (1983), Dobbin (1989), Mackie (1988), The (1989).

from the indigenous rulers, such as the collection of port duties and the manufacturing and distribution of salt. They were mostly single or had left their families behind. They intermarried with local non-Muslim or only nominally Muslim women. Their offspring formed the pre-war *peranakan* Chinese community, which was highly concentrated on Java and some urban regions on the Outer Islands, which was involved in intermediate trade and moneylending. By the time they showed a high degree of assimilation, and due to their knowledge of local languages and Dutch, they were also employed in Dutch or Chinese business firms. Their descendants, the post-war *peranakan*, also show a high degree of assimilation, and the majority of them applied for Indonesian citizenship.

The *totok* Chinese immigrants came in great numbers during a period of political upheavals in China at the end of the nineteenth and early twentieth centuries. In contrast to the earlier migration wave, they were accompanied by their families and settled largely in groups apart from the local population. As a result they maintained their Chinese customs and manners and showed little willingness to assimilate. The local language was only learned and used for the necessary daily conversation with Indonesians. On densely populated Java, the *totok* Chinese also participated in trade since they had to find an occupational gap among the indigenous, largely agricultural population, while on the less populated Outer Islands they engaged in a variety of jobs, including work in the manufacturing sector. Many of them worked as coolies, labourers in mines and plantations. Some became fishermen or farmers, although the Dutch officially did not allow foreigners to possess land. Coolie labour by far outnumbered other occupations. Nowadays the descendants of the *totok* immigrants who were locally born display a higher degree of assimilation, especially on Java, although much less so than the *peranakan* Chinese. Wertheim (1980) applied this view in his article on *Trading Minorities in Southeast Asia*.

With the arrival of the Europeans and increasing control of foreign trade by the Westerners, the Chinese were gradually pushed into or adapted to various intermediary functions. The first half of the seventeenth century with Governor General J.P. Coen was considered the 'heyday' of the Chinese business community on Java (The 1989: 159). This development was related to the sale of estates and the letting of whole villages to wealthy Chinese, in which they obtained seigniorial rights to levy taxes and corvée, as well as leases of various monopoly rights. All this raised revenue for the VOC. However, by 1720 the immigration of Chinese was restricted, which was followed by an anti-Chinese pogrom in 1740. During the later VOC period, a more friendly policy towards the Chinese was resumed. They were employed as intermediaries in the sale of salt and opium, the purchase of sugar, tobacco, coffee, indigo, etc. and for delivery to the VOC as well as contracting of public work. The revenue farms were even extended in the course of the nineteenth century (The 1989: 159-60). However, eventually the Dutch took legal action against the Chinese as a private business group, which was increasingly considered parasitic on the indigenous population. In 1823 land leases for Chinese and Europeans were abolished and restrictions on free travel, trade and settlement of 'foreign Orientals' were introduced. These measures severely affected the average Chinese trader and moneylender. While in 1837 new immigration of Chinese was prohibited, the shortage of skilled labour soon led to annulment of this regulation. The abolition of revenue farms in the course of the late nineteenth and early twentieth centuries and the introduction of the popular credit system and public pawnshops further affected Chinese business.

Towards the end of the nineteenth century anti-Chinese sentiments came to the fore again. With the emergence of the feeling to be responsible for the destiny of the 'natives', the Chinese and Arabs increasingly became the scapegoats for the exploitation of the indigenous population, because they were said to have no moral sentiments. In regions where many Chinese lived they could keep control of local and second-level, i.e. domestic, trade but in other regions indigenous people increasingly took up the retail trade. Wholesale trade, however, was primarily in the hands of Europeans with only few Chinese involved (The 1989: 167-8).

Government measures and growing competition from indigenous traders created an ethnic consciousness among the Chinese and they organized themselves during the first decade of the twentieth century in Chinese chambers of commerce (*Sianghwee* or *Tiong Hwa Siang Hwee*). According to Willmott (1960: 27-8), these associations represented Chinese business interests to the Dutch government and did local social and welfare work. In addition they formed a major link between the Chinese communities in Indonesia and both the Manchu and the Republican governments in China. Coppel (1983: 22) argued that these chambers of commerce were probably the model for the Muslim Indonesian competitors who formed the Islamic commercial union (*Sarekat Dagang Islam*) in 1911.

For an impression of involvement in trade and moneylending, according to ethnic division, the Javanese *Volkstelling* (census) of 1930 provided the following data. The share of *pribumi* (indigenous people) in large-scale and intermediate trade was 6,551 or 0.7 percent of all *pribumi* in trade and similar occupations. In this category, the Chinese had a share of 1,892 or 1.8 percent and Europeans of 3,498 or 37 percent. Among small-scale retail traders, on the other hand, there were 837,200 *pribumi* or 92.1 percent of all *pribumi* in trade and related occupations, 92,849 Chinese or 88.1 percent, and 2,957 Europeans or 31.3 percent. In contrast to this distribution of trade, the census outlined the following distribution of credit provision: *pribumi* numbered 13,725 or 1.5 percent of *pribumi* occupied in trade and related occupations, Chinese 5,336 or 5 percent and Europeans 1,798 or 19.1 percent (Suryadinata 1978: 82).

Statistics on moneylending are generally questionable since most moneylenders combine credit provision and trade or other economic activities and therefore are counted as traders, landlords, and so on. In spite of this limited validity, the data reflect the tendency. While both the Chinese and *pribumi* were predominantly engaged in small-scale trade, the Chinese had an overproportionate share in credit provision. The high European involvement in credit provision is due to European banks and the popular credit system.

After this short review of the history of Chinese migration to Indonesia, I shift my attention to their moneylending activity. Detailed statistics are available on Chinese moneylenders in early nineteenth-century Buitenzorg which were reinterpreted by Boomgaard (1986a). These statistics prove that, in this region at least, cash loans were customary even in 1805 which puts the stereotype of the subsistence-oriented

Javanese village into question. The statistics were compiled on the Order of the Government-General of 15 February 1805. Chinese moneylenders from Buitenzorg had to report to the Commissioner of Native Affairs how much money the inhabitants of the Buitenzorg Regency owed them. Buitenzorg was not representative of rural Java. It was a border region between the city of Batavia and its commercialized hinterland, the Ommenlanden, and the much more traditional, less monetized Priangan Regencies, where hardly any wage labour existed and barter was common. Therefore Buitenzorg already fits what Gonggrijp (1922) called one century later an 'intermediate sphere of credit'. I should emphasize that the traveling restrictions to foreigners were imposed three decades later. I shall give a brief review of the statistics and Boomgaard's interpretation.

To begin with, the statistics reveal that high officials in Buitenzorg had enormous debts, either to European or Chinese moneylenders and often to both of them. The regent's debts alone amounted to 38,744 Rds[5] silver and 6,340 Rds paper, which were, however, not included in the statistics. 620 inhabitants of Buitenzorg had loans amounting to a total of 13,550 Rds silver, copper or paper from Chinese moneylenders, which was small compared to the amount of the regent alone. However, considering the monetary and non-monetary average income of the population, a bachelor wage-labourer, for example, would have worked around 200 days to repay an average debt. For a peasant the average loan was 45 percent of his gross income per year. Boomgaard assumed that the redemption in ten annual installments together with interest, which was around 40 percent p.a., would have cost him 10 percent of his gross income over ten years – always provided that he had not taken up any additional loans.

All creditors surveyed in this document were Chinese; however, this may have been a distortion of reality due to the nature of the statistics and does not imply that no other moneylenders existed. The Chinese moneylenders' reputation among the Dutch colonial officers was very bad.

> "Commissioner Engelhard calls them in 1794 'the plague of the upland areas', which included Buitenzorg. He then proceeds to describe their role as merchants-cum-moneylenders, and their usurious practices. They monopolized the trade in rice, sugar and peanuts. Similar complaints are voiced in 1808 by the Commission for the Inspection of the Jakarta & Priangan Regencies (...) By their usurious practices the Chinese had become owners of the rice-fields" (Boomgaard 1986a: 51).

Most of the 26 moneylenders, of whom only one was female, were moneylenders-cum-merchants. The mean of all loans averaged Rds 520, with a high standard deviation. Five moneylenders provided more than 50 percent of the money outstanding. Not all lenders used the same pattern of lending. While some had spread their capital in petty sums among many borrowers, other lenders had provided few but large-scale loans. Eight lenders were in fact merchants, since their loans were trade loans. Boomgaard summed up that the Chinese moneylenders in the region of early nineteenth-century Buitenzorg did not form a homogeneous group. The poorest among them were probably less wealthy than the richest debtors (Boomgaard 1986a: 50-2).

---

[5] The statistics for early nineteenth-century Java provided a variety of measures, weights and monetary units. To make them comparable, Boomgaard recalculated the statistics in the report on the basis of Rixdollars (Rds), which were valued differently according to the material: silver, copper and paper.

The debtors were socially and ethnically stratified, but no typical patterns were found among the clusters of Javanese, Chinese or *priyayi* borrowers. Most borrowers were male Javanese and only a few Chinese and *priyayi*. In these statistics Boomgaard identified the following types of credit: on mortgages, namely *sawah* and buffaloes, on personal security, and shop credit. For credit on *sawah* mortgages, which had a share of almost 11 percent of all loans, an interest rate of 40 percent p.a. or more was common. It seems that interest was not expressed in cash, but in paddy, to take into account inflation and seasonal price differences. The rates were similar among the different lenders. This and the comparatively low interest rates point to a rather competitive market. Loans against the security of buffaloes amounted to 15 percent of all loans, and the interest was probably fixed at 50 percent per annum. On average secured loans were provided for 2.6 years, with 1.6 years of interest payments still outstanding. Personal loans totaled 22 percent of all loans, and interest rates of 50 percent p.a. were common. On average these loans were already outstanding for 4 years, for which 2.5 years were still due. The large majority of credit (almost 70 percent) was shop credit. For such credit only concealed interest was charged. The price that the debtor had to repay was higher than the value of the merchandise sold.

As long as the activity of alien moneylenders was not severely curbed by travel and settlement restrictions, the village moneylender seemed to be indispensable in Javanese village life, as reported by De Wolff in 1901 from the Preanger (Adat Rechtsbundels 1911b). Such village moneylenders worked with surprisingly large amounts of capital that many of them had obtained from larger town moneylenders. The village lender was satisfied with the verbal promise of the borrower to repay according to the loan conditions. If the loan sum exceeded f 25, he required a promissory note or the mortgage of agricultural land, fish ponds, houses, and so on. For legal recognition such a loan transaction had to be witnessed by the village administration. However, in practice most moneylenders renounced the official seal to avoid the fee of f 1.50 and believed in customary forms of pressure on the borrower.

According to Vleming (n.d.: 141), customers of Chinese village and particularly town moneylenders came from all sections of the population. The biggest ones lent on mortgages to Chinese and Europeans and frequently accepted deposits from small savers, who received a certain interest on savings. For 1901 De Wolff mentioned the following interest rates. For a loan of f 50 the usual interest rate was 5 to 25 percent per month, depending on the security provided, while the interest rate for small-scale loans of f 5 and below was f 1 to f 2.50 per month, which amounts to 20 – 50 percent. For large-scale loans the standard interest rate was three to five percent per month, which was considered to be moderate by Dutch colonial officers. In many cases interest expressed in paddy worth f 20 to 30 for every 100 guilders was also common (Adat Rechtsbundels 1911b: 70-1). Other typical interest on loans exceeding f 25 was the benefit derived from usufructuary mortgages.

Another practice of Chinese town moneylenders was the requirement that for larger loans the borrower had to sign a receipt higher than the loan, which was reported to occur among Arab moneylenders, too. This practice covered the commercial character of the loan. Coolhaas (n.d.: 111) provided an example of a very high interest rate from the late 1930s, which contrasts with De Wolff's observations of almost four decades earlier that large-scale loans were quite cheap. For a loan of f 100, the borrower had to sign a receipt for f 150 or even f 200 and repay in six or ten monthly installments. Calculated upon an annual basis, the interest rate usually amounted to 100 – 120 percent of the principal and was actually much higher still because the loan amount decreased continually over time with every installment, while the interest rate was always calculated on the principal sum. The risk involved was fairly low, and Coolhaas considered such loans usurious. If payment were delayed fines were common. Usually they amounted to 20 percent per month counted from the last installment paid, and the borrower was forced to sign another receipt that he had obtained an additional loan. According to another form of contract the borrower had to agree to repay the principal and interest in a lump sum. In such cases a borrower, who obtained a loan of say f 100, had to sign a receipt that he had obtained f 200. However, the lender promised verbally that the debt would be paid off with the repayment of f 120 within one month, f 140 in two months and so forth. The problem with such an agreement was not so much that the lender did not keep his promise but rather that the borrower was incapable of repaying the lump sum within the specified period. Such agreements resulted in a continuous monthly payment of f 20 in interest, while the signed loan sum of f 200 was not paid off.

Another observation from the 1930s was that town moneylenders employed lawyers to set up mortgage contracts for larger loans. These contracts contained the clause that in case of the borrowers' defaulting, the lender could sell the mortgaged property (land, a house, a car or expensive furniture) to cover his losses. Since the mortgaging of land or houses to aliens was allowed only in particular cases, such mortgages were covered in contracts of sale with the right of repurchase (Coolhaas n.d.: 111-2) as already described.

Town moneylenders used to give such loans to people with a regular income, such as civil servants and employees. As in the case of Arab lenders, on salary days moneylenders would lurk outside the offices of their customers to collect the installments.[6] Such lenders did not usually urge their customers to repay the principal sum borrowed, since their business was the collection of interest. For civil servants and employees Coolhaas (n.d.: 111f) reported flat interest rates of 100 – 120 percent in the 1930s.

Burger (1930: 400) referred to cases of large-scale Chinese moneylenders in the Pati regency. One of them had outstanding loans of f 354,600 in 1928, which secured an interest of f 41,295 annually (the rates were quite moderate ranging from 9 to 18 percent p.a.). Another one provided loans ranging from f 600 to f 2,000 against solid collateral. Burger maintained that it is wrong to assume that such large-scale lenders provided large-scale credit only. They used every business opportunity and offered small-scale credit, too. The *Landraadarchief* to which Burger referred contained various files of civil cases in which Chinese village and town moneylenders took legal action against their customers. These suits shed some light on their modes of operation. During a one-year period 1926/27, there were 143 cases in the Regency of Pati of which 111 were directed against common people and 32 against civil servants. 111

---

[6] This description was provided by Coolhaas. He reported that the offices '(. . .) *omgeven zien door woekerars, die op hun slachtoffers wachten*' (Coolhaas n.d.: 112), which means that the offices were surrounded by usurers waiting for their victims.

Chinese were known to operate as moneylenders. The reports called the clauses of the loan contracts reasonable. One case, for example, was a loan of f 80 to be repaid in 10 monthly installments of f 8 and a fine of f 2.50 per month (i.e. 2 percent) in the case of late payment of installments. Other cases were similar. Many borrowers, however, complained that the contracts which they had to sign did not correspond with the real conditions. In the example shown the borrower did not receive f 80 from the lender as mentioned in the document, but only f 50. However, he had to repay f 80 in installments plus fine, which is equivalent to an anticipated interest of f 30 or 24 percent for ten months (Burger 1930: 400-1).

Whether Chinese town and village moneylenders and merchants-cum-lenders as described in the previous paragraphs belonged to *peranakan, totok* or both categories is difficult to decide with the material used because reports and statistics did not apply these terms. Nevertheless, I assume that such sedentary moneylenders were in many cases *peranakan* who lived among the indigenous people, while the following category of Chinese moneylenders, the *tjina mindering,*[7] itinerant moneylenders on Java and to a lesser extent on the Outer Islands, largely belonged to the *totok*. In many cases the *tjina mindering* combined small-scale moneylending and petty trade by selling particular goods on credit to indigenous people, whereby repayment took place in installments, or by providing small-scale installment credit. They peddled their goods by bicycle or on foot in the surrounding markets and villages to their customers. Recent field work in Indonesia has shown that the *tjina mindering* can still be found in rural Java (Heru-Nugroho 1993). The term for the sale on credit, initially of linen, later other colonial goods such as coffee, sugar, and so on, was according to Van Gutem (1919) *mindringan tjita*, whereas the term for credit in money was *mindringan oewang*. This scholar, whose report is the key article on *tjina mindering*, provided the following rough description of their appearance:

> "*Afgezien van de speciale gelaatsnit, kenmerkend voor de Chineesche stammen, waaruit deze lieden voortkomen, herkent men hen aan het pak katoentjes, dat zij over den schouder dragen, ondersteund door eene ellenmaat, dan wel achter op hunne fiets gegespt. Die bundel sisten is –zooals aanstonds nader blijken zal – in velen gevallen nauwelijks meer als koopwaar te beschouwen, en is dan feitelijk niet anders, dan een beroepsinsigne. Voorts zijn daar de eigenaardige dubbele zak van linnen die over den schouder geslingerd of om de stuurstang van het rijwiel geknoopt wordt, de ouderwetsch Chineesche lederen hopau of buikbeurs onder het baadje, en last but not least, de paraplu tegen zon en tegen regen, alles onmiskenbare attributen van het beroep. Zoo uitgerust ziet men de 'Tjinga mindringan' allerwege, op de markten, langs de landwegen, in desa's, vlijtig bezig om hunne uitstaande schulden in te vorderen en nieuwe leeningen te plaatsen*" (Van Gutem 1919: 107).

To sum up this description, they carried a double-pointed piece of linen around their shoulders (which during the early twentieth century was no longer a trading article but only a symbol of their profession), its ends having been nodded around the handle bars of their bicycles, a yardstick, the old-fashioned Chinese abdominal purse under the jacket, and the umbrella against sun and rain.

---

[7] *mindering*: Dutch, reduction (of installment credit). Other synonymous terms used are *tjina mindringan* or *toekang renten*, whereas *tjina* is an ethnic category referring to Chinese only and *toekang* a functional term used for non-Chinese with the same profession (Ong Eng Die 1943: 118).

A newcomer, who migrated from the departments Hok Tsija, Hok Tsijoe and Hing Hoa in China, usually settled on Middle and East Java where kinfolk, friends or village folk already practiced moneylending. These had set themselves apart from *peranakan*, who lived as shopkeepers, traders or pursued other professions among the indigenous population, and had formed *kongsi* (business and residential houses containing sometimes three but up to thirty and even more moneylenders) in which the newcomers were integrated. These *kongsi* were multi-functional institutions. They were places of information exchange; they formed the basis for internal rotating credit associations and for inter-*kongsi* credit transactions. *Kongsi* members provided working capital to other members against personal security or collateral (property) (Van Gutem 1919; Vleming n.d.: 140).

One can assume that such *kongsi* are ethnicity-based counter parts to Chettiar temples (see Evers, Pavadarayan and Schrader 1994). Ethnicity (or more precisely: language group), the same profession and the living together created a feeling of solidarity, defined the boundary between internal and external morality, and pre-structured business, although business took place on each individual's own account and competition among them seemed to occur frequent. But there is insufficient information to determine in how far *kongsi* members perhaps formed oligopolies or regional monopolies of credit provision. However, there has been no mention of *kongsi* fixating of interest rates, as reported among the Chettiar, or a collective fund other than of internal RoSCAs.

The newcomer needed a patron who taught him the business and provided him with some starting capital. Initially this was a parcel of linen to be sold on installment credit. After repaying the market value of this linen to his patron, the newcomer would start business on his own as an itinerant peddler who sold on credit and lent money. If a *tjina mindering* left the country, his claims would be transferred to a colleague against compensation, whom he would introduce to his debtors.

Comparative data from the early twentieth century show that the number of Chinese moneylenders, of whom the majority were *tjina mindering*, increased significantly. Van Gutem (1919) explained this by an increased demand for credit of the indigenous population. Burger (1930: 397), and before him other scholars, argued that this increase was closely connected to the abolition of the requirement that the Chinese apply for travel documents to travel within Java. Van Gutem held against this view that the main increase of moneylenders occurred around 1910, which was before the abolition of the travel and settlement restrictions in 1915 (Ind. Stb. No. 212).

The following table provides some data from 1919[8] of their numbers on Java. The table supports the hypothesis that *tjina mindering* settled according to place of origin which correlated largely to language group.

---

[8] It is difficult to assess in how far these data are an overestimation or underestimation. On the one hand, Van Gutem counted among the *tjina mindering* Chinese buyers of the standing crop under the *idjon* system and some large-scale moneylenders; on the other hand, statistics on moneylenders are always vague, because it is difficult to decide who is and is not a moneylender, due to a variety of occupations.

Tab. 8: Number of Tjina Mindering, Java 1919

Region of origin	HokTsija	HokTsijoe	Hing Hoa
Madioen	115-120	–	45-50
Tjaroeban	12-15	–	–
Oeteran	7-8	–	–
Kanigoro	4-5	–	–
Ponorogo	30	–	25
Magetan	20	–	7-8
Ngawi	–	–	25
Djombang	–	100	–
Plosso	–	15	–
Modjokerto	25	100	–
Modjosarie	–	30	–
Soerabaja	1,000	–	–
Lamongan	12	–	–
Babat	20-25	–	–

Source: Van Gutem (1919: 115-6)

The advantages and disadvantages of customers taking credit from *tjina mindering* are those which are generally listed as informal credit. Money was quickly available, at least by the next morning in cases when the sum required exceeded the liquidity of the lender, so that he himself had to borrow from another lender. If a transaction exceeded his capacity, he could hand over the business to a colleague and would receive compensation. Another advantage to the borrower was the informality of business. The moneylender did not ask for the purpose of credit or contact a village official to obtain a reference for the borrower. He judged his customer according to his own experience, which involved the risk of wrong assessment. Installments were adapted to the borrower's requirements (for example, traders obtained installments on market days). Since *tjina mindering* lent on the promise of their debtors only, they were not in danger of losing land or their means of production, such as buffaloes. Nevertheless, they contributed to increasing rural indebtedness.

The customers of *tjina mindering* were largely *pasar* traders and small cultivators, whereas civil servants, factory workers and employees rarely counted among their customers. In the morning they used to go to the *pasar* either in their place of abode or in the next village to collect installments and to provide new credit. After ten a.m. they peddled on foot, by bicycle or dogcart around the countryside, where they met the peasants at lunch time. Van Gutem reported that most *tjina mindering* were illiterate. They knew only a few Chinese letters to carry out their business. In most cases they did not receive receipts for the loans provided, and they did not usually offer receipts for the installments paid. In some exceptional cases they put a mark on the *pasar* tickets of traders as a form of receipt for the installment received.

Characteristic of the *tjina mindering* is that they visited their customers. The rule was that if the lender did not go to collect his installments, the Javanese would not pay.

Potential customers had nothing to do but wait until a moneylender passed by. This reduced the borrower's transaction costs (time spent for obtaining credit, fares, etc.) but increased the lender's expenses. Nevertheless, the latter were quite low. Their working equipment consisted of a note book, a pencil, perhaps a bicycle or a small fare. No office rent was involved, and time was not taken into account.

For the *tjina mindering*, Van Gutem (1919) reported loan amounts ranging from f 1 to f 30, sometimes from f 50 or f 100. One decade later scholars, including Burger (1930), mentioned averages of f 30 to f 50, while the Anti-Usury Commission from 1937 again reported rates not very different to those reported by Van Gutem. Since Burger's data cover the depression period, it is possible that credit contracted and that moneylenders were more cautious in lending. Perhaps they developed a strategy to provide credit to the better-off among their customers only, which would have increased the average loan sum. To provide some examples of typical loan schemes: Common for petty traders was the borrowing of f 1 in the morning and repayment of f 1.01 to f 1.05 at noon. Similar loan schemes were the borrowing of f 1, to be repaid in 12 installments per market day each f 0.10, i.e. f 1.20 total; f 5, to be repaid in 30 days each f 0.20, or in 60 days each f 0.10, or in 12 weeks each f 0.50, or in six weeks each f 1 or in five weeks each f 1.20, i.e. f 6 total. The internal provision of working capital by *kongsi* members involved an interest rate of around 7 – 9 percent, while at least double this amount could be obtained by on-lending (Van Gutem 1919: 133ff., Vleming n.d.: 140).

All scholars referring to *tjina mindering* debated in how far they were usurers. Van Gutem (1919) emphasized that neither in Malay nor in Javanese nor Chinese is there an equivalent to the term 'usury', while there are terms for interest or lending. On the other hand, the prohibition of *riba*, according to Muslim law, considers every form of interest usurious. Western scholars, however, discussed the matter from a European point of view, which legitimized high interest on account of the high risk and labor cost of the moneylender. Burger (1930: 398) explained the high risk as resulting from lack of legal security (no written contracts and promissory notes). If a borrower died, for example, or moved away, the heirs were usually unwilling to pay the debt because the moneylender could not prove his claims. Coolhaas (n.d.: 111) argued in the late 1930s (after the Great Depression) that the high risk resulted not so much from the lack of willingness of the borrowers to repay than rather from a lack of ability due to declining welfare and increasing poverty. Van Gelderen (1927: 70) explained the high interest rates as resulting from capital scarcity in the economy, while according to Boeke (1938: 52) it was not capital but money that was scarce. The production factor capital, he argued, was rather unimportant for the indigenous household, while consumption credit was needed, which is money and not capital. Here Boeke failed to note that also the *pasar* trader used such small-scale credit as working capital.

This point was taken by the first Anti-Usury-Association in Yogyakarta (passim). Peddlers in the *pasar* did not consider the interest rates usurious, since they generated an income with the loan (quoted by Ong Eng Die 1943: 123-4). In the same sense Fruin (1938: 113) argued that the interest was high if calculated on a monthly or annual basis, but most credit was very short-term and generated an income. Van Gutem (1919: 94ff.) also emphasized that the image of *tjina mindringan* among the

Javanese was that while they took high interest, they did not cheat their customers. He estimated that the *tjina mindering*'s income amounted to 10 to 15 percent of the pretax turnover, which is about f 30 per month. The occasional attacks on Chinese even during the colonial period seemed to contradict this view, however; they were directed toward the economic supremacy of the Chinese as a whole and carried out against the weakest among them, namely small traders and moneylenders. On a whole, however, the Dutch position towards the Chinese was ambivalent. On the one hand, the Chinese and other moneylenders were potentially blamed for increasing rural indebtedness; on the other hand, the Chinese in particular held the *compradore* position between the Dutch and the indigenous population and facilitated the colonial economy (of exploitation). In addition, during the second half of the nineteenth century, the credit provided by moneylenders ensured timely revenue payments by the local people as it did in India.

Having so far analyzed the types of credit in the Netherlands Indies, I identified on the informal side largely the Arab, Chinese and Indian small-scale itinerant and sedentary moneylenders or moneylenders-cum-traders, who financed petty traders and small-scale cultivators, and some medium-scale moneylenders from these ethnic groups, as well as some European lenders, who provided loans to factory workers, employees and some larger cultivators and traders. With the introduction of the popular credit system and public pawnshops at the turn to the twentieth century, which I discuss in another chapter, alternative formal sources of small-scale credit were introduced. The top sphere of finance, on the other hand, was formed by trade credit from Dutch import-export firms and government loans, which were abolished during the mid-nineteenth century and eventually replaced by commercial banks. Like in India, this sphere of credit, however, was hardly relevant for the indigenous population or non-Western commerce and, with the exception of some alien contractors or commercial intermediaries, it was confined to European customers and enterprise only.

Considering this pattern of credit supply, compared with the Indian pre-colonial and colonial periods, it is striking that in India a medium- and large-scale sphere of indigenous finance developed even during the pre-colonial period and continued to operate, although on a different level, during the colonial and to some extent even post-colonial periods. In colonial Indonesia, however, this sphere was developed only marginally by some larger Arab, Chinese or Indian lenders. As individual cases and with regard to their credit volume they can perhaps be compared to some indigenously developed bankers in India. However, these cases were much fewer in number and the material from the Netherlands Indies suggests that they worked more or less individually, while in contrast many Indian merchant bankers had constituted elaborate networks to efficiently distribute money from surplus to deficit regions and to finance domestic trade in distant places. Since for the Netherlands Indies direct evidence to comparable networks is lacking, I shall attempt in what follows to find indirect evidence, which can – if at all – be expected to be found among the Chinese, the leading non-Western commercial group in Indonesia. Is it perhaps possible that they had established ethnic commercial networks and an internal financial system without producing specialized financial agents?

11.5. Chinese Patronage Networks

To provide a potential answer, I shall now take a look at the Chinese elites. Rush (1990: 83-107) described the role of Chinese in opium farms. These revenue farms were introduced rather late in 1809 and replaced in 1904 by the Dutch-managed opium bureau, the *regie*. They were the most lucrative regional monopolies and generated enormous profits. They were found all over Java except in certain 'forbidden areas' such as the Preanger. Revenue farmers, however, in many cases held high official positions simultaneously, which was possible in a political system of indirect rule, and these positions gave them considerable power over the Chinese community. It is worthwhile to look more closely at these revenue farmers-cum-officers to analyze how far they financed the Chinese community.

Under the Cultivation System the presence of Chinese officials increased sharply from only thirteen cities in 1832 to thirty-three by the mid-nineteenth century. The collective office of this ethnic administrative unit became known as the Chinese Council (*kongkoan*), which functioned as an intermediary between the Dutch administration and the Chinese community. It investigated crimes in which Chinese were involved with its own political force and pursued offenders against government tax and monopoly laws. The officers were even given powers to inspect Chinese shops, warehouses, firms, and so on. Sometimes officers were asked by the Dutch to collect the poll tax from which the officers themselves and Chinese revenue farmers in general were exempt. According to Willmott (1960: 148ff.), three factors determined the eligibility for office: wealth, connection with Dutch officials, and influence in the Chinese community. In many cases Chinese officers recruited family members for other official positions.

During the period of the Cultivation System, when the colonial government introduced the law of confining 'foreign Orientals' to certain neighborhoods and severely restricted their ability to move freely within Java by obliging them to apply for travel documents, the revenue farmers and officers were exempt from these restrictions (the former at least temporarily). Rush (1990) argued that this decree aimed at restricting Chinese opportunities in the inland trade to enforce the Cultivation System. Exemptions from this decree made such positions even more desirable.

For 1850 it was estimated that about 14,000 Chinese lived as officers and revenue farmers of various regional or local monopolies with exemptions in the interior of Java. In addition to opium farms, the following 'small means' existed: (a) bazaar leases (i.e. the right to tax goods offered for sale in the bazaars) which were abolished in 1851; (b) the slaughter of cattle and pigs; (c) fishing and the supply of fishing nets; and (d) the sale of arrack and liquor (these revenue farms being abolished in 1864); (e) the practice of certain occupations; (f) the collection of the Chinese poll-tax; (g) the import and cultivation of tobacco; (h) the collection of tolls at bridges, river crossings and sluices; (i) the harvesting of birds' nests; (j) the cutting of timber in forests; (k) the trade in products from the *Duizend Eilanden* (Thousand Islands) close to Batavia; (l) the lease of the right to *wayang* performances; and (m) pawnshop and gambling house leases (The 1989: 161). By the nineteenth century, the *Cabang*

Atas, the elite of tax-farmers and (or -cum-) officers, was a clearly recognizable class with endogamous marriage rule. Nevertheless, this elite admitted talented newcomers. The *Cabang Atas* spent a fortune on charitable institutions and temples. In contrast to the frugality of well-off Chettiar or Marwaris in India, the important officer-cum-opium farmers built Chinese-style luxury family compounds which I explain with the Hindu and Confucian religious ethics. Various opium-farm-cum-officer constellations existed, and each constellation represented a complex network of economic relations, family liaisons, and ethnic and contractual obligations.

> "Broadly viewed, these constellations were hierarchical (. . .) At the top stood the group patrons, senior Chinese officers, opium farmers and farm guarantors. Beyond them were lesser members of the opium farm *kongsi*, sub-farmers, and lower-ranking Chinese officers, including relatives and protégés of the major patrons. At yet another level stood those in a direct, personal relationship (receivers of credit, employment, or other sorts of patronage) to the core group, or to the kongsi as a corporate group; beyond these were hundreds of others who in smaller amounts, and several links removed from the center, enjoyed the patronage of the constellation in the form of credit, employment or influence (. . .) All sorts of economic activity was financed ultimately via the patronage of the dominant opium farm interests. Reaching out from the center of these constellations was a wide and diversified network of patrons and clients, along the chain of which the wealth of the few financed the enterprise of many" (Rush 1990: 96-7).

While the usual distinction of *peranakan* and *totok* Chinese suggests a sharp dividing line between both groupings, Rush maintained that, although the center of such patronage networks formed *peranakan*, many *totok* Chinese were absorbed into such networks, too. They represented clear-cut boundaries of economic power and patronage, although they were not necessarily mutually exclusive. They included various economic activities, such as revenue farms, commercial agriculture, light industry, and commercial networks for the transport of inland produce to the ports and for the distribution of imports in the country, where they were sold in shops and by *tjina mindering*, in cash or on credit. An opium farm was important for economic dominance within a particular region and was in most cases supported by other regional or local 'small means'.[9] In most cases members of the same *kongsi* held all these monopolies within the same region. Additionally the Chinese elite entered into government contracts, such as the transportation of certain state-controlled commodities, the selling of salt, and so on. These contracts were farmed out, too, and in the cases where Europeans had won the contracts, the *Cabang Atas* became sub-contractors.

During the mid-nineteenth century the economy was liberalized and the Agrarian Laws opened a space for private commercial agriculture. Private plantations emerged and the infrastructural development of Java required construction work and transport facilities. The Chinese quickly set up such businesses and again obtained exemptions from residence and travel restrictions for these contracts. In addition, whereas possible the Chinese took up estate production on rented or leased land and engaged in the processing of rice wine, bread, oil or leather and, most importantly, the refining of sugar. During the 1870s almost half of the private sugar mills on Java were Chinese-owned.

Another important source of Chinese income was the retail trade, which consisted of

---

[9] In 1874, 913 of the 922 pawnshop farms, for example, were run by the Chinese (Rush 1990: 99).

"a multitude of small, discrete economic activities, transactions between Javanese villagers and small traders on the one side, and Chinese shopkeepers, moneylenders, and rice and produce dealers on the other. Copper pennies (. . .) and credit were the primary media of exchange in this rural economy. The Chinese were essential to the circulation of the first and to the availability of the second" (Rush 1990: 103).

Opium farms generated the necessary assets of the *kongsi* to make advances to cultivators under the *ijon* system or to provide credit to other customers. Javanese farmers borrowed small sums from the Chinese to pay their taxes, to repay other debts, to be able to rent a buffalo or to pay daily labourers, to organize a social event or to make a living in the slack agricultural season. Local small-scale traders borrowed their working capital. *Tjina mindering* again obtained their working capital from their *kongsi*. Although it was shown that Chinese credit provision, particularly that of *tjina mindering*, was not considered usurious by most Dutch scholars, the borrowers were in many cases unable to repay the loans and became increasingly indebted as time went by. This was not, however, only the result of loan contracts but was due to declining welfare arising from world trade cycles and colonial policy. Statistics on rural indebtedness are rare, but it is obvious from various reports that rural indebtedness increased during the nineteenth and twentieth centuries at least until the Great Depression and was common in Central and East Java.

Dutch laws did not succeed in excluding the Chinese from the village sphere, and it is questionable whether this was really intended. As a matter of fact, the Dutch depended upon the Chinese *compradores* in trade, transport and rural finance, which explains the privileges of the Chinese elite. Due to a lack of competition among the Chinese elite, its manifestation of power through the patronage networks, and because of the privileges the elite became more and more powerful, economically and socially, until the revenue farms were abolished during the early twentieth century. Nevertheless, Rush maintained that no constellation could monopolize the control within a residency, since at least some of the contracts and revenue farms were incorporated by another Chinese patronage network.

The abolition of the opium and other monopolies in the early twentieth century, and their control by government deprived the Chinese elite of a large part of their incomes. Adaptation to other professions was necessary. This was facilitated by the capital accumulated through leases and other businesses. However, considering the Chinese business community as a whole, most of these enterprises were medium or small-scale family firms only, *tokos* or even itinerant peddling enterprises, such as *tjina mindering*. Only a small number entered heavy industry or developed into multicorporate enterprises.

An example of the latter is the Oei Tiong Ham Concern with its head office in Semarang (see Wilmott 1960: 49-50). Oei Tiong Ham inherited his father's produce business. He engaged in the sugar market and accumulated enough capital to lease the opium monopoly in 1890. Oei Tiong Ham was able to hold the opium farm for thirteen years until its abolition, and he and three other Chinese are said to have extracted profits amounting to 18 million guilders from this monopoly. With the acquired revenues he expanded and diversified his businesses. Because of his wealth and social standing he was finally appointed Major of the Chinese community by the Dutch. Oei

Tiong Ham was charitable, as would be expected from such a wealthy man, to the Chinese community. He had five or six wives and twenty-six children. Eight sons were trained to take over the business. By the late 1950s the Oei Tiong Ham Concern developed into the biggest and best-organized Chinese enterprise in Indonesia, with offices in nine major Indonesian cities and fifteen overseas commercial centers, including London, Amsterdam, and New York. The concern owned at least ten factories and sugar, kapok, rubber and other mills, a bank and insurance company (which was, however, largely confined to the internal financing of the enterprise) and a vast amount of real estate property. It imported textiles, drugs and chemicals, flour, machinery, news print, glassware and miscellaneous goods, and exported rubber, sugar, kapok, rice, tea, leather, and so on. In Semarang the concern owned a pharmacy, a number of large warehouses, and the biggest Chinese building and construction company. Oei Tiong Ham, who died in 1924, operated a 'modern' concept of personnel policy. In contrast to Chinese tradition, he put abilities and training before family connections. Nevertheless, the top managerial positions were still occupied by members of the Oei family, several generations of whom constituted to be employed in the enterprise.

A valuable contribution to an assessment of the Chinese position in Indonesian production, commerce and industries from the liberalization period onward was provided by Robison (1986: 7-30). He argued that until 1870 the Chinese were engaged in plantations, but were eventually replaced by Dutch trading corporations and agricultural banks. From 1870 until independence foreign enterprises underwent a major expansion, and with growing capital investment requirements, private plantation owners were eventually displaced by foreign banks and large trading houses. There was a shift in production on Java to the Outer Islands, in which the Chinese were also involved.[10] British and American capital was invested in plantation estates, petroleum and large manufacturing ventures of the tire industry, tobacco, oil, and so on, while 'domestic' investors, i.e. the Dutch and the Chinese, largely remained in estates, petroleum and commerce, only few entering industries. Considered as a whole, the dominant capitalists were the British, the Americans and the Dutch estate corporations with associated banking and trading houses. These were followed by the Chinese patronage networks with multiple economic activities (estate business, some industrial involvement, the marketing of agricultural produce, wholesale and retail of imported commodities, the provision of rural credit and the establishment of small manufacturing enterprises). A Javanese landowning class barely developed. During the liberalization period, Javanese landowners preferred to let their land to tenants or foreigners instead of engaging in large-scale agriculture on a wage-labour basis.

Considering the economic sectors of internal trade and industries in particular, in the early days of the VOC both Chinese and Javanese were engaged in trade. The

---

[10] For 1921, Cator (1936: 64, quoted by The: 173) estimated a total investment by the Chinese of f 340 million or 10.6 percent, compared to f 2,350 million or 73.4 percent of Dutch investment and f 300 million or 9.4 percent of British investment. Mackie (1988: 238ff.) presented data on the occupational structure during the late colonial period, based on the 1930 Census. Of the almost 470,000 Chinese in the Netherlands Indies, including 183,000 on Java and Madura, 313,000 and 76,000 respectively were foreign-born. 170,000 and 101,000 of the foreign-born were engaged in trade, and of these 5,700 and 4,400 respectively were involved in the credit business. For Java and Madura, the latter figures were 5,300 and 4,300.

decline of the Javanese merchant princes (see Van Leur 1955) during the seventeenth century left only one dominant group of merchants, the Chinese, who became increasingly the intermediary force between the Dutch and the indigenous population. Robison considered the position of the *compradore* a tactical construct of colonial authorities, due to the social vulnerability of minorities among the population and hence their dependence on the foreign authority. The gradual opening-up of the country to private capital led the Chinese extend their businesses into foreign trade, as well as continuing the collection and domestic marketing of produce and moneylending. The rapid development of the money economy, including money taxation, and the diminishing state control, as well as capital being set free from the monopolies, gave rise to the accumulation of merchant capital. Growing peasant indebtedness and dependency on Chinese moneylenders led the Chinese to increasingly control the rural commodity markets and agricultural prices. Nevertheless, compared to the large-scale operations of foreign capital, most of the Chinese enterprises remained fairly small. Based on family businesses, many firms tended to decline after several generations, and few firms managed to dominate trade and credit for an extended period. During the twentieth century, however, Javanese *santri* traders experienced some growth. Once travel restrictions on the Chinese were lifted, the latter expanded their businesses into the Javanese domains, resulting in competition and anti-Chinese sentiments. This view is confirmed by Coppel (1979), but it stands in contrast to Wertheim's (1964) *santri* hypothesis that put forward the growth of an indigenous Muslim traders' class (*santri*) and takeover of market shares of the formerly Chinese domain as the cause of racial tension.

In industry the pattern was the same as in trade. Larger mechanized factories belonged to foreign Western capital, partially mechanized medium and small-scale factories engaged in food processing and batik, for example, were owned by Chinese. Nevertheless, the Chinese were able to consolidate their dominance in certain large-scale manufacturing industries, such as *kretek* (clove cigarette) production. It was difficult for indigenous producers to rise above the petty-production level. Some indigenous manufacturers managed only occasionally to bypass Chinese middlemen.

Robison (1986) concluded that the economic success of the Chinese during the colonial period compared to the indigenous people was caused by exogenous as well as endogenous factors: their economic position which supported the colonial economy and their kinship and ethnic business associations and networks

> "which provided an exclusive and mutually supportive trade and credit framework within which family-based firms operated. Not only did Chinese merchants have a much larger capital base, but they had the structure to sustain the accumulation process. With the entry of *totok* or *singkeh* (new immigrant) Chinese in the late nineteenth century, leading sectors of this network of credit and trade were expanded beyond Indonesia to operate on a regional basis. Most importantly, leading elements of the Chinese business community, primarily the *totok*, were able to use their networks of credit, collection, import, wholesale and retail distribution to entrench capital investment in the production process" (Robison 1986: 266-7).

Indigenous merchants and traders had no incentive to enter manufacturing to compete against the Dutch. Instead, they sought confrontation with the Chinese merchants and manufacturers. A reaction to the abolition of travel restrictions on Chinese after

1904 was the formation of the *Sarekat Dagang Islam* from 1909, which was renamed *Sarekat Islam* in 1912. The movement advocated a boycott against Chinese merchants and sought joint action by indigenous merchants against the Chinese. Initially the Muslim leadership was held by the indigenous merchants, but after 1918 it shifted to the village *kiyayi* (Muslim religious leaders) who condemned the modernist reforms of the Muslim merchants. At the national level, many members of *Sarekat Islam* joined the communist/trade union wing.

A matter that scholars have not so far examined in detail are the remittances of overseas Chinese to China during the colonial and contemporary period. The question is in how far these flows were based on Chinese financial or trading networks and, if they existed, where they were based.[11] As a matter of fact, however, this outflow of capital indicates the reluctance of Chinese migrants to re-invest the accumulated capital in the host countries.

The analysis of the Chinese business community in colonial Indonesia reveals that there were indeed some multi-functional Chinese networks which to some extent included the financing of trade from the inland to the ports. However, much of the financing remained concealed, and surprisingly no Chinese specialized large-scale credit agents emerged as they did in India, at least not before independence. I shall later try to find an explanation for this discrepancy.

---

[11] Recently G.L. Hicks (1993) edited a book on 'Overseas Chinese Remittances from Southeast Asia 1910-1940', which I was unfortunately no longer able to consider in this study. A review of this book, however, mentioned that different channels of remittances existed: post offices, returning Chinese, couriers, private postal exchanges and banks, which seems quite different from the flow of capital within the networks of indigenous-style bankers who used their own negotiable credit instrument, the *hundi*.

12. Formal Finance during the Colonial Period

For an understanding of the financial landscape in colonial Indonesia, I shall examine the emergence of commercial banks, as well as the formation of a popular credit system and public pawnshops in response to declining welfare.

12.1. Banks and Trading Companies

The gradual shift from government to private cultivation during the nineteenth century, and the eventual abolition of government credit for contracting enterprise during the second half of the nineteenth century, created a need for capital among Western and some 'foreign Oriental' entrepreneurs. Until then the capital requirements of private business were fairly small because its opportunities were strictly limited. The contracting enterprises obtained government credit through the *Javaasche Bank* from 1827 or, under the Cultivation System, advances for consignments by the *Nederland-sche Handel-Maatschappij* (hereafter NHM), which had been founded in 1824 as a monopolistic trading company to arrange the transport of export crops raised under the Cultivation System to the Netherlands. Until 1883 the NHM refrained from general banking.

According to Helfferich (1914) and Van Laanen (1990), the rising need for entrepreneurial credit during the period of liberalization created a scarcity of available capital, what led commerce and plantation owners apply to the government for the establishment of banks in 1862. During 1850-1881 the following banks were opened: the *Nederlandsch-Indische Escompto Maatschappij* (NIEM), the *Rotterdamsche Bank*, the *Nederlandsch-Indische Handel-Bank* (NIHB), the *Internationale Crediet en Handelsvereeniging "Rotterdam"*, the *Handelsvereeniging "Amsterdam"*, the *Koloniale Bank*, (all Dutch), the Chartered Bank of India, Australia and China, and the Hong Kong and Shanghai Banking Corporation (both British). The Dutch commercial banks, however, had overestimated the credit needs of commerce in Indonesia, which caused them to enter the business of agricultural banks with its specific task of provision of long-term loans. Only the British banks were involved in pure banking, while the Dutch banks were largely trading houses or *cultuurbanken* (plantation banks), which concentrated on the financing of the large-scale agricultural sector. Like the NHM, they established relations with the estates, predominantly on Java, on the basis of consignments.

The provision of credit on consignment of the harvest was a risky business and some plantation banks suffered major losses. Before 1870, mortgages were possible only on private land, but the Agrarian Laws included *erfpacht* land (hereditary leasehold), too. However, rented land could not be mortgaged, – and the sugar estates used to raise sugar cane in such land. The loans to most sugar estates were therefore made on personal security only. Another risk was involved in the particular culture raised. Advances were made to all plantations – sugar, coffee, pepper, indigo, tobacco, tea, and so on –regardless of the length of time it took to harvest the crops. The risk was of course higher with slowly-growing produce.

According to Helfferich (1914: 37ff.), another danger in the management of these banks was the optimistic belief in growth, which was severely shaken by the world sugar crisis in 1883-4. In 1883 the Dutch banks had a total capital and debts amounting to f 36.5 million and agricultural loans of f 50.2 million. A total of 83 sugar plantations and 74 coffee plantations were on the list of the debtors. With the onset of the crisis the prices of agricultural produce dropped sharply. The debtors were unable to fulfill their obligations, which in turn caused difficulties for the banks with regard to their liabilities towards their Dutch investors. Several banks faced insolvency because a large portion of their assets was tied up in long-term agricultural loans. The bankruptcy of several other banks could be avoided only due to the rational conduct of the Dutch financiers. The banking system as a whole lost about 40 million guilders. This caused the reorganization of the Indonesian banking system, whereby a distinction was introduced between general banking business for short- and medium-term credit and agricultural banking business for long-term loans. With the exception of the NHM and NIHB, commercial banks withdrew from their agricultural engagement, while the *Nederlandsch-Indische Landbouw-Maatschappij* (Colonial Bank and Principalities Agricultural Company) was set up as a specialized agricultural bank, which was partly financed by bonds.

From the domestic perspective, banks survived the depression better than many of the estates. An effect of the crisis was that the banks started credit rationing, providing loans to the soundest enterprises only. Additionally they entered the decision-making process of these enterprises by taking shares as collateral.

A royal decree from 1886 further increased the security of the banks, since the taking into pawn of the harvest or the store houses became possible. In case the debtor was unable to fulfill his obligations, the bank could even take over decisions of the enterprise, organize the harvest and transport and set off the sales price against their claims and costs. Such clauses were now introduced in the contracts between banks and plantations.

For the purpose of consolidation, the banks paid only a small or even no shareholder dividends during the two decades following the sugar crisis. After this period, however, they were on such a sound basis that, during the period 1905-12, they were able to pay dividends ranging from three to almost 30 percent, depending on the institution.

The *Javaasche Bank* according to Furnivall (1956, quoted by Wardhana 1971: 338ff.) was created as a private bank for the purpose of 'colonizing Java with capital rather than with men'. Investors, however, initially showed little interest in the shares, so that the capital had to be provided by the government and the NHM. At the outset the bank's primary task was the discounting of promissory notes. Until 1850 this bank was the only private institution which offered credit to traders who were subject to the provisions of the Cultivation System. Other trading houses providing agricultural credit only loaned money from the Java Bank. The main concern of the bank in the initial years was the financing of Dutch private enterprise and, to a limited extent, the issuing of bank notes, which was the Java Bank's own credit instrument. Since the issuing was not limited by a maximum, credit extension rose to an unhealthy degree and caused almost bankruptcy. In 1846 the real money supply and money printing process became regulated. In 1875 a system of proportional cover was introduced. With respect to credit extension to private bodies the Java Bank increasingly lost ground to more specialized bank institutions, in spite of entering into competition with these agencies. As late as 1922, the Java Bank was formally granted the right to become the only bank circulating currency in Indonesia. The economic policy the bank was supposed to pursue as the central bank was the unification of the Indonesian currency and its linkage to the Dutch currency by maintaining the official rate of exchange between both currencies at one-to-one parity. This, and the fact that the money market for Indonesian funds was in the Netherlands, explains why the central bank could not develop independently of the Netherlands.

Van Laanen (1990: 252) concluded that the Java Bank cannot be considered a real central bank – 'a bank on which private banks can fall back in order to bolster their liquidity'. During the colonial period there was no functioning formal Indonesian money market. In many cases the Java Bank administered only transfers from the Netherlands to Indonesia and vice versa. This bank should be considered a private bank with the exclusive right to issue notes, although these notes became legal tender as late as in 1914. It was a bank which behaved like a commercial bank in financing plantation business, import-export trade, and so on. But it also performed some of a central bank's functions, such as the stabilization of the domestic value (purchasing power) as well as the external value (exchange rate) of the Indonesian guilder.

According to Van Laanen (1990: 249), capital supply in colonial Indonesia outside the popular credit system was more or less Dutch (80 percent of the capital value in businesses was in Dutch hands). It largely consisted of:

- Capital tied to the country by the virtue of the nationality of its owner, e.g. Chinese, Arabs, and some well-to-do Indonesians. This capital was invested in real estate, stocks and *desa*-credit extension (the purchase of rice, commodity trade and credit provision by the Chinese, Arabs or Indians).

- Assets supplied by Europeans as securities, bank deposits and life insurance premiums.

- Reserve funds of enterprises with head offices in Indonesia (securities and bank de Reserve posits).

Van Laanen argued that

> "the conclusion that the control of funds in Netherlands India amounted to no more than simple cash management would appear overdrawn. But available funds that could not be invested on a short-term basis were often transferred abroad, either directly, by means of commodity exports, or indirectly, with the banking system as an intermediary for products sold within Netherlands India. In normal circumstances, the Netherlands Indian banks held only a small amount of liquid company-balances. There was scarcely any suggestion of a money market in its own right or,

consequently, of the Java Bank's being able to implement an autonomous monetary policy" (Van Laanen 1980: 33).

12.2.   The Popular Credit System

The development of the popular credit system in the Netherlands Indies emerged on the basis of savings generation and credit provision through distinct institutions. From 1853 onward private savings banks and from 1886 onward provident banks emerged, but both were confined to only a few cities. In 1898 the first post savings bank opened with the aim to increase thrift in the whole country. On the side of credit provision, various *priyayi* banks developed, which provided loans to indigenous government employees to combat their dependency on private moneylenders. In what follows I shall briefly look at the savings aspect (Handbook of the Netherlands Indies 1924: 197; 1930: 141), before turning to the credit side.

Postal and Private Savings Banks

Pure savings banks by definition only provide the service of savings mobilization, rather than credit. This also holds true for the savings banks of the Netherlands Indies. Savings administration offered a customer the service of the safekeeping of his money and simultaneously the opportunity to stimulate his own savings capacity. Such banks aimed at lower- and medium-income people. It was generally assumed by the Dutch that part of the indigenous population, such as traders and employees, were capable of saving, whereas peasants were considered too poor to save. This perspective was maintained for a long time in development planning. Only recently, the perspective was changed in that in rural finance both savings generation and credit provision have to go hand in hand in a single institution. From this perspective, the contemporary criticism of postal savings banks is that they mobilize rural savings and channel the funds into the main centers instead of investing where the funds were raised.

The Postal Savings Bank which operated through a wide network of post-offices and branch offices and, during 1920s, expanded its operation in East Java through the offices of government pawnshops, developed at the same time as the roots of the *Volkscredietwezen*, which was designed to satisfy rural credit needs. The Postal Savings Bank had its head office in Weltevreden (Batavia). It was founded in 1898 and worked with revenues independent of the government. The maximum deposit allowed was only f 2,400 per saver. In 1920 the number of European customers constituted 34.84 percent, while they had a share of assets of 73.17 percent. The figures for the indigenous population were 59.10 percent and 23.28 percent and of non-Western foreigners (*freemde Oosterlingen*) 6.06 and 3.55 percent, respectively. Total savings amounted to 19.25 million guilders. Over time the share of indigenous savings increased. At the end of 1928 60.9 percent of savings originated from Europeans, 32.7 percent from the indigenous population and 6.4 percent from non-Western foreigners. Total savings amounted to 22 million guilders.

In addition to the Postal Savings Bank, several private savings banks were founded in the early twentieth century, such as the Batavia Savings Bank, the General Savings Bank in Batavia, the Savings Bank in Bandung, and so on. There were nine in 1928, five of which were on Java and four on the Outer Islands. While Europeans were mainly customers of private savings banks, postal savings banks found more widespread acceptance among the indigenous population.

The Volkscredietwezen

Schmit (1991) analyzed the emergence and operation of the *Volkscredietwezen* in great detail. The roots of the People's Credit System can be found in the late nineteenth century. It was conceived as a government reaction to increasing rural indebtedness arising from the world sugar crisis, population growth and an increasing scarcity of land. These developments coincided with the increasing importance of the Chinese in rural trade, moneylending and estate business. De Wolff van Westerrode's idea was therefore – after the only partial success of the Agrarian Laws to prohibit the transfer of land to moneylenders – to introduce a popular credit system which could compete with private moneylenders. According to Boomgaard (1986b, quoted by Schmit 1991), growing nationalist, anti-colonial feelings constituted another threat. However, instead of addressing them, the official undertaking was to devise an anti-usury policy directed against Chinese and other alien moneylenders. This was to legitimize strong government intervention under the banner of protecting the indigenous people. The Home Ministry

> "opted for a dual policy of separation of the various ethnic domains of action and for decentralization of the welfare services. Under this dual strategy the indigenous rural population was defined as a 'pre-capitalist' category with weak economic 'instincts'. The Chinese population was labeled as an 'ultra-capitalist' category with strong economic 'instincts'. The cooperative formula was supposed to suit the pre-capitalist institutions of the rural population and legal segregation of ethnic domains was seen as the most appropriate way to control the Chinese segment of the population" (Schmit 1991: 45-6).

However, it should be emphasized that strong anti-Chinese sentiments were already expressed during the early nineteenth century when the Dutch regained the Netherlands Indies. These feelings submerged for some time only to break out again towards the end of the century with growing market integration, the expansion of Chinese business and indigenous people's increasing dependency on Chinese moneylenders and traders.

It was commonly assumed by colonial scholars that the credit 'hunger' of the indigenous people for consumption purposes resulted from an accelerated economic development that social change could not keep pace with. Towards the end of the century, there was an increasing demand for state intervention on behalf of Javanese welfare. The fight against usury was seen as a government task and taken up by the cooperative movement and grassroots-level credit institutions, such as *Bank Priyayi*

Poerwokerto. This bank is usually considered as the foundation of the People's Credit System.[1]

In 1901 Queen Wilhelmina proclaimed the 'ethical colonial policy' in the Netherlands, which took up the question of popular credit explicitly, along with agricultural improvement, an irrigation system, the cooperative movement and government pawnshops. The popular credit schemes aimed at the provision of cheap credit to Indonesians, under the condition that cost should be minimized. In addition the population should be encouraged to produce more.

- The cooperative movement and popular credit provision were two competitive approaches, although they were thought to complement each other, and until the 1930s the latter was continuously criticized by the protagonists of the former. The Ethical Policy favored the more pragmatic system of village paddy banks, which were introduced on Java only, and village banks. Originally designed as self-help groups with the village headman as the manager, these plans failed due to the incompetence of village headmen and a lack of administrative and bookkeeping skills on the village level, so that eventually the government authorities came to regulate bank affairs. In 1903 the popular credit structure was as follows: 19 *priyayi* banks (later called *volksbanken* [in Java and Madura *afdeelingsbanken*] or district banks) supervised 1,240 *desa lumbungs* (village paddy banks), and various *desa banken* (village banks). Three years later there were already 33 district banks, 7,424 village paddy banks and around 300 village banks. The officers employed were mostly indigenous people (Schmit 1991: 46-7).

- *Desa lumbungs* lent rice to cultivators for consumption or as seed, which had to be repaid in kind in a few installments after the harvest.[2] Furnivall (1934a) maintained with reference to Boeke, that village paddy banks flourished only where there was largely subsistence-oriented agriculture and a dense population. Demand varied according to season. A village paddy bank was active only after the harvest and from October to January when there was great need for paddy loans. Profits were smaller than those of village banks, because the turnovers were lower and there was usually some damage to the paddy stored, for example, through rat and mice infestations.

- *Desa banken* provided small-scale credit in cash to be usually repaid in ten installments. The advances made were in general on the level of the *tjina-mindering* loans and small traders (most of whom were women) and craftsmen used to take up such loans for working capital requirements. Usually cultivators did not apply for such a credit.

---

[1] The founder of this institution has remained in the dark until now. Various versions of the story exist, most of which agree that the reason of institutionalization was the indebtedness of *priyayi* officials to moneylenders. This resulted in the loss of prestige of the bureaucracy and simultaneously lent support to nationalist and radical Islamic movements. It was mentioned that, in spite of the Agrarian Laws, Chinese and European moneylenders took possession of the land of such indebted officials (see Schmit 1991: 49-51).

[2] An average loan of *desa lumbungs* in the mid-1930s amounted to 90-100 kilograms of paddy per borrower (Fruin 1938: 161ff.).

- *Afdeelingsbanken* aimed at providing credit to those target groups of the largely Chinese and European middle-class which were beyond the scope of commercial bank institutions. Loan amounts varied considerably from a few guilders up to tens of thousands.[3] The loan conditions depended on the borrower's occupation and income. The installments were generally fixed for a period of twelve months.

In 1906 the Home Ministry advised officials to consider the promotion of popular credit provision one of their prime tasks. In 1908 district and village banks were exempted from the prohibition of banks to take collateral from the borrowers. In 1910 it was confirmed that the village banks and village paddy banks were to maintain their decentralized status and that the district banks were to keep their philanthropic character, too. In the same year the *Inlandsche Gemeente Ordonnantie* maintained that the money reserves of village councils were to be deposited in village banks for the purpose of lending. A problem was the dual role of village leaders-cum-bank managers, which induced corrupt practices. Therefore plans emerged to integrate the three separate institutions into the *Volkscredietwezen* to reduce the autonomy of village banks and village paddy banks and to exert stronger government control. The *Centrale Kas* (Central Cash Office) was designed as the head organization of formal finance. The district banks were to deposit money in the *Centrale Kas* on a voluntary basis and receive interest, and these deposits were to flow to the lower level institutions in the form of subsidized loans. This reorganization went alongside with an increasing level of professionalization, which contradicted to the originally philanthropic character of the whole system (Cramer 1929).

In 1913 the *Volkscredietwezen* and the *Centrale Kas* were institutionalized and a distinction was made between two different services: (a) the central cash service, which was concerned with the *afdeelingsbanken*; and (b) the popular credit service, which was concerned with *desa banken* and *desa lumbungs*. To put it another way, the philanthropical credit provision was largely left to village banks and village paddy banks and separated from the district banks. These, however, were kept under government control because their customers were mainly Chinese and European traders, and these banks were prevented from evolving into commercial banks. The extension of government control was legitimized by the enforcement of government's anti-usury policy. The *Centrale Kas* obtained a fund worth five million guilders. Schmit (1991) maintained that this reorganization was also necessary for bureaucratic reasons because the popular credit system had expanded too much to be administered by the Home Ministry alone. At this time there were 75 district banks, more than 12,400 village paddy banks and 1,336 village money banks.

State intervention was thought to be temporary only until the cooperative movement, which was designed to provide productive credit, had gained sufficient prominence. These plans caused a debate between Boeke and others. Boeke (1926a,b), who in 1916 was offered a position in the Head Office of the *Volkscredietwezen*, argued in favor of the existing structure, in that consumption credit was necessary and that a successful operation of cooperatives could not be expected in the near future.

---

[3] According to Fruin (1938: 116ff.), the average loan during the mid-1930s was f 53 on Java and, due to plantation business, f 134 on the Outer Islands.

Boeke's critics attacked his assumption of the credit 'thirst' and the *Volkscredietwezen* as a whole, because it neglected the savings capacity of the rural population. For the second decade of the twentieth century, Van Gutem (1919), for example, argued that the credit 'thirst' of the rural people was nothing but a great need for consumer goods in a region which was drawn into the market. This demand, however, could not be satisfied sufficiently by the *Volkscredietwezen*. Boeke responded by dividing the rural population into two categories: one group with a credit 'thirst' and another more affluent rural elite, and maintained that the two services, central cash service and popular credit service, aimed at these two distinct categories (Boeke 1919, 1920; quoted by Schmit 1991: 54-5). Other critics favored the support of cooperatives to provide production credit to cultivators, to promote their savings capacity and to restructure the marketing system to combat the dependency on crop dealers.

Schmit argued that

> "the primary functions of the *Volkscredietwezen* were containment and appeasement of the commercial, nationalist and religious aspirations of various categories of the rural population by means of an anti-Chinese policy. In this respect Wertheim has observed that despite many differences, a certain parallel between the overtly anti-Chinese character of the 'Ethical Policy' and the events in Nazi Germany is undeniable" (Schmit 1991: 56, quoting Wertheim 1964, 1980).

In 1920 Boeke became adviser for cooperative matters to the *Volkscredietwezen* and was joined by Fruin who was the adjunct-adviser of the *Volkscredietwezen*, and later the adjunct-director of the *Centrale Kas*. Both pushed forward with the centralization of the system. Boeke supported group lending on the basis of joint-liability groups, which was rediscovered with the Grameen Bank and the linkage concept during the 1970s and 80s. Between 1920 and 1928 both men subordinated the district banks to the Home Ministry. The value of district bank and village bank operations increased consistently during this period. However, the share of the *Centrale Kas* remained below ten percent. This proves that the district banks retained their funds rather than voluntarily transferring them to the Central Cash Office. The village bank institutions operated very efficiently with arrears of outstanding loans below one percent. Interest rates were around 40 to 45 percent per annum. Unprofitable banks were closed.

By 1925 it became obvious that the *Centrale Kas* could not fulfill its control function nor its function to absorb the surplus funds of the lower levels of the organization. Fruin therefore proposed to reorganize the *Volkscredietwezen* in so far that the assets were concentrated in the *Centrale Kas*,[4] that the district banks should be centrally controlled and that a welfare service was created. These proposals again stimulated a heated debate, this time with Hirschfeld from the Rotterdam School of Economics who argued that Fruin's proposals would not create a sound credit policy as the premises of a rural population with a need for consumption credit were wrong (Hirschfeld 1926, quoted by Schmit 1991: 62). Boeke (1926b) again defended his credit policy.[5] A third group around Van der Kolff favored a pragmatic approach of

---

[4] After 1925, the district banks were obliged to deposit 30 percent of their reserves in the *Centrale Kas*.

[5] Considering this controversy around the People's Credit System, the two opposing groups belonged to Leiden University, including Boeke and Fruin, who favored a culturalist and protectionist policy, and the Rotterdam School of Economics, including Hirschfeld and Gonggrijp, who adhered to a technocratic, more production-oriented than welfare policy. Hirschfeld therefore rejected normative objectives and

group-based crop credit. The national and communist uprisings in 1926 were used by Boeke and Fruin to emphasize that centralization was even more necessary. With the passing of the Cooperative Law, however, a number of village banks were converted into cooperatives. It was at this point that Boeke retreated and accepted a chair for colonial economics in Leiden. Soon afterwards Fruin changed his policy and transformed the *Volkscredietwezen* into a state corporation.

Proposals for the reorganization of the *Volkscredietwezen* through the formation of the *Algemeene Volkscredietbank* (AVB) were already made by Fruin in 1931. In 1927 the number of paddy banks had decreased to about 6,000, with 1.7 million picols of rice, while the number of village banks had increased to 5,569, with reserves of 8 million guilders and an annual turnover of 46 million guilders.[6] There were 110 cooperatives, almost half of which were on Java and Madura. The AVB was designed as a non-profit and multi-functional welfare institution. It was supposed to include the centralization of the management 90 district banks, 6,264 *desa* banks and 5,545 *desa lumbungs* with total reserves of 63 million guilders and outstanding loans of 35 million guilders in 1933. The then 233 cooperatives should also be included. However, it was not until the end of the Depression that the AVB was institutionalized.

The Great Depression resulted in credit contraction, which made the indigenous population again turn to subsistence production and to private moneylenders. The credit arrears of the district banks during this period increased heavily from 3.1 percent in 1929 to 55.7 percent in 1933. Two debt settlement programs were started. The number of borrowers on the village level remained quite stable, and arrears amounted to only seven percent in 1934. However, the total value of lending dropped by 63 percent and the average loan amounts from 41.6 to 16.1 guilders.

With the formation of the AVB, the question again arose whether the institution should adopt a policy to stimulate agricultural and entrepreneurial activity or continue to provide consumption credit to compete with moneylenders. For a short period the first strategy was pursued and the Indonesian middle class was designed as the target group of the AVB. In addition, group credit facilities were to be provided to cultivators. In 1936 Fruin was replaced by a board of directors, which again shifted the issue to the agricultural class. However, the emphasis was moved from consumption credit to marketing relations, which were exploited by Chinese crop dealers. Debt-relief was offered to farmers exploited. In this way the cooperative movement, which had been oppressed so far, gradually began to be considered more apt than the *Volkscredietwezen*.

By 1939, ten percent of total loans or three million guilders outstanding were loans to debt-relief groups. Cooperatives numbered 574, of which 530 were on Java and Madura. 53 of them were pure debt-relief cooperatives and 385 (including the former ones) savings and credit cooperatives.

---

argued in favor of taking general economic laws as the basis for political decisions (Schmit 1991: 62-3). This anticipates the controversy between neoclassical and welfare economics.

[6] It is still not possible to decide whether the decline in the volume of credit and number of village paddy banks was a consequence of advanced monetization of Java or whether it was caused by a political measure to promote monetization.

District banks were turned into AVB branch offices. The policy pursued after 1935 was to regain old loans worth 6.5 million guilders and provide new loans worth 9.3 million guilders. Until 1939 the value of old loans declined to only 0.6 million guilders, and the new loans amounted to 20.1 million guilders. Arrears amounted to only 3.3 percent. On the village level outstanding loans rose from 2.6 million and 595,000 borrowers to 3.4 million and 865,000 borrowers (Schmit 1991: 75-6). During World War II, the Japanese incorporated the AVB into their own financial system. The village banks were renamed into the *Syomin Ginko* corporations and the AVB branch offices were subordinated to the Yokohama Specie Bank.

After this description, some statistical data on the *Volkscredietwezen* may be helpful. The growth of the People's Credit System during the period 1910-40 – including government pawnshops – is shown in the following figure.

Fig. 3: People's Credit System, Indonesia 1910-1940 (in thousands)

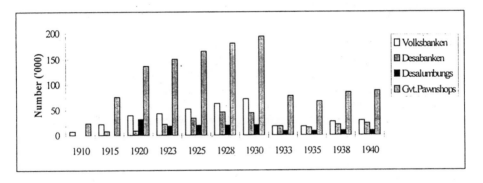

Data: Van Laanen (1990: 262)

The rates of interest under the People's Credit System were as follows:

Tab. 9: Rates of Interest, People's Credit System, Java and Madura, 1905-1937 (percent per annum)

Year	Volksbanken	Desabanken	Desalumbungs
1905-1913	12-18	24-45	
1913-1926	13-19	40-60	30-60
1929-1937	8-15	30-40	25-30

Source: Van Laanen (1990: 262).

Government Pawnshops

The recognition of pawnshops in the Netherlands Indies goes back to 1746 with the *Bank van Leening te Batavia*, which largely belonged to the VOC. In 1811 Raffles privatized the existing pawnshops and introduced their licensing, and in 1814 switched to the farming out of pawnshop monopolies (*pachtstelsel*) up to a maximum loan amount of f 100. With the restoration of the Netherlands Indies to the Dutch, the latter maintained this system, which spread all over the East Indies, except in the Preanger and the Vorstenlanden.

An article in the *Tijdschrift voor Nederlandsch Indie* (n.n. 1857) heavily attacked the colonial practice of farming out pawnshops. It considered pawnshops as institutions for the poor, while they were misused by the government to raise funds. The argumentation ran as follows: Interest rates of pawnshops, as regulated by the *Indische Staatsblad*, 1849, no. 52 are immense. The pawnshops, however, legally take 3.25 percent and for small amounts until six percent per month from people who are officially considered poor. Private moneylenders on Java, on the other hand, are accused to take usurious interest of 1 to 2.5 percent per month. The reason for such unjust legislation can be explained only by the high revenue for the state (in 1854 f 300,000, while some years before it was f 100,000 only). This revenue for the state can be only appropriated if the pawnshops provide sufficient profit to the revenue farmers. Such high interest rates are therefore sanctioned by the state (translation and summary of the argument).

Revenue farmers were predominantly Chinese. In 1870 the farming out of pawnshops, which then provided the Dutch with revenue of f 375,000 annually, was abolished and the licensing system reintroduced. The result was a steep increase in the number of pawnshops from 242 in 1869 to 986 in 1875, while government revenues decreased by more than f 200.000 to f 56,000 only. Ten years later the revenue farms were reinstalled, except for a few regions in the west where revenues for such monopolies had been very low. However, it was agreed that revenue farmers should be better controlled by the government. The Chinese reacted with reduced interest in such revenue farms and this demand gap resulted in the reorganization of the pawnshop system at the turn of the century by introducing public pawnshops in addition to private ones. In 1900 revenue farms were completely abolished, and in 1903 the government, in accordance with the Ethical Policy, monopolized the running of pawnshops on Java and Madura up to a loan amount of f 100, with the exception of the Principalities, where pawnshops were continued to be licensed. The government pawnshop monopoly was not extended outside Java until 1921 (see Keers 1928; Kat Angelino 1931; Furnivall 1934b; Coolhaas n.d.; Van Laanen 1990).

One very important aspect of pawnshops was the converting of savings in commodities into money. impersonal nature of credit. Van Laanen (1990: 263) argued that borrowers could not fall into arrears. Credit was always below the value of the pawn. Even if a borrower defaulted and the pawn was auctioned, he was able to repurchase it later.

Customers of pawnshops were cultivators, small traders and artisans. Average loan amounts were on the level of small-scale credit; however, many clients pawned several items at the same time. According to Fruin (1938), many traders pawned jewelry and other valuables in order to obtain working capital. The use of pawnshop was cyclical according to the agricultural calendar. Outstanding loans were lowest after the second crop, which was usually raised for sale. Re-pawning was not limited to a certain period, as long as the client paid regular interest per month. In the case of non-payment the pawn was sold by auction. If auctioning the item was profitable, the former owner received the difference. Furnivall (1934b: 10-11) argued that pawnshops are particularly useful during a period of transition from a subsistence to a market economy, because people can transform their valuables into cash, which can be re-used for productive purposes.[7] He added that pawnshops do not offer easy credit, since the borrower has to make a sacrifice (the pawn) before he obtains credit as a first step.

To provide some further statistics: the interest rates of public pawnshops during the period 1901-1940 were as follows.

Tab. 10: Government Pawnshop Service, Rates of Interest (per annum), 1901-1940

Loan Size (f)/ Year	0-0.50	0.50-25	25-50	50-75	75-100
1901-1919	72%	72%	60%	48%	36%
1920-1924[8]	48%	36%	16%	12%	?
1924-1940	72%	72%	60%	48%	36%

Source: Van Laanen (1990: 264), based on official sources

Furnivall provided the following time series on pawnshops in the Netherlands Indies from 1901-30.

Tab. 11: Pawn Shops in the Netherlands Indies, 1901-30 (in thousands)

Year	Shops	Transactions	Advances	Total income	Total costs	Profit
1901	1	39.5	78.2	23.9	23.9	–
1905	23	1788.5	2958.7	381.9	263.0	118.9
1910	165	15159.8	20777.2	3205.6	2478.9	726.8
1915	313	34636.9	75897.4	10467.8	5915.0	4552.8
1920	360	35790.3	136518.1	13111.7	10786.7	2324.9
1925	398	47923.6	166250.0	23430.3	10972.8	12457.6
1930	453	51547.6	194141.6	25826.4	14265.7	11560.7

Source: Furnivall (1934b: Appendix).

---

[7] Recent research shows that pawnshops flourish in developing countries with high inflation rates and an underdeveloped banking system, as well as in Western countries during economic crises. From a sociological point of view, valuables such as jewelry and ornaments, which form social capital to some extent, can be easily transferred into economic capital and vice versa (see Bourdieu's [e.g. 1977]. thoughts on cultural and social capital).

13. Anti-Usury Legislation and Anti-Usury Associations

With the spread of the Ethical Policy, legal action was also taken against moneylenders. An indirect measure were the Agrarian Laws which restricted the sale of land to foreigners. In 1875 another Act even tightened control. Furthermore, the letting of land to foreigners was put under the supervision of the authorities. However, in practice various ways were found to evade such acts and regulations. For example, foreign moneylenders employed indigenous touts (often their house-maids) in whose name the transfers were registered. Other indirect measures were the popular credit system and cooperatives, both of which were discussed in the previous chapter.

Direct government legislation against usury was passed even later than in India. Before 1938, the only direct attack on usury was the *koninklijk Besluit van 17 Juli 1916*, no. 23 (Royal Ordinance from 17 July 1916), which was published in the *Indische Staatsblad* No. 643. Nevertheless, this was much earlier than in the Netherlands where the first moneylenders' act was introduced as late as 1933. Boeke (1916) was to discuss this royal order.

> "*Indien bij eene overeenkomst eene der partijen, misbruik makende van de lichzinnigheid, onervarenheid of noodtoestand der wederpartij, voor zich of voor een derde eeinig voordeel heeft bedongen, dat hare eigen uit de overeenkomst voortvloeiende verpflichting zoodanig in waarde overtreft, dat, in verband met de omstandigheid van de wederzijdsche verbintenissen buitensporig is, kan de rechter, op verzoek der benadeelde prtij, de verplichting dier partij matigen of de overeenkomst nietig verklaren en zal hij bij zijn uitspraak in het geding tevens de gevolgen voor beide partijen naar billijkheid regelen, met dien verstande dat, ingeval van nietigverklaring van de overeenkomst, partijen zoovel mogelijk zullen moeten worden hersteld in den staat, warin zij zich vóór het aangaan van de verbintenis bevonden. Het bewijs door getuigen is in alle gevallen toegelaten*" (*koninklijk Besluit van 17 Juli 1916, no. 23*, quoted by Boeke 1916).

In the subsequent *Indische Staatsblad* No. 644 a royal order of the same date was added as a new article 135a:

> "*De president is bevoegd om, indien hij dit voor den goeden en geregelden gang der zaak noodig acht, partijen bij de behandeling van de zaak de noodige voorlichting te geven en haar opmerksaam te maken op de rechts- en bewijsmiddelen, welke zij kunnen aanwenden*" (ibid.).

To summarize in English, usury was defined as an agreement according to which one party exploited the recklessness, inexperience or need of the other party to obtain a personal advantage. Boeke emphasized that this act was very similar to the German Usury Act, which treated usury as a matter of private law. In the Netherlands Indies, every district administrator obtained the right to judge usury cases, reduce the loan amount or even declare the agreement void. However, like in India he could intervene only, if people called on him for justice, which was one of the main deficiencies of most usury laws. Common people are usually reluctant to call for justice, since courts are socially and spatially distant, and borrowers are afraid that they might not find an alternative credit source, since moneylenders exchanged information on their clients. Boeke maintained that the indigenous people did not even consider usury an offense, so that the enforcement of penal law even offended against indigenous feeling. Compared to the German Act, however, this royal ordinance included usury in sales contracts with the right of repurchase, pawning, and the fictive sale of products on credit, in short: contracts which Muslims applied in loan transactions to cope with *riba*, the prohibition of interest in the Qur'an, and other people to circumvent the laws.

Much more significant than the Royal Ordinance of 1916 were three provisions from 1938: (a) the Moneylenders Ordinance (*geldschietersordonnantie 1938*, Staatsblad 1938 No. 523); (b) the Usury Ordinance (*woekerordonnantie 1938*, Stb. 1938 No. 524); and (c) the less severe punishment with respect to hard labour (Stb. 1938 No. 360).[1]

(a) The Moneylenders Ordinance for Java, Madura, Sumatra's east coast (the Chettiar area of activity) and Aceh aimed at professional moneylenders, and the question of usury was not taken into consideration. The term 'usury' was therefore avoided in the text. To mention some of the regulations: according to the ordinance, the business of moneylending required a license from the Assistant Resident or Resident that had to be renewed every three years. Moneylenders were defined as persons or institutions whose profession or firm (in Dutch: *beroep of bedrief*) was concerned with the provision of credit. Excluded from this ordinance were small-scale loans up to f 10, which was mainly the domain of *tjina mindering* and public pawnshops, and loans exceeding f 500 as well as formal financial institutions.

An agreement with a moneylender without license was legally invalid. In the case of such agreements the borrower did not have to repay more than the principal sum. In case that the full amount had not yet been repaid, a judge could fix installments. For every installment the lender was obliged to provide a receipt to the debtor. Agreements in which the loan was in cash and the repayment in kind were treated like cash loans. In case a mortgage secured the loan, the creditor could not take it in charge without the authorization of a judge. Disregarding the ordinance was punished by fines or even imprisonment.

(b) The Usury Ordinance replaced the *Royal Ordinance from 17 July 1916*. It extended the right of courts to intervene, which they could do now either at request of a borrower or even by themselves. The ordinance was valid for monetary loans as well as for loans in kind and could also be applied retroactively.

(c) The punishment of imprisonment for debts (*lijfsdzwang*) was eased in the following way. People above 65 and people whose health could be expected to be damaged by such punishment were excluded from being kept hostage *(gijzeling)*. Also excluded were people who were incapable of repaying. The maximum period for *gijzeling* was reduced from three to one year. These three ordinances had a major impact on usury in that many professional moneylenders discontinued their businesses.

Another measure against usury were the anti-usury associations, which emerged during the 1920s and 1930s. The first anti-usury association was founded in Ban-

---

[1] I took this information from a speech to the members of the Rotary Clubs in Solo and Djember, which was printed in *De Woeker* 56 (n.n. 1941: 2-13).

dung in 1927. Other associations followed in Makassar, Semarang, Bandung, Kedri, Malang, Batavia, Surabaya, Yogya, and Medan to mention only a few. The office hours were adapted to the needs of customers. In 1933 the associations formed the *Verbond van Anti-Woekervereenigingen in Nederlandsch-Indie* (Union of Anti-Usury Associations in Netherlands-India). According to their self-understanding,[2] they were a service organization for borrowers. Every complaint by a debtor was considered in detail with regard to the borrowing conditions, which was more difficult than it seems because every lender tried to avoid any written evidence of interest actually taken. The association considered an interest rate of two percent per month reasonable. If the association thought a loan relation was usurious, the borrower was advised to stop his repayment. If the lender called for the judge, the borrower was supported by the association and in many cases succeeded in getting the debt reduced. Another task of the associations was to apply for public credit on the borrower's behalf at the *Algemeene Volkscredietbank* with which the creditor could be paid out. In some cases the direct negotiations of the associations with the lenders led to the reduction of the debt when he was paid out, in other cases lenders agreed to accept repayment by installment.

A report of an anti-usury association of 1931[3] emphasized that, contrary to the common opinion that borrowers had debts only to a single lender, borrowers used to combine different credit sources, which made the work of such associations and the courts to rehabilitate borrowers more difficult. The following example which was explicitly mentioned to be an ordinary case will illustrate this and the work of such associations. An indigenous borrower had debts to six lenders, three Chinese and three Arabs. From the first lender he had obtained credit twice, once f 250 to be repaid in ten installments of f 45 (totaling f 450), another time f 80 to be repaid in ten installments of f 12 (totaling f 120). The second lender had provided f 300 to be repaid in ten installments of f 46 (totaling f 460), the third f 100 to be repaid in ten installments of f 17 (f totaling 170). From the fourth lender he had obtained f 50 to be repaid in five installments of f 15 (totaling f 75), from the fifth lender f 60 to be repaid as one single sum of f 72 or, what is more realistic, with ten installments of f 12 per month (totaling f 120). Lender six then had provided f 40 to be repaid in five installments of f 12 (totaling 60). The total sums obtained were f 880, the total sums to be repaid f 1,455. The borrower had already repaid a total of f 133 with and a total of f 365 without receipts. The further monthly total installments were f 175, while the maximum total installments which he was able to repay was f 100 only, according to the calculations of the association. Therefore an installment plan was proposed by the association which the lenders agreed to. The installments per lender were in some cases reduced, so that the total installments did not exceed f 100 (translated and summarized from Anti-Woeker Vereeniging Bandoeng 1931: 56-7).

What was considered 'not extraordinary' by the association, were loans which I do not any longer count among small-scale loans. This leads me to assume that borrowers who sought help from the anti-usury associations were not the customers of small-scale lenders. In addition, although these associations were widespread on Java, they

---

[2] This self-understanding was expressed in a speech to the members of the Rotary Clubs in Solo and Djember, which was printed in *De Woeker* 56 (n.n. 1941: 2-13).

[3] Anti-Woeker Vereeniging Bandoeng (1931): 5e Jahrverslag 1931. Bandung

could be found in towns and cities only, so that the clients of the associations originated from an urban context and probably belonged to the urban middle-class.

For the latter speaks the design of the journal of the associations called *de woeker*[4] (usury) which was first published in 1935. The journal was written in Dutch. It contained news and reports of the various anti-usury associations and of the *Anti-Woeker Verbond*, of the history of usury, of moneylenders' practices, judicial cases, and so on. The cover speaks for itself. An oversized black spider keeps a white, motionless man in its net and claws.

In 1937, a commission for the scaling down of debt was introduced. Its tasks were already in line with the policy to strengthen cooperatives. The commission had access to a welfare fund. Its target group were people from large parts of Java and Menado who had been disadvantaged by the *idjon* system. The methods applied varied according to the socio-economic context, for example, the establishment of their own marketing organizations or the provision of credit. Until the end of 1938, a total of 16,310 people obtained f 937,021. Some local authorities even stopped giving permission to the operation of *tjina mindering* in market-places and instead offered small-scale public credit to traders (Coolhaas n.d.: 117).

---

[4] De woeker. Tijdschrift voor de Woekerbestrijding in Nederlandsch-Indie. Uitgave von het Verbond van Anti-Woekervereenigingen in Ned.-Indie. This journal was a monthly publication and in the early 1940s had a circulation of 25,000 copies.

14. The Contemporary Financial Landscape

My argument so far has been that there was no chance for informal large-scale finance in Indonesia to develop in a period of potential world market-expansion, because the VOC and the Netherlands Indian government practiced state capitalism with heavily restricted markets. Once these were liberalized, foreign capital from outside the Netherlands Indies filled the gap of large-scale finance by institutionalized banks. In this chapter I take a final look at the contemporary financial landscape in Indonesia and the role of informal finance, in particular.

For long policy makers have tried to restrict informal finance. The main resentment and prejudice are that informal lenders exploit their clientele, that informal credit is used only in an unproductive way and that informal finance is not under the control of financial legislation and may undermine financial policy. The colonial and post-colonial administration tried to legally prohibit informal finance or provided subsidized credit and public finance to the people to create competition with the high informal interest rates to bring them down. This market-compatible policy is in contrast to former market restrictions through government monopolies and tax farms. Only recently, policy makers realized that formal and informal finance may not necessarily be in competition but indeed may complement each other, as both aim at different target groups. Strategies applied to cope with informal finance are the downgrading of formal finance to the village sphere, the upgrading of financial self-help groups by formalizing them and the interlinking of banks and self-help groups. As a first step, I provide a description of the current financial landscape in Indonesia with regard to both formal and informal finance and their relation. As a second step, I consider the present role of Chinese capital and its involvement in finance. The point in question is whether they could use their accumulated wealth and knowledge from their intermediary function during the colonial period (see Schrader 1994a, b, c) to defend their dominant position in commerce, industries and banking in independent Indonesia.

14.1. Financial Policy: From Regulation to Deregulation

McLeod (1994) characterized Indonesia's post-colonial politico-financial development in a short and apt way.[1] Sukarno, he argued, interpreted the Indonesian constitution in such a way that it aimed to establish an economy with more collective rather than private enterprise. The state was to control particular key sectors of the

---

[1] For a more detailed description which put an emphasis on the relation between foreign, Chinese, indigenous and state capital, see Robison (1986). For a description of formal finance, see Panglaykim (1974), Lee (1982), Arndt (1987), Bank Bumi Daya (1988); for a review of rural finance, see Schmit (1991). A good contribution on the Sukarno era was made by Dahm (1978).

economy, such as certain industries and banking. The 'socialist' command economy,[2] mere state capitalism that regulated markets and prices, was the response to colonial exploitation which was assumed to be representative of capitalism. Overlooked was the fact that the Dutch colonial system was far from being a liberal market and private enterprise characteristic of capitalism. In addition to the Dutch, Chinese private enterprise and its *comparadore* (intermediary) position in the colonial economy were made responsible for colonial exploitation during the colonial period and the Chinese were considered one main factor impeding post-colonial development.

The first OPEC boom in 1973, which turned Indonesia's balance of payment into black figures, concealed the weaknesses of its command economy, because a transfer of money between sectors became possible which hid the non-profitability of various state enterprises (see Robison 1986). Resources were also available to design large subsidized financial programs to eradicate the supposed dependence of small-scale businesses (farmers, fishermen, and so on) on self-finance and informal finance.

Until 1983 formal finance was tightly regulated. The policy aimed at replacing informal finance by formal and semi-formal one and was characterized by the channeling of large funds into the formal financial sector to promote a highly dispersed rural infrastructure of the state-owned smallholders' bank (Bank Rakyat Indonesia, BRI), which set up 3,600 village units. On the other hand, the government simultaneously restricted the growth of formal finance. In 1968 the New Order reformed the banks and laid down the banking structure (see Lee 1982).[3] After 1971 no new banks were permitted to be established (there were scores of private domestic banks, the seven large state banks, twenty-seven provincial banks, and eleven foreign banks), and the banks required official permission to extent their branch networks. In addition the government fixed growth limits to the banks in order to control the money supply. On the basis of this structure and the 1971 decree, the growth of existing 'hybrid' decentralized institutions such as *Bank Kredit Desa* or *Bank Pasar* (the roots of which go back to the Netherlands-Indian *Volkscredietwezen*) was restricted, while simulta-

---

[2] This belief was strongly and consistently held during the Sukarno era. Under the New Order, the regime's policy changed several times from a command economy to greater freedom for private enterprise and vice versa. Robison (1986) argued that this political orientation resulted from the power of the technocrats in the National Development Planning Board, *Bappenas*, who had been trained in the US, on neo-liberal grounds. Their power has always risen and fallen with the dependency of Indonesia on foreign capital. During the second half of the 1980s, this dependency became so overwhelming that the whole economy had to be deregulated on the pressure of IMF and World Bank.

[3] Five government-owned banks were integrated into one institution with five units: Bank Negara Indonesia (BNI) Unit 1, now Bank Indonesia, the Central Bank; BNI Unit II, now split into Bank Rakyat Indonesia and Bank Exspor Impor Indonesia; BNI Unit III, now Bank Negara Indonesia (1946); BNI Unit IV, now Bank Bumi Daya; and BNI Unit V, now Bank Tabungan Negara. The General Law of Banking of 1967 reorganized the banking structure into four categories, namely: commercial banks (state commercial banks, national private banks and foreign banks), savings banks (state-owned and private), development banks (state-owned and private) and other (rural) banks. The New Legislation of 1968 dissolved the five BNI units under the roof of the BNI into eight state-owned banks: Bank Indonesia, the central bank (established in 1953); five commercial banks: Bank Negara Indonesia 1946, Bank Rakyat Indonesia, Bank Ekspor Impor Indonesia, Bank Degang Negara, and Bank Bumi Daya; the government-owned development bank Bank Pembangunan Indonesia (Bapindo); and the savings bank Bank Tabungan Negara. Besides these government-owned banks there were a number of small, private indigenous and foreign banks. The last were allowed only in Jakarta. Outside the capital they had to seek domestic financial institutions as partners.

neously various provincial government credit institutions and government programs emerged (see Kern 1986: 120-1).

Rural credit provision belonged to the *Bimas* (mass guidance) Program, which was implemented in 1965 to promote Indonesia's rice production to the level of self-sufficiency by providing seed, fertilizers, pesticides etc. on cheap, subsidized credit to groups of farmers. On the whole, three different sub-programs were introduced. With the *Group Bimas* emphasis was placed upon cooperative organization; with the *Bimas Gotong Royong* foreign contractors helped to supply the means of production; and the *Improved Bimas* gave support for using modern technology, loan organization and procedure, learning the distribution of the means of production to the cultivators and the purchasing, processing and harvesting to obtain good profits and prices. The credit program categorized the borrowers into four loan groups with different loan purposes and loan conditions.[4] The main problem of the credit scheme was the risk in the field of agricultural loans, such as natural disasters and pests. The *Bimas* was given as a parcel containing the means of production like fertilizer, seed and insecticide, together with cash to help the farmer until harvest (for details see A.I.D. Spring Review 1973; Schmit 1991). Loans were distributed by the BRI branch network and the BRI was refinanced by the central bank with subsidized rates. The scheme was ultimately a misfortune because of a very high default rate and a continuous flow of state bank funds into the program.

Another program was the KIK/KMKP (*Kredit Investasi Kecil/Kredit Modal Kerja Permanen*) small business program (see e.g. McLeod 1980, 1983), which was operating in a similar way, but also supplied credit to individuals. But this time the credit risk was insured by the government-owned *PT Askrindo* insurance company. This scheme was less disastrous, although it also required subsidies and was finally terminated in 1990. These and similar programs, which are characteristic for this period in a number of developing countries, have been increasingly criticized because they neglected the savings side of finance.

Interference with the financial market went further. The government tried to reactivate the Jakarta stock exchange, but it overestimated private demand for shares. The government therefore established a national investment fund, *PT Danareksa*, which was to purchase large quantities of shares and resell them in very small bundles to the poor. But this scheme was not successful either. The target group preferred traditional informal savings or bank savings.

According to McLeod (1994) the government itself was the primary obstacle to the growth of the formal financial sector. Another factor which restricted growth was the continued flow of funds from the state bank to the state owned-commercial banks. On

---

[4] Group I: 12 percent interest per annum for loans in the fields of fertilizer import and distribution and for special areas like *bimas*, rice; Group II: 15 – 18 percent interest per annum for loans in the field of poultry farming, crude rubber production and export of Java tobacco; Group III: 21 – 24 percent interest per year for loans in the field of export products and for the distribution of nine basic commodities, agricultural products, animal husbandry, fisheries, industries and public transport; and Group IV: 25-36 percent interest per year for loans in the field of trade and other distribution activities not covered in the other groups. The total credit volume was divided among the groups (Group I 10 percent, group II 10 percent, group III 45 percent, group IV 35 percent).

the whole, the Sukarno regime and, until 1983, the New Order more or less suppressed the price mechanism in the financial market. All state bank loans had subsidized rates and were in turn subsidized by the state bank. In spite of this policy, the aim of supplanting informal finance by providing cheap formal credit to the poor, with an extensive rural branch system and government credit programs, was only partly achieved. In spite of the fast growth of small, medium and large firms, many of these continued to finance themselves, at least to some extent, through informal sources, while certain private large- and medium-scale enterprises benefited from subsidized credit. According to Robison (1986), these were particularly Chinese and indigenous enterprises under the patronage of the government or military and bureaucratic capitalists who went into partnership with WNI Chinese.[5]

Being aware of the limited results of financial policy and the unintended side-effects, and on the advice of the IMF and World Bank, the government introduced two major packages of deregulation in 1983 and 1988, and various laws in 1992 to regulate banking, insurance and pension funds. Broadly speaking, the state partly withdrew from the control of the financial market and created more room for private initiative.

The 1983 deregulation of the financial landscape opened the market for the setting-up of new banks which have since mushroomed in Jakarta and other commercial places in Indonesia. How far Chinese, the colonial non-Western commercial elite, are involved in private banking shall be investigated in the second part of this chapter. Most interest rate controls were ended. When the banks began to offer high savings interest rates, bank deposits could be substantially increased. Lending rates rose by 24-30 percent. Currently they cover inflation and reflect market conditions. Comparatively speaking, Indonesia's formal interest rates are among the highest in the whole region which has reduced capital exports.[6] According to Seibel (1989):

> "the present financial situation in Indonesia bears the marks of both old and new, regulated and free market policies. Financial markets are segmented into formal, informal and semi-formal financial markets. Banks are the core institutions of the **formal financial sector**. This sector also includes a number of small second-tier institutions, which are defined as non-banks, such as BKK[7] in central Java (...) and others, which are supervised by primary banks (...) as well as registered cooperatives (...) which fall under the cooperative law. There are numerous **informal financial institutions** (...) which operate without legal status and outside state control: moneylenders, financial self-help groups (rotating and non-rotating savings and credit associations, unregistered credit unions) and numerous other groups with secondary financial functions (...). **Semi-formal financial institutions** include PVOs as well as GOs [private voluntary organizations and government organizations, H.S.], which act as intermediaries between domestic or foreign donors and informal self-help groups or final individual borrowers. They are extra-legal in their financial activities, but so far have obviously enjoyed the tacit tolerance of the state. In addition, one may include officially recognized but unregistered pre-cooperatives in this sector" (Seibel 1989: 10-11).

---

[5] WNI: *warga negara Indonesia*, i.e. Chinese with Indonesian citizenship.

[6] In 1983 the nominal deposit rate in Indonesia was fixed to 18 percent, which means that only then the real deposit rates turned into positive figures. Time deposits amounted to between 16 and 24 percent. The deposits per economically active population increased from about US 50 in 1983 to US 150 in 1990. The annual nominal lending rates increased to more than 20 percent during the 1980s, which means that the real lending rates amounted to more than 10 percent (UN Statistics, own calculations, see Schrader 1993).

[7] *Badan Kredit Kecamatan*, a regional government credit program for rural finance (see below).

The deregulation package terminated different credit programs, such as the *Bimas* in 1983, and the state banks had to do without the subsidies of BI. They therefore heavily increased their time deposits. To maintain their market shares private banks followed the example. The whole banking sector experienced considerable growth with competition between state and private banks.[8] By 1983-1987 the number of banking offices increased from 1,210 to 1,460. The largest share of banking offices were found on Java (excluding Jakarta) with 32.64 percent, Sumatra with 24.07 percent and DKI Jakarta with 14.97 percent, whereas the rest of Indonesia had a share of only 10.3 percent. From the perspective of assets, the non foreign-exchange private national banks experienced the fastest growth. They held the largest average share of banking funds with 68.41 percent. During 1983-87 banking credit grew by an average of 26.5 percent. The state foreign-exchange banks held the largest average share with 67.12 percent of total value. In second position were the national private foreign exchange banks which supplied an average of 9.02 percent per year. Development banks supplied an average of 7.7 percent, but experienced a downward trend throughout the whole period. Non-foreign-exchange national private banks had an average share of 7.45 percent, with an upward trend throughout the period. Foreign banks had an average share of 4.61 percent with a downward trend. The savings banks had the smallest share with 4.1 percent, with a slight upward trend. Considering the average growth rates of credit supply per year of the different institutions, private foreign-exchange banks had growth rates of 47.94 percent, non-foreign-exchange banks of 42.27 percent, savings banks of 30.97 percent, state foreign-exchange banks of 24.8 percent and development banks of 20.02 percent. Considering the allocation of bank credit the largest share was distributed in Jakarta (averaging 53.1 percent per year) followed by Java (excluding Jakarta, 25.09 percent) and Sumatra (12.45 percent). Kalimantan's share averaged 4.16 percent, Sulawesi's 2.68 percent and Malakku and Irian Jaya's share was 1.11 percent (Bank Bumi Daya 1988). Outside the banking system, a number of heterogeneous financial institutions are mushrooming, such as insurance companies, capital investment companies and pension-fund corporations.

The 1988 deregulation package removed barriers to institutional development, such as the regulated access to the banking sector and the opening of new branches. This resulted in a doubling of the number of private domestic banks (126 by the end of 1991) and an increase of the new foreign joint venture banks. The number of branches increased from 1,700 in 1988 to more than 4,200 in 1991, with a share of one quarter and half of private banks, respectively. In addition, 600 new secondary banks (*Bank Perkreditan Rakyat*, BPR) were established. According to McLeod (1994), the growth of banks is inhibited by the necessity to maintain an appropriate balance between the asset portfolio and capital available to absorb potential losses.

---

[8] According to Arndt (1987) the contemporary state commercial banks are: (1) Bank Bumi Daya (specializing mainly in export production, estates, mining, with 76 branches); (2) Bank Dagang Negara (export production, mining, 93 branches); (3) Bank Negara 1946 (industry, agriculture, export production, with 218 branches including sub-branches); (4) Bank Rakyat Indonesia (agriculture, livestock, 293 branches including payout stations, mobile units and village units); and (5) Bank Ekspor Impor Indonesia (export production, estates, with 49 branches).

Downgrading, Upgrading and Linking

With the abolition of the *Bimas* program in 1983 and the KIK/KMKP program in 1990, BRI downgraded its banking services to the village level by offering new banking services under market conditions (or almost market conditions) through the existing branch network. The strategy to refrain from subsidized credit emerged during the 1980s as a response to the failure of such programs and was applied in two credit schemes: *Kupedes* and *Simpedes*. *Kupedes* is a loan for either investment or working capital supplied to individuals. The *Kupedes* interest rates are still below the market rates (33 percent p.a.) but rather high compared to the *Bimas* program (9 percent p.a.). They cover the costs of funds, transaction costs, a reserve for bad debts and a profit margin, and contrary to former experiences with subsidized programs the repayment rate is almost 98 percent. *Kupedes* loans range from Rp. 25,000 to Rp. 2 millions (Seibel 1989). *Simpedes* is a rural savings program, which was introduced in 1986 and has enjoyed great success.

Another example of downgrading is BKK (*Badan Kredit Kecamatan*), a regional government rural credit program in Central Java, which has been operating since 1972 through almost 500 independent small delivery units. Each BKK is owned by the local government of the *kecamatan* (sub-district), supervised and refinanced by BPD, the Provincial Development Bank, and technically assisted by USAID. This program belongs to semi-formal finance, since it does not fall under the control of the credit law. BKK loans are small-scale, short-term and determined by market conditions. Transaction costs are minimized by having mobile offices, teams traveling throughout the region according to a fixed schedule. From the beginning of 1972 to December 1986, a total of Rp. 4.8 million in small and very small loans were granted to small farmers, tenants and micro-entrepreneurs. The rate of repayment was, according to Seibel (1989), close to 98.8 percent. The operational costs (costs of fund, salaries, administrative expenses, default losses) are covered by the interest margin.

Contrasting the strategy of downgrading is one of upgrading private voluntary organizations and self-help groups in Indonesia to form their own banks. An example are the LPN (*Lumbung Pitih Nagari*), savings and credit associations in West Sumatra, which have been integrated into the formal regional banking system. In the late 1980s, 40 percent of the LPN, the self-help LPN, operated successfully with repayment rates of almost 100 percent, while many government LPN which consider themselves as agencies channeling government funds to the target groups were less successful. Self-help LPN rely mainly on their own funds, i.e. the savings of their members and profits. Loans issued to members run mostly between six and eight months, with a maximum of twelve months, and vary between 10,000 Rp. and 1 million Rp. The effective interest rate is about 40 percent per annum (Seibel 1989).

A third strategy of rural finance is the provision of formal credit to borrowers who individually have no security to offer but who form joint liability groups to compensate for this lack. APRACA[9] is an Asian-Pacific association of central banks, rural development banks and commercial banks, which aims at constructing a financial in-

---

[9] Asian and Pacific Regional Agricultural Credit Association, originally promoted by the UN Food and Agriculture Organization (FAO).

termediary system between existing banks and grassroots micro-entrepreneurs around self-help groups. The emphasis is placed on both the credit and the savings sides, which will be linked in such a way that joint-liability groups build up their own savings, which are placed in the banks. Credit is delivered at market rates and the groups decide how to distribute this credit among their members. In Indonesia a pilot project was started in cooperation with BI. Grassroots groups function as intermediaries for small-scale entrepreneurs to minimize transaction costs. The interest rates include the costs of funds, gross margin for the bank (including transaction costs, reserves for bad debts, profit), gross margin for self-help primary institutions, and gross margin/incentive payment to the self-help group. Defaults have been minimized to less than five percent (Seibel 1989).

Reasons for the shift in Indonesian financial policy from heavy regulation to deregulation are manifold: successful experiences of other Southeast Asian countries with private financial markets; the decreasing oil price (so that petrol-dollars can no longer compensate for the losses of state enterprise and subsidize credit programs); the bad experiences with high default rates in subsidized credit programs; the capital exports from Indonesia; the cultivation of development aid and pressure of supra-national organizations; the attempt to develop Jakarta as **the** nodal point of the Asia-Pacific trade zone; and growing confidence in private enterprise.

14.2. Informal Finance

Having so far shown the shift in financial policy in Indonesia from heavily regulated financial markets with heavily subsidized but rather unsuccessful credit programs for the grassroots level to less restricted financial markets and the current strategies of downgrading formal finance, of upgrading self-help groups to formal institutions and of linking self-help groups with banks to reach the poor, the question remains how the different suppliers of informal finance developed within this changing financial landscape. First of all, it is obvious that informal finance developed earlier than formal finance and always adapted to the changing circumstances. However, with growing importance and integration of the economy, the necessity of formal finance has increased, because the complexity of financial affairs in a differentiated economy exceeds the capacity of informal financial agents and requires an integrated financial network. One important reason that the state supports the growth of formal finance at the expense of informal finance is that the latter operates outside the scope of control of the state.

On the other hand, the acceptance of and confidence in banks by the public is a very long process which took several centuries in Europe and was concluded in the twentieth century. It is however, too simplistic to believe that this slow change is only a matter of tradition. Informal and formal finance each have certain, largely antipodal advantages and disadvantages. The following reasons are mentioned as advantages of informal financial intermediaries. They are spatially closer to the borrowers and often well-known; credit is available easily and quickly; installment schemes are adapted to the requirements of the borrowers; the lenders usually accept an interruption in installment payments in emergency cases (although very often they take some advantage of such postponement); they do not ask for the loan purpose; security is only required for new customers, while old customers obtain preferential rates; borrowers want to maintain their long-established credit link, while they are afraid in a new, impersonal relation with a bank, and so on. Disadvantageous are the high interest rates (which often reflect the insecurity of a loan), the limitation of funds, a lack of refinancing possibilities, no provision of additional services such as consultancy, no savings facilities for borrowers, etc. From such a perspective, contemporary informal finance and the continuous change in financial intermediaries are both a reaction to common peoples' requirements and state laws. In Indonesia moneylending and private pawnbrokerage have been legally prohibited by the Indonesian government since independence but can easily be circumvented in practice. Most financial legislation refers to the sphere of formal finance and has hardly affected informal finance.

In this paragraph I refer to a number of micro- and macro-studies on credit in rural Java. First of all, it has been commonly agreed that in Indonesia (as in most developing countries) the share of informal finance has been decreasing over the last three decades. The heavy expansion of formal finance into rural regions on Java in particular creates competition with informal finance. But a decreasing share of informal finance does not necessarily mean a reduction in absolute numbers. It means no more than that the growth rate of formal finance is higher than the informal one. Sectoral developments are not visible from such a ratio. For example, recent estimates suggest that informal finance is still expanding in the petty and medium-scale trading sector.

Micro-studies point out that borrowing is an everyday affair in the rural as well as the urban context. Almost every household needs credit at least once a year. What is important is that the choice of creditor by the borrower does not depend so much on the rate of interest, but on credit amount and reason for borrowing, as well as the collateral that the borrower can offer (Hardjono 1987).

In his 1987 survey on rural and urban households on Java and Bali for a comparative study of the Asian Development Bank (Ghate 1992), Prabowo et al. (1989: 5) found that 90 percent of the total values of loans used by individuals came from informal sources (semi-formal sources such as credit unions were counted among the informal ones).[10] Since the study includes the urban context, it goes beyond the scope of most studies. Nevertheless, such aggregated estimations are of course not very reliable. The report emphasized that the informal financial markets are segmented and cover a broad spectrum of agents, institutions and arrangements. Commercial lenders and credit arrangements are professional, part-time and semi-professional lenders, private pawnshops and commercialized rotating savings and credit associations (RoSCA). Non-commercial are the traditional RoSCA, credit unions, public pawnshops and neighbors, friends and relatives. I take a closer look at this spectrum and include the findings of several other studies.

---

[10] It was based on questionnaires to 70 lenders and 240 borrowers in rural regions of Central and East Java, as well as 50 lenders and 187 borrowers in the cities of Jakarta, Semarang, Surabaya (all Java) and Denpasar (Bali).

14.2.1.   The Spectrum of Financial Intermediaries

Professional moneylenders are more prevalent in urban than in rural regions. They are called *rentenir*. The typical moneylenders of the colonial period (peddling Chinese *tjina mindering* in rural regions, Chinese and Arab lenders in towns and cities on Java, and the Chettiar at the east coast of Sumatra, see Schrader 1995) have lost ground compared to Indonesians, although some Chinese moneylenders are still operating in Jakarta. Among the professional Indonesian moneylenders are a number of Batak who operate outside their home region (Prabowo et al. 1989; Ghate 1992). According to Bouman and Moll (1992) professional moneylenders largely operate with own funds from their homes or offices in urban regions around market places and business centers, and they only occasionally accept savings.[11] They provide credit to small and medium-scale industries, commerce and farmers. Empirical evidence suggests that they limit their number of clients to a maximum of 30. If they serve more clients, they employ brokers who often form the link to rural regions. If they operate successfully, they may set up as independent operators.

In his in-depth study on moneylenders in a sub-district town on Java, Heru-Nugroho (1993) observed that the majority of professional moneylenders are Javanese women, which contrasts the colonial period both in terms of ethnicity and gender. In many cases they were formerly engaged in trade. The partners of practicing moneylenders mostly work in trade and commerce, while a few male professional moneylenders were formerly involved in the administration or the military. To set up a moneylending business, one needs a stock of capital achieved by savings, or one has to take a loan and obtain information from a large-scale moneylender. There is some competition between the moneylenders on the same level of business, but not between different levels. Interest for such starting capital usually amounts to ten percent per month, which is half the interest the smaller lenders acquire by on-lending to their clientele. In many cases the large-scale moneylender has access to bank credit or bank savings accounts but he or she uses it only if there is a shortage of capital. Banks take 2.5 percent interest per month.

Among the professional moneylenders, Hardjono (1987) and Prabowo et al. (1989) identified so-called mobile bankers (*bank keliling* or *bank plecet*).[12] They have opened a 'bank' office or 'cooperative' to obtain a license but peddle from door to door. They provide small and medium-scale installment credit to traders and factory workers without collateral and without long procedures and charge interest rates of 10 – 20 percent per month.

In addition to professional moneylenders, there are various occasional moneylenders, people with some wealth or the wives of husbands with regular incomes from teaching, civil service, etc. who prefer the option of moneylending to the alternative of savings in a bank because of higher returns. Since they often have access to formal credit, the more enterprising take a bank credit themselves to enlarge their working

---

[11] In Denpasar (Bali) Prabowo (1987) came across moneylenders who paid their depositors a share of the profit.

[12] On Java they are often called *bank plecit*, meaning that the lender hunts the borrower and there is no way of escaping timely repayment.

capital and on-lend to informal borrowers. Bouman (1989) observed for India that this group is growing rapidly at the expense of professional lenders, and this is probably also true for Indonesia. For both professional and part-time moneylenders interest rates range from ten to twenty percent per month. I agree with Bouman and Moll (1992) that these relatively high interest rates are not so much due to monopoly profit than reflect the nature of the financial services offered and the characteristics of the borrowers. They cannot offer collateral, require small-scale and short-term loans, the default rates are high, and so on.

In rural regions moneylending is almost always combined with other occupations. Semi-professional lenders, who usually do not consider themselves as moneylenders, include shopkeepers, crop merchants, suppliers of fertilizers and farm machinery, landlords, millers, craftsmen, transport dealers and peddling traders. They either provide cash credit to be repaid in kind like landlords and crop merchants, or they sell on credit. Dewey (1964), Hardjono (1987) and Bouman and Moll (1992) maintained that the purpose of lending of such credit suppliers is not only, if at all, to make large profits by lending, but to facilitate other exchanges. For example, shop owners sell on credit and charge no interest or hidden interest through higher prices. The reason is that in many cases they do not undercut each other with prices (since the profit margins in the price calculations are already at the minimum level) but offer preferential conditions to their customers. Another reason is that in many cases customers cannot pay in cash but have to balance their bills with their next income. Most shop-owners, both urban and rural, have obtained their stock on credit (see e.g. Alexander 1986) and most small-scale industries and artisans obtain trade credit from input suppliers and themselves offer trade credit to wholesalers and retailers, so that complex networks of trade credit can occur. *Ijon*, the selling of the green crop to an agricultural trader, and similar arrangements of crop dealers are not very different from those during the colonial period. *Ijon* was prohibited by Law No. 2/1960, *sewa* (land lease) and *gadai* (land pawning) by Article 53 of the basic Agrarian Law. Nevertheless these systems are still flourishing.[13]

Until the 1950s most itinerant moneylenders-cum-traders were Chinese, but the Javanese subsequently took over this business. They peddle from house to house and sell a variety of products, such as glassware, plastic ware, textiles, and small electronic goods on installment credit, whereas the lending of cash seems to be less common. No contract is signed. The installments are fixed to every five days, comprising an interest rate of 20 to 30 percent per month, so that it becomes obvious that these lenders, the *mendriks*,[14] earn more from the interest than from the goods sold. Nowadays *mendriks* are also popular in towns.

Whether in the urban or the rural context, moneylenders have good knowledge of their customers. Officially moneylending is illegal. Prabowo et al. (1989) reported

---

[13] *Gadai* is allowed up to seven years after which the loan is considered to be repaid. With shorter *gadai* the principal sum is automatically reduced in proportional. As a result of these laws, many transfers of land as a result of credit are made 'under the table'.

[14] *Mendrik* or *mendring* has been derived from *tjina mindering* (see Schrader 1994a, b, c), which was, however, applied to Chinese itinerant lenders only. Hardjono (1987) mentioned another term that is applied, namely *tukang kredit*.

that one strategy of the lenders to avoid legal confrontation is not to attract attention by keeping their clientele and radius of action small. Another strategy is the bribing of officials. Most moneylenders in rural Indonesia provide credit without collateral, while in urban regions collateral in the form of luxury or consumer goods or titles (electronics, jewelry, motorcycles or cars, land titles, household items, insurance licenses and pension documents) is frequent. The value of collateral always exceeds the value of the loan.

Arisan are the Indonesian RoSCAs, which are wide-spread, ranging from non-commercial to commercial forms. The *arisan call* is highly commercialized and functions by bidding. To minimize the encounters with legal authorities, the meetings are kept secret or bidding is even done on phone.[15]

Friends, relatives and neighbors are usually a source of non-commercial credit. In rural Indonesia, loans from friends and relatives, which are small-scale, are usually interest-free, while credit among neighbors very often takes the form of a rice loan with an interest rate of 50 percent until the next harvest. With increasing differentiation of the economy social obligations such as reciprocal interest-free loans to closely-knit members of the community seem to decline.

Another supplier of credit are the private and public pawnshops, the former being informal, the latter formal institutions. As pawn brokerage existed already during colonial times and is by now a state monopoly, all private pawnshops are illegal. As in many other Third-World countries, the majority of Indonesians invest their savings in gold and jewelry due to high inflation and devaluation, and these valuables are occasionally pawned. Gold shops, for example, sell gold to their customers and provide the guarantee to re-purchase it a the current market rate and sell it back to the former owner at the current market rate, too. This works because the gold price has been rising steadily. Skully (1994) mentioned a number of around 500 public pawnshops in 1990. Pawns in Indonesia, in addition to gold, ornaments and luxury goods, are a variety of household articles, the latter of which is untypical for private pawnshops in most Southeast Asian countries, most of which accept jewelry and gold only. Loans amount to between 84 and 89 percent of the value of the pawn, which private pawnshops offer for gold only. Bouman and Moll (1992) reported that the turnover of public pawnshops increased from Rp. 31 billion in 1975 to Rp. 156 billion in 1981 (US$ 124 and 468 million at the time). The redemption rate was almost 100 percent. Pawning is an everyday-affair of many people and pawnshops have been called the 'poor peoples' banks'. Although public pawn houses take an interest of 3 to 4 percent only, many people prefer the pawning at private shops in spite of much higher interest, because they receive larger sums for the pawns.

14.2.2.   Loan Size and Interest Rates

Prabowo et als' (1989) survey data demonstrate that the acceptance of formal finance is not very high. In the rural areas of Central Java almost 26 percent of the 120

---

[15] This telephone bidding gave its name to this *arisan* 'call'. For a detailed discussion of RoSCAs, see e.g. Bouman (1983, 1994); Schrader (1991).

respondents borrowed from registered cooperatives, close to 22 percent from BKD (*Bank Pembangunan Daerah*, the provincial development bank) and about 14 percent from BKK (*Badan Kredit Kecamatan*), a regional government credit program for rural finance in Central Java. In east Java almost 16 percent borrowed from BRI and 9 percent from cooperatives. In Semarang only some well-off people borrowed from the formal sector, and in Surabaya and Denpasar at the same time from informal agents and institutions, too. In Jakarta, on the other hand, most respondents had access to bank credit. From these data it is difficult to assess the size of informal loans, since borrowers tend to take up formal and informal loans at the same time. Nevertheless, I suggest that at least 50 percent of credit in Central Java and considerably more in East Java and other islands being from informal or semi-formal sources, seems justified, while for West Java different conditions apply inside and outside DKI Jakarta.

Prabowo et als' (1989) sample provides further information. With regard to loan size, 65 percent of the respondents borrowed up to Rp. 500,000 and 35 percent above Rp. 500,000 from informal sources. The average size of formal credit was more than Rp. 1,600,000, which was about twice as large as the loan size from informal sources (about Rp. 950,000). The sample's total amount of formal credit was about Rp. 23 million (with 14 borrowers), while that of informal credit was Rp. 202 million with 217 borrowers (whereby the report does not state the mean). Much of the informal credit was given on an installment basis, and the repayment schemes were adapted to the requirements of the borrowers.

Heru-Nugroho (1993) outlined five different types of credit which are adapted to the requirements of the customers in length and installment payments. The length and maximum loans are 12 days and Rp. 20,000, 24 days and Rp. 50,000, 30 days and Rp. 100,000, 60 days and Rp. 300,000 and one year and up to Rp. 100 million. While the former four types usually imply interest rates of 20 percent per month, the latter amounts from 6 – 10 percent. Large business loans, however, usually require collateral.

From the point of view of use of funds, Prabowo's report emphasized the increasing demand for credit for special occasions (e.g. Hindu festivals or start of tourist season in Bali, the start of the school year which requires school fees, purchase of books, etc.).[16] Such seasonally fluctuating credit demand leads to a temporary increase in interest rates. In Central Java, the main reasons for borrowing were household, subsistence and working capital requirements. Other reasons were emergency needs, schooling, house repairs, and so on. In urban regions, the average rate of interest was lower than in rural regions, and a large array of different credit sources were available. The demand for informal credit was higher in cities.

The sampled lenders consisted mainly of middle-aged women with higher education (high school 70 percent). More than half of the respondents were already in this business for more than five years. Moneylenders and itinerant traders used to charge higher interest than other informal lenders, and short-term credit was more expensive than long-term credit.

---

[16] Fifteen years ago Prabowo found that around 75 percent of the respondents in rural areas borrowed in one way or another for subsistence purposes.

Considering the interest rates and conditions of loans, formal and informal market rates vary over a wide range. This is due to the fact that both markets are largely complementary with different clienteles. Interest costs for formal loans are lower than informal ones. However, from an economic point of view these costs are only one component of total borrowing costs, which are the sum of interest costs and non-interest costs: transport costs, opportunity costs and miscellaneous other costs like fees for transaction and sometimes even bribe. These total borrowing costs of formal and informal credit are not much different, since the non-interest costs of banks are much higher than those of informal credit. Prabowo et al. (1989) maintained that informal rates, which typically ranged from 40 to 60 percent per annum in the survey year, express the market price of money better than the bank rates of 25 – 35 percent per year.

Financial policy has taken account of the fact that, from the borrowers' point of view, the level of interest is only one – and in many cases not the decisive – component of making the decision from which source to borrow. Micro-economics analysis has therefore elaborated broader cost-concepts (transaction costs, opportunity costs in addition to the costs of interest), which measure components such as spatial distance, but they have also understood that psychological components, such as social distance and long-established credit relations with a moneylender that cannot be measured in monetary terms, are equally important for the decision-making process. These additional cost-components and psychological factors are explained by the imperfection of the financial markets in developing countries (monopoly profit of moneylenders, lack of information of the borrowers, and so on) and by the partly traditional behavior of the borrowers. Heru-Nugroho (1993) even found that one cannot assume moneylenders to act entirely means-ends rational. Because of competition, they apply mixed strategies to maintain or gain a clientele. They provide economic incentives to their customers, persuade them to borrow and even utilize spells and magic hoping to bind the customers to themselves and thereby acquire business success.

To summarize the first part of this chapter: Like in many other Asian countries the absolute size of formal finance increased in Indonesia during the past decades while that of informal finance decreased. However, it is not obvious whether these changes result from a growing acceptance of formal finance in the public or whether they are related to the booming of certain cities, economic sectors and large-scale enterprise while the average population, including medium- and small-scale enterprise are still hesitant to have confidence in these new, impersonal financial institutions or are even afraid of the ponderous bureaucratic procedures of credit application.

A number of surveys from within and outside Indonesia demonstrate that there is indeed demand of capital not only on the higher, but also on the lower plain of the economy and reality shows that those who have access to formal finance combine it with informal finance to maximize their credit volume. I think this should be a lesson for a number of development planners. It is against the requirements of the population to try to extinct informal finance and substitute it against formal one, without being able to offer substitutes for its advantages. With regard to this I believe that the strategies of upgrading and linking are promising attempts. They are based on the assumption that formal and informal finance complement each other.

14.3.   Chinese-Owned Capital

The second part of this chapter reconsiders the economic position of the Chinese in contemporary Indonesia and their relation to finance. Were they able to maintain the dominant position in colonial trade and moneylending and did they use their accumulated wealth and knowledge to conquer the key positions in commerce and industries?

Even during the colonial period, but particularly during the post-colonial period the Chinese were physically attacked by the indigenous population. Buchholt (1992) argued rightly that contemporary Indonesian-Chinese conflicts are related to the colonial past because of their intermediary function and resulting economic benefits. Envy and their collaboration with the colonial system made them the target of indigenous attacks, which were, however, very often initiated by the colonizers to divert the aggression expressed against the colonial regime. During the late colonial and post-colonial periods, increasing competition occurred between indigenous people and trading minorities in the commercial field, but it is again too simplistic to see economic reasons as the only cause of pogroms. Before considering this particular question, I shall look at political and legal restrictions to private business in general and Chinese business in particular in post-colonial Indonesia.

During the Sukarno era, policy was directed towards the nationalization of foreign and the restriction of Chinese capital. The basic idea of the 'Guided Economy' was to develop the economy with state-owned capital. Private indigenous and Chinese enterprises were almost excluded from the most profitable economic spheres. Some of them, however, managed to have close relations with political and military leaders who provided them with licenses for imports and exports or state credit. Some indigenous groups entered the import trade, too.

During the 1950s the *benteng* (fortress) policy tried to supplant the Chinese from import and export. In 1959 the monetary purge severely affected private capital, much of which was Chinese capital, when all bank deposits exceeding Rp. 25,000 lost 90 percent of their value. This experience caused many businessmen and industrialists in Indonesia to keep capital low and to run foreign accounts abroad or to invest in stock. Much more restrictive was PP 10 (*Peraturan Presiden*), a presidential decree in 1959, which prohibited Chinese to settle and retail in rural regions. This decree forced 400,000 people of Chinese descent to transmigrate, and this may perhaps explain why the number of Chinese moneylenders in rural regions decreased in favor of indigenous ones. On the level of personal strategies, many Chinese businessmen reacted by employing indigenous touts, by capital exporting or by even emigrating. However, considered as a whole, they maintained their economic dominance. The early 1960s again limited private imports by fixing certain quotas for bank credits to private businessmen and sectors. The anti-Communist/anti-Chinese subsequent to the fall of the Sukarno regime are well-known.

Robison (1986) and Suryadinata (1988) emphasized that with the demise of Sukarno and the more economically liberal policy of the New Order, which welcomed foreign investment, the Chinese once again attained favorable conditions for their business. To my mind, this is true for the circumstances of private capital in general. With regard to the Chinese, this applies to Chinese large-scale business and industry only, while the average Chinese trader and shopkeeper was restricted by existing anti-Chinese legislation and suffered from the more or less regular looting of his property or even loss of life. In large-scale business and industry, an increasingly functional relation ('strategic group', see Evers and Schiel 1988) was established between the military and Chinese. *Cukong* is the term used for a big Chinese businessman who collaborates with a member of the Indonesian power elite, usually a high military officer. The *cukong*, the Chinese businessman runs the business and provides the capital, while the power elite provides protection (Suryadinata 1988). According to Robison (1986) these *cukongs* obtained trading monopolies and privileged access to state bank credit and government contracts. In addition, they were part of Chinese overseas networks throughout Asia and attracted international investment capital.[17]

During the era of the New Order various Chinese-owned business conglomerates emerged with investment in manufacturing, forestry, trade, shipping and transport, banking, property and construction. While in Chinese family-firms all staff members were Chinese, many large firms, including these consortia and conglomerates, also employed Indonesians. However, the top-level employees who were involved in decision making, were still Chinese.

In the early 1970s the pressure upon the *Bappenas* group to discourage foreign and promote indigenous capital, and the subsequent shift in policy also affected the Chinese. The state faced the dilemma of restricting Chinese capital by simultaneously being closely interlinked with this capital. In 1973/74, after anti-Chinese and anti-government riots in Jakarta and Bandung, the National Economic Stabilization Board introduced the following change: capital equity share of Indonesians was to achieve 51 percent in new joint ventures within a period of ten years. All foreign investment projects were to involve Indonesian partners. In those cases where local partners were not indigenous Indonesians, i.e. mainly WNI Chinese, half of all shares were to be sold through the stock exchange to indigenous Indonesians within a shorter period. Certain investment areas were closed to foreign capital. Investment credit by the state bank was provided to indigenous Indonesians only. Domestic investment projects were to involve 75 percent indigenous equity, except in those cases where the management was largely in indigenous hands. Here the share was only supposed to be 50 percent (Robison 1986: 167, 189).

Considered as a whole, the New Order policy favored the development of indigenous private capital on a small- and medium-scale level in manufacturing, forestry, hotels and tourism, shipping and finance. For large-scale indigenous capital, however, the patronage of the military or officials and joint ventures with Chinese or foreign capital were a prerequisite. The other side of the coin of this policy was a restriction to Chinese small- and medium-scale capital. The position of large-scale Chinese capital, however, remained strong because of its close coalition with the military. It coped with the equity-problem by raising its loan capital abroad.

---

[17] For example, the Bangkok Bank, a Chinese-owned bank, provided finance to various Chinese conglomerations in Indonesia, while indigenous entrepreneurs did not generally have access to finance.

Robison (1986: 278ff.) provided a list of Chinese conglomerates in Indonesia, of which several are involved in banking, finance and insurance business, too. An example is Tan Tjoe Hing (Hendra Rahardja). Besides property development, manufacturing, a motor cycle agency and a cement plant, it runs P.T. Bank Harapan Santosa, P.T. Bank Tonsea Menado, P.T. Bank Pasar Gunung, P.T. Inti Harapan, the P.T. Asuransi Harapan, P.T. Cahaya Harapan and P.T. Sumber Cipta Harapan Sakti. Another example is the Liem Group, and it is worth looking at the history of this firm. An immigrant in 1936, Liem joined his brother in peanut oil trading and the clove trade. Eventually he expanded into manufacture and became a supplier of the Indonesian army. In the 1950s he established the Bank Windu Kencana (which is now military-owned but still managed by Liem) and purchased the Bank Central Asia, of which he holds a share of 24 percent. This bank is now the largest private, domestically owned bank with assets of US $ 277 million in the mid-1980s. Nowadays the Liem group forms a major regional and international financial and industrial group (manufacture, automobiles, trade, finance) which has close relations with the military but is no longer in a *compradore* position.[18]

During the 1980s Liem also expanded internationally around trade and finance (Hong Kong, USA, Liberia, the Netherlands, the Netherlands Antilles). It makes sense to explain this international expansion by the political risk of concentrating the entire group holdings in Indonesia, because under the present regime success depends upon patronage. Since Suharto may retire in a few years, the future with regard to relations with a new political leader are uncertain. In addition, the alliance of politico-bureaucrats, *cukongs* and foreign capitalists has been increasingly criticized and led to anti-Chinese riots during the 1970s and 1980s. However, since military and Chinese big businessmen cannot be physically attacked, those who suffered were again the small and medium Chinese enterprises.

Because of their well-developed networks of finance both at the local and regional levels, their connection with international and indigenous capital and the centers of politico-bureaucratic power, the *cukongs* have maintained if not even strengthened their economic position. Robison (1986: 317) emphasized that the power of the Chinese conglomerates results from the fact that they not only dominate the distribution networks as before, but that they are capitalists. Their position has been strengthened from the decline in the oil revenues onward, which forced the government to rely increasingly on investment finance.

In many cases the *cukongs* transformed themselves from traders-cum-lenders during the colonial period to large-scale businessmen, industrialists, bankers and even international conglomerates. However, research on the Chinese patronage systems in colonial Indonesia and its development during the post-colonial period is barely available. One reason is that the Chinese try to conceal their business affairs with regard to

---

[18] According to Robison (1986: 317), Liem finances the activities of the conglomerate in a four-fold way: through the Bank Central Asia for the daily needs, through equity funds, through attracting large-scale international bank credit and through informal credit networks between the major Chinese business groups. The Bangkok Bank seems to be involved in this network, too. Joint ventures exist between the Liem Group and the Suharto family.

internal finance. In addition, the close connection between large-scale Chinese capital and the military may discourage scholars from research.

The investigation of the financial landscape of pre-colonial and colonial Indonesia reveals that, in contrast to India, informal specialized financial agents providing large-scale credit, hardly emerged until independence. Having so far explained the different financial landscapes of both countries from the perspective of the domestic economies, I shall attempt to give a potential answer from the international point of view.

Part IV   THE WORLD-ECONOMY OF THE FAR EAST AND THE MODERN WORLD-SYSTEM

15. The World-Economy of the Far East

According to Braudel (1986a, b) the medieval world consisted of four world-economies, the European, the Russian, the Islamic-Osmanian and the Far Eastern world-economy. He defined a world-economy as an autonomous sector from the economic perspective which is more or less self-sufficient and shows a degree of organic unity from the point of view of internal exchange (1986b: 18-9). Chaudhuri (1990) provided the following description of the Far Eastern world-economy:

"The economic development of the Indian Ocean regions was the consequence of three struc-tural features. A highly productive agriculture supported a complex system of political and social institutions. Industrial production for the export markets introduced some elements of capitalist principles governing the relationships between the artisans and merchants. Economic exchange primarily took the form of local and long-distance trade and the market for agricultural and in-dustrial goods operated on the allocation principle of relative prices indexed by money and cur-rency. The distribution of natural endowments, of course, determined in the last instance whether a particular community or region was to enjoy relative affluence or remain trapped in a cycle of bare survival and destructive starvation (. . .) A central contradiction in all Asian economies was the coexistence of non-market and market relations. Farmers tilled their fields to raise crops which mainly went to feed their immediate families. Where the opportunity for marketing of high-value food crops and agricultural raw materials for industrial manufacture existed, peasants allocated some of their land to cash crops [long before Western intrusion, H.S.] (. . .) Where the state claimed a physical share of crops, the services of financial intermediaries were required in order to transform the revenue in kind into cash incomes. Money assessment on the other hand involved not only a detailed survey of land and the annual calculation of areas sown with cash crops but also the prediction of average prices and the cash revenue of farmers. That peasant pro-ducers should pay rents and taxes to the state and the dominant warrior classes controlling land was taken as axiomatic. What was less than clear was the degree of force which should be applied to determine the 'economic' relationship between the tax-payers, the rentier, and the state agents" (Chaudhuri 1990: 39).

Medieval and early modern Asia were characterized by an important country trade, i.e. an inner-Asian long-distance trade along the coastal lines. Commodities were not transported between two distant poles, but they passed along the trade routes, were exchanged on the way against other goods, and so on. Chinese, Javanese, Indian, Arab traders and others were involved in this movement of goods, each of them operating a particular route. Since the economy of many smaller islands and coastal regions involved in this country trade was only partly monetized, an accepted medium of exchange other than money was Indian hand loom from Gujarat and the Coromandel Coast, which was bartered against local goods (Chaudhuri 1982: 386-7).

Van Leur (1955) described this inner-Asian trade as being organized by itinerant peddlers, traveling around with a minimum of baggage but very expensive trade goods: spices, pearls, perfumes, pepper, diamonds and so on, which caused him to argue that the Asian trade was backward and limited. Braudel (1986a: 123ff.), Dasgupta (1982: 414-6) and others questioned this description emphasizing that the larger part of trade was in necessary goods of the cheaper kind rather than luxury goods. In line with Meilink-Roelofsz (1969), Braudel assumed that the traders of the Indian Ocean formed a broad spectrum, of whom Van Leur's peddlers trading on their own account constituted a minority only. The majority, however, were ship owners and carriers of long-distance trade who had insufficient capital to finance this trade. Many Muslim traders borrowed money from wealthy Indian merchants, merchant-bankers or the nobility under the condition of repaying double the amount after a successful journey (the financiers shared the risk of ship-wreck). The borrowers offered their labour and that of their family members as collateral. In the case of misfortunes other than ship-wreck they would become bonded labourers until the debt was repaid. Another group was formed by Armenian traders who traveled between the Middle East and India. They traded on account of large-scale merchants in Turkey, Russia, Europe, and so on. Contracts stipulated that these merchants financed the whole enterprise and that the traveling trader obtained one quarter of the profits. Chinese junks traveled from China to the Southeast Asia trading entrepots in South Malaysia, Java and Sumatra also used to trade on account of Chinese merchants. None of these traders fits Van Leur's description.

According to Chaudhuri (1985: 12), the business communities in such trading cities had their own rules of the game which facilitated the overcoming of the lack of international legal security. Traders who defaulted lost their credit-ability and reputation not only in the particular city but also in other places, because of the flow of information within the trading networks. The flourishing of the trading cities depended on the fairness of legal transactions. Most rulers guaranteed protection to foreign merchants and provided them a certain measure of judicial independence. They also kept the tribute on the merchants within limits. Once a trading port lost its reputation, it was close to bankruptcy. Considered as a long-term process, there were fluctuating fortunes for port cities along the coastal lines of South and Southeast Asia (Clifford 1990).

While the financing of Asian carriers was usual, the Europeans, according to Braudel (1986b: 234-5), initially had only partial access to the indigenous financial networks, which meant that they had to pay in cash. Either they sold European goods, participated in Asian country trade to make gains and pay for the exports, or carried precious metal from Europe to Asia to balance the accounts. Since European goods were not in great demand in Asia, the two other possibilities were more common. All European traders were involved in such country trade, in addition to a continuous flow of precious metal (mainly silver) from Europe to the Far East which, during the 'long sixteenth century', had been extracted from the then already colonized Latin America.

An understanding of the different commercial and financial landscapes of pre-colonial India and Indonesia is impossible without taking their role in this territorially largest, Far Eastern world-economy of the fifteenth to the eighteenth century into account. This world-economy comprised the Muslim World of the Middle East to India, India, the Southeast Asian trading entrepots and China, with rising and falling centers of power, intertwined trading networks and price chains, a world-economy which was eventually incorporated in the course of expansion of the capitalist world-economy. I shall confine my analysis to India and Indonesia.

The description of medieval India, the former Hindustan, which territorially comprised large parts of present-day India and Pakistan, showed its high commercial development and involvement in long-distance trade, before the East India Company in particular captured most of its territory in the course of the eighteenth century. To provide an overview of this Far Eastern world-economy at the turn of the fifteenth century, this trade was largely in the hands of Gujarati Muslim merchants. They dominated the trade between India and Malacca and regularly ventured to the Red Sea and the Persian Gulf, but the latter carrying trade was dominated by a Cairo-based mercantile organization called the Karim. The Chinese had a trading monopoly in the South China Sea, and the trade from Malacca to the Spice Islands on small trading vessels and other spice-producing areas was predominantly in Javanese and Malayan hands.

India's main export goods were cotton textiles. The bulk of it, both to the Red Sea and Southeast Asia, was of the cheap variety for commoner people, and the more expensive cloth did not sell well. Other exports were common foods like rice and pulses, wheat and oil, coconut products, minor spices, pepper, sugar and raw silk. The picture of exports remained almost the same throughout the twelfth until the early eighteenth century. Indian imports were restricted to spices and horses and smaller quantities of materials like tin, ivory and dye woods. The export surplus was balanced by bullion imports (Dasgupta 1982: 407-18).

East Sumatra, West Malaya and West Java formed an important entrepot region in the Far Eastern world-economy because of their geographical position. Long-distance trade from India to Southeast Asia crossed the Indian Ocean and passed through the Straits of Malacca or the Sumatra Straits, and from China it traversed the South China Sea.

According to Braudel (1986b), India's contacts with Southeast Asia date back to somewhere around the year zero and that of the Chinese to around the fifth century. In contrast to the latter, the Indians, in addition to trading culturally penetrated the region. Hinduism spread on Java and Bali, and later they also impacted Islam to Southeast Asia which, however, had a stronghold in the coastal regions only. Such trading contacts led to an economic expansion of the entrepot regions, in particular Sri Vijaya (South Sumatra) from the seventh to the thirteenth century, Majapahit (Java) from the thirteenth to the fifteenth century and Malacca (fifteenth to seventeenth century).

In 1403 Malacca on the Malayan Peninsula grew from a small village of sea-rovers and fishermen to become the central entrepot. While both Majapahit and Siam claimed suzerainty over the Peninsula, Malacca managed to gain the recognition of the Ming dynasty which tried to increase its economic influence in Southeast Asia. Malacca expended rapidly because of its control of trade through the Straits. It became an emporium of Indian, Chinese, Javanese and other traders to exchange their goods. First of all, both Indians and Chinese aimed at buying spices from the Spice Islands and Sumatra, but there was some direct trade between them, too. Indians purchased Chinese porcelain and silk. While the Chinese had no interest in Indian cotton textiles, the pepper supply of Sumatra was insufficient, and hence they bought a considerable amount of pepper from the Indians (which originated in Malabar) in addition to sandalwood, incense and probably opium. This direct exchange, however, did not by far reach the volume of spice exports (Dasgupta 1982: 409). Javanese and Malays traded in spices. The exchange was previously handled via Majapahit but shifted to Malacca. The Southeast Asian traders acquired, among other things, Indian textiles. The Javanese share of trade in the archipelago was controlled by aristocratic Javanese families, the so-called 'merchant princes' (see, for example, Van Leur 1955). These and Javanese traders adopted Islam which was spread by Western Indian traders in Malacca and from there to the coastal regions of Java, while the people in the island's interior stayed predominantly Hindu or animist.

Malacca was described as a vast market, whose economic well-being largely depended on foreign traders. It only provided the infrastructure of an entrepot, but it had the reputation of being the most famous market of 'India'. The dominant traders were Western Indian Gujarati, many of whom were financed by Surat bankers; other traders were form the Coromandel coast, Bengal, the Mon kingdom of Lower Burma, from Pasai in North Sumatra, from Palambang, Java, the Moluccas and the Bandas, Borneo, the Philippines and China. Many Javanese themselves settled in Malacca. Since the entrepot had no hinterland, it depended on imports of food from Java and India, which were paid by the trading tribute.

When the Europeans entered the Asian arena they participated in the well-established indigenous trading and financial networks until they had consolidated their power. According to Braudel (1986b: 551ff.), they began to conquer the Indian subcontinent and Southeast Asia from the sea. India's problem was that it dominated the Far Eastern world-economy only from the economic point of view. Politically it remained passive towards this world-economy by not trying to get a military stronghold beyond the Indian subcontinent. On the sub-continent India had a well-equipped army to defend its territory. At sea, however, the poorly-armed Indian trading vessels were vulnerable. The gradual conquest, which began in the late fifteenth century and led to the incorporation of the world-economy of the Far East into the European world-economy, started with the control of the Indian Ocean: selling safe-conduct passes, providing escorts, attacking ports or making sea blockades (Chaudhuri 1982: 384-5; 1985: 86).

> "The opportunity for peaceful trading in Asia was open to the Dutch and the English. They did not take it, because they believed that neither the Portuguese nor the powerful Asian rulers in whose kingdoms they traded would allow them to do so without the sanction of arms. This argument was of course only a part of the current political ideology. The VOC, and later the East India Company, needed no explicit act of violence offered to them to justify attacks on Asian merchants and shipping" (Chaudhuri 1985: 87).

The next steps were the establishment of trading settlements (factories) and the negotiation and enforcement of advantageous conditions of trade. Step by step the Indian and other Asian traders were pushed out of the Asian country trade, while the Europeans increased their share of trade and divided large parts of the Far Eastern World-economy among themselves.

The Portuguese were the first Europeans who were active in regular trade in the regions of the Indian Ocean. This trade was largely Asian country trade, rather than Asian-European trade. During the first half of the sixteenth century, they came to control the spice trade, based upon their naval superiority over Asian ships. In 1510 they annexed Goa and thus laid the foundation of the future Portuguese empire. They soon captured Malacca in 1511, which they ruled until they were expelled by the

Dutch. This was followed by opening trading settlements at the Coromandel coast, Hugli and Chittagong (Bengal), Macao (China) and Colombo (Ceylon). This maritime empire later acquired the name of *Estado da India*.

The conquest of Malacca by the Portuguese had an impact on the Indian trade, since Malacca became an important center of missionary activity and an attack on Islam. Gujarati Muslim ship owners were opposed to the Portuguese from the beginning. They were involved in the defense of Malacca and, when Malacca fell, they boycotted the entrepot and began to trade between India and Achin (West Sumatra, the contemporary Acheh) or Bantam. Malacca remained for some time the nodal point of Christian, Hindu and Chinese traders between the Pacific, India and Europe. The Portuguese later dropped their anti-Muslim attitude in Malacca to regain the superiority of this entrepot, but only with partial success. On the whole the Portuguese only temporarily affected Indian trade in Southeast Asia, but they pushed Sumatra and the Malayan peninsular in particular further into the world-economy by promoting commercial pepper production and gold and tin mining.

At the beginning of the seventeenth century both the Dutch and the English and their newly founded trading companies appeared on the scene. In the early years these companies steered their ships to the Indonesian archipelago and Spice Islands, where the Portuguese opposition was weaker than in India. However, it was difficult to finance spice exports to Europe without participating profitably in Asian country trade. This again required access to Indian cotton textiles, particularly in Gujarat and on the Coromandel Coast. The Dutch and the English therefore extended their trade to India in the first decade of the seventeenth century and soon established trading settlements, too. At the same time Indian textiles increasingly gained importance in trade with Europe. In the course of the seventeenth century the VOC expelled the Portuguese from their trading post in the Indian Ocean by systematically attacking their ships and their settlements. While the Mughals disposed of them in Bengal in 1632, the Dutch besieged Goa from 1636 onward, conquered Malacca in 1641 and controlled the Coromandel Coast, incorporated the cinnamon trade of Ceylon with the conquest of Colombo (1655-6) and finally took Cochin (1659-63).[1] But the emerging English East India Company was an inconvenient competitor which continuously grew in size. With the rise of France as the leading power in Europe, the *Companie des Indes Orientales* came into being occupying the east coast of India from the 1660s onward. This company eventually also competed with the Dutch and the English. Such rivalries culminated in the Anglo-French wars.

With the expulsion of the Portuguese from Malacca, the gradual establishment of the spice trading monopoly and the shift in control of Southeast Asian trade into the

---

[1] For a comparison of VOC trade in India and Indonesia during the seventeenth century, see Van Goor (1992). He established the following differences: First, Indonesian trade was mainly based on primary-sector goods, while the Indian trade consisted of draperies and cotton goods or the produce of home industries. Second, in Indonesia payment took place in the form of barter or imported coins, while the Indian mercantile system was already highly monetized. A third difference was the strong connection between rulers and economic activity in the Indonesian archipelago, while it was less strong in India. Indonesia was fragmented and the states much weaker than the well-organized Mughal state. Fourth, while in India free wage labour was available owing to the Indian economy, labour in the Indonesian archipelago consisted of slave labour and Chinese labourers.

hands of the VOC, Batavia came to replace the other entrepots. Because of declining opportunities in the spice trade, Gujarati traders gave up Achin after 1618 and almost totally withdrew from Southeast Asia.

On the whole India's involvement in foreign trade expanded in the course of the seventeenth and early eighteenth centuries. This growth was due to Dutch, English and French participation in country trade from and to India, while the Indians defended their former volume of trade. However, European involvement wrought major changes in the Indian pattern of trade. The Southeast Asian share of the Indians declined, while Western trade to the Middle East increased. Dasgupta (1982: 432-3) considered the late seventeenth century as the golden period of Indian maritime trade, which was short-lived, however. Its sharp decline in the early eighteenth century resulted from political collapses in India and Persia. However, additional factors contributed to this fall. One explanation is that the high volume of exports had caused a glut in the Arabian markets and reduced prices, so that journeys to the west became unprofitable. Hence, Indian financiers withdrew their investment in shipping. Political unrest in North India further accelerated the decline. During the first half of the eighteenth century, Surat's turnover decreased by two-thirds, but as late as the middle of the eighteenth century, English factors which had by then become powerful, met with fierce resistance from Gujarati merchants in Western trade (Dasgupta 1982: 432-3).

A reason related to this glut of Indian products on foreign markets is India's cheap labour which resulted in cheap exports. According to Braudel (1986b: 583-4), this cheap labour formed not only the basis of Indo-Arab trade but of Indo-European trade, too. Referring to Chaudhuri (1985), he argued that the flourishing of the old-established pattern of cotton exports led India to miss the chance to make technical improvements, in contrast to the Europeans.

Braudel summed up the European position in the Far Eastern world-economy as follows. Until the formal conquest of India by the English with the Plassey events in 1757, the Europeans were no more than 'parasites on a foreign body' (Braudel 1986b: 554). They used the established infrastructure and opened their factories close to the production zones and markets on the important trade routes. Braudel warned us, however, against misinterpreting this metaphor. Although the Europeans were few in numbers, they were allied with Western capitalism. Moreover, they were not opposed to the Asian masses but to an indigenous merchant class which dominated inner-Asian trade and commerce. These merchants initiated the Europeans into the functioning of this country trade, partly by force and partly by free will, and started the process which towards the end of the eighteenth century led to an English monopoly which controlled 85 – 90 percent of the Indian foreign trade. In the course of the eighteenth century, however, the volume of trade and turnover of the English East India Company began to supersede the VOC (Hall 1985: 221-32).

Having so far described the involvement of Indian, Chinese and Indonesian traders in the Far Eastern world-economy, it becomes obvious that, before the conquest of Malacca by the Dutch at least, the lion's share of long-distance trade on the Indian Ocean was with Indian traders, who were largely financed by wealthy Indian investors. The emergence of the Dutch spice trade monopoly squeezed them out of Southeast

Asian business. The decline in this trade, however, could be compensated for some time by the growth of trade to the Middle East.

Considering the role of the Southeast Asian entrepot region in the Far Eastern world-economy before the establishment of Dutch control, I argue that from the meta-level of world trade there was no real necessity for an indigenous Southeast Asian finance. The main long-distance traders from and to these entrepots were Indian and Chinese traders who were financed by well-established home-based financial apparatuses. The Javanese trade restricted itself to inner-archipelago trade. It was conducted by merchant princes and sojourning traders on board of small vessels, while the Indian ships and Chinese junks were somewhat larger. The merchant princes could fall back upon state revenue to finance this trade, while Van Leur's peddling trade did not require much financing. The entrepots only provided the infrastructure and were content to collect trade revenue, while they were hardly involved in active trading themselves.

16. The Netherlands, England and the Companies

Let us discuss the European perspective. I confine myself to the two main European competitors in the penetration of the world-economy of the Far East: the English and the Dutch, the latter of whom were chiefly responsible for the Portuguese withdrawal from Southeast Asia. But it is unnecessary to emphasize that the French, the Portuguese, the Spaniards and other Europeans were similarly involved in this process.

According to Wallerstein (1980b: 37ff.), around 1600 the core of the world-economy was in Holland and Zeeland, the Home Countries, East Anglia and northern and western France. During the period 1600 – 1750, which the historians call Mercantilism,[1] the Dutch dominated fishery, agriculture and industrial production. Spurred by the Eighty Years' War and the Thirty Years' War, the import of raw materials was promoted by the government, and the industry expanded. The structure changed from artisan guilds to manufacturing and the putting-out system of production. Historians emphasized that the Netherlands were the first country which attained self-sustained growth.

During the seventeenth century Dutch shipping dominated world trade. It grew ten times between 1500 and 1700, and in 1670 the Dutch owned three times the tonnage of the English. The latter were engaged in their Civil War, so that Dutch ships developed as carriers of world trade, including English textiles. One can consider them as middlemen and the factors and brokers of Europe. They ventured to the East and West Indies, the Mediterranean, Africa and the Baltic Sea. As already shown, Asian-European long-distance trade and country trade were inseparably intertwined. Braudel (1986b: 238) gave a vivid description of the Dutch country trade. They bought Indian textiles in Surat, Bengal or on the Coromandel coast. Some of these were offered in Sumatra in exchange for pepper, gold and camphor. In Siam they could not make large profits with Indian cotton, due to intensive competition. However, there was Siamese demand for spices, pepper and coral and they in turn offered tin, gold, elephants and deer furs; the latter were in great demand in Japan, and elephants in Bengal. In contrast to inner-Asian country trade, the Asian-European trade – the transfer of goods from one world-economy to another – was fraught with difficulties because trade was subject to the laws of the market. Other European traders were attracted to participate in Asian country trade and Asian-European long-distance trade. Increasing European demand for spices raised prices in Asia, while the increasing supply of Asian goods in Europe reduced their prices, so that profits declined on a whole.

One possibility of solving this problem of declining profits that was due to competition in favor of the Dutch was to incorporate the East Indies as a colony; the other possibility was to carry out administered trade (see Polanyi 1957) in the traditional mode

---

[1] Mercantilism has been defined as 'the belief that the economic welfare of the state can only be secured by government regulation of nationalist character' (Coleman 1969: 1).

of long-distance trade between world empires. While the directorate of the VOC, *de Heren Zeventien*, favored the administered trade, the then residing governor-general, Jan Pieterzon Coen, pursued the option of annexation. He aimed at reorganizing the system of production and exporting a settler class to supervise cash-crop production and create a market for European exports (see Hall 1985: 306ff.). However, the decision went in favor of administered trade, since the short-term benefits of the VOC were considered more important than the long-term ones, and the annexation was launched after 1750. With the exception of their privileges in Japan, the Dutch were able to introduce and maintain one efficient monopoly only: spices, nutmeg, cloves, and cinnamon, which was introduced and defended in the same manner. Production was restricted to one particular island only, so that competition from elsewhere was excluded. Prices were kept high by keeping outputs low. With the spice monopoly the Dutch enjoyed an advantage for some time compared to other European traders, but eventually rivaling companies emerged and substitutable products were imported from other regions. At the same time the maintenance of the monopoly also involved an expanding, costly apparatus of control, armed confrontations with indigenous rulers and even rivaling trading companies. Considered as a whole, however, the balance of trade of the VOC was positive during the seventeenth century.

Detailed studies of the VOC were produced by Glamann (1958) and Bruijn et al. (1979-87) and of the East India Company by Chaudhuri (1978, 1985, 1990). The former was the product of a merger between different competing trading companies in 1602, the latter was founded two years earlier. These two companies were the most successful merchant organizations in the early modern era. In contrast to the organization of non-Western trade, their organization was modern. They transformed the traditional pattern of merchant trading capital being provided for one single trading enterprise only into a pattern of fixed or permanent capital, with a separation between capital owners and managing company which consisted of professional merchants and salaried administrators. Chaudhuri (1985: 81-2) considered this organizational form as a reflection of emerging capitalism. According to Neal (1990: 195), this transformation of the VOC occurred by 1612, of the East India Company by 1659. After this transformation both companies became joint-stock companies. They sold shares which were traded in the stock exchanges of Amsterdam and London. Part II of this book pointed out that this step in business organization and finance was not taken by Indian merchants and bankers, what some scholars considered the reason for their declining business.

In the late sixteenth and early seventeenth centuries, the Dutch held the lion's share of Asian-European long-distance trade because of their technological superiority. In comparison with the VOC, the Dutch West India Company was much less successful. Dutch superiority resulted from the triangular trade, which provided Europe with cotton, sugar and tobacco from the West Indies and spices and tea from the East Indies. Nevertheless, trade profits largely went to the English and French, which among other things was due to the fact that the Dutch as the pioneers invested heavily in infrastructure while the others entered on developed areas. At least until 1660 the Dutch were able to maintain their dominance in international trade. Their largest profits resulted from marketing and stapling in the entrepot of Amsterdam. They enjoyed superiority in commercial organization, too. They pooled the savings in partnerships, created a system of buffer stocks which reduced risks for the individual merchant (since it was organized in a monopolistic way) and his dependence on the staple prone to fluctuating supply and costs. They provided a network of commission agents who found a customer for the producer, took goods on consignment and received a commission on the bill paid by the purchaser to the producer.

The Amsterdam stock exchange was the leading one in the seventeenth century, and Amsterdam was then the center of the international money market. The productive and commercial strength and control of the international money market made Dutch capital exportable which brought in remittances generating surpluses much higher than what they produced themselves. Commercial advantages in maritime trade and insurance were sufficient to create a surplus in the balance of payments. Dutch state credit was to a high degree responsible for its military success, and the United Provinces formed a safe place for deposits. All this overvalued the currency. The *Wisselbank van Amsterdam*, which was founded in 1609, became the center for European deposits and exchange. Amsterdam developed a highly efficient bill-of-exchange business, too, and between 1660 and 1710 it formed the center of a multilateral payment system. Dutch currency became the preferred specie of world trade, and the Dutch had the lowest interest rates. Due to the fact that Amsterdam was both the leading commercial and monetary center, it was also the most important place of investment.

> "The United Provinces seemed to be the great exception to the predominance of mercantilist ideology in the seventeenth century. From this fact, many persons draw the curious inference that the Dutch state was weak. It seems to me that exactly the inverse was true: in the seventeenth century, the Dutch state was the *only* state in Europe which enjoyed internal and external strength such that its need for mercantilist policies was minimal" (Wallerstein 1980b: 60).

Not only did this state afford protection, it also created the condition for the success of private enterprise. The ideology of Dutch hegemony was *mare liberum*, while at the same time they kept away non-Dutch merchants from the coast of Africa and the East Indies. The strength of the state at home coincided with its strength abroad, which was challenged between 1651 and 1678: Dutch hegemony was so strong that both English and French decided to attack it by force. I agree with Wallerstein (1980b: 61-5) and Gills (1993: 117ff.) that hegemony cannot persist for long in a capitalist world system because of rivalling politico-economic powers, whereas I shall postpone the discussion for a short while what actually constitutes a world system.

The seventeenth century was characterized by deteriorating relations between England and the Netherlands, and frequently conflicts occurred between the traders of both companies. Eventually the superiority of the Dutch began to change during the mid-seventeenth century. The Thirty Years' War and the Eighty Years' War had ended, and the internal conflicts in France and England had come to a halt. These states now sought intrastate confrontation against the Dutch economic hegemony. According to Glaman (1958), Chaudhuri (1978, 1985) and Braudel (1986b: 239ff.), the turning point of dominance among the European trading companies was the result of a change in the Asian trading pattern. Until 1718 the tea trade went via Batavia. However, when the Dutch decided to offer the Chinese fixed prices at a much lower rate than previously, the Chinese refused to travel to Batavia for the next five years, and the European competitors began to trade tea directly with the Chinese, after China had opened her doors to European traders. The English East-India Company quickly stepped into this new trade, established regular tea imports from Canton in 1717 and experienced considerable growth until 1760. Tea was paid for by precious metal. The VOC missed the chance and relied on the old-established barter of tea against spices and corals with Chinese junks in Batavia. The English, however, established the Bengal-China trade (tea against cotton and silver, later opium). Although in the long run the Dutch adapted to this new trade pattern, they were in a much more inferior position compared to the English. The VOC missing this chance was, according to Braudel, one of the decisive factors which led to a change of dominance among the trading companies, and therefore the decline and ultimate ruin of the VOC at the end of the eighteenth century.

In contrast to this view that concentrates on a single event, Neal (1990) argued that not only the changing pattern of tea trade in favor of the East India Company was decisive for the loss of superiority of the VOC, but the growing competition from new trading companies in general, particularly the French, to take part in the fight for supremacy in Asian trade. The greater rigidity of the VOC organization and its trading patterns were responsible for slower adaptability compared to the East India Company.

> "The marketing areas of the VOC were always continental Europe, whereas the EEC (East India Company, H.S.) concentrated on its growing home market, and re-exports of its imports were directed increasingly to the growing Atlantic empire of the British. Country trade within Asia was undoubtedly more important in quantity and value for each company than the intercontinental trade, however. The Dutch dominated the southern Asian seas and the trade in exotic spices, whereas the English developed trade at the very edge of the Muslim world (. . .) The greater success of the English company in meeting the economic competition of the French, Austrians, and Scandinavians during the 1730s and 1740s enabled them eventually to achieve military victories over the French in India as well as in the Atlantic during the course of the Seven Years' War" (Neal 1990: 222-3).

To provide proof for his hypothesis, Neal (1990) analyzed the share prices of both companies. The outcome was that, during the second half of the seventeenth century until around 1720, both companies' shares fluctuated with the same trends, so that one can assume that both experienced the effects of stronger competition in Europe or Asia. From 1723-94, however, the fluctuations were inverse. The East India Company gained at the expense of the VOC

According to Braudel (1986b), the exact turning point of the VOC's well-being is difficult to assess, since the manner of recording makes it impossible to make a calculation of the total balance of payment. The dividends paid by the VOC over-assessed its profits, and he asked how far this was intended. Additional factors for the fall of the VOC were declining profits in the inner-Asian country trade, and the defrauding of company agents; the latter, however, occurred in other companies, too. To complete the story of these two companies, the flourishing English East India Company was brought under the control of the government in 1772, while the heavily indebted VOC was wound up at the end of the century by the Netherlands Indian Government.

17. The Incorporation of South and Southeast Asia

How then did the annexation of India and Indonesia as colonies take place? According to Wallerstein's world-system theory (1989: 129ff.), the expansion of the modern world-system occurred in different spurts and periods of consolidation, the second expansion during 1733-1850 with the incorporation of the Indian subcontinent, the Ottoman Empire, Russia and West Africa. This theory has undergone much criticism. In the next paragraphs I summarize Wallerstein's perspective, which is followed by a summary of recent critique.

Wallerstein (1979: 155-9) considered both world-economies and world empires as world systems. While a world empire is characterized by political unity, he defined a world-economy as a single division of labour within which multiple cultures are located but which has no overarching political structure. The long sixteenth century (1450-1640) engendered the modern world-system which came to cover the entire globe.[1]

In the course of the expansion of the European world-economy, Wallerstein distinguished three successive movements for a 'zone': 'being in the external arena, being incorporated and being peripheralized'. The process of incorporation lasted about one century.

> "Incorporation means fundamentally that at least some significant production processes in a given geographic location become integral to various of the commodity chains that constitute the ongoing division of labour of the capitalist world-economy (. . .) A production process can only be considered to be thus integrated if its production responds in some sense to the ever-changing 'market conditions' of this world-economy (. . .) in terms of efforts by those who control these production processes to maximize the accumulation of capital within this 'market' (. . .) Incorporation involves 'hooking' the zone into the orbit of the world-economy in such a way that it virtually can no longer escape, while peripheralization involves a continuing transformation of the mini structure of the area in ways that are sometimes referred to as the deepening of capitalist development" (Wallerstein 1989: 130).

On the national level, production and mercantile enterprises had to become larger (plantations or larger trading companies which took control of many petty producers through debt obligations), and producers had to be influenced in their decisions on production and production inputs (machines, materials, capital and labour). This happened in particular regions. Taking this view, I would even go further than Wallerstein. Chapter 7.3 showed the financial and commercial link of moneylenders-cum-traders with domestic trading networks which organized the flow of cash-crops to the ports

---

[1] Wallerstein (1984: 13) introduced the hyphenation to distinguish the term from the common understanding of the world-economy as 'international economy' of separate, national economies which trade with each other, the sum of which forms the international economy. Palat et al. (1986: 174-5) emphasized that the existence of long-distance trade does not in itself indicate the existence of a world-economy. In agreement with Wallerstein (1980b) he referred to a hierarchical division of labour, which emerged in the regions surrounding the Indian Ocean around 1600.

and the up-country distribution of imports. I argue that in many cases producers' debt obligations to village moneylenders were therefore sufficient to determine their production decisions. The parallel to the weak position of developing countries with contemporary debt obligations to industrial ones (world debt crisis) is obvious.

The newly emerging pattern of exports and imports reproduced the core-periphery dichotomy (or, in other words, the international division of labour). In the formerly external arenas the following changes in the production processes occurred: world market-oriented cash-crop production and analogous forms in the primary sector expanded and local manufacturing activities were eliminated. Particular areas were transformed into cash-crop producing areas and these were no longer available for subsistence production. Cash-crop producers or wage labourers had to purchase their own food, which required the production and distribution of food for sale in addition to export crops.

In the mid-eighteenth century both Great Britain and France had replaced the Netherlands as the centers of the capitalist world-economy and expanded into the external arenas. During the period 1650-1750, the older centers of international trade in India (Masulipatnam, Surat and Hugli) declined in importance, while new centers of European trade emerged, such as Calcutta, Bombay and Madras.

Wallerstein (1989: 140) identified the initial period of incorporation with the linkage of the Ganges trade via Calcutta to the world-economy after the English incorporation of Bengal in 1757, and a parallel expansion which occurred in South India after 1800.[2] The period 1750-1850 was marked by the East India Company's combination of economic and political control of India. During the first half of the nineteenth century indigo, raw silk, cotton and opium were the four major raw materials (which amounted to 60 percent of the total) of which the former two went to Europe, the latter two to China. Indigo production, which was already an important export good under the Mughals, expanded fourfold under British rule. Cotton was an old product of Gujarat which before 1770 had never been exported to places other than Sindh, Madras and Bengal. Increasing world demand for cotton seemed to have been one factor in the annexation of Surat in 1800. Only the expansion of opium production had no impact on production elsewhere in the world-economy.

The other impact of the reconstruction of import-export patterns in the former external arenas, argued Wallerstein, was the decline of indigenous manufacturing. Before 1800 the standard of textile production on the Indian subcontinent was comparatively high. However, England closed its market for Indian textiles, systematically weakening the Indian cottage industry and eventually built up its own, more capital-intensive production (see Alavi 1962; 1979). On the whole, the Indian economy was reversed in the process of colonization. There was tribute and a drain of wealth from India to Europe, deindustrialization and deurbanization, the general dislocation of indus-

---

[2] 'Rothermund catches the shift from external arena to incorporation precisely in the changing functions, as he describes them, of the (trading) factory: it went from buying and selling aboard ships to placing special orders to financing these orders by advances to using the advances to stimulate production to organizing production via the putting-out system and operating workshops' (Wallerstein 1989: 154, quoting Rothermund 1981: 76). However, in a recent book Rothermund (1994) attacked the weak conception of external arena.

trial and agricultural production. The result was a different international division of labour. India was pushed back onto the level of raw material production and a market for British products.

Of these four export goods, indigo was the most important and plantation-oriented. During the late eighteenth century, various English private traders opened plantations. They offered credit to small-scale producers and reclaimed it when the recession set in. This led to forfeitures and land concentration. The putting-out system was also used for indigo production during this period.

> "In either case – direct production or a system of advances to petty producers – the indigo planters kept the basic production decisions in their hands, using either 'petty oppression' or 'debt servitude' to realize their objectives. Similarly, in the production of raw cotton, as it becomes more export-oriented, there came to be an 'increasing grip of usury and trading capital over production', as the 'real burdens of rent and interest became (...) heavier'" (Wallerstein 1989: 153, quoting Guha 1972: 18, 28).

Once a particular zone was incorporated into the world-economy, this normally had consequences for the adjacent zone. For example, when India was incorporated, China became part of the external arena. England bought tea from China and provided Bengal silver in exchange. Indian cotton replaced the former silver payment. In a final step, cotton was substituted for opium which was forced on China (Wallerstein 1989: 167-8).

> "Incorporation into the world-economy means necessarily the insertion of the political structures into the interstate system. This means that the 'states' which already exist in these areas must either transform themselves into 'states within the interstate system' or be replaced by new political structures which take this form or be absorbed by other states already within the interstate system. The smooth operation of an integrated division of labour cannot operate without certain guarantees about the possibility of regular flows of commodities, money and persons across frontiers. It is not that these flows must be 'free'. Indeed, they are hardly ever free. But it is that the states which put limitations on these flows act within the constraint of certain rules which are enforced in some sense by the collectivity of member states in the interstate system (but in practice just a few stronger states)" (Wallerstein 1989: 170).

By 1750 the Mughal empire was undergoing the disintegrative process of succession wars. However, it took one century until it was fully incorporated in the new administrative unit of non-sovereign India. The inner political situation of the subcontinent during the mid-eighteenth century showed Europeans that political interference might work for their economic interest. For some time, however, there was strong English reluctance to take direct control. The annexation of Bengal demonstrated that it was a profitable enterprise. It resulted in the decrease of bullion outflow from England, because Indian exports were paid by the revenues raised. There was armed confrontation with the French for Bengal's control until England's final victory in the third Anglo-French war. By 1837 the British established *the* power over India.

I want to stress again that I interpret the changing functions of indigenously developed bankers as resulting to a considerable degree from these world system processes, since their business was closely related with trade. Initially the position of Indian traders and financiers was still quite strong. However, the penetration of European traders and powers in the world-economy of the Far East undermined the position of

Indian traders. As a first step they withdrew from Indonesian trade because of declining trading opportunities compared to the Europeans, thus concentrating on trade with Arabia. However, this trade eventually declined, too, because of the saturation of the Arabian markets, leading to the further decline of Indian maritime trade. Indigenous-style bankers, as the financiers of and participants in foreign and domestic trade as well as providing state finance, were similarly affected by this structural change. The remaining business opportunities of informal financial agents during and after the annexation were the financing of domestic trade as an important constituent of the newly emerging international division of labour and, in particular, agricultural finance, which transformed subsistence producing into cash-crop producing areas and opened up unploughed land for market production. The broad spectrum of moneylenders in colonial India, their support of the colonial apparatus by pre-financing the land revenue, and their link with higher-level finance, domestic and international commerce was discussed in Part II in detail.

In contrast to his detailed analysis of incorporation of India into the modern world-system, Wallerstein did not explicitly deal with the annexation of the Indonesian archipelago by the Dutch and its final the peripheralisation. However, this process was also long-term and distinctive of different parts of Indonesia. I am aware of the fact that the control of the periphery by the center is not necessarily bound to territorial control of whole regions, since economic control is sufficient in itself. However, the historical processes of colonization – or to use Wallerstein's terminology, the incorporation of external arenas and their final peripheralisation – was accompanied by territorial control, whereas pure economic control of virtually independent countries is largely a post-colonial phenomenon. Historical maps on the expansion of Dutch authority in the East Indies (see e.g. Soedjatmoko 1965) indicate this long-term process. A look at Java alone shows that the enforcement of Dutch authority took more than two centuries. While Dutch control of Batavia and the surrounding areas was already achieved in 1619 with the establishment of a Dutch factory, large parts of Central Java were not under their control until the 1830s. On the Outer Islands (for example, the interior of Borneo or Celebes) control of large parts was not gained until the early twentieth century. For Java one can perhaps consider the introduction of the Cultivation System in 1830 as a decisive shift to economic dependency from the Netherlands, and for the Outer Islands the emergence of large-scale plantation business and mining on Sumatra, Borneo, and so on, during the second half of the nineteenth century.

Having so far described what according to Wallerstein happened to the Indian subcontinent in the course of expansion of modern world-system I shall continue with critiques to this view, because I believe that Wallerstein's theory has to be modified. A main point of critique refers to his definition of 'world-system'. Nederveen Pieterse (1988) argued that this understanding is a system rhetoric rather than a system theory which has conceptual weaknesses with regard to social change and action. The basis of analysis are 'social systems', one of which is the 'modern world-system'. In particular, the approach has some difficulty to deal with structural change. The transition from one social system or mode of production to another is logically impossible. This question is approached in combination with dependency theory and conventional Marxism. The following weaknesses have been adapted: the centrism from dependency theory and the materialism and determinism from conventional Marxism. Finally, world system theory revives the view that capitalism can be overcome with Socialism, which is one of the weakest theorems in Marxism.

Rothermund's (1994: 114ff.) critical comments started from the same point of departure. He argued that world-system theory leaves room for only an internal differentiation because the modern-world system is assumed to encompass the entire globe. However, instead of introducing more or less autonomous sub-systems Wallerstein developed the spatial-hierarchical order of core, semi-periphery and periphery. The construct of 'external arena' prior to the period of colonization underestimates the importance of international long-distance trade. I agree with Rothermund. The description of India's, China's and Southeast Asia's position within the world-economy of the Far East poses the question whether the latter did not form a 'hinterland' (Gills and Frank 1993: 94-5) of India and China.[3] This hierarchical relationship causes me to disagree with Palat et al. (1986: 174-5) that the world-economy of the Indian Ocean emerged around 1600. To my mind this happened far earlier, as will be discussed below.

With regard to Wallerstein's neglect to consider the Dutch colonial power in Indonesia Rothermund ironically remarked that unfortunately this region does not fit Wallerstein's scheme – probably because the Dutch colonial attempts to control the producers of their trade goods started before 1750 – the year that Wallerstein identified as the beginning incorporation of the Indian subcontinent into the modern world-system. He explained this turning point from external arena to period of incorporation with a decrease in the flow of precious metal from Europe to Asia. The same flow, however, started once again some time later. Taking Wallerstein's argument one might turn it the other way around that the periphery fell back into the state of external arena. This, however, is impossible in world-system theory.

Rothermund's conclusion: Wallerstein's theory is characterized by a wrong periodical interpretation and a simplistic tri-polarity; a weak concept of 'external arena'; and a unilinear interpretation of development processes, so that every country has to be pressed into this threefold pattern. Neither dissociation nor particular developments are possible. Asia's historical state as an external arena, as well as its contemporary rapid growth processes seems to be a problem for world-system theory.

In their recent reader with the challenging title *The World System – Five Hundred or Five Thousand?* Frank and Gills (1993) allude to the birth date of the modern world system. These scholars went beyond the deconstruction of world-system theory and provided a new interpretation of 'world system' as having an at least 5,000 year-old history. They argued that the rise and dominance of Europe and the West in this world system is only a recent event which may perhaps even pass. According to Gills (1993), instead of considering transitions between different discrete modes of production (as Wallerstein does) the world system can be seen as a series of hegemonic reorganizations or 'hegemonic transitions' which characterize shifts in the locus of

---

[3] While Wallerstein (1980b, 1989) used the term 'hinterland' in the sense being external to the expanding capitalist world-system, Gills and Frank held against this view that it neglects the structural and systemic significance of zones being 'outside' but related to the hegemonic center.

accumulation in the world-economy. The process of capital accumulation is the motor force of history. While Wallerstein emphasizes the particularity of accumulation under the capitalist mode of production in the modern world-system, Frank and Gills (1993) replied that accumulation before 1500 was not much different. In the same way the center-periphery structure and the concepts of hegemony and rivalry are applicable to previous periods.

> "We recommend the world system as the locus, and the process of accumulation within it as its motor force of development, as the primary determinants of the historical process. In this regard we are very much in agreement with Wallerstein, Amin, Abu-Lughod, and others as far as they go. However, (. . .) we want also to apply the same methodology much further in space and time. We believe that Marxist and neo-Marxist histography also should not be confined in its self-imposed 'isolationist' orthodoxy. Rather, historical-materialist analysis, Marxist or otherwise, should move in ever more holistic and inclusive directions, which were proposed by earlier materialist economic historians " (Frank and Gills 1993: 30).

Amin (1993) and Wallerstein (1993) defended their theses that the modern world-system began around 500 years ago. They argued that the capitalist mode of production is fundamentally different from world empires and other hegemonic forms. The particularity of accumulation in the modern world-system is an imperative to accumulate 'ceaselessly' in order to accumulate at all.

Janet Abu-Lughod (1989, 1993) took a position between Frank/Gills and Wallerstein/Amin. She maintained that the rise of the West followed the fall of the East and resulted in a hegemonic shift from East to West, perhaps due to overextension and political economic decline in various parts of the East. She identified the birth of the modern world-system around 1250. Frank and Gills (1993) agreed that the rise of the West did not just constitute a new modern world-system. It was part of a continued development of hegemonic shift within the old world system. A world system is not always dominated by only one hegemon. There may be a number of coexisting core powers that become increasingly integrated by means of conflictual and cooperative relations. Changes in the configuration of relations can have an important impact on the history and social development which is as important as or even greater than the impact of class struggle. The world system as a whole never 'falls', rather the interlinking of hegemonial powers changes. Frank and Gills, however, criticized her because like Wallerstein she is not willing to accept a single world system with a cyclical development. An explanation is perhaps their 'overembedded' view of ancient society. This view has to be dropped. Only then can one open one's eyes for transregional economic processes which involved the transfer of goods and capital across ancient Eurasia and their effects within ancient empires.

I agree with Frank's and Gills' position of hegemonic shifts, whereas Nederveen Pieterse's and Rothermund's critique to a blurred understanding of 'world system' as 'system' also seems to me applicable to this interpretation. Perhaps it makes more sense to drop this term and replace it with 'world-economy' – a term theoretically and empirically open to expansion and contraction. To my mind Wallerstein took a eurocentric view explaining the world from the perspective of European expansionism. Certainly, colonialism is a historical fact which, however, can also be explained with a shift of hegemonic power. Whether this shift from East to West was the result of rivaling hegemony in Europe causing competitive armament, technical and organizational progress which was finally decisive for the conquest of large parts of the world (a position that many historians take), or whether the rise of the West was in the last analysis only possible because of a preceding decline of the hegemony of the East caused by the plague (see Abu-Lughod 1989, 1993), is still undergoing a discussion among historians and theorists.

18. Colonial Policy and Practice

I shall now leave the meta-level of world-system theory and its critique and turn to the question of how the colonies were governed, since in my opinion this governance had a decisive effect upon the structure of the emerging financial landscapes. Furnivall (1956) argued in his famous book *'Colonial Policy and Practice'* that, as a matter of fact, colonial policy is not independent of domestic policy, which again is partly determined by certain social, economic and political doctrines and ideologies. Colonial practice, however, differed immensely in India and Indonesia, as the following paragraphs reveal.[1]

British colonial practice in Asia developed on the premise of Liberalism: individual freedom and freedom of property and trade were seen to lead to progress. The monetization of rural regions was pushed forward with the requirement to pay land revenue in cash, which provided a large part of the colonial state's finance. It was assumed that, once expelled from the subsistence economy, the cultivator's wish for individual gains would be awakened. Individual profit was to be increased by output growth (increase of productivity and/or arable land) that required productive investment. Since peasants were too poor for such investment, they were in need of credit. Due to the fact that this credit was mainly supplied by non-Western lenders, these had to obtain legal security for the loan provision. This was one of the reasons why the British put in place the legal framework for a market of production factors. Land became private property, could be mortgaged and – where necessary – its transfer enforced by court decree. Indigenous merchants and merchant bankers were to deliver cash crops and raw materials to the ports for export and to distribute the industrial goods imported by the British. The import-export trade itself was dominated by the East India Company and British private capital. The ultimate political aim of the British was the freedom of the colonies which, it was argued, could be achieved by means of education only. An Indian government on the British model and an efficient administration which ranged from the highest city level to the village level were to be introduced.

While until the mid-nineteenth century colonial exploitation was largely mercantile,[2] the heyday of imperial rule was the second half of the nineteenth century until the First World War with a shift towards industrial colonial exploitation (British-owned jute factories). According to Palat et al. (1986), this industrialization, which exploited the Indian labour conditions, was rather exceptional for a colony. These in-

---

[1] Furnivall (1956) distinguished colonial policy and practice. Both British and Dutch colonial policies were based on the ideology of Liberalism, while their colonial practices developed differently: Roughly speaking, British India changed from 'direct' to 'indirect' rule and the Netherlands Indies from 'indirect' to 'direct' rule – with regional differences in each colony. The common preference in colonial policy was indirect rule, if the indigenous population was to develop along its own lines, and direct rule, if the policy was to find a place for the indigenous people in a society with European-style institutions.

[2] I understand mercantile exploitation in the sense that it was largely confined to the obtaining natural resources.

dustries which, at least until the Great Depression, were dominated by British capital, complemented British interests, although British national jute textile production was displaced. This period coincided with a more efficient organization of government to manage India to Britain's advantage, an aim, that was never stated explicitly.

However, unexpected side-effects of *laissez-faire* capitalism became apparent from the mid-nineteenth century onward, such as increasing rural indebtedness and land alienation, which contrasted with the British assumption that the morality of Hinduism was an indigenous protection against the disruptive forces of the market. Nevertheless, there was a reluctance to state intervention in the market for some time because moneylenders played a decisive role in the peasantry's timely revenue payments. Chapter 7.3 showed the ambivalent attitude displayed by the British colonial officials towards moneylenders and moneylending. This may help to explain why legislation regarding moneylenders and usury was not fixed until the late nineteenth and early twentieth centuries, as well as the half-hearted attitude to setting up cooperatives. In the same way, the British did not introduce a popular credit system as the Dutch did in Indonesia. Paradoxically, this strategy would have been more compatible with Liberalism than the interventionism by law.

Colonial practice in Indonesia was quite different. In line with the tenor of Furnivall's description is Tichelman's (1980: 113-125) contribution, which leads us back to the macro level of analysis. He started from the point that, in contrast to other colonies, the industrial-capitalist period of colonial exploitation of Indonesia began very late because of the increasing weakness of Dutch capital. While in the first phase of expansion of the European world-economy Holland was the leading commercial and industrial country, the situation changed in the course of the eighteenth century. According to Suroyo (1987: 67), the Netherlands during the nineteenth century were less industrialized and prosperous than England. The VOC trade monopoly had not drained enough surplus into the Netherlands to produce general welfare. Because of the continuous wars in Europe and the Netherlands Indies, and due to the take-over of the VOC debts, the state treasury was in deficit.

The British interlude (1811-1816) had only limited success in bringing the Javanese peasant into direct touch with the market because of the stagnation of the whole society, the absence of any dynamic capitalist sector and deficits in the administration. The Dutch considered Raffles' policy highly 'illiberal' and unsuited for the indigenous population. Instead a 'liberal policy adapted to its character and institutions' (Furnivall 1956) was pursued under the doctrine of indirect rule with regard to the administration, legal system and so on, and state trading monopolies in the shape of Cultivation and Consignment Systems. Alexander and Alexander (1991: 388-90) emphasized that the colonial state favored a division of labour between the indigenous people and the Chinese in that the former were 'protected from the disruptive forces of the market', and their economic activity largely confined to subsistence agriculture, forced cultivation and low-level commerce, while the latter were found in coolie labour, tax farms and on all levels of commerce. Irrespective of their commercial abilities, rural Javanese entrepreneurs who tried to expand their business had to enter unequal partnerships with Chinese.

Paradoxically, in spite of this strong-arm policy in the economic sphere, Dutch government control was never as strong as the British. The Dutch were constantly drawn into wars. From the beginning indirect rule was – on Java at least – applied to the highest level of administration only, while on the intermediate and lower levels *bupati* (indigenous administrators) were employed, that is to say, former rulers and new bureaucrats.

With the 1870 Agrarian and Sugar Laws private estate enterprise became possible on land which had been declared a government domain (*domeinverklaring*) or on land hired or rented from Indonesians. In all colonial phases, Tichelman (1980) argued, Indonesian products were brought on the world market by the Dutch, while the indigenous people were prevented from entering that market and from capitalist development. High finance in the Netherlands showed no inclination to invest in the Netherlands Indies until the early twentieth century, when a number of small entrepreneurs had successfully taken the pioneering risk and proved the profitability of investment.

Only from 1870 onward, but particularly during the twentieth century, private capital began to fitter into Indonesia, which weakened the colonial bureaucracy that still continued to play the role of the 'protector' of the Indonesian society. The late nineteenth and early twentieth centuries involved much heavier exposure to the money economy, much higher tax obligations and labour services for the indigenous population than the period of the cultivation system. A major decline in the Javanese standard of living could be observed, which was due to enormous population pressure in addition to economic reasons. Interestingly, rural people reacted by falling back on subsistence production (which can hardly be explained with orthodox Marxism). The ethical period (1904-1914) produced specific programs to increase the welfare of the population, such as the People's Credit System and government pawnshops, which was a threat to private lenders. While the former strategy was market-compatible, the latter was a continuation of the earlier policy of state monopoly capitalism. Nevertheless, Wertheim (1964: 96) argued, that the Ethical Policy was not purely altruistic, because Dutch industrialists expected rising Indonesian imports from the Netherlands with this policy, since welfare was likely to increase Indonesian demand for Dutch products. During this decade of 'ethical imperialism' the attention of foreign investors was drawn to the Outer Islands, and the Chinese invested to some extent in cultivation of rubber, coconut, tobacco, etc. The years of anti-colonial struggle (1918/19 and 1923-27) took the Dutch by surprise. In the economic sphere these years produced increasing competition with foreign capital. The Dutch response was reactionary and strengthened the centralist and authoritarian conservative bloc. In this framework the rudimentary attempts to industrialize were suppressed, which did not contribute to the development of Indonesian capitalism. This period was characterized by the maintenance of the status-quo and a de-liberalization of the Ethical Policy (see Kat Angelino 1929-30).

Colonial practices in Indonesia and India can be explained in terms of the economic and political conditions in the Netherlands and England themselves. Tichelman argued that for the Netherlands the particular evolution of (industrial) capitalism – characterized among other things by the concentration and centralization of capital and production, by monopoly formation, and by the intertwining of banking and industrial capital, by the growing trend toward falling profit rates and by surplus capital export – had barely begun in the Netherlands in the course of the late nineteenth century. To put it another way: the Dutch, unlike the British, did not build their own industry on the import of raw materials from their colonies to process and re-export them as ready-made products to the colonial markets, nor invest in colonial industry to exploit cheap labour. For some time they perpetuated a mercantile (not to say, Mercantilist)[3] exploitation policy by appropriating raw materials and produce and selling them on the world market. The related monopoly export trade inhibited the development of Indonesian trade and shipping and restricted Java and most of the Outer Islands to agricultural and estate production. An imperialist perspective to open up Indonesia as a market for Netherlands products occurred only at the turn to the twentieth century but was retarded further by the colonial government.

The lack of specialized large-scale financial agents in Indonesia during the colonial period, which could be compared with indigenously developed bankers in India, can be explained by various factors on both the micro- and macro-levels. First of all, large parts of pre-colonial Indonesia were subsistence-oriented and barely monetized. Only a few cash-crop producing coastal regions and particular harbor principalities were integrated into the world-economy of the Far East. Perhaps we can apply Gills' terminology that Southeast Asia was a 'hinterland' of India (and possibly China). This view supports my argument that the large-scale financing of trade in its entrepots was unnecessary because the traders involved in long-distance trade to India or China were largely aliens, both Indians and Chinese, who traded on account of merchant bankers in their home countries or at least obtained finance from them. Large-scale state finance, such as in Mughal India, does not seem to have played an important role either. The Indonesian states financed themselves by appropriating land revenue (mostly in kind), corvée labour, and –depending upon the region – some state trading and tribute. Merchant princes used their treasuries to finance trade to the spice islands, while the sojourning petty traders described by Van Leur (1955) did not require high finance.

Second, in the course of European expansionism into Asia, non-Western traders were increasingly squeezed out of the Asian country trade and confined to domestic trade, while the European trading companies increased their share of both country trade and Asian-European trade. I showed that the heyday of indigenously developed bankers in India had then already passed, although they adopted particular roles in colonialism (compradore functions), which supports my argument that no indigenous finance was necessary in Indonesia either.

Third, during the colonial period the British shifted from mercantile colonialism to imperialism in the second half of the nineteenth century, while the Dutch continued their mercantile policy that aimed at a more or less one-sided movement of produce

---

[3] The Dutch also adhered to the doctrines of Liberalism which challenged the former Mercantilist doctrines. However, from the point of view of strong government intervention in the market from the early nineteenth century to at least 1870, they applied a Mercantilist policy. The same argument can be applied to the period when the English East India Company had monopolized foreign trade between England and India.

and mineral resources from the Netherlands Indies to the Netherlands. In such a colonial economy private credit demand and supply were rather limited. The transport to the ports was partly financed by trade credit from the exporting firms to Chinese intermediaries, partly by Chinese-internal networks, but specialized financial agents hardly emerged. During the period of the Cultivation System, the estates and specific processing industries obtained government credit and later bank credit which, similar to India, financed only certain sectors of the economy. In addition, most Indonesian estate production was not very capital intensive. The step towards imperialism, with foreign investment in domestic industries, was for some time delayed in Indonesia. To sum up my argument for the colonial period: large-scale professional moneylenders were not necessary in this kind of state monopoly capitalism because the opening up of the country to the market with private capital was not pursued and sometimes even prohibited. Private investment was suppressed at least until 1870 and then allowed to grow only hesitantly, particularly on the Outer Islands.

A factor which supported this retardation was the stratum of capital owners. In India, the national movement developed in close relation with the high-level indigenous economic stratum, and this stratum worked politically for an independent India in expectation of economic advantages for themselves. They invested in Indian industries. Among these investors were many indigenously developed bankers, who reorganized their economic activity. In Indonesia, however, the highest non-Western economic stratum was composed of the Chinese. Not that their politico-economic function was very different from the indigenous-style bankers in India. On the whole both had collaborated with the colonial regime in the position of *compradores* and revenue farmers. However, the Chinese were aliens occupying the commercial sphere, while Indonesians tried to get a foothold in this economic field. The Indonesian national movement was only supported by Indonesians who attacked both Dutch and Chinese. The more or less regularly occurring pogroms against the latter and the nationalist policy that continued after independence may perhaps explain the reluctance of many Chinese until the mid-1960s to make long-term, large-scale capital investments that are the constituents of industrialization, in a lucrative but very hostile environment. In so far as the Chinese invested, they did so in the estate business and light industries where the capital inputs were limited in amount and time. The last three decades, however, showed growing Chinese investment on the basis of joint ventures with the military/bureaucrats and a diversification and internationalization of their business, as described in Chapter 14.3. These joint ventures provide the necessary political patronage and protection. The victims of the still continuing anti-Chinese pogroms are the majority of Chinese in Indonesia on the small-scale and medium-scale levels of trade.

Finally, this study requires me to return to my research hypotheses outlined in Chapter 2. With regard to the first hypothesis concerning large-scale finance I specify that, from a general point of view, large-scale professional moneylenders and merchant bankers are a structural phenomenon of expanding merchant capitalism, who have been largely replaced by banks in the long process of transformation of the economy and society and the expansion of the capitalist mode of production. However, I would argue, with regard to the two different colonial histories of India and Indonesia, that the extent to which such financial agents emerge depends on specific endogenous and exogenous factors. While I discussed a number of endogenous explanations in Parts I – III, I analyzed exogenous factors in Part IV, such as the historical integration of a particular country into world trade, as well as on state and colonial policies which determine the limits of private capital and the relative freedom of its markets.

I also argued that small-scale moneylenders have always existed throughout all historical periods. I interpreted their pre-colonial activities as having been constrained by the moral economy. They were expected to help villagers in need. In addition to public arrangements of social security they provided a private service for the risk management of bad harvests and other disasters. To put it another way, the lender-borrower relation was to a high extent embedded in the village life. I called this relation during this period patron-client relationship. In contrast to large-scale financiers, whose heyday was the flourishing Far-Eastern world-economy, moneylenders and agricultural lenders experienced a considerable growth during the colonial period because they had important functions within the colonial economy. Not only did they pre-finance the land revenue which formed the basis of colonial rule, but they organized trade and crop purchases in rural regions, supporting the incorporation of these regions into the world market. Their business was backed by Western legislation, which defined property, mobilized the production factor land and made it desirable. I argued that particularly this change in the political and legal framework disembedded the lender-borrower relation from village life, because it dissolved the narrow constraints of economic action which was set by the moral economy for both lenders and borrowers. Their relation became impersonalized, the credit conditions no longer being adjusted to the requirements of the borrower and the uncomfortable enforcement of lenders' claims being left to the courts. Only when rural indebtedness became a severe problem posing a threat to colonial authority, did the colonial administration begin to intervene in informal finance with moneylenders' legislation and popular credit. The extent to which moneylending and agricultural finance flourished in a particular country depended on the degree of its embeddedness and political interference.

From the structural perspective contemporary moneylenders and a number of other informal financiers are not a residue of the past slowing down development and eventually disappearing with the onset of modernization. The statistics of developing countries speak against this. In many cases informal finance constitutes more than 50 percent of total finance, even though its relative share declined. The reason is that until recently at least government policies aimed at expanding formal and confining informal finance. Already in the late colonial period, but particularly from independence until the 1980s the Indian and Indonesian governments heavily regulated the financial landscape. Then they were forced by the World Bank, the IMF and other transnational financial institutions to take up the favored development strategy of market deregulation.

I went further by saying that informal finance even supports capitalism because it provides purchasing power in the form of consumer credit to marginalized people beyond the scope of banks and links them to the commodity market as consumers. The analysis has shown that this hypothesis can be maintained if not even extended as far as developing countries are concerned. Informal borrowers are not only people on the bottom rung of society. There are large numbers of them in rural as well as in urban regions. They are not only consumers but in many cases small-scale and medium-scale producers, such as young entrepreneurs who do not have as yet any security to offer, or they are customers from the service sector. The degree to which contemporary informal finance is flourishing varies from one country to another and hinges on the extent of economic, political and legal constraints.

If I should assess the future development of the two financial landscapes considered here, I nevertheless expect a homogenization (which, however, does not mean: eradication of informal finance, due to the fact that it is so flexible to always quickly adapt to changing circumstances). The reason for this homogenization is that the ongoing process of globalization sets limits to the independence of political decision-making on the national level whereas the political authority of transnational organizations grows. A supranational financial policy which provides a similar political framework in which financial landscapes develop, will in the long run perhaps give rise to similar financial actors, intermediaries and institutions – both formal and informal – on a world scale.

Bibliography

ABU-LUGHOD, J. 1989: *Before European Hegemony. The World System: 1250 – 1350.* New York: Oxford University Press.

ABU-LUGHOD, J. 1993: Discontinuities and Persistence. In: A.G. Frank and B.K. Gills (eds.): *The World System – Five Hundred or Five Thousand?* London: Routledge.

A.I.D. Spring Review of Small Farmer Credit 1973: *Small Farmer Credit in Indonesia.* Vol. XVII. Washington, D.C.

ADAMS, D.W., D.H. Graham and J.D. v. Pischke (eds.) 1984: *Undermining Rural Development with Cheap Credit.* Boulder, Colorado: Westview.

Adat Rechtsbundels II 1911a: Java en Madoera. Serie B West Java No. 1, D: Schuldenrecht: 26-55.

Adat Rechtsbundels II 1911b: Java en Madoera. Serie B West Java No. 2: Rapport De Woff van Westerrode 1901: 57-82.

Adat Rechtsbundels XVIII 1919: Serie C. Middel-Java No. 41: Landbouwkrediet en Adatrecht (1906): 71-73.

Adat Rechtsbundels XXXIV 1931: Serie B. West Java. No. 53: Pandrecht in West Java (1911): 92-102.

AG BIELEFELDER ENTWICKLUNGSSOZIOLOGEN (eds.) 1979: *Subsistenzproduktion und Akkumulation.* Bielefelder Studien zur Entwicklungssoziologie Band 5. Saarbrücken and Ford Lauderdale: Breitenbach.

ALAVI, H. 1962: *Capitalism and Colonial Production.* London: Croom Helm.

ALAVI, H. 1979: Indien und die koloniale Produktionsweise. D. Senghaas (Hrsg): *Kapitalistische Weltökonomie.* Frankfurt/M.: Suhrkamp.

ALEXANDER, J. 1986: Price Setting in a Rural Javanese Market. *Bulletin of Indonesian Economic Studies* 22, 1: 88-112.

ALEXANDER, J. and P. 1991: Protecting Peasants from Capitalism: The Subordination of Javanese Traders by the Colonial State. *Comparative Studies in Society and History* 33, 2: 370-394.

All India Debt and Investment Survey 1977: Indebtedness of Rural Households and Availability of Institutional Finance (1971-72). Bombay: Reserve Bank of India.

All India Rural Credit Survey 1955: The General Report. Bombay: Reserve Bank of India.

AMIN, S. 1993: The Ancient World-Systems Versus the Modern World-System. In: A.G. Frank and B.K. Gills (eds.): *The World System – Five Hundred or Five Thousand?* London: Routledge.

ANDRESKI, S. 1984: *Max Weber on Capitalism, Bureaucracy and Religion. A Selection of Texts.* London, Boston and Sydney: Allen and Unwin.

ANTI-WOEKER VEREENIGING De Bandoeng 1931: 5e Jaarverslag. Bandung: Visser.

ARASARATNAM, S. 1979: *Indians in Malaya and Singapore.* Peteling Jaya, Selanger: Oxford University Press.

ARISTOTLE 1962: *The Politics.* Harmondsworth: Penguin Books.

ARNDT, H.W. 1987: The Financial System of Indonesia. *Savings and Development* 11, 3: 305-315

BAECKER, D. 1991: *Womit handeln Banken? Eine Untersuchung zur Risikoverarbeitung in der Wirtschaft.* Frankfurt/M.: Suhrkamp.

BAGCHI, A.K. 1972: *Private Investment in India: 1900-1939.* Cambridge: Cambridge University Press.

BAKKER, P. 1936: Eeninge Beschouwingen over het Geldverkeer in de Inheemsche Samenleving van Nederlandsch-Indie. Proefschrift (Doctor in de Rechtsgeleerdheid). Rijksuniversiteit Leiden. Groningen en Batavia: Wolters.

BALAMOHANDAS, V. et al. 1991: *Rural Banks and Rural Credit.* New Delhi: Discovery Publishers.

BALDWIN, C. and R. Wilson 1988: Islamic Finance in Principle and Practice. C. Mallat (ed): *Islamic Law and Finance.* London/Dordrecht/Boston: Graham and Trotman.

BANK BUMI DAYA 1988: *Perbankan di Indonesia.* Jakarta.

BELL, C. 1990: Interactions Between Institutional and Informal Credit Agencies in Rural India. *The World Bank Economic Review* 4, 3: 297-327.

BHARGAVA, B.K. 1934: *Indigenous Banking in Ancient and Medieval India.* Bombay: D.B. Taraporevala.

BHATTACHARYA, S. 1982: Eastern India. D. Kumar (ed): *The Cambridge Economic History of India*, Vol. II. New Delhi: Orient Longman and Cambridge University Press.

BLOCH, M. 1989: The Symbolism of Money in Imerina. J. Parry and M. Bloch (eds.): *Money and the Morality of Exchange.* Cambridge: Cambridge Univ. Press.

BMZ, GTZ and DSE 1987: *Rural Finance: Guiding Principles.* Ed. by R.H. Schmidt and E. Kropp. Eschborn: GTZ.

BOEKE, J.H. 1916: De Indische Woekerwet. *Koloniale Studien* 2: 61-82.

BOEKE, J.H. 1919: De controle op de Afdeelingsbanken. *Blaadje van de Centrale Kas te Batavia* 7, 9: 147-155.

BOEKE, J.H. 1920: De controle op de Afdeelingsbanken. *Blaadje van de Centrale Kas te Batavia* 8, 2: 22-28.

BOEKE, J.H. 1926a: Inlandse Budgetten. *Koloniale Studien* 1.

BOEKE, J.H. 1926b: Dr. Hirschfeld over het Volkscredietwezen in Nederlandsch-Indie. *Koloniale Studien* 2: 811-822.

BOEKE, J.H. 1938: *Inleiding tot de economie der inheemsche samenleving in Nederlandsch-Indie.* Amsterdam: H.E. Stenfert Kroese.

BOEKE, J.H. 1942: *The Structure of Netherlands Indian Economy.* New York: Institute of Pacific Relations.

BOEKE, J.H. 1946: *The Evolution of the Netherlands-Indian Economy.* New York: Institute of Pacific Relations.

BOEKE, J.H. 1953: *Economics and Economic Policy of Dual Societies as Exemplified by Indonesia.* New York: Institute of Pacific Relations.

BOEKE, J.H. 1980: Dualism in Colonial Societies (repr. from Indonesian Economics). H.-D. Evers (ed): *Sociology of Southeast Asia.* Kuala Lumpur: Oxford University Press.

BOEKE, J.H. n.d.: Agrarian Reforms in the Far East. *American Journal of Sociology* LVII.

BOHANAN, P. 1959: The Impact of Money on an African Subsistence Economy. *The Journal of Economic History* 19: 491-503.

BÖHM-BAWERK, E. 1970: *Capital and Interest –A Critical History of Economic Theory.* (repr. 1922). New York: A.M. Kelly.

BONDER, M. und B. Röttger 1993: Eine Welt für alle? Überlegungen zu Ideologie und Realität von Fraktionierung und Vereinheitlichung im globalen Kapitalismus. *Nord-Süd aktuell* 7, 1: 60-71.

BOOMGAARD, P. 1986a: Buitenzorg in 1805: the Role of Money and Credit in a Colonial Frontier Society. *Modern Asian Studies* 20,1: 33-58.

BOOMGAARD, P. 1986b: The Welfare Service of Indonesia, 1900-42. *Itinerario* 10, 1: 57-82.

BOOMGAARD, P. 1989: *Children of the Colonial State. Population Growth and Economic Development in Java, 1795-1880.* Amsterdam: Free University Press.

BOOTH, A. 1989: Exports and Growth in the Colonial Economy, 1830-1940. A. Maddison and G. Prince (eds.): *Economic Growth in Indonesia 1829-1940*. Dordrecht: Foris.

BOSE, S. 1986: *Agrarian Bengal: Economy, Social Structure and Politics, 1919-1947*. Cambridge: Cambridge University Press.

BOTTOMLEY, A. 1983: Interest Rate Determination in Underdeveloped Rural Areas. J.D. Pischke et al. (eds.): *Rural Financial Markets in Developing Countries*. Baltimore and London: Johns Hopkins.

BOUMAN, F.J.A. 1983: Indigenous Savings and Credit Societies in the Developing World. J.D. von Pischke et al. (eds.): *Rural Financial Markets in Developing Countries*. Baltimore and London: Johns Hopkins.

BOUMAN, F.J.A. 1989: *Small, Short and Unsecured: Informal Rural Finance in India*. New Delhi: Oxford University Press.

BOUMAN, F.J.A. 1994: RoSCA and ASCrA: Beyond the Financial Landscape. F.J.A. Bouman and O. Hospes (eds.): *Financial Landscapes Reconstructed. The Fine Art of Mapping Development*. Boulder: Westview.

BOUMAN, F.J.A. and H.A.J. Moll 1992: Informal Finance in Indonesia. D.W. Adams and D. Fitchett (eds.): *Informal Finance in Low-Income Countries*. Boulder: Westview.

BOURDIEU, P. 1977: *Outline of a Theory of Practice*. Cambridge: Cambridge University Press.

BRAUDEL, F. 1981: *Civilization and Capitalism, 15th-18th Century*. Vol. I: *The Structure of Everyday Life*. New York: Harper and Row.

BRAUDEL, F. 1982: *Civilization and Capitalism, 15th-18th Century*. Vol. II: *The Wheel of Commerce*. New York: Harper and Row.

BRAUDEL, F. 1984: *Civilization and Capitalism, 15th-18th Century*: Vol. III: *The Perspective of the World*. New York: Harper and Row.

BRAUDEL, F. 1986a: *Sozialgeschichte des 15.-18. Jahrhunderts*. Band 2: *Der Handel*. München: Kindler.

BRAUDEL, F. 1986b: *Sozialgeschichte des 15.-18. Jahrhunderts*. Band 3: *Aufbruch zur Weltwirtschaft*. München: Kindler.

BREMAN, J. 1980: *The Village on Java and the Early Colonial State*. Casp I. Rotterdam: Erasmus University.

BRUIJN, J.R., F.S. Gaastra, and I. Schöffer 1979-87: *Dutch-Asiatic Shipping in the 17th and 18th Centuries*. 3 volumes. The Hague: Martinus Nijhoff.

BRUNHOFF, S. de 1973: *Marx on Money*. New York: Urizen Books.

BUCHHOLT, H. 1990: *Kirche, Kopra, Bürokraten: Gesellschaftliche Entwicklung und strategisches Handeln in Nord Sulawesi, Indonesien.* Bielefelder Studien zur Entwicklungssoziologie Band 44. Saarbrücken, Fort Lauderdale: Breitenbach.

BUCHHOLT, H. 1992: Der niemals endende Konflikt? Händlerminoritäten in Südostasien. *Sociologus* 42, 2: 132-156. Berlin: Duncker und Hublot.

BURGER, D.H. 1930: Het niet-officieele crediet in het Regenschap Pati in 1927. *Koloniale Studien* 14, 2: 395-412.

BURGER, D.H. 1939: De outsluiting van Java's binnenland voor het wereldverkeer. Dissertation. Wageningen: Veeman and Jonen.

BURGER, D.H. 1975: *Sociologisch-economische geschiednis van Indonesie,* deel II. S'Gravenhage: Martinus Nijhoff.

CATANACH, I.J. 1970: *Rural Credit in Western India 1875-1930.* Berkeley, Los Angeles, London: University of California Press.

CATOR, W.J. 1936: *The Economic Position of the Chinese in the Netherlands Indies.* Oxford: Basil Blackwell.

CHANDRAVAKAR, A.G. 1982: Money and Credit, 1858-1947. D. Kumar (ed): *The Cambridge Economic History of India,* Vol. II. New Delhi: Orient Longman and Cambridge University Press.

CHARLESWORTH, N. 1985: *Peasants and Imperial Rule. Agriculture and Agricultural Society in the Bombay Presidency, 1850-1935.* Hyderabad: Orient Longman.

CHAUDHURI, B.B. 1969: Rural Credit Relations in Bengal, 1859-1885. *Indian Economic and Social History Review* 6.

CHAUDHURI, K.N. 1978: *The Trading World of Asia and the East India Company, 1660-1760.* Cambridge: Cambridge University Press.

CHAUDHURI, K.N. 1981: The World-System East of Longitude 20: The European Role in Asia, 1500-1750. *Review* 5, 2: 219-245.

CHAUDHURI, K.N. 1982: Foreign Trade and Balance of Payments (1757-1947). D. Kumar (ed): *The Cambridge Economic History of India,* Vol. II. New Delhi: Orient Longman and Cambridge University Press.

CHAUDHURI, K.N. 1985: *Trade and Civilisation in the Indian Ocean. An Economic History from the Rise of Islam to 1750.* Cambridge: Cambridge University Press.

CHAUDHURI, K.N. 1990: *Asia Before Europe. Economy and Civilization of the Indian Ocean from the Rise of Islam to 1750.* Cambridge: Cambridge University Press.

CHEESMAN, D. 1982: 'The Omnipresent Bania': Rural Moneylenders in Nineteenth-Century Sindh. *Modern Asian Studies* 16, 3: 445-462.

CIRVANTE, V.R. 1956: *The Indian Capital Market*. Bombay: Oxford University Press.

CLARK, J.B. 1907: *Essentials of Economic Theory as Applied to Modern Problems in Industry and Public Policy*. New York: Macmillan.

CLIFFORD, H. 1990: *Further India. The Story of Exploration*. Bangkok: White Lotus.

COLEMAN, D.C. (ed) 1969: *Revisions in Mercantilism*. London: Methuen.

Congress Agricultural Enquiry Committee Report 1982 (repr.). Gurgaon: Nisha Jain.

COOLHAAS, W. n.d: *Insulinde. Menschen en Maatschappij*. Deventer: Van Hoeve.

COPPEL, C.A. 1983: *Indonesian Chinese in Crisis*. Kuala Lumpur: Oxford University Press.

CRAMER, J.C.W. 1929: *Het Volkskredietwezen in Nederlandsch Indie*. Amsterdam: H.J. Paris.

DAHM, B. 1978: Indonesien, Geschichte eines Entwicklungslandes (1945-1971). *Handbuch der Orientalistik*, Dritte Abt., erster Bd: Geschichte. Leiden: Brill.

DALTON, G. and P. Bohannan (eds.) 1962: *Markets in Africa*. Evanston: Northwestern University Press.

DARLING, M.L. 1977: *The Punjab Peasant in Prosperity and Debt* (repr.). New Delhi: P.L. Printers.

DASGUPTA, A. 1982: Indian Mercants and the Trade in the Indian Ocean. T. Raychaudhuri and I. Habib (eds.): *The Cambridge Economic History of India*, Vol. I. New Delhi: Orient Longman and Cambride University Press.

DEWEY, A. 1964: Capital, Credit and Savings in Javanse Marketing. R. Firth and B.S. Yamey (eds.): *Capital, Savings and Credit in Peasant Societies*. London: Allen and Unwin.

DHANAGARE, D.N. 1991: *Peasant Movements in India, 1920-50*. New Delhi: Oxford University Press.

DJOJOHADIKUSOMO, R.M. Sumitro 1943: *Het volkscredietwezen in de depressie*. Haarlem: De Erven F. Bohn.

DOBB, M. 1976: *Studies in the Development of Capitalism* (repr.). New York: International Publishers.

DOBBIN, C. 1989: From Middleman Minorities to Industrial Entrepreneurs: The Chinese in Java and the Parsis in Western India, 1619-1939. *India and Indonesia. Comparative History of India and Indonesia*, Part IV. Leiden, New York: Brill

DODELL, H. 1910: Economic Transition in India. *The Economic Journal* 5.

DURKHEIM, E. 1964: *The Division of Labor in Society.* New York: Free Press.

EINZIG, P. 1949: *Primitive Money.* Oxford: Pergamon.

ELWERT, G. 1987: Ausdehnung der Käuflichkeit und Einbettung der Wirtschaft. Markt und Moralökonomie. K. Heinemann (Hrsg): *Soziologie wirtschaftlichen Handelns. Kölner Zeitschrift für Soziologie und Sozialpsychologie*, Sonderheft 28.

ELWERT, G., H.-D. Evers und W. Wilkens 1983: Die Suche nach Sicherheit: Kombinierte Produktionsformen im sogenannten informellen Sektor. *Zeitschrift für Soziologie* 12, 4.

ENTHOVEN, R.E. 1979: *The Tribes and Castes of Bombay* (repr. 1920). New Delhi.

EVERS, H.-D. (ed) 1980: *Sociology of Southeast Asia.* Kuala Lumpur: Oxford University Press.

EVERS, H.-D. 1987: Chettiar Moneylenders in Southeast Asia. D. Lombard (ed): *Marchands et hommes d'affaires asiatiques.* Paris: Editions d l'EILESS. 199-219.

EVERS, H.-D. 1988: Traditional Trading Networks of Southeast Asia. *Archipel* 35: 89-100.

EVERS, H.-D. 1994: The Traders' Dilemma: A Theory of the Social Transformation of Markets and Society. H.-D. Evers and H. Schrader (eds.): *The Moral Economy of Trade. Ethnicity and Developing Markets.* London: Routledge.

EVERS, H.-D., J. Pavadarayan and H. Schrader 1994: The Chettiar Moneylenders in Singapore. H.-D. Evers and H. Schrader (eds.): *The Moral Economy of Trade. Ethnicity and Developing Markets.* London: Routledge.

EVERS, H.-D. und T. Schiel 1988: *Strategische Gruppen – Vergleichende Studien zur Staatsbürokratie und Klassenbildung in der Dritten Welt.* Berlin: Dietrich Reimer.

EVERS, H.-D. and H. Schrader (eds.) 1994: *The Moral Economy of Trade. Ethnicity and Developing Markets.* London: Routledge.

FASSEUR, C. 1978: *Cultuurstelsel en Koloniale Baten. De Nederlandse Exploitatie van Java 1840-1860.* Leiden: Universitaire Press.

FIRTH, R. 1964: Capital, Savings and Credit in Peasant Societies. R. Firth and B.S. Yamey (eds.): *Capital, Savings and Credit in a Peasant Society.* London: Allen and Unwin.

FOKKENS, F. 1896: *Inlandsch landbouwcrediet op Java.* Verslagen der Algemeene Vergaderingen van het Indisch Genootschap 1896: 31-59.

FRANK, A.G. and B.K. Gills 1993: The 5,000-Year World System – An Introduction. A.G. Frank and B.K. Gills (eds.): *The World System – Five Hundred or Five Thousand?* London: Routledge.

FRUIN, T.A. 1938: Popular and Rural Credit in the Netherlands Indies. *Bulletin of the Colonial Institute of Amsterdam* 1, 2 Parts. February.

FURNIVALL, J.S. 1934a: State and Primitive Money Lending in Netherlands India. *Studies in the Social and Economic Development of the Netherlands East Indies* IIIb. Rangoon: Burma Book Club.

FURNIVALL, J.S. 1934b: State Pawnshops in the Netherlands Indies. *Studies in the Social and Economic Development of the Netherlands East Indies* IIIc. Rangoon: Burma Book Club

FURNIVALL, J.S. 1939: *Netherlands India.* Cambridge: Cambridge University Press.

FURNIVALL, J.S. 1956: *Colonial Policy and Practice.* New York: New York University Press.

GADGIL, D.R. 1955: Indian Economic Organization. S. Kuznett (ed): *Economic Growth: Brazil, India, Japan.* Durham: Duke University Press.

GAMBETTA, D. 1988: Can We Trust Trust? D. Gambetta (ed): *Trust – Making and Breaking Cooperative Relations.* New York: Basil Blackwell.

Gazetteer of India 1972: Tamil Nadu State. Madras.

Gazetteer of the Bombay Presidency 1885 Vol. XIX: Sátára. Bombay.

Gazetteer of the Bombay Presidency 1877 Vol. II: Gujarat. Bombay.

Gazetteer of the Bombay Presidency 1884 Vol. VIII: Káthiáwár. Bombay.

Gazetteer of the Bombay Presidency 1884 Vol. XVII: Ahmadnagar. Bombay.

GEERTZ, C. 1963a: *Agricultural Involution. The Process of Ecological Change in Indonesia.* Berkeley, CA: University of California Press.

GEERTZ, C. 1963b: *Pedlars and Princes – Social Change and Economic Modernization in Two Indonesian Towns.* Chicago, London: University of Chicago Press.

GERMIDIS, D. 1990: Interlinking the Formal and Informal Financial Sectors in Developing Countries. *Savings and Development* 14, 1:] 5-22.

GERSCHENKRON, A. 1966: *Economic Backwardness in Historical Perspective.* Cambridge, Mass.: Belknap.

GHATAK, S. 1976: *Rural Money Markets in India.* New Delhi: Macmillan.

GHATAK, S. 1983: On Interregional Variations in Rural Interest Rates. *Journal of Developing Areas* 18: 21-34.

GHATE, P. 1988: Informal Credit Markets in Asian Developing Countries. *Asian Development Review* 6, 1.

GHATE, P. 1992: *Informal Finance: Some Findings from Asia.* Hong Kong: Asian Development Bank and Oxford University Press.

GHOSE, B.C. 1943: *A Study of the Indian Money Market.* London: Oxford University Press.

GILLS, B.K. 1993: Hegemonic Transitions in the World System. A.G. Frank and B.K. Gills (eds.): *The World System – Five Hundred or Five Thousand?* London: Routledge.

GILLS, B.K. and A.G. Frank 1993: The Cumulation of Accumulation. A.G. Frank and B.K. Gills (eds.): *The World System – Five Hundred or Five Thousand?* London: Routledge.

GLAMANN, K. 1958: *Dutch-Asiatic Trade, 1620-1740.* Copenhagen: Danish Science Printers.

GOLDSMITH, R.M. 1987: *Premodern Financial Systems.* A Historical Comparative Study. Cambridge: Cambridge University Press.

GONGGRIJP, G. 1922: Het Crediet in de Indische Volkshuishouding. *Koloniale Tijdschrift* 11: 529-552.

GONGGRIJP, G. 1957: *Schets eener economische geschiednis van Indonesie.* Haarlem: De Erven S. Bohn.

GOSWAMI, O. 1985: Then Came the Marwaris: Some Aspects of the Changes in the Pattern of Industrial Control in Eastern India. *The Indian Economic and Social History Review* 22, 3: 225-249.

GOSWAMI, O. 1989: Sahibs, Babus, and Banias: Changes in Industrial Control in Eastern India, 1918-50. *Journal of Asian Studies* 48, 1 and 2 (1989).

GOVERNMENT OF INDIA 1956: *Agricultural Legislation in India.* Vol. I: Regulations of Moneylending. New Delhi.

GOYAL, O.P. 1979: *Financial Institutions and Economic Growth of India.* New Delhi: Life and Light.

GRANOVETTER, M. 1985: Economic Action and Social Structure: The Problem of Embeddedness. *American Journal of Sociology* 91, 3: 481-510.

GRANOVETTER, M. 1992: Economic Action and Social Structure: The Problem of Embeddedness. M. Granovetter and R. Swedberg (eds.): *The Sociology of Economic Life.* Boulder: Westview.

GREGORY, C.A. 1988: Village Moneylending, the World Bank and Landless in Central India. *Journal of Contemporary Asia* 18, 1.

GUHA, A. 1972: Raw Cotton of Western India: Output, Transport and Marketing, 1750-1850. *Indian Economic and Social History Review* 9, 1: 1-42.

HABIB, I. 1960: Banking in Mughal India. T. Raychaudhury (ed): *Contriburions to Indian Economic History,* Vol. I. Calcutta: Firma K.L. Mukhopadhyay.

HABIB, I. 1964: Usury in Medieval India. *Comparative Studies in Society and History* 4.

HABIB, I. 1982: Non-Agriculatural Production and Urban Economy. T. Raychaudhuri and I. Habib (eds.): *The Cambridge Economic History of India,* Vol. I. New Delhi: Orient Longman and Cambridge University Press.

HABIB, I. 1990: Merchant Communities in Pre-colonial India. J.D. Tracy (ed): *The Rise of Merchant Empires.* Cambridge: Cambridge University Press.

HALL, D.G.E. 1985: *A History of Southeast Asia* (4th ed.). Macmillan Asian History Series. Hong Kong: Macmillan.

Handbook of the Netherlands East Indies 1924. Div. of Commerce and Dpt. of Agriculture, Industry and Commerce. Java.

Handbook of the Netherlands East Indies 1930. Div. of Commerce and Dpt. of Agriculture, Industry and Commerce. Java.

HARDJONO, J. 1987: *Land, Labor and Livelihood in a West Java Village.* Pusat Penelitian Kependudukan. Yogyakarta: Gadjah Mada University Press.

HARRIS, O. 1989: The Earth and the State: the Sources and Meanings of Money in Northern Potosí, Bolvia. J. Parry and M. Bloch (eds.): *Money and the Morality of Exchange.* Cambridge: Cambridge Univ. Press.

HARRISS, B. 1981: *Transitional Trade and Rural Development: The Nature and Role of Agricultural Trade in a South Indian District.* New Delhi: Vikas.

HARRISS, B. 1983: Money and Commodities: Their Interaction in a Rural Indian Setting. J.D. v. Pischke et al. (eds.): *Rural Financial Markets in Developing Countries.* Baltimore and London: Johns Hopkins.

HARRISS, B. 1992: Secret Agents, Private Agro-Commercial Moneylending and Formal Sector Credit in India. Paper for the Institute of Development Studies, Sussex, Workshop.

HARVEY, G.E. 1945: *The British Rule in Burma, 1824-1942.* London: Faber and Faber.

HEINEMANN, K. 1969: *Grundzüge einer Soziologie des Geldes.* Stuttgart: Ferdinand Enke.

HEINEMANN, K. 1987: Soziologie des Geldes. K. Heinemann (ed): *Soziologie des wirtschaftlichen Handelns.* Sonderband. *Kölner Zeitschrift für Soziologie und Sozialpsychologie* 28.

HELFFERICH, K. 1914: *Die Niederländisch-Indischen Kulturbanken.* Jena.

HENDERSON, J.W. et al. (eds) 1971: *Area Handbook for Burma.* Washington D.C.: US Government Publishers.

HERU-NUGROHO SOEGIARTO 1993: The Embeddedness of Money, Moneylenders and Moneylending in a Javanese Town. Ph.D. thesis. University of Bielefeld.

HEWISON, K. 1988: The Structure of Banking Capital in Thailand. *Southeast Asian Journal of Social Science* 16, 1.

HICKS, G.L. (ed) 1993: *Overseas Chinese Remittances from Southeast Asia 1910-1940.* Singapore: Select Books.

HIRSCHFELD, H.M. 1926: Het Volkskredietwezen in Nederlandsch-Indie. *Koloniale Studien* 2: 548-569.

HIRSCHMAN, A.O. 1977: *The Passions and the Interests: Political Arguments for Capitalism before Its Triumph.* Princeton: Princeton University Press.

HIRSCHMAN, A.O. 1986a: The Concept of Interest: From Euphemism to Tautology. A.O. Hirschman: *Rival Views of Market Society and Other Essays.* New York: Viking.

HIRSCHMAN, A.O. 1986b: Rival Views of Market Society. A.O. Hirschman: *Rival Views of Market Society and Other Essays.* New York: Viking.

HOMER, S. 1963: *A History of Interest Rates.* New Brunswick, New Jersey: Rutgers University Press.

HOSELITZ, B. 1963: Entrepreneurship and Traditional Elites. *Explorations in Entrepreneurial History* 2, 1: 36-49.

Indian Central Banking Enquiry Committee Report 1931. Calcutta.

INTERNATIONAL MONETARY FUND 1989: *International Financial Statistics 1988.*

IQBAL, F. 1988: The Determinants of Moneylender Interest Rates: Evidence from Rural India. *Journal of Development Studies* 24, 3: 364-78.

ISLAM, M.M. 1985: M.L. Darling and the Punjab Peasant in Prosperity and Debt: A Fresh Look. *The Journal of Peasant Studies* 13.

ITO, S., 1966: A Note on the 'Business Combine' in India – with Special Reference of the Nattukottai Chettiars. *The Developing Economies* 4, 3: 367-380.

JAIN, C. 1929: *Indigenous Banking in India.* London: Macmillam.

JONES, J.H. 1994: A Changing Financial Level in India. Micro and Macro Level Perspectives. F.J.A. Bouman and O. Hospes (eds.): *Financial Landscapes Reconstructed. The Fine Art of Mapping Development.* Boulder: Westview.

KARKAL, G. 1967: *Unorganized Money Markets in India.* Bombay: Lalvani Publishing House.

KARTODIRDJO, S. 1973: *Protest Movements in Rural Java.* Singapore: Oxford University Press.

KAT ANGELINO, A.D.A. De 1929-30: *Staatkundig Beleid en Bestuurzorg in Nederlandsch-Indie.* S'Gravenhage: Martinus Nijhoff.

KAT ANGELINO, A.D.A. De 1931: *Colonial Policy, Vol. II. The Dutch East Indies.* The Hague: Martinus Nijhoff.

KEERS, J. 1928: Het Pandcrediet op Java. *Koloniale Studien* 12: 367-418.

KERN, J.R. 1986: The Growth of Decentralised Rural Credit Institutions in Indonesia. C. MacAndrews (ed): *Central Government and Local Development in Indonesia.* London: Oxford University Press.

KESSINGER, T.G. 1982: North India. D. Kumar (ed): *The Cambridge Economic History of India,* Vol. II. New Delhi: Orient Longman and Cambridge University Press.

KESSLER, D., A. Lavigne, and P.A. Ullamo 1985: Ways and Means to Reduce Financial Dualism in Developing Countries. Working Paper. OECD Development Centre.

KHAN, I.A. 1976: *The Middle Classes in the Mughal Empire.* Proceedings of the 36th Session of the Indian History Congress, Aligarh, 1975. New Delhi: Indian History Congress.

KNEBEL, J. 1901: Varia Javanica. Over Kalangs. *Tijdschrift voor Nederlandsch Indie* 44: 24-23.

KNIGHT, G.R. 1992: The Java Sugar Industry as a Capitalist Plantation: A Reappraisal. *The Journal of Peasant Studies* 19, 3 and 4: 68-86.

KRAHNEN, J.P. and R.H. Schmidt 1994: *Development Finance as Institution Building.* Boulder, San Francisco and Oxford: Westview.

KRISHNAN, V. 1959: *Indigenous Banking in South India.* Bombay: Bombay State Co-operative Union.

KROPP, E. et al. 1989: *Linking Self-help Groups and Banks in Developing Countries.* Eschborn: GTZ-Verlag.

KUMAR D. (ed.) 1982: *The Cambridge Economic History of India.* Vol. 2: c. 1757 – c. 1970. New Delhi: Orient Longman and Cambridge University Press.

KUMAR, R. 1965: The Deccan Riots of 1875. *Journal of Asian Studies* 24, 4: 613-35.

LAMBERTE, M.B. and A.A. Jose 1988: The Manufacturing Sector and the Informal Credit Markets: The Case of Trade Credits in the Footwear Industry. WP No. 88-07. Philippines Institute for Development Studies.

LE GOFF, J. 1979: *The Usurer and Purgatory.* Centre for Medieval and Renaissance Studies: The Dawn of Modern Banking. New Haven and London: Yale University Press.

LE GOFF, J. 1980: *Time, Work and Culture in the Middle Ages.* Chicago: Univ. of Chicago Press.

LE GOFF, J. 1988: *Wucherzins und Höllenqualen: Ökonomie und Religion im Mittelalter.* Stuttgart: Klett-Kotta.

LE GOFF, J. 1989: *Kaufleute und Bankiers im Mittelalter.* Frankfurt/Main: Fischer

LEE, S.Y. 1982: *Financial Structures and Monetary Policies in Southeast Asia.* London: Macmillan.

LEONARD, K. 1979: The 'Great Firm' Theory of the Decline of the Mughal Empire. *Comparative Studies in Society and History* 21: 151-167.

LEONARD, K. 1981a: Banking Firms in Nineteenth-Century Hyderabad Policies. *Modern Asian Studies* 15, 2: 177-201.

LEONARD, K. 1981b: Indigenous Banking Firms in Mughal India: A Reply. *Comparative Studies in Society and History* 23: 309-313.

LIPTON, M. 1976: Agricultural Finance and Rural Credit in Poor Countries. *World Development* 4, 7.

LUHMANN, N. 1973a: *Vertrauen: Ein Mechanismus der Reduktion sozialer Komplexität.* Stuttgart: Ferdinand Enke.

LUHMANN, N. 1973b: Knappheit, Geld und bürgerliche Gesellschaft. *Jahrbuch der Sozialwissenschaften* 23.

LUHMANN, N. 1988a: *Die Wirtschaft der Gesellschaft.* Frankfurt: Suhrkamp.

LUHMANN, N. 1988b: Familiarity, Confidence, Trust: Problems and Alternatives. D. Gambetta (ed): *Trust – Making and Breaking Co-operative Relations.* Oxford: Basil Blackwell.

LUXEMBURG, R. 1966: *Die Akkumulation des Kapitals.* Berlin: Vorwärtz Dietz.

MACKIE, J.A.C. 1988: Changing Economic Roles and Ethnic Identities of the Southeast Asian Chinese: A Comparison of Indonesia and Thailand. J. Cushman and Wang Gungwu (eds.): *Changing Identities of the Southeast Asian Chinese Since World War II.* Hong Kong: Hong Kong University Press.

MALAMOUD, C. 1981: On the Rhetoric and Semantics of Purusarthaa. *Contributions to Indian Sociology* 15, 1 and 2: 35-54.

MALAMOUD, C. 1983: The Theology of Debt in Brahmanism. C. Malamoud (ed): *Debts and Debtors.* Delhi: Vikas.

MALINOWSKI, B. 1964: *Argonauts of the Western Pacific.* London: Routledge and Kegan Paul.

MALLAT, C. (ed.) 1988: *Islamic Law and Finance.* London, Dordrecht and Boston: Graham and Trotman.

MAMORIA, C.A. 1982: *Rural Credit Markets in India.* Alahabad: Kitab Mahal.

MARX, K. 1970: *Capital.* Volume I and III. New York: International Publishers.

MASUBUCHI, T. 1966: Wittfogel's Theory of Oriental Society (or Hydraulic) Society and the Development of Studies of Chinese Society and Economic History of Japan. *The Developing Economies* 6, 3: 316-333.

MAUSS, M. 1925: *The Gift. Forms and Functions of Exchange in Archaic Societies.* Glencoe, Ill.: Cohen and West.

MAUSS, M. 1990: *Die Gabe. Form und Funktion des Austauschs archaischer Gesellschaften.* Frankfurt/Main: Suhrkamp.

McLEOD, R. 1980: Finance and Entrepreneurship in the Small-Business Sector in Indonesia. Ph.D. thesis. Australian University. Canberra.

McLEOD, R. 1983: Concessional Credit for Small-Scale Enterprise. A Comment. *Bulletin of Indonesian Economic Studies* 19, 1: 83-89.

McLEOD, R. 1992: Indonesia's Changing Financial Landscape: The Evolution of Finance Policy in Indonesia. Conference Paper 'Financial Landscapes Reconstructed'. Wageningen: 17-19 Nov.

MEILINK-ROELOFSZ, M.A.P. 1969: *Asian Trade and European Influence in the Indonesian Archipelago between 1500 and about 1630.* The Hague: Martinus Nijhoff.

MENKHOFF, T. 1993: *Trade Routes, Trust and Trading Networks – Chinese Small Enterprises in Singapore.* Bielefeld Studies on the Sociology of Development No. 54. Saarbrücken and Fort Lauderdale: Breitenbach.

MENON, R. 1985: Banking and Trading Castes in the Colonial Period: The Case of the Nattukottai Chettiars of Tamil Nadu. *South Asia Bulletin* 5, 2.

METCALF, T.R. 1979: *Land, Landlords, and the British Raj. Northern India in the Nineteenth Century.* New Delhi: Oxford University Press.

MICHIE, B.H. 1978: Baniyas in the Indian Agrarian Economy: A Case of Stagnant Entrepreneurship. *Journal of Asian Studies* 37: 637-652.

MIRACLE, M.P., D.S. Miracle and L. Cohen 1980: Informal Savings Mobilization in Africa. *Economic Development and Cultural Change* 28, 4: 701-724.

MORRIS, M.D. 1982: The Growth of Large-Scale Industry to 1947. D. Kumar (ed): *The Cambridge Economic History of India*, Vol. II. New Delhi: Orient Longman and Cambridge University Press.

MUNDLE, S. 1979: *Backwardness and Bondage. Agrarian Relations in a South Bihar District.* New Delhi.

MYRDAL, G. 1968: *Asian Drama.* 2 volumes. New York: Pantheon.

N.N. 1857: Eene Stem uit Java over de Pandjes- of Lombard-huizen in Nederlandsch Indie. *Tijdschrift voor Nederlandsch Indie* 19, 2: 221-241.

N.N. 1859: *Tijdschrift voor Nederlandsch Indie* 21, 2: 58-61.

N.N. 1924: Verslag van den Economischen Toestand der Indlandsche Bevolking, Deel I.

N.N. 1941: Propaganda voor de Woekerbstrijding. *De woeker.* Tijdschrift voor de woekerbestrijding in Nederlandsch Indie 56.

NAFZIGER, E.W. 1978: *Class, Caste and Entrepreneurship: A Study of Indian Industrialists.* Honolulu: University Press of Hawaii.

NAYAR, C.P.S. 1973: *Chit Finance.* Bombay: Vora.

NAYAR, C.P.S. 1982: Finance Corporations: An Informal Financial Intermediary in India. *Savings and Development* 6, 1: 5-39.

NEAL, L. 1990: The Dutch and the East India Companies Compared: Evidence from the Stock and Foreign Exchange Markets. J.D. Tracy (ed): *The Rise of Merchant Empires.* Cambridge: Cambridge University Press.

NEDERVEEN PIETERSE, J. 1988: A Critique of World System Theory. *International Sociology* 3, 3: 251-266.

NISBET, C. 1967: Interest Rates and Imperfect Competition in the Informal Credit Market of Rural Chile. *Economic Development and Cultural Change* 16: 73-90.

ONG ENG DIE 1943: *Chineezen in Nederlandsch-Indie.* Assen: Van Gorcum.

ONGHOKHAM 1975: The Residence of Madium: Priyayi and Peasants in the Nineteenth Century. Unpublished Dissertation.

OTSUKA, H. 1966: Max Weber's View of Asian Society – with Special Reference to His Theory of the Traditional Community. *The Developing Economies* 6, 3: 275-298.

PALAT, R. et al. 1986: The Incorporation and Peripherization of Southeast Asia, 1600-1950. *Review* 10, 1: 171-208.

PANGLAYKIM, Y. 1974: Financial Institutions in Indonesia: Some Notes. *The Indonesian Quarterly* 3 (1974): 60-75.

PANJABI, C. 1961: Multani Bankers – Their Role in the Indian Money Market (2 parts). *Journal of the Indian Institute of Bankers.* October and December (1961).

PARRY, J. 1989: On the Moral Perils of Exchange. J. Parry and M. Bloch eds. (1989): *Money and the Morality of Exchange.* Cambridge: Cambridge University Press.

PARRY, J. and M. Bloch 1989: Introduction: Money and the Morality of Exchange. J. Parry and M. Bloch eds. (1989): *Money and the Morality of Exchange.* Cambridge: Cambridge University Press.

PARTADIREJA, A. 1974: Rural Credit: the Ijon System. *Bulletin of Indonesian Economic Studies* 10, 3: 54-71.

PATINKIN, D. 1968: Interest. *International Encyclopedia of Social Sciences*, Vol. 7. New York: Macmillan.

PAVADARAYAN, J. 1986: The Chettiars of Singapore: A Study of an Indian Minority in Southeast Asia. Ph.D. thesis. Faculty of Sociology. University of Bielefeld.

PENDERS, C.L.M. (ed.) 1977: *Indonesia. Selected Documents on Colonialism and Nationalism 1830-1942.* St. Lucia, Queensland: University of Queensland Press.

PISCHKE, J.D. 1992: RoSCA: State-of-the-Art Financial Intermediation. D.W. Adams and D.A. Fitchett (eds.): *Informal Finance in Low-Income Countries.* Boulder: Westview.

PISCHKE, J.D. von, D.W. Adams and G. Donald (eds.) 1983: *Rural Financial Markets in Developing Countries. Their Use and Abuse.* Baltimore and London: Johns Hopkins.

POLAK, J. 1989: *Financial Policies and Development.* OECD Development Centre.

POLANYI, K. 1957: The Economy as an Instituted Process. K. Polanyi, C.M. Arensberg and H.W. Pearson (eds.): *Trade and Markets in Early Empires.* New York: Free Press.

POLANYI, K. 1978: *The Great Transformation* (German Ed.). Frankfurt/Main: Suhrkamp.

POLANYI-LEVITT, K. 1990 (ed): *The Life and Work of Karl Polanyi.* Quebec: Black Rose.

POPKIN, S. 1979: *The Rational Peasant.* Berkeley, Los Angeles and London: University of California Press.

PRABOWO, D. 1987: The Role of Informal Financial Intermediation in the Mobilization of Household Savings and Allocations in Indonesia (paper based on a survey carried out for the Asian Development Bank).

PRABOWO, D. et al. 1989: Study on Informal Credit Market in Indonesia. Report for the Asian Development Bank, Manila. Yogyakarta: Faculty of Economics, Gadjah Mada University.

Preliminary Report of the Bengal Board on Economic Enquiry 1935: NAI, Government of India, Finance Department, File No. 22 (25)-F.

RAJU, A.S. 1941: *Economic Conditions in the Madras Presidency, 1800-1850.* Madras: University of Madras.

RAU, B. Ramachandra 1938: *Present-Day Banking in India.* Calcutta: Calcutta University.

RAVAILLON, M. 1990: Rural Indebtedness in the Punjab 1878: Results of a Household Survey. *Explorations of Economic History* 27: 178-198.

RAY, R.K. 1979 *Industrialization in India. Growth and Conflict in the Private Corporate Sector, 1914-47.* New Delhi: Oxford University Press.

RAYCHAUDHURI, T. 1982: The Mughal Empire. T. Raychaudhuri and I. Habib (eds.): *The Cambridge Economic History of India,* Vol. I. New Delhi: Orient Longman and Cambridge University Press.

RAYCHAUDHURI, T. and I. Habib (eds.) 1982: *The Cambridge Economic History of India,* Vol. I: c. 1200 – c. 1750. New Delhi: Orient Longman and Cambridge University Press.

REID, A. 1980: The Structure of Cities in Southeast Asia, Fifteenth to Seventeenth Centuries. *Journal of Southeast Asian Studies* 11: 235-50.

RAFSC, see Report of the Agricultural Finance Sub-Committee

Report of the Agricultural Finance Sub-Committee 1945 (1965 repr.). Bombay: Government Press.

Report of the Punjab Provincial Banking Enquiry Committee 1929-30. Calcutta.

Report of the Study Group on Indigenous Bankers 1971. Bombay: Government Press.

Report of the Study Group on Non-Banking Financial Intermediaries 1971. Bombay: Government Press.

RINGROSE, J.H. 1940: Crediet in de Nederlandsch-Indische Samenleving. *Tijdschrift voor Economische Geographie* 3: 65-72.

ROBISON, R. 1986: *Indonesia: The Rise of Capital.* Sydney: Allen and Unwyn.

ROTH, H.-D. 1983: *Indian Moneylenders at Work. Case Studies of the Traditional Rural Credit Market in Dhanabad District,* Bihar. New Delhi: Vikas.

ROTHERMUND, D. 1978: *Government, Landlord and Peasant in India. Agrarian Relations Under British Rule 1865-1935.* Schriftenreihe des Südasien-Instituts der Universität Heidelberg 25. Wiesbaden: Franz Steiner.

ROTHERMUND, D. 1981: *Asian Trade in the Age of Mercantilism.* New Delhi: Manohar.

ROTHERMUND, D. 1982a: Einleitung: Weltgefälle und Weltwirtschaftskrise. D. Rothermund (ed): *Die Peripherie in der Weltwirtschaftskrise.* Paderborn: Schöningh.

ROTHERMUND, D. 1982b: Die Interferenz von Agrarpreissturz und Freiheitskampf in Indien. D. Rothermund (ed): *Die Peripherie in der Weltwirschaftskrise.* Paderborn: Schöningh.

ROTHERMUND, D. 1985: *Indiens wirtschaftliche Entwicklung.* Paderborn: Schöningh UTB.

ROTHERMUND, D. 1989: *An Economic History of India* (repr.). New Delhi: Manohar.

ROTHERMUND, D. 1992: *India in the Great Depression 1929-1939.* New Delhi: Manohar.

ROTHERMUND, D. 1994: *Geschichte als Prozeß und Aussage: eine Einführung in Theorien des historischen Wandels und der Geschichtsschreibung.* München: Oldenbourg.

RUDNER, D. 1989: Banker's Trust and the Culture of Banking Among the Nattukottai Chettiars of Colonial South India. *Modern Asian Studies* 23, 3: 417-458.

RUSH, J.R. 1990: *Opium To Java. Revenue Farming and Chinese Enterprise in Colonial Indonesia,* 1860-1910. Ithaca and London: Cornell University Press.

RUSSEL, R.V. 1975: *Tribes and Castes of the Central Provinces of India* (repr. 1916). New Delhi: Cosmo Publications.

SAHLINS, M.D. 1972: *Stone Age Economics.* Chicago: Aldini-Atherton.

SANDHU, K.S. 1969: *Indians in Malaya: Some Aspects of their Immigration and Settlement (1786-1957).* Cambridge: Cambridge University Press.

SAYERS, R.S. 1952: *Banking in the British Commonwealth.* Oxford: Clarendon Press.

SCHMIT, L.Th. 1991: *Rural Credit Between Subsidy and Market. Adjustment of the Village Units of Bank Rakyat Indonesia in Sociological Perspective.* Leiden Development Studies No. 11. Leiden.

SCHOORL, S.J. 1926: De Chetti en zijn bedrijf. *Koloniale Studien* 10,1: 68-87. Weltevreden: G. Kolff & Co.

SCHRADER, H. 1989: Chettiar Moneylenders – An Indian Minority in Burma. Working Paper No. 121. Sociology of Development Research Centre. University of Bielefeld.

SCHRADER, H. 1990: The Origin and Meaning of Money. A Discourse on Sociological and Economic Literature. Working Paper No. 136. Sociology of Development Research Centre University of Bielefeld.

SCHRADER, H. 1991: Rotating Savings and Credit Associations – Institutions in the "Middle Rung" of Development? Working Paper No. 148. Sociology of Development Research Centre. University of Bielefeld.

SCHRADER, H. 1992: The Socioeconomic Function of Moneylenders in Expanding Economies: The Case of the Chettiars. *Savings and Development* 16, 1: 69-82.

SCHRADER, H. 1993: Some Reflections on the Accessibility of Banks in Developing Countries: A Quantitative, Comparative Study. Working Paper No. 188. Sociology of Development Research Centre. University of Bielefeld.

SCHRADER, H. 1994a: A Discussion of Trade in Social Science. H.-D. Evers and H. Schrader (eds.): *The Moral Economy of Trade.* London: Routledge.

SCHRADER, H. 1994b: Changing Financial Landscapes in India and Indonesia – Sociological Aspects of Monetisation and Market Integration. Unpublished Research Report (Habilitationsschrift). University of Bielefeld: Faculty of Sociology.

SCHRADER, H. 1995: Chettiar Finance in Colonial Asia. *Zeitschrift für Ethnologie* 120: 1-26.

SCHRIEKE, B. 1929: Native Society in the Transformation Period. B. Schrieke (ed): *The Effect of Western Influence.* Batavia: Kolff.

SCHRIEKE, B. 1966: *Indonesian Sociological Studies.* The Hague: Van Hoeve.

SCHUMPETER, J.A. 1912: *Theorie der wirtschaftlichen Entwicklung.* Leipzig: Duncker und Humblot.

SCHUMPETER, J.A. 1974: *The Theory of Economic Development.* Oxford: Oxford University Press.

SCHUMPETER, J.A. 1990: *The Economics and Sociology of Capitalism* (ed. by R. Swedberg). Princeton: Princeton University Press.

SCHWEPPENHÄUSER, H.G. 1982: *Das kranke Geld. Vorschläge für eine soziale Geldordnung von morgen.* Frankfurt/Main: Fischer.

SCOTT, J.C. 1976: *The Moral Economy of the Peasant.* New Haven, Conn.: Yale University Press.

SEDDON, D. (ed.) 1978: *Relations of Production. Marxist Approaches to Economic Anthroplogy.* London: Cass.

SEIBEL, H.-D. 1989a: Linking Informal and Formal Financial Institutions in Africa and Asia. J. Levitsky (ed): *Microenterprises in Developing Countries.* London: Intermediate Technology Publications.

SEIBEL, H.-D. 1989b: Finance with the Poor, by the Poor, for the Poor. Financial Technologies for the Informal Sector. With Case Studies from Indonesia. K.M. Leisinger, P. Trappe (eds.): *Social Strategies Forschungsberichte 3, 2.*

SEIBEL, H.-D. 1991: Development by Deregulation: Innovative Rural Finance in Indonesia. Paper Presented at Bina Swadaya, January 30, 1991. Jakarta.

SEIBEL, H.-D, and M.T. Marx 1987: *Dual Financial Markets in Africa.* Saarbrücken and Fort Lauderdale: Breitenbach.

SEIBEL, H.-D. and U. Parhusip 1990: Financial Innovations for Microenterprises – Linking Formal and Informal Financial Institutions. *Small Enterprise Development* 1, 2. Intermediate Technology Publications. Cranfield School of Management. London.

SELTMANN, F. 1987: *Die Kalang. Eine Volksgruppe auf Java und ihre Stammesmythe.* Wiesbaden: F. Steiner.

SGIB, see Report of the Study Group on Indigenous Bankers

SHAH, K.J. 1981: Of Artha and the Arthasastra. *Contributions to Indian Sociology* 15, 1 and 2: 55-73.

SHATZMILLER, J. 1990: *Shylock Reconsidered: Jews, Moneylending and Medieval Society.* Berkeley and Los Angeles, Oxford: Univ. of California Press.

SHERMAN, D.G. 1990 *Rice, Rupees and Ritual. Economy and Society Among the Samosir Batak of Sumatra.* Stanford: Stanford University Press.

SHIOZAWA, K. 1966: Marx's View of the Asian Society and His "Asiatic Mode of Production". *The Developing Economies* 6,3: 298-315.

SIMMEL, G. 1989: *Philosophie des Geldes* (Hrsg. O. Rammstedt). Frankfurt/Main: Suhrkamp.

SINGH, J. 1989: Banks, Gods and Government. Institutional and Informal Credit Structure in a Remote and Tribal Indian District (Kinnaur, Himachal Pradesh) 1960-1985.

SINGH, K. 1968: Structural Analysis of Interest Rates on Consumption Loans in an Indian Village. *Asian Economic Review* 10.

SINGH, K. 1983: Structure of Interest Rates on Consumption Loans in an Indian Village. J.D. v. Pischke et al. (eds.): *Rural Financial Markets in Developing Countries.* Baltimore and London: Johns Hopkins.

SIVAKUMAR, S.S. 1978: Aspects of Agrarian Economy in Tamil Nadu: A Study of Two Villages. Part III, Structure of Assets and Indebtedness. *Economic and Political Weekly,* 20 May: 846-51.

SKINNER, G.W. 1976: *The Study of Chinese Society.* Stanford: Stanford University Press.

SKULLY, M. 1994: The Development of the Pawnshop Industry in Asia. F.J.A. Bouman and O. Hospes (eds.): *Financial Landscapes Reconstructed. The Fine Art of Mapping Development.* Boulder: Westview.

SMITH, A. 1976: *An Inquiry into the Nature and Causes of the Wealth of Nations* (ed. by E. Canaan). Chicago: University of Chicago Press.

SOEDJATMOKO 1965: *An Introduction to Indonesian Histography.* Ithaca: Cornell University Press.

SOENARIO 1939: *Verschulding en economische toestand op Java's platteland.* Batavia: Lux.

SOMBART, W. 1919: *Der moderne Kapitalismus.* Band 1 und 2. München, Leipzig: Duncker und Humblot.

SOMBART, W. 1927: *Der moderne Kapitalismus.* Band 3. München, Leipzig: Duncker und Humblot.

SPENCER, G.W. 1968: Temple Moneylending and Livestock Redistribution in Early Tanjore. *Indian Economic and Social History Review* 5, 3: 277-293.

STIEGLITZ, J.E. 1986: The New Development Economics. *World Development* 14: 257-265.

STIEGLITZ, J.E. 1989: Motives, Information and Organisational Design. *Empirica* 16: 3-29.

STOKES, E. 1978: *The Peasant and the Raj. Studies in Agrarian Society and Peasant Rebellion in Colonial India.* New Delhi: Vikas.

SUBRAMANIAN, L. 1987: Banias and the British: the Role of Indigenous Credit in the Process of Imperial Expansion in Western India in the Second Half of the Eighteenth Century. *Modern Asian Studies* 21, 3: 473-510.

SUJARIYAPINUM, P. 1988: Pawning Behavior in Bangkok. M.A. thesis. Faculty of Economics. Thammasat University. Bangkok.

SUNDARAM, K. and V.N. Pandit 1984: Informal Credit Markets, Black Money and Monetary Policy: Some Analytical and Empirical Issues. *Economic and Political Weekly* 19, April-June.

SUROYO, A.M. Juliati 1987: Some Preliminary Remarks on Colonial Exploitation Systems in Java and India in the Nineteenth Century. *Itinerario 11, 1: Special Issue: India and Indonesia from the 1830s to 1914*. The Heyday of Colonial Rule: 61-82.

SURYADINATA, L. 1978: *Pribumi, Indonesians, the Chinese Minority and China*. Kuala Lumpur, Singapore, Hong Kong: Heinemann.

SURYADINATA, L. 1988: Chinese Economic Elites in Indonesia: A Preliminary Study. J. Cushman and Wang Gungwu (eds.): *Changing Identities of the Southeast Asian Chinese Since World War II*. Hong Kong: Hong Kong University Press.

SURYO, Djoko 1987: Land Tenure Systems and Rural Development in India and Indonesia in the Colonial Period. A Comparative Study. *Itinerario 11, 1. Special Issue: India and Indonesia from the 1830s to 1914*. The Heyday of Colonial Rule: 265-276.

THAKRANONTHACHAI, T. 1982: Orient's Oldest Financial Institution: The Pawn Shop. *ABAC Journal* 2, 2.

THE SIAUW GIAP 1989: Socioeconomic Role of the Chinese in Indonesia. A. Maddison and G. Price (eds.): *Economic Growth in Indonesia, 1820-1940*. Dordrecht: Foris.

THORNBURN, S.S. 1886: *Musalmans and Moneylenders in the Punjab*. Edinburgh.

THURNWALD, R. 1932: *Economics in Primitive Communities*. London: Oxford University Press.

TICHELMAN, F. 1980: *The Social Evolution of Indonesia. The Asiatic Mode of Production and its Legacy*. Studies in Social History, Issued by the International Institute of Social History, Amsterdam. Martinus Nijhoff.

TIMBERG, T. 1978: *The Marwaris*. New Delhi: Vikas.

TIMBERG, T. and C.V. Aiyar 1980: Informal Credit Markets in India. *Economic and Political Weekly*, Annual No., Feb.: 279-302.

TOENNIES, F. 1959: Gemeinschaft und Gesellschaft. A. Vierkant (Hrsg): *Handwörterbuch der Soziologie*. Stuttgart: Ferdinand Enke.

TOMLINSON, B.R. 1979: *The Political Economy of the Raj, 1914-1947*. London: Macmillan.

TOMLINSON, B.R. 1981: Colonial Firms and the Decline of Colonialism in Eastern India 1914-47. *Modern Asian Studies* 15, 3: 455-486.

TORRI, M. 1991: Trapped Inside the Colonial Order: The Hindu Bankers of Surat and Their Business World During the Second Half of the Eighteenth Century. *Modern Asian Studies* 25, 2: 367-401.

TUN WAI, U 1953: *Burma's Currency and Credit.* Bombay, Calcutta, Madras: Orient Longman.

TUN WAI, U 1980: The Role of Unorganized Financial Markets in Economic Development and in the Formulation of Monetary Policy. *Savings and Development* 6, 4.

VAN DER KOLFF, G.H. 1929: European Influence on Native Agriculture.   B. Schrieke (ed): *The Effect of Western Influence.* Batavia: Kolff.

VAN DER KOLFF, G.H. 1937: *The Historical Development of the Labour Relationship in a Remote Corner of Java as They Apply to the Cultivation of Rice.* Batavia: Institute of Pacific Relations.

VAN DER KROEF, J.M. 1953: The Arabs in Indonesia. *The Middle East Journal* 7, 3.

VAN DEVENTER, V.Th. 1904: *Overzicht van den Economischen Toestand der Inlandsche Bevolking van Java en Madoera.* S'Gravenhage: Martinus Nijhoff.

VAN GELDEREN, J. 1927: *Voorlezingen over tropisch-koloniale staatshoudjunde.* n.p.

VAN GELDEREN, J. 1929: Western Enterprise and the Density of the Population in the Netherlands Indies. B. Schrieke (ed): *The Effect of Western Influence.* Batavia: Kolff.

VAN GOOR, J. (ed.) 1986: *Trading Companies in Asia 1600-1830.* Utrecht: Hes Uitgevers.

VAN GOOR, J. 1992: India and the Indonesian Archipelago from the 'Generale Missiven der VOC' (Dutch East India Company). *Itinerario* 14, 2: 23-37.

VAN GUTEM, V.B. 1919: Tjina Mindering. Eenige aanteekenigen over het Chineesche geldschieterswezen op Java. *Koloniale Studien* 3, 1: 106-150.

VAN LAANEN, J.T.M. (ed) 1980: *Changing Economy in Indonesia.* Vol. 6: Money and Banking 1816-1940. The Hague: Martinus Nijhoff.

VAN LAANEN, J.T.M. 1990: Between the Java Bank and the Chinese Moneylender: Banking and Credit in Colonial Indonesia. A. Booth, W.J. O'Mally and A. Weidemann (eds.): *Indonesian Economic History in the Dutch Colonial Era.* Monograph Series 35, Yale University Southeast Asia Studies. New Haven.

VAN LEUR, J.C. 1955: *Indonesian Trade and Society.* The Hague: Van Hoeve.

VAN NIEL R. 1972: Measurement of Change under the Cultivation System in Java, 1837-1851. *Indonesia* 14: 89-109.

VLEMING Jr., J.L. n.d.: Het Chineesche Zakenleven in Nederlandsch-Indie. Belasting-Accountantsdienst in Nederlandsch-Indie.

WALLERSTEIN, I. 1979: *The Capitalist World-Economy.* Essays. Cambridge: Cambridge University Press.

WALLERSTEIN, I. 1980a: *The Modern World System, Vol.I: Capitalist Agriculture and the Origins of the European World Economy in the 16th Century.* New York: Academic Press.

WALLERSTEIN, I. 1980b: *The Modern World System* II. New York: Academic Press.

WALLERSTEIN, I. 1984: *The Politics of the World-Economy.* Essays. Edition de la Maison des Sciences de l'Homme, Paris. Cambridge University Press.

WALLERSTEIN, I. 1986: The Incorporation of the Indian Subcontinent into the Capitalist World-Economy. *Economic and Political Weekly* 21, 4.

WALLERSTEIN, I. 1989: *The Modern World System* III. San Diego: Academic Press.

WALLERSTEIN, I. 1991: *Unthinking Social Science. The Limits of Nineteenth-Century Paradigms.* Cambridge: Polity Press and Basil Blackwell Inc.

WALLERSTEIN, I. 1993: World System Versus World-Systems. A.G. Frank and B.K. Gills (eds.): *The World System: Five Hundred or Five Thousand?* London: Routledge.

WARDHANA, A. 1971: The Indonesian Banking System: The Central Bank. B. Glassburner (ed): *The Economy of Indonesia: Selected Readings.* New York: Cornell Univ. Press.

WEBER, M. 1947: *The Theory of Social and Economic Organization.* New York: Oxford University Press.

WEBER, M. 1950: *The Protestant Ethic and the Spirit of Capitalism.* Frome and London: Butler and Tanner.

WEBER, M. 1964: *The Sociology of Religion.* Boston: Beacon Press.

WEBER, M. 1968: *The Religion of China.* New York: Free Press.

WEBER, M. 1972: *Gesammelte Aufsätze zur Religionssoziologie Bd. 2: Hinduismus und Buddhismus.* Tübingen: Mohr.

WEBER, M. 1978: *Economy and Society* (ed. by G. Roth and C. Wittich). Berkeley: University of California Press.

WEBER, M. 1985: *Wirtschaft und Gesellschaft* (Hrsh. J. Winckelmann). Tübingen: Mohr.

WERTHEIM, W.F. 1964: *Indonesian Society in Transition* (2nd ed.). The Hague: Van Hoeve.

WERTHEIM, W.F. 1980: The Trading Minorities in Southeast Asia. H.-D. Evers (ed): *Sociology of Southeast Asia*. Kuala Lumpur: Oxford University Press.

WEST, R. 1892: Agrarian Legislation for the Deccan and Its Results. *Journal of the Society of Arts* 41: 705-31.

WESTENENK, L.C. 1922 De Chetti. *Koloniale Studien* 6, 2: 1-17.

West Bengal District Gazetteers 1969: Malsa. Calcutta.

West Bengal District Gazetteers 1972: Hoogly. Calcutta.

WILLMOTT, D.E. 1960: *The Chinese of Semarang. A Changing Minority Community in Indonesia*. Ithaca: Cornell University Press.

WITTFOGEL, K.H. 1931: *Wirtschaft und Gesellschaft Chinas*. Leipzig: Junius.

WITTFOGEL, K.H. 1957: *Oriental Despotism. A Comparative Study of Total Society*. New Haven: Yale.

WOLF, E.R. 1966: Kinship, Friendship and Patron-Client Relations in Complex Societies. M. Banton (ed): *The Social Anthropology of Complex Societies*. London.

WORLD BANK 1983: *Indonesia Rural Credit Study*. Washington D.C.: World Bank.

Market, Culture and Society

edited by Helmut Buchholt, Hans-Dieter Evers, Rüdiger Korff, Gudrun Lachenmann, Günther Schlee, and Heiko Schrader

Helmut Buchholt; Erhard U. Heidt;
Georg Stauth (Hrsg.)
Modernität zwischen Differenzierung und Globalisierung
Kulturelle, wirtschaftliche und politische
Transformationsprozesse in der sich
globalisierenden Moderne
Bd. 1, 1996, 256 S., 48,80 DM, br.,
ISBN 3–8258–2782–8

Heiko Schrader
Changing Financial Landscapes in India and Indonesia
Sociological Aspects of Monetization and
Market Integration
Bd. 2, 1997, 400 S., 48,80 DM, br.,
ISBN 3–8258–2641–4

Empirische Wirtschaftsforschung

herausgegeben von Prof. Dr. Helmut Hergeth
und Prof. Dr. Franz W. Peren

Jochen Schübbe
Tourenplanung für die Entleerung von Bringsystemen zur Wertstoffsammlung in Stadtgebieten
Bd. 18, 1992, 200 S., 69,80 DM, gb.,
ISBN 3–89473–400–0

Ingo Kracht
Verschnittoptimierung in der Kunststoff-Fenster-Fertigung
Eine empirische Analyse für den Zuschnitt
von Rahmenprofilen, dargestellt am Beispiel
eines ausgewählten Kunststoff–Fenster–
Konfektionärs
Bd. 21, 1992, 183 S., 58,80 DM, gb.,
ISBN 3–89473–315–2

Hans Peter Ickrath
Standortwahl der "neuen technologieorientierten Unternehmen (NTU)"
Eine empirische Untersuchung zum Einfluß
von speziellen Agglomerationsvorteilen
auf die Standortwahl der NTU, dargestellt
an ausgewählten Großstädten in der
Bundesrepublik Deutschland
Bd. 22, 1992, 208 S., 58,80 DM, br.,
ISBN 3–89473–452–3

Arnd Verleger
Risikostrukturen am deutschen Aktienmarkt
Bd. 23, 1993, 196 S., 78,80 DM, gb.,
ISBN 3–89473–617–8

Frank Siegmann; Heinz-Jürgen Pinnekamp
EDV-gestützte Kurzfristprognosen mit Hilfe modifizierter Verfahren der Saisonbereinigung
Dargestellt am Beispiel textilwirtschaftlicher
Zeitreihen
Bd. 24, 1993, 248 S., 38,80 DM, br.,
ISBN 3–89473–682–8

Volker Bechtloff
Computergestützte Befragungssysteme bei der Datenerhebung und ihr praktischer Einsatz in der Bundesrepublik Deutschland
Bd. 25, 1993, 200 S., 48,80 DM, gb.,
ISBN 3–89473–720–4

Thomas Altenseuer
Die Preisentwicklung von Wohnimmobilien
Eine empirische Untersuchung für die
Bundesrepublik Deutschland von 1973 bis
1994
Bd. 26, 1995, 272 S., 58,80 DM, gb.,
ISBN 3–8258–2619–8

Thorsten Runde
Arbeitskampfaktivitäten im Verarbeitenden Gewerbe der Bundesrepublik Deutschland
Eine empirische Analyse begrenzter
Abhängigkeiten bei kombinierten Längs- und
Querschnittsdaten
Bd. 27, 1996, 208 S., 58,80 DM, gb.,
ISBN 3–8258–2727–5

Christine Miller
Informationsmodellierung in öffentlichen Verwaltungen
Dargestellt am Beispiel einer
Universitätsverwaltung
Bd. 28, 1996, 232 S., 58,80 DM, br.,
ISBN 3–8258–2808–5

LIT Verlag Münster – Hamburg – London
Bestellungen über: Dieckstr. 73 48145 Münster Tel.: 0251 – 23 50 91 Fax: 0251 – 23 19 72